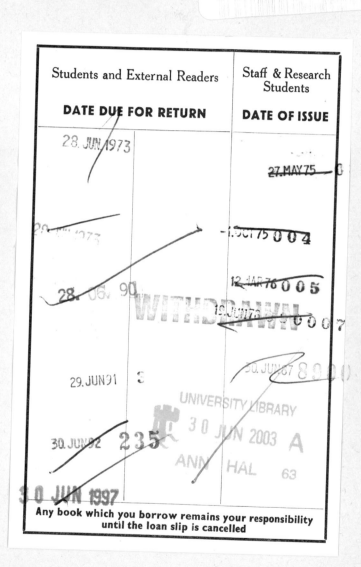

Students and External Readers	Staff & Research Students
DATE DUE FOR RETURN	**DATE OF ISSUE**
28. JUN. 1973	
	27. MAY 75
29 1973	-1. OCT 75 **004**
28. 06. 90	12 MAR 76 **005**
	19 JUN 76 **007**
29. JUN 91	30. JUN 87 **8**
30. JUN 92 235	UNIVERSITY LIBRARY
	3 0 JUN 2003 A
3 0 JUN 1997	ANN HAL 63

DISESTABLISHMENT
AND LIBERATION

William H. Mackintosh

Disestablishment and Liberation

*The Movement for the Separation of
the Anglican Church from State Control*

LONDON
EPWORTH PRESS

SBN 7162 0202 6

Inquiries should be addressed to The Dis-
tributors, The Methodist Book Room, 2 Chester
House, Pages Lane, Muswell Hill, London
N10 IPZ

Printed in Great Britain by
Ebenezer Baylis and Son Limited
The Trinity Press, Worcester, and London

DEDICATION

*First and foremost to my wife, Eva, and my children;
also to Mr and Mrs William H. Wilson, of Polmont,
Stirlingshire; to the Rev. and Mrs Jeffrey R. Plowman,
the Rev. and Mrs Brian A. A. Whiting, the Rev. and
Mrs Geoffrey E. Beck, the Rev. and Mrs Thomas C.
Stiff; to Mr and Mrs Frederick J. Thomas, Mr and Mrs
F. Bruce Shepherd, Mr and Mrs Sidney G. Bates, Mr
and Mrs Sidney Collis, and the people of Wheatley and
Witney Chapels, Oxfordshire; and to a host of friends
and loved ones on both sides of the Atlantic who helped
me find the time over the years to put all these materials
together.*

Foreword

THE STORY of the Liberation Society and of its agitation for the separation of Church and State constitutes far more than a footnote to the history of Victorian England. It provides an important clue to many of the ecclesiastical and political developments and attitudes from the days when Peel was Prime Minister to those of Asquith. The French historian, Elie Halévy, recognized this and he has been followed by H. J. Hanham, Kitson Clark and John Vincent. Only the last named, however, in *The Formation of the Liberal Party* (1966), has made use of the records of the Society, which are now to be found in the Greater London Record Office, County Hall, London.

Dr W. H. Mackintosh had earlier access to those records and here presents a detailed study of the activities of the Society. In its early days the British Anti-State-Church Association, as it was originally called, had the support of John Bright. The Society played an important part in the General Elections of 1857 and 1865. Led by Edward Miall, Edward Baines, Samuel Morley and other Nonconformist M.P.s, it had a large share in securing the removal of a number of the civil disabilities suffered by Nonconformists. In the closing decades of the nineteenth century the Society could secure the help of men as diverse as Joseph Chamberlain, John Morley and C. H. Spurgeon. In its later days Lloyd George frequently spoke on the Society's platform.

Writing to a friend in 1874, Gladstone said: 'I do not feel the dread of disestablishment which you may probably entertain: but I desire and seek, so long as standing ground remains, to avert, not to precipitate it.' By then the Irish Church had been disestablished. The Welsh Church lost its established position in 1912, though World War I delayed the consequent changes. The Church of Scotland, though established, has made clear its independence of state control. The question of the relationship of the Church of England to the State remains an unresolved issue, but a still important one.

Popular agitation by Free Churchmen has ceased. They are less logic-ridden, less sure of the right answers than they were. The Liberal Party has all but disappeared. The old Liberation Society no longer exists. But Anglicans are troubled about the state connexion of their Church in a way they were not in Victorian times. A whole series of commissions and committees has considered the method of Crown appointments and the wider question of the relations between Church and State in England. The scheme of union between the Church of England and the Methodist Church, as set out in 1963, envisaged as part of Stage 2 'a radical revision and repeal of the Acts of Parliament by which the Church of England is now governed'.

There is therefore present relevance as well as historical value in what is recorded in the following pages.

July 1969   ERNEST A. PAYNE

Preface

THE WORDS 'Disestablishment' and 'Liberation' have a radical and revolutionary sound and are not usually in the vocabulary of the average quiet-living Christian. In considering such a book as this, therefore, the reader may well ask, What is its relevance to me and the contemporary life of my Church? What could a history of the movement for Disestablishment and Liberation of the Church of England in the nineteenth century have to do with religious-social movements today that are utterly different?

This is a practical study of what happened to the Establishment of one of the great Churches of the world after the Industrial Revolution; the lessons should be studied carefully by all Churches concerned, lest the cry for Disestablishment rise again. In the year 1972, a century after the Disestablishment of the Church of Ireland, there are murmurings of the former discontent. With the extension of the Industrial Revolution into the technological revolution in the vast urban centres today, there are serious questions concerning the adequacy of established religious institutions to meet human needs.

A good test for an Established Church and its claim to be so regarded by the leaders and people of the State is its ability to relate with other Churches and denominations in the country. It must be comprehensive in its appeal and its embrace. When an Established Church cannot be in communion with Christians of other major ecclesiastical bodies it loses its value as the publicly accepted channel for drawing men together in the love of God and in the name of Christ. The plans for a merger, hopefully, between Methodists and Anglicans should prove that Churches can share their benefits and traditions, and emerge stronger.

I shall leave my readers to judge how far the Church of England, and the Church of Scotland, is meeting the test, and which Church is best qualified to remain as it is at present established. Both national Churches have shown a willingness for 'conversations' with representatives of other denominations in the interest of unity, but there has been no corresponding success in overcoming the theological and doctrinal differences. Interpretation of teaching, of course, is vital; but not more so than the peace and strength of the whole body of Christ.

The day may be near when the Ministers and Clergy who mark time with their endless talking will be overruled by a well-informed Laity of the nation, demanding that their unreasonable quarrels be resolved. This could mean the administrative control of the Churches eventually being taken out of the hands of the ordained professionals because of their slowness of heart to move. There are signs that the twenty-first century may bring a new Reformation of the entire Church, with organized laity taking the initiative in directing its course. As leading laymen become disenchanted and shed their natural timidity to raise their voices in challenge to the clergy, some radical remedies will be demonstrated by the people.

Although the Presbyterian communion throughout the world is relatively open, the Church of Scotland is generally suspicious of steps toward unity with the Episcopalians. The Anglican Church remains relatively tight on the questions of inter-communion and apostolic succession. Standing in a favoured position with the allegiance of the Crown, it finds difficulty in recognizing other of Her Majesty's subjects who are not confirmed or ordained according to its own tenets. Thus, to the Church of Scotland there appears to be a greater future in the path of union with the Baptists, Congregationalists, Methodists, and the Free Church of Scotland. Among the members of these Churches there is more common ground and a greater incentive to come together.

Furthermore, any exclusive constitutional status given to one Church should be for the general public welfare; otherwise, the honour should be forfeited to a body that can minister in a spirit of genuine friendship to people outside the Church. There is no little arrogance and false pride in the dialogue of some clergy in England and Scotland with the 'unrespectable' elements of the population. When this feeling stands as a wall to the world, that Established Church should be liberated.

Clearly, if a modern Church is adequately to fulfil its role in modern society, the policy of mutual dependence of Church and State must go. The threat today is no longer State interference, but State indifference to the Christian faith. The more the powerful secular institutions shape the character of the nation, the greater need is there for the Church to participate in national life – though not as a department of the Government. The principle of the separation of Church and State in America, traditionally advocated in that country by leaders of the movement for religious equality, has there produced a multitude of confusing sectarian voices, and is now less in favour. But the broad aim of the Liberationists to remove the monopoly of privilege from a national Church keeping itself aloof is in some ways still valid.

This book may well be considered a manual for those wishing to study the techniques of political education used by various Church leaders acting together. The involvement of the Churches in political, social and economic questions today is no new thing, as this record will show. If any Church agency is to achieve any goal in the power structure of the State it is here clear that reliance upon the Will of God must be manifest in methods of organization for educating public opinion.

Two great lessons for the contemporary Church emerge from the pages of this history. One is the need for closer co-operation by Churches in local projects, and the pooling of their resources to meet the threats of the forces of anti-religion. The second is the need for a fearless message to man to help him to judge rightly the difference between the true and the false, the moral and the immoral, the kingdom of this world and the kingdom of God.

The dramatic work of the Society for the Liberation of Religion from State Patronage and Control, the history of which is here compiled for the first time, ranged widely through the fields of Church unity, power politics and social change. It was a powerful instrument in creating other influential bodies such as the Free Church Federal Council, the National Liberal Federation, and the National Education Association. Among the outstanding figures on this stage were those of Edward Miall, the fiery Minister–Journalist–Member of Parliament leading the Liberationists, and William Gladstone, the scholarly and dignified upholder of the Establishment. In these pages are hitherto undiscovered letters of the four-times Prime Minister, revealing his underlying respect for the Nonconformist conscience. Three subsequent Prime Ministers appeared on the Liberation Society's platforms and championed its principles – Henry Campbell-Bannerman, Herbert Asquith, and David Lloyd George. The fortunes of the Liberal party were closely linked with this kindred Society.

The Churches in the Industrial Revolution ministered directly to both sacred and secular concerns in Church and State with an evangelical and intellectual fervour. The person today interested in the ministry of the Church in higher education should read the chapters on Oxford and Cambridge (7, 14, 20). The person interested in the story of the Churches' missionary enterprise should read the chapters on the Colonies (8, 15, 22). The person interested in taxation and financial support of the Church should read the chapters on Rates and Taxes (5, 13). The person interested in the question of religious instruction in schools should read the chapters on Elementary Education (3, 26). The person interested in the social background of forms of worship should read the chapters on Burials and Marriages (9, 16, 21). The reader will observe that the ordinary layman in the Victorian age was far more energetic in determining the position of his Church than he is today.

The 'Introductory' Chapter in each Part of this book gives a chronological account of the internal history of the Liberation Society. Successive chapters deal with the specific parliamentary measures and the external political history which the Society helped to fashion. Should the reader wish for fuller details, he may consult the doctoral thesis on this subject submitted by me and to be found in the Bodleian Library, Oxford. Today there is a *new* Liberation Society, for greater freedom from State interference in religious affairs, with an account for subscribers and supporters at the Royal Bank of Scotland, Knightsbridge, London s.w. 3.

I wish to acknowledge my debt to several eminent Church leaders who have guided my thinking and study that lie behind the writing of this book:

the Rev. Dr Ernest A. Payne as my tutor and mentor at Oxford University; the Rev. Prof. Kenneth Scott Latourette, late of Yale University; the Rev. F. C. White, the late General Secretary of the Liberation Society; the Rev. Dr John Marsh and the Rev. Dr Nathaniel Micklem, former Principals of Mansfield College, Oxford; and the Very Rev. Dr R. F. V. Scott at St Columba's Church of Scotland in London. Their personal views are, of course, not necessarily to be identified with those expressed in this work.

My thanks go also to the present and former Deans of Regis College in Denver, Colorado: the Rev. Eugene E. Grollmes s.j., and the Rev. Harry R. Klocker s.j.; also to my faculty chairman, the Rev. Francis J. Malecek s.j. – all exceptional scholars who have opened doors for me to serve as a professor in this combined area of History, Theology and Philosophy. Mrs Dona Smidt kindly spent many patient hours in typing the final script. I am especially grateful to Herbert Rees Esq., of Bradford-on-Avon, England, for his superb guidance and assistance in preparing the typescript of this work for publication.

My ministries over the past years at St Columba's and Crown Court Church in London, St Cuthbert's in Edinburgh, and St Michael's in Linlithgow have enriched my appreciation of current problems facing the Established Churches in their relations with the State in Britain. I am indebted to these local churches for their help to me personally and as a Minister of the Church of Scotland. I owe deepest thanks to my friend and Supervisor, the late Regius Professor of Ecclesiastical History and Canon of Christ Church, Oxford, the Rev. Dr Claude Jenkins, whose vast learning and love of the Church of England was always to me an inspiration.

Trinity Parish Church   WILLIAM H. MACKINTOSH
Coatbridge, Lanarkshire

Contents

PART FIVE

DECLINE AND RECESSION, 1886–1895

Introduction

> The abuse of the reformer, as well as the blood of the
> martyr, becomes the seed of the Church, and when the evil
> day is past the good seed springs up to life.
>
> JOHN TULLOCH[1]

D ANIEL DEFOE once made the remark that he who would serve
man must anger him. The foundation of the Society for the Liberation of Religion from State Patronage and Control in the year
1844 introduced an era of revolution in the relations between Church and
State. Here was simply a desire to cleanse the Temple. And as in all human
history, the challenge of the new and the resistance of the old resulted in a
righteous anger on both sides, but it also brought new life.

The hitherto unexplored collection of massive minutes and papers of the
Liberation Society reflects dramatically the burst of new energy and skill
within the Industrial Revolution during the mid-nineteenth century. This
fascinating story must, however, be carried further back if we are to understand the real service rendered by the Society to both the Free and the
Established Churches of the British Empire.

A. *The Idea of Liberation*

The Established Church in the early 1800s was but one among several fixed
societies undergoing the process of social change. Like Parliament, the
Municipalities, the Universities, and other national establishments, the
Church had come to be regarded too much as for the benefit of the privileged
few, and too little as an institution endowed for great public good. Since the
passing of the Act of Uniformity in 1662, Disestablishment had been
generally conceived of as the separation of Church and State, the redistribution of national religious endowments for the benefit of all Christian
citizens, and the placing of the Established Church on the same legal footing
as the other major Churches in Britain.

The Church of England was the most frequent target of this aim of
liberation, but the Church of Ireland and the Church of Wales as sister
Episcopal bodies also felt its full effect. The Church of Scotland too came

---

[1] *Movements of Religious Thought in Britain during the Nineteenth Century* (London 1885),
p. 61.

under reproof, but because its link with the Crown did not interfere with its freedom under the General Assembly to govern itself democratically, Liberationists were inclined to leave that Church to work out its own reforms.

At the beginning of Queen Victoria's reign, Disestablishment was looked upon by most Churchmen as a naughty heresy. Earlier, it had been suspected that it was aimed at the estates of the Church by grasping innovators as the easiest means of supplying an exhausted exchequer. But at the close of the nineteenth century, although the Liberation Society had declined, Disestablishment proved to be a workable ideal in socio-political progress. In the view of William Addison, this new association in British society 'gave impetus and focus to a powerful force in favour of an organised and sustained attack upon the Establishment . . . the fountain head of all those several inequalities of which Nonconformists complained'.[1]

In attacking the bond between Church and State, the Society assaulted public opinion by stages, selecting its point of pressure according to the circumstances of the day and the prevailing temper of the public mind. Thus, the following measures achieved a gradual disestablishment of the Church of England:

1854. Act for reform of Oxford University;
1855. Act for extending licences of Dissenting Places of Worship;
1856. Act for reform of Cambridge University;
1858. Act for admission of Jews to Parliament;
1860. Act for opening Grammar Schools to Dissenters;
1866. Act for removing Religious Oaths for Public Offices;
1867. Act for removing Religious Disabilities of Roman Catholics;
1868. Act for abolition of Compulsory Church Rates;
1869. Act for removing Clerical Restrictions in Grammar Schools;
1869. Act for Disestablishing and Disendowing the Irish Church;
1871. Act for abolition of Religious Tests at the Universities;
1880. Act for amendment of the Burial Laws;
1882. Act for removing Clerical Restrictions in Oxford and Cambridge;
1883. Act for revision of the London Parochial Charities;
1887. Act for restriction of Church of England Patronage;
1891. Act for recovery of Tithe Rent-Charge;
1898. Act for registration of Nonconformist Marriages.

Furthermore, these measures marked out the history of the Liberation Society and the progress of religious equality in the latter half of the Victorian age. Through them the Nonconformists sought to penetrate the Anglican armoury of supremacy, but not, as some said, 'to destroy the Church'. In this movement, as in the case of other great legislative reforms, the practical and steady character of the British mind proved equal to the occasion.

The leaders of the Liberation Society openly asserted that America provided a worthy example of what they really desired for Britain. And indeed this study may, in some ways, afford a useful background for a proper

---

[1] *Religious Equality in Modern England 1714–1914* (London 1944), p. 91.

understanding of American Church history. Thousands of liberty-loving immigrants to the United States had brought with them bitter memories of the effects of the tie between Church and State in European countries. The American Constitutional principle of separation of Church and State made wide appeal to all persecuted religious minorities. Religion seemed to stand all the firmer in the nation by standing on its own strength.

Matthew Arnold, who looked upon America chiefly as 'that Paradise of sects',[1] aligned the leaders of the Liberation Society with those philistines who determined the barbarian instincts of the age. He declared that 'the dissidence of Dissent and the Protestantism of the Protestant religion' (the motto of the *Nonconformist* newspaper) had some of mankind's deepest instincts against them, and in the end would fail. For him the science of improving the temper and making the heart better was the concern of the State Church, and would prove more lasting if left in its care.

In view of the loose way in which people referred to those outside the Established Church, a brief word should be said concerning the usage of the terms 'Dissenter', 'Nonconformist' and 'Radical'. In most cases they have been used interchangeably, although each has certain distinct features.

The designation 'Radical' was used most commonly by later writers of the Victorian era to refer to either Nonconformists or Dissenters and any others who exerted 'pressure from without' for fully democratic institutions in Church and State.[2] But to a moderate Conservative like Viscount Goschen, the modern Radical, who expected Government 'to lay its hand on every trade, to remedy abuses, and to adjust the relations between capital and labour', in short 'to do what older Radicals and political economists thought that men should do for themselves', was advocating 'the reign of numbers' and endangering 'the teaching that made Englishmen self-reliant'.[3] Thus, Edward Miall, the founder of the Society, John Morley, Joseph Chamberlain, Charles Dilke, and Robert Dale were the great Radicals among the Liberationists.

The term 'Dissenter' was the oldest of the three and, more than the other two, had definite religious connotations. In 1832, Dr Renn Dickson Hampden, Principal of St Mary Hall, Oxford, defined Dissent as the 'difference of opinions arising out of the different conclusions drawn by different minds out of the same given elements of Scripture'.[4] Writing a century later, Bernard Lord Manning deplored the negative names for those who were not inside the Church of England. They went out of it, he said, to obtain an inheritance, not to avoid one. For him, orthodox Dissent had its foundations not on

---

[1] *Last Essays on Church and Religion* (London 1877), p. 227. Elsewhere in this work, however, Arnold pointed out that there were 138 bodies of Dissenters in England, which he describes as 'Ranters, Recreative Religionists, and Peculiar People' (p. 205).

[2] S. Maccoby, *English Radicalism 1832–1852* (London 1935), p. 8.

[3] A. D. Elliot, *Life of Viscount Goschen* (London 1911), i, 164.

[4] *Observations on Religious Dissent: with particular Reference to the Use of Religious Tests in the University* (Oxford 1834), p. 4; Hampden was Principal of St Mary's Hall, Oxford.

political opinions, but on a distinctive ministry of the Word and Sacraments.[1]

Dissenters were distinguished during the first half of the nineteenth century as belonging to either 'religious' or 'political' platforms. Those in the latter category became more generally known as 'Nonconformists' – the title popularized by the Liberation orators. Nonconformists were usually called upon to exercise more courage than mere Dissenters. And so R. W. Dale made it clear that it was no 'crime for religious men to interfere in political struggles'.[2]

But whatever they were called, the men and women in the non-Episcopal tradition found their witness difficult. It demanded an effort and meant cutting themselves off, not so much from the foundations of holiness, but from the main privileges of national life. Very often the petty persecutions gave them a sense of social inferiority.

The successes of the Liberationists during this period were to a large extent governed by the attitudes of the Queen and her Prime Ministers. Victoria generally took care not to offend her Dissenting subjects, and they seldom spoke against her, but it was Gladstone whom they truly respected. With few exceptions they accounted him above other Ministers of the Crown as their courteous friend.

Gladstone's true feelings on the proper relations between Church and State were often enshrouded in mystery. And this seemed to be characteristic of his profound but at times enigmatic style of expression.[3] His Parliamentary career (1841–94) roughly paralleled the Liberation Society's period of effectiveness. He sent letters to their leaders[4] but never accepted their platform. His views on Disestablishment in private, and as leader of the Liberal party, were not the same. Throughout his life he fluctuated between his early Conservative creed and his later Liberal conscience. He was ever a loyal and devout Anglican of the Oxford school, but he was prepared to condone disestablishment of the Anglican Church in countries where it was no longer the Church of the majority. For this reason he promoted schemes for Disestablishment in Ireland, Scotland, and Wales – but not in England. Gladstone could not be classed with those Whigs whose philosophy was said to be

> To save the Church, and serve the Crown
> By letting others pull them down;

---

[1] *Essays in Orthodox Dissent* (London 1943), preface (unpaged).

[2] 'Religion and Politics', lecture to the Manchester Nonconformist Association; *Liberator*, Oct. 1887, p. 148.

[3] cf. Lord Macaulay, in his review of Gladstone's essay, 'The State in its relations with the Church', quoted in *Nonconformist*, 10.vi.74, 'Is Church Patronage property or a trust?', p. 547.

[4] The Gladstone Letters to the Liberation Society, which are derived from the Society's minutes and incorporated in the present work, are found nowhere else in print. D. C. Lathbury's *Correspondence on Church and Religion of William Ewart Gladstone* (2 vols, London 1910) does not adequately represent Gladstone's associations with Free Church leaders.

To promise, pause, prepare, postpone,
And end by letting things alone.

His predecessors, Lord John Russell and Lord Palmerston, although having no great fondness for the Dissenters, welcomed their support from political expediency. Palmerston admitted that 'in the long run English politics will follow the consciences of the Dissenters', but he was not eager to follow their advice. Russell, who was more of a democrat, had more patience with the Dissenters. He looked upon the behaviour of many of the Anglican clergy

> with the amused contempt of the average Englishman, who regarded the squabbles over robes and ritual as very much of a matter of women's clothes – important to the feminine type of priest, but of no particular significance to the masculine world of politics.[1]

Disraeli was in many ways the arch-enemy of the Dissenters. Before becoming Prime Minister in 1852, he had often wooed the Radicals to combine with the Tories against the Whigs. Afterwards, with his personal ambitions realized, he often seemed to abhor their presence in the House. Of the Liberation Society he once said:

> As I hold that dissolution of the union between Church and State will cause permanently a greater revolution in this country than foreign conquest, I shall use my utmost energies to defeat these fatal machinations.[2]

B. *The Meaning of Disestablishment*

J. A. Froude stated that to be entirely just in our estimation of other ages is not difficult – it is impossible. This is particularly true of any effort to set forth the background to Disestablishment in the Victorian age. The opening of the nineteenth century brings into this study cross-currents of socio-religious ideals and events far too complex for separate analysis.

> In all directions the ancient bands of sentiment and tradition were being weakened; in religion, literature, and politics the ideas which attracted the age were new creeds of universal brotherhood and enfranchisement, dreams of 'pantisocracy', new births of liberty and equality; . . .[3]

The derivation of some of the ideas in the Disestablishment controversy went back to the sixteenth century, when the distinctive teaching of the Church of England first appeared in its formularies.[4] At the time of the

[1] A. Wyatt Tilby, *Lord John Russell: a study in civil and religious liberty* (London 1930), p. 116.

[2] Monypenny & Buckle, *The Life of Benjamin Disraeli, Earl of Beaconsfield* (London 1929), ii, 365.

[3] Francis Warre Cornish, *The English Church in the Nineteenth Century* (London 1910), i, 182.

[4] A. C. Headlam, *The Church of England* (London 1924), p. 52; cf. H. Hensley Henson, art. 'Establishment': '. . . the essential incidents of Establishment must still be sought within the precincts of the sixteenth century.' Henson (ed.), *Church Problems: A View of Modern Anglicanism* (London 1900), p. 58.

Reformation, two teachers, Calvin and Erastus, were responsible for two competing views on Church and State. The German Erastus taught the subordination of the Church to the State, and rejected the idea of either possessing an independent government. The Sovereign or Christian prince should exercise ecclesiastical discipline. Most English monarchists accepted Erastianism and established the King as head of the Church. The Frenchman Calvin taught the subjugation of the State and its people to the absolute sovereignty of God. The laws of the State must be in accordance with the laws of God. The Church must possess independence and could own allegiance to no earthly master. The English Puritans accepted Calvinism and propounded the doctrine of the crown rights of the Kingdom of Christ.

The ministers in pre-Victorian England were divided very much along these same lines. There were the dissenting branches of the old Puritan trunk, whose members believed that their labour and industry was primarily their duty toward God. The Evangelical revival had inspired them to preach individual salvation and to practise social improvement – and they did so with patient sobriety and with the stamina of marathon runners.[1] They taught of 'the gathered Church' as being apart from 'the world'. They believed that the body was at war with the spirit, and therefore could rightly insist upon the separation of Church and State. They steadfastly held that 'where the Spirit of the Lord is, there is liberty'.

These Dissenters and their communities were frequently ridiculed in fashionable circles. In 1841, the year in which *Punch* first made its appearance, Samuel Warren (the son of a Methodist minister) wrote *Ten Thousand a–Year*,[2] which described the Reverend Dismal Horror and his partner in hypocrisy, the Reverend Smirk Mudflint, with positive brutality. Archdeacon George A. Denison in his *Church and State Review* was at times hard on the Dissenters. Episcopal charges and pastoral letters were often warnings to parishioners to beware of the Dissenters. Dickens, Thackeray and Trollope mercilessly satirized the Nonconformist's pride and priggishness and ridiculed his place of worship.

In a wholly different setting were the English clergy, the bulk of whom were reasonably educated, refined, and God-fearing men. According to Henry Wakeman, however, they 'had no high standard of clerical duty. They were content to live and to work as their predecessors had done.'[3] They had an exaggerated fear of fanaticism and of cant. Their services were conducted with an austere formality and their sermons were unbearably dull. Not a few

[1] cf. R. H. Tawney, *Religion and the Rise of Capitalism* (London 1926), p. 202: '. . . the chosen seat of the Puritan spirit seemed to be those classes in society which combined economic independence, education, and a certain decent pride in their status, revealed at once in a determination to live their own lives, without truckling to earthly superiors, and in a somewhat arrogant contempt for those who, either through weakness of character or through economic helplessness, were less resolute, less vigorous and masterful, than themselves.'

[2] 3 vols (Edinburgh & London 1841).

[3] *An Introduction to the History of the Church of England* (London 1897), p. 459.

farmers grumbled that their tithes went to feed idle mouths, whilst numerous townspeople enjoyed the pictures of parsons in the novels of Jane Austen and Maria Edgeworth. On the whole, the Anglican clergy raised the tone of the life around them and formed worthy centres of culture and manners. But often they lived too comfortably and differed little from other country gentlemen.

The rivalry between these two types of religious personalities was in fact at the bottom of the Disestablishment controversy. To vindicate their righteous causes they fell back upon the language of ridicule and scorn. Both Anglican and Nonconformist were grossly guilty of attempting to catch the transient popularity of the hour by hurling sarcasm. Edward Miall described Disraeli's style of debating as that of 'a wild boar at bay, he is reckless whom he wounds'.[1] Matthew Arnold described R. W. Dale's manner of lecturing as that of a pugilist from the Birmingham arena, who went occasionally to London to give public exhibitions.[2] Thus it continued.

One of the most formidable circumstances which gave rise to Disestablishment was the Broad Church movement. This rising liberalism and progressive churchmanship within Anglican circles was first recognized in the writings of Archdeacon William Paley and Bishop Richard Watson of Llandaff. The Broad Churchmen wished to purge the Church, they said, of 'all common dregs of popery'. Called also Latitudinarians, they tried to adapt traditional theological beliefs to scientific conclusions, and used critical reason in historical research to combat the catchwords of ecclesiastical parties. They favoured the abolition of subscription to doctrinal tests and the revision of church liturgy. They believed that the clergy should be no more confined to the theology of the Fathers, Scholastics, or Reformers than professors should be confined to the problems of Aristotle, the metaphysics of Plato, and the astronomy of Ptolemy. Their most ardent disciples were known as Noetics, or 'intellectuals', of whom Oriel College, Oxford, became the centre. There, Edward Copleston, Renn Dickson Hampden, and Richard Whately spoke as the practical interpreters of Scripture rather than tradition. All three sought always to penetrate the real meaning of customary phrases. Copleston rejected the theory of transmitted powers from Apostolic times and the sacramental character of the ministry. Hampden favoured simplicity in creeds and the admission of Dissenters to the ancient seats of learning. Whately openly advocated Disestablishment (without Disendowment) because the alliance of Church and State violated the teaching of Christ on the spirituality of His Kingdom, and because the complex ecclesiastical organization was not in accord with the Scriptures.[3]

Not a few Anglicans now began to feel that the ground was shifting beneath their feet. It was not any threat from without that bothered them most, but

[1] Arthur Miall, *Life of Edward Miall* (London 1884), 'Parliamentary Sketches', p. 176.

[2] A. W. W. Dale, *The Life of R. W. Dale of Birmingham*, 3rd ed. (London 1899), p. 379.

[3] cf. T. Mozley, *Reminiscences chiefly of Oriel College and the Oxford Movement* (London 1882), i, 20–1.

the one working within their midst. Bishop Blomfield of London charged his clergy in 1850:

> I cannot but think that we have more to apprehend from the theology of Germany than from that of Rome.[1]

The plans for Disestablishment were complicated by attempts to understand what was implied by the phrase 'established by law'. According to the *Encyclopaedia Britannica* (tenth edition), the word 'establishment' in its general sense is concerned principally with law. The words in the Coronation Oath, 'the Protestant Reformed Religion as by law established', refer to a legal fact not a matter of doctrine. Hence, H. W. Cripps, the authority on English ecclesiastical law, states:

> The process of establishment means that the State has accepted the Church as the religious body in its opinion truly teaching the Christian faith, and given to it a certain legal position, and to its decrees, if rendered under certain legal conditions, certain civil sanctions.[2]

There was little disagreement here, but where the learned lawyers differed most seriously was on the question of when this establishment took place. Eventually two main lines of opposite argument were followed by the liberators and the defenders of the Church of England.

On the one hand, Roundell Palmer, the Earl of Selborne (Lord Chancellor in 1872), put forward Dr Samuel Johnson's definition of 'establishment': 'Confirmation of something already done; ratification.'[3] Selborne, in his *Defence of The Church of England against Disestablishment*, cited Richard Hooker and William Gladstone in support of his thesis that the Establishment existed from the days of the primitive Church of England. This meant that from time to time 'the temporal legislature has recognised and added certain sanctions to the institutions and laws of the Church'. But these institutions and laws did not originate in acts of the State. The statutes of the realm and other public documents simply confirmed what was already in existence, meaning that the present Anglican Church held a direct continuity with that of Roman Catholic times. The break with the Church of Rome was doctrinal and gradual – not structural nor at a fixed point in history. An Act of Dis-

---

[1] Cited by J. R. H. Moorman, *A History of the Church of England* (London 1953), p. 355.

[2] *A Practical Treatise on the Law relating to the Church and Clergy*, 8th ed. (London 1937), ed. Kenneth M. Macmorran, p. 2. Some of the other possible meanings, which show that the terms assert the fact, but not the exact nature, of the connexion or relationship between Church and State: (1) Mutual right of intervention, (2) Co-operative partnership or 'marriage', (3) Co-existence, (4) Public recognition of Christianity, (5) Incorporation of ecclesiastical law into constitutional law, (6) Protection or absorption by the State, and (7) Created by law.

[3] Samuel Johnson, *A Dictionary of the English Language* (Dublin 1775), i, 644: the second meaning. The English word is derived from the Latin 'stabilire', meaning 'to make firm or stable'. This is the sense used in Psalm 90:17: '. . . establish thou the work of our hands upon us; yea, the work of our hands establish thou it.' cf. also Psalm 68:28. See *The New English Dictionary* (Oxford 1897).

establishment therefore would shatter the constitutional basis of English society. Professor Edward A. Freeman was inclined to agree:

> From the time when there first arose a Kingdom of England, the National Church was closely bound up in the national constitution. This would lead some to say that establishment was in existence at this time. The fact constituted establishment.[1]

On the other hand, historians like Bishop Short of St Asaph contended that the alliance between Church and State dated from the time of the Reformation, when King Henry restored the National (English) Church.[2]

> The alliance may be said to have commenced in the twenty-second year of the reign of Henry VIII, in which year, when the whole clergy of this realm were supposed to have incurred the penalties of a *praemunire*, they implored the clemency of the King, and petitioned in convocation for a remission of those penalties; and in their petition the King was, for the first time, styled the protector and supreme head of the Church and clergy of England.[3]

By the Acts of Supremacy and of Submission, the English Sovereign, in the Church of his domain, succeeded to the headship of the Pope. In this sense Royal Supremacy and 'establishment' were equivalent, and the Church *in* England became the Church *of* England.[4] In the years after this occurred, the terms 'established' and 'established by law' came into common usage. It was then that there arose other religious bodies in England which had to be distinguished from this English Church, and then that Richard Hooker's dictum in his *Laws of Ecclesiastical Polity* (London 1662), required qualifying: 'We hold, that seeing there is not any man of the Church of *England*, but the same man is also a member of the Common-wealth; nor any member of the Common-wealth, which is not also of the Church of *England*. . . .'

The Liberation Society followed this up by saying that 'the Church of England is what it is as the result of the action of the Legislature, which founded it, and shaped it throughout'.[5] Parliament had embodied in the Church of England much of the old system which had existed from the

---

[1] *Disestablishment and Disendowment, What are They?* (London 1874), p. 35. Note J. S. Brewer, *The Endowments and Establishment of the Church of England*, 2nd ed. (London 1885), ed. Lewis T. Dibdin, pp. 288–9: 'Establishment in any given country is the complex resultant of *all* the mutual dealings between Church and State, since both have existed in that country.'

[2] Thomas Vowler Short, *A Sketch of the History of the Church of England to the Revolution 1688* (Oxford 1832), i, 154: 'The existence of the church of England as a distinct body may be dated from the period of the divorce, and her final separation from Rome.' cf. William Stubbs, *Lectures on Medieval and Modern History* (Oxford 1900), pp. 292–6.

[3] Cripps, op. cit., p. 2.

[4] Sir Robert Phillimore, *The Ecclesiastical Law of the Church of England* (London 1895), vol. i, pp. 6–8, sets forth the supremacy in four categories: (a) Common Law, (b) Statute Law, (c) Canons of the Church, and (d) the Thirty-nine Articles. For a legal analysis of 'The Supremacy of the Sovereign as introduced by the Reformation', see Felix Makower, *Constitutional History and Constitution of the Church of England* (London 1895), pp. 251–9.

[5] *The Case for Disestablishment* (Liberation Society 1884), p. 47.

beginning, but in other respects gave to it features and characteristics which were wholly new. And what Parliament had done and created Parliament, so it was argued, could safely undo in an Act of Disestablishment.

The friends of the Liberation Society failed in accomplishing the separation of Church and State, but they succeeded in liberating the Church from a great deal of State patronage and control. The impatience with State control had, however, been made clear in the Church itself, by the desire of its parties for greater freedom of action. High Churchmen would centre control in exclusively clerical assemblies, Broad Churchmen would confer it upon parishioners, and Evangelical Churchmen would seek it in a truly Protestant (and revised) prayer-book. It was when certain socialists indicated that they would grant control to those who were not associated with the Church that the Disestablishment movement began to decline. Liberationists who sympathized with that idea were accused of working for the freedom of religion from religious control – a thing which was far from their original aim and was a subtle form of persecution.

But the Dissenters had experienced real persecution, and Disestablishment was to them the only sure way of ending it. To be tolerated only irritated their wounds. They sought complete religious equality with the Church which they had been forced to leave because they believed that it had forsaken its Protestant heritage. Had the Establishment remained true to the Reformed tradition, the demand for separation of Church and State might never have been made by these descendants of the Puritans.

PART ONE

Setting and Beginning
1834 – 1849

CHAPTER 1

Introductory

I believe that when Daniel, in ancient days, was performing
his duty as the minister of Darius, he as much felt himself
under a sacred obligation, as when praying to God three
times a day. In carrying out our movement we must, I think,
endeavour to impress upon all that their duty, though it
refers to a secular matter, rests on a sacred obligation.

> JOSEPH STURGE: from speech on May
> 2nd, 1884, at first
> Anti-State-Church
> Conference.[1]

ONE OF the main pillars in the Nonconformist ecclesiastical setting
of this period, according to one writer, was 'the divine right of
Voluntaryism'. Having been put to its first severe test in Scotland
between the years 1834–43, it was not found wanting. Sympathetic observers
in other parts of the British Isles soon built up strong support. They claimed
to have found the authentic and Apostolic basis for all social and religious
life. The Voluntaries taught that no acceptable or effectual service could be
rendered in spiritual or temporal affairs which did not first rest on individual
conviction and individual conscience.

> The voluntary principle, by throwing the support of religious institutions upon
> the members of society, instead of upon government, operates in perfect union
> with this individual sense of responsibility. . . . Enterprize is the salt of society. . . .
> That restlessness among a people of any land which prompts them to be ever
> seeking an improvement of their state, like the tides of ocean, preserves society
> from stagnant corruption. . . . Throw but the religion of a land upon its own
> resources, and the spirit of active enterprize it evokes for its own support prompts,
> enters into, and informs, all other undertakings.[2]

This principle was also demonstrated in the economic and political spheres
of the period. In 1847 came the triumph of *laissez faire* doctrines in the repeal of
the English Corn Laws, and in 1848 the sweep of republican ideals in the fall

---

[1] *Nonconformist*, 6.v.44, p. 312.

[2] Edward Miall, *Views of the Voluntary Principle* (London 1845), pp. 85, 163–4; cf. the
same author's *The Fixed and the Voluntary Principles: Eight Letters to the Right Hon. the
Earl of Shaftesbury* (Liberation Society 1859).

3

of the French monarchy. Common to such phenomena as these was the theory that State protection and intervention was not essential to the welfare of the nation.

Even Utilitarianism furthered this principle of Nonconformity by seeking to put the parishes of the State Churches to secular use. On the whole Voluntaryism implied approval of this idea, but noted a clear difference of motive. For the secular philosophy, the motive was the greatest happiness for the greatest number, whereas with the religious system it was the liberty of the individual and the freedom of his conscience.[1]

But while it was a time of new and revolutionary reform, the seeds of the old and orthodox reaction were deeply planted. In planning their course ahead, therefore, militant Dissenters had to reckon with the counter-attraction designed by high Anglicans. In 1834 Edward Baines (M.P., Leeds) presided at the first public conference on Disestablishment and in 1835 Canon E. B. Pusey (Regius Professor of Hebrew, Oxford) joined the band of Tractarians at the University. Each party gave incentive to the other to propagate with untiring zeal – hence, the formation of the British Anti-State-Church Association and the conversion of the Rev. John Henry Newman to Rome were but one year apart. The Liberation and Oxford movements competed side by side, fostering denominationalism and Tractarianism respectively.

Those standing between these opposites hardly knew at times which way to turn. But the imprisonment of the Rev. James Shore in 1849 for renouncing Anglican Orders by declaring himself a Dissenter, and the secession of the Rev. and Hon. Baptist Noel from the Established Church, were telling signs. Other indications were evident in the increase of the 170,000 Congregationalists and 125,000 Baptists in 1837, to 400,000 and 340,000 by the close of the era. In their quest for civil and religious equality, the former were better leaders in politics, and the latter better students of the Bible. The Wesleyans on the whole stood by with uncertainty because they were closer to the Evangelical Churchmen,[2] and the Presbyterians walked by themselves because of their anti-Trinitarian controversy. The great bulk of Nonconformity, however, was with the Rev. Joseph Angus when he prophesied in 1839 that within twenty years Church and State would be completely cut asunder.

> Come it must, and upon the zeal and enlightened devotedness of Christians it depends whether it be speedily in peace, or later in tears and in blood.[3]

Some Anglicans were ready to cut the connexion themselves for the sake of

[1] The production of happiness, declared the *Nonconformist* (13.ix.43, p. 633), was not within the sphere of Government, but the protection of life, liberty and property – allowing each subject to go in quest of the greatest happiness, taking care that none trespass upon his neighbour's rights.

[2] According to E. R. Taylor, *Methodism & Politics 1791–1851* (Cambridge 1935), pp. 150–1, Methodism occupied a middle position between the Church and Nonconformity, but Natural Rights, Individual Liberty, and Democracy seemed scriptural enough to most Methodists.

[3] Joseph Angus, *The Voluntary System* (London 1839), p. 207, quoted by Ernest A. Payne, *The Free Church Tradition in the Life of England* (London 1951), p. 129.

greater freedom, but hesitated because of the pain it would inflict. They believed that 'the Church was so closely bound up with the national life that many fibres would be severed in the process'.[1]

A. *Preceding Movements and Organization*

If Lord John Russell or Earl Grey or anybody else supposed that the Dissenters would rest after the repeal of the Test and Corporation Acts (1828), the emancipation of the Roman Catholics (1829), and the passage of the great Reform Bill (1832), they were mistaken. This legislation equipped the forces of radical Dissent with implements for the most drastic assault of all.

The first serious talk of Disestablishment dated from the mid-1830s. Voluntary Church Associations, thriving in towns of Scotland before the Disruption, spread across the border and were formed in several large industrial cities in 1834. In the same year several months after the abolition of slavery throughout the Empire, a group of Dissenters met in the Congregational Library calling for the end of the union between Church and State to ensure the full freedom and equality of all British subjects. Also in 1834, the Tory-Chartist Minister, Joseph Rayner Stephens, was expelled from Methodist circles for proclaiming and prophesying Disestablishment:

... ere long the very existence of the Established Church will be like a tale that is told ...[2]

Sporadic attempts had thus been made to organize agencies in England to promote directly and indirectly the 'idea of Disestablishment'. None of these succeeded in gaining a firm grip on the public mind, largely because of lack of practical determination and vigorous leadership. Further, the Act against Political Corresponding Societies (1794) prohibited Dissenters from establishing throughout the country any branch or auxiliary association with which they might maintain connexion and from which they might receive funds. This difficulty had to be overcome before any such movement could make serious headway.

With the threat of Lord Sidmouth's Bill in 1811 for restricting the licences of Nonconformist lay preachers, there came into existence the Protestant Society for the Protection of Religious Liberty. The Society later achieved distinction by its role in the repeal of the Test and Corporation Acts. Although this body was not specifically concerned with the Disestablishment issue, it laid the foundation of the Liberation Society. It sought to unite all Protestants upon a policy of 'protection' in religious matters and to eliminate petty persecutions. Under leaders like John Wilks (M.P., Boston) and William Smith

---

[1] L. E. Elliott-Binns, *Religion in the Victorian Era* (London 1936), p. 474.

[2] George Smith, *History of Wesleyan Methodism* (London 1857–61), iii, 213. The specific offence was the role he played in the inauguration of the Church Separation Society at Ashton-under-Lyne on 27 January 1834. He became secretary shortly afterwards and drew up a Disestablishment Memorial signed by 100 Methodist laymen. He was charged with violating the injunction of John Wesley and the principles of the Methodist Conference (see pp. 209–41).

(M.P., Norwich) the Protestant Society succeeded for the first time in uniting the support of Methodists with that of the older Church bodies.

Exertions by members of this Society on Parliament were effective and contributed to a number of minor victories for Dissenters. They witnessed the rejection of Lord Sidmouth's Bill. By a 'new Toleration Act' in 1812, the Conventicle and Five Mile Acts[1] were formally repealed and J.P.s were required to administer oaths in instances where they had formerly refused. Unitarians were placed on the same footing with other Nonconformists in 1813, and chapels were exempted from local rates in 1815. In 1820 the Society assisted in the defeat of Lord Brougham's Education Bill for rate-supported schools under the direction of the Anglican clergy.

The influence of the Protestant Society may be judged by those liberal-minded Whigs presiding at its annual meetings – among them Lord John Russell, Lord Holland, the Duke of Sussex, Lord Brougham, and Sir James Mackintosh. After the last public meeting of the body in 1839, those who had taken its lead were left to choose between the more liberal Religious Freedom Society, and the more conservative Evangelical Voluntary Association.

In May 1820, a Society for Promoting Ecclesiastical Knowledge was formed for the publication and circulation of literature on ecclesiastical property, Church establishments, and the principles of Dissent. It sought to advance the idea of Disestablishment through 'the calm medium of literature'. Among its founders were leading Nonconformist Ministers, educators, and literary figures. Benjamin Hanbury, author of *Memorials Relating to Independents*, and an editor of Hooker's *Laws of Ecclesiastical Polity* took the chair at the formation of the Society.

Under the guidance of Dr James Bennett, himself an historian of Dissent, the Society published a variety of works by such men as Dr Francis A. Cox, Dr Robert Vaughan, Dr Thomas Price, Dr John Pye Smith, and John Blackburn, the editor of the *Congregational Magazine*. This band of journalists and scholars was dissolved in 1843, in view of the pending national conference on separation of Church and State.

The 'United' Committee on Dissenting Grievances was formed in 1833 under the guidance of the Protestant Dissenting Deputies. The Wesleyans and Quakers held themselves aloof from the other three denominations in representation on this committee. Its aims were set forth in a list of six practical grievances: (1) compulsory conformity to the Prayer Book in marriage, (2) the want of a legal registration of Dissenters' births and deaths, (3) liability to Church Rates and other ecclesiastical demands, (4) alleged liability of places

---

[1] The Conventicle Act prohibited every person of 16 years and upwards from attending any Nonconformist service at which five or more persons were present. For the third offence the accused was liable to a fine of £100 or, in default, transportation to one of his Majesty's colonies. The Five Mile Act prohibited Nonconformist Ministers who would not take the oath against any alteration of government, either in Church or State, from residing within five miles of any city or corporate town. Robert W. Dale, *History of English Congregationalism* (London 1907), pp. 427–30.

of worship to poor rates, (5) denial of the right of burial by their own Ministers in parochial Churchyards, and (6) virtual exclusion from the benefits of Oxford and Cambridge Universities.

Twice, deputations were sent from the United Committee in London to Earl Grey. They politely presented him with a 'Brief Statement of the Case of Protestant Dissenters', which purposely avoided reference to the ticklish question of Disestablishment. The Prime Minister promised to be sympathetic with 'any reasonable measure'.

Meanwhile, Dissenters 'who were less in touch with the Government' pressed for a national meeting to launch a movement for the separation of Church and State. The United Committee hesitated to co-operate because of the irritation it might cause to the Whig leaders and the harm it might bring to their alliance with the Dissenters. The 'Provincial Dissenters', however, overruled these objections and called a general conference in Nottingham in May 1834 – the first ever held in England for the total abolition of the Church Establishment. Edward Baines (M.P., Leeds) was in the chair, and speakers included John Angell James, Josiah Conder, Charles Hindley, and John Howard Hinton. The practical results of this assembly were the withdrawal of Lord Althorp's Church Rate Bill of that year (preparing the way for the Church Rate Abolition Society in 1836), and the formation of Voluntary Church Associations in cities like Liverpool, Birmingham, and Ashton. Another deputation to Earl Grey was determined upon, and William Howitt, an energetic Quaker, was delegated to act as spokesman.

> After some further discussion, Earl Grey, quite bewildered, exclaimed, 'What is it you really do wish? Do you want entirely to do away with all establishments of religion?' 'Precisely,' was the prompt reply. Earl Grey said he was very sorry for it; the suggestion of such sweeping changes would alarm parliament and startle the country, and he considered it the sacred duty of every government to maintain an establishment of religion. 'People are not so easily frightened at changes nowadays,' replied Mr. Howitt; and he proceeded to argue that 'to establish one sect in preference to another was to establish a party and not a religion'.[1]

This United Committee had a checkered existence down to 1843 when it bore the brunt of opposition to Sir James Graham's Factory Education Bill. After that success, little was heard of it as a separate body.

Josiah Conder (the Editor of the *Patriot* and the *Eclectic Review*) issued proposals in 1839 for a general union of all religious equalitarians – thereby providing Edward Miall with a kind of pattern to copy five years later. Conder was sceptical as to the effectiveness of the 'quiet propaganda' of the Ecclesiastical Knowledge Society, and had induced several of his friends to withdraw from it.[2] It had not been progressive enough in its programme.

[1] Thomas Archer, *William Ewart Gladstone and his Contemporaries* (London 1898), i, 111–12.

[2] Conder was on intimate terms with the poets Robert Southey, John Foster and James Montgomery. See private correspondence quoted in Eustace R. Conder, *Josiah Conder: A Memoir* (London 1857), pp. 128–207.

At a dinner given to inaugurate a Religious Freedom Society in May 1839, Charles Lushington (M.P., Tower Hamlets) was elected chairman, and adherents to each of the major religious faiths in the country clearly declared themselves against the union of Church and State. On its council were Edward Baines, Francis A. Cox, John Howard Hinton, David King, Thomas Price, and Ralph Wardlaw. This Society differed from all others by freely opening its fellowship to all sympathetic Roman Catholics, Jews, Dissenters, and Churchmen. Its three fundamental resolutions were: (1) freedom of worship, (2) freedom from ecclesiastical taxation and compulsion, and (3) freedom from state favouritism and patronage in religion. Its organization provided for a central committee, local associations, an annual meeting of representatives, and the diffusion of printed information throughout the year.

The Society found later that its scope of membership was too wide to be practical. Whether or not Utilitarians ought to be permitted to join their ranks posed a perplexing question and one which became a source of division. Should the movement go forward in the name of religion or utility? It eventually committed itself to the Disestablishment principle mainly as a dissenting body, working primarily from religious motives. The tendency towards too much organization and not enough spirit was responsible for its decline in 1843. By 1844 it had practically evolved into the formation of the British Anti-State-Church Association.

Another group, the Evangelical Voluntary Association, endeavoured to unite Evangelicals within and without the Church of England around the voluntary principle. They defined their principle as the power of the religion of Christ to maintain and increase itself by the spirit kindled in the hearts of those accepting it. On 4 December 1839, the Association elected Sir Culling Eardley Smith (Anglican) as chairman and treasurer. The bulk of business was handled by three secretaries headed by Dr F. A. Cox (Baptist), together with a committee of twenty-five comprising such men as Dr John Pye Smith, the Rev. Joseph Angus, Hull Terrell, and T. Rundle (M.P., Tavistock).

As Voluntaryists they raised their banner against the worldly alliance of the Church with the State, the 'totalitarian practices' of the Roman Church, and the Puseyite pretensions in the English Church. The movement was to be guided in action by what was scriptural and by the basic conviction that the divine law-giver of the Church had expressly ordained voluntary exertions, individual and collective, for the propagation of the Gospel. The second rule of the Association stated:

> This Society shall not take part in any appeals to the legislature of the country; but its simple business shall be – in the spirit of meekness and charity towards those of our Christian brethren, whether in or out of the Establishment, who dissent from its object, and with the view of convincing and/or persuading their minds – to advocate and extend, by means of public lectures, and through the press, and in every other practicable way, the principle of Voluntary Churches.[1]

[1] 'Proceedings at a Meeting for the Formation of the Evangelical Voluntary Church Association' (London, Tracts on Dissent, privately printed, 1840), p. 1.

At the first meeting of the Association, Dr Cox declared that their struggle was not for a particular government and administration, but for the emancipation of religion from secular ties.

Such a position eventually ran counter to that of Edward Miall, who saw the need for a radical transformation in the actual composition of the government before proper religious equality could be achieved. To succeed in his aims, he believed that Nonconformity should drop the separatist or sect idea, and seek the right kind of 'worldly' and political alliances. The most marked difference between the Voluntary Association and the Liberation Society lay in the preference of the former for calm investigation and prayerful seeking, instead of the latter's tumultuous cry for agitation.

Five years after its inception the Association languished from lack of support and financial indebtedness. The organization was dissolved shortly after Sir Culling's return from a trip to Rome in 1844.

The oldest of these organizations, the Dissenting Deputies, had deliberated several times throughout their history, dating from 1732, on the question of Disestablishment. On such questions as involved an open fight, however, they reacted 'with caution'. The Liberation Society later looked upon the Deputies as a purely defensive organization.

In 1834 enterprising Dissenters were impatiently calling for a dissolution of the alliance between the Church and State. The Deputies and their United Committee condemned the demand in somewhat pious tones:

> The United Committee feared that wild rumours about a Disestablishment and Disendowment campaign were being used to alarm opinion and to prevent any redress of grievances. . . . They disclaimed all connexion with 'the intrigues of faction and the designs of infidelity' and wished to use only dispassionate argument and scriptural authority.[1]

To the surprise of some, the Deputies willingly arranged and financed, in March 1839, a series of eight lectures by Dr Ralph Wardlaw of Glasgow on the voluntary principle. These were in answer to the arguments of Dr Thomas Chalmers of Edinburgh who had lectured the previous year on Church establishments and their support by the State. Early in 1844, however, the general committee of the Deputies could not come to agreement on resolutions of a sub-committee for Disestablishment. This uncertainty was upsetting to the Radical-Nonconformists who were tired of 'piece-meal' tactics.

The intransigence of the Deputies during the 'thirties and 'forties on this issue may have been due to the moderating influence of the Presbyterian-Unitarians on the committee who generally disapproved of radical methods of any kind. All along, however, the mass of Nonconformists in England were being prepared for 'wholesale assault' upon the source of their practical grievances. There was a growing opinion that much effort had been wasted on the periphery, and that denials of religious equality could ultimately be overcome only by going to the centre of their complaints, the Establishment itself.

---

[1] Manning, *Essays in Orthodox Dissent*, p. 389.

3

Not until after the National Anti-State-Church Conference and the apparent enthusiasm which it produced did the Deputies come to a more positive stand.

During a time of hearty co-operation in good works between many evangelical Churchmen and evangelical Dissenters, the Oxford Movement occurred. According to John Henry Newman in his *Apologia pro Vita Sua*, its beginning dated from the Assize Sermon of John Keble, at St Mary's, Oxford, on 14 July 1833, which condemned the interference of the State with the sacred affairs of the Church as a sign of 'National Apostasy'. Considerable discussion and argument, however, began with Lord Althorp's Bill, in February 1833, to save £60,000 of Church money in Ireland by reducing the number of bishoprics from 22 to 12.[1]

Joined by the much admired Hurrell Froude and the influential Canon Pusey, these Tractarians attacked the growing liberal criticism of the Bible and attempted to revive in England the received tradition of the ancient Church. Opposed to this, R. D. Hampden, the Professor of Moral Philosophy, published his *Observations on Religious Dissent* in 1834, maintaining that doctrinal statements should not be confused with basic religious truth.

Serious controversy did not develop, however, until the appearance in 1841 of Tract XC, which aimed at showing the consistency of Roman Catholic dogmas and the Thirty-Nine Articles. To the vast majority of Anglicans the movement now seemed to endanger the orthodox Protestant doctrines and securities of the Established Church. Francis Warre Cornish has commented:

> Catholic emancipation opened the door; Wiseman, more than any one else, stood on the threshold welcoming the newcomers, helping them to feel that by becoming Romans they did not cease to be Englishmen, . . .[2]

Most historians agree that the Anglo-Catholic crusade was part of a general resurrection of the 'corporate' as against the 'individual' spirit – or, romanticism versus realism – which was appearing in most areas of life in the nineteenth century. But to challenge liberalism by claiming to speak with the voice of Heaven, 'quod semper, quod ubique, quod ab omnibus creditum est' required a certain rigid independency of its own. Thus, Dr A. M. Fairbairn in his book, *Catholicism: Roman and Anglican*, was later to refer to it as a 'pseudo-Catholicism' with the worst kind of sectarian vanity.[3]

In 1845 came the 'catastrophe' of Newman's migration to Rome and the consequent bridge he created for others after him. Henry Manning maintained that the common bond of those stepping away from the *via media* was 'their want of truth'.[4] And in the words of Dean Church, the wonder was, 'human nature being what it is, not that so many went, but that so many stayed'.[5]

With the popularity of this celebrated Tractarianism, there came also an

---

[1] Henry Bettenson, *Documents of the Christian Church* (Oxford 1943), pp. 434–5.

[2] *The English Church in the Nineteenth Century*, i, 338.

[3] *Catholicism: Roman and Anglican* (London 1899), p. 348.

[4] John Morley, *Life of William Ewart Gladstone* (London 1908), i, 234.

[5] R. W. Church, *The Oxford Movement: Twelve Years, 1833–1845* (London 1891), p. 270.

increasing dislike of the declared authority of the State in the offices of the Church. Numerous High Churchmen, therefore, favoured Disestablishment on grounds of their own – not because of religious equality, nor from objection to State endowments, but because they desired freedom to worship with their own liturgical discipline. Hurrell Froude had no hesitation in saying:

> If a national Church means a Church without discipline, my argument for discipline is an argument against a national Church; and the best thing we can do is to unnationalise ours as soon as possible; let us tell the truth and shame the devil; let us give up a *national* Church and have a *real* one.[1]

B. *Edward Miall and 'The Nonconformist'*

The leader of 'the second Puritan War' and the author of the Liberation Society was one Edward Miall (1809–81), journalist, and Member of Parliament. From the day of the founding of the British Anti-State-Church Association[2] until the day of his death, Miall was the guiding influence in all the proceedings of the notorious organization. By 1885, J. S. Brewer and Sir Lewis Dibdin could confidently write that there was 'as much likelihood' of the Church of England 'being disestablished as there is that Mr Miall and his friends will disestablish the solar system'.[3] But while the fearless Nonconformist lived, many Anglicans nervously expected anything to happen.

Miall possessed many unusual qualities of leadership and therefore became the object of suspicion and ridicule. But as a party leader he remained unruffled and unsparing in his denunciation of political injustice and priestly privilege. At Wymondley Theological College, London (afterwards Coward College), he had read Classics and English Literature with distinction, cultivating at the same time no mean oratorical and literary abilities. In early years his humble father had advised him to follow one path if he would achieve excellence. It was something he never forgot.

The Rev. J. Guinness Rogers in his autobiography described his friend as a man 'absolutely dominated by conscience. . . . His arguments were biting, but his words were never rude or vulgar'.[4] In Miall, said Henry W. Clark, 'the disestablishment idea came to its rightful place . . . in the ultimate Nonconformist ideal'.[5] Dr R. W. Dale referred to the man's gentle, devout, and fair-minded traits:

> While he held with resolute firmness the substance of the evangelical faith, he

[1] ibid., p. 47. Elliott-Binns (op. cit., p. 474) claims that John Keble once said: 'the union of Church and State as it is now understood is actually sinful.'

[2] This name was dropped at the 1853 Triennial Conference in favour of the less negative form 'The Society for the Liberation of Religion from State Patronage and Control', shortened to 'The Liberation Society'. Similar changes had been suggested at the first (1847) Triennial Conference.

[3] *The Endowments and Establishment of the Church of England*, p. 165.

[4] *An Autobiography* (London 1903), p. 93.

[5] *History of English Nonconformity* (London 1911, 1913), ii, 413. He defined this 'ideal' as the imparting of a divine life from Christ the Head, directly to the individual Christian disciple, and by that life energizing the Church and Society (cf. pp. 381, 375).

was charitable and generous to men of every religious creed and of none; . . . He was . . . regarded with passionate admiration by tens of thousands of people in every part of the country; but his personal life was lonely and meditative.[1]

It must be admitted that he made impressions of a distinctly different kind not only upon Tory Churchmen, but upon his fellow Dissenters as well. The older school of Ministers, though much disturbed by the spread of the Oxford Movement, were by no means disposed to follow Miall. As Principal W. B. Selbie later put it, 'He was a Radical, and they were not. He was a disturber of the peace of Israel, and they preferred to let sleeping dogs lie.'[2] Dr John Campbell, the Editor of the British Banner, after six years with the British Anti-State-Church Association, severed his connexion on the grounds that it had become 'a school of anarchy'. Miall simply dismissed men of this kind as being fearful of righteous commotion and unfaithful to sacred principles. He admitted that he liked agitation because it opposed stagnation and stirred up the truth.

The radical zest with which he set about his work originated, he claimed, in the repeal of the Test and Corporation Acts, and the consequent beginning of a new era in the advancement of religious liberty. Similar influences were afterwards brought to bear upon him in the disruption of the Scottish Church, the revolution on the Continent, the unrest in Ireland, the great Reform Bill, the Factory Education Bill, and the revival of Catholic principles in the Anglican Church. But the single event that fired his hostility most and moved him to drastic action was the imprisonment of William Baines, a member of his church in Leicester, for his refusal to pay an Anglican Church Rate in 1840.[3]

From that time onward, he became unrelenting, almost fanatical for the one end he had in view, total dissolution of the alliance between Church and State. His means was to be none other than the organization of Nonconformist public opinion. He said in a bitter message to those who were ready to act with him against every form of religious persecution:

I appeal to the honest, the thinking, the manly Dissenters of this kingdom. What have you gained by your silence and inactivity? Not peace. For every petty officer of the State Church, emboldened by your apathy, ventures forth to insult you. Not a more kindly consideration of your claims, for no questions are treated by the Legislature with such haughty and supercilious derision as questions

[1] History of English Congregationalism, pp. 635–6.

[2] Nonconformity: Its Origin and Progress (London 1912), p. 212.

[3] This had also been the fate of John Thorogood of Chelmsford, John Childs of Bungay and John Simonds of Aylesbury. Herbert S. Skeats & Charles S. Miall, History of the Free Churches of England 1688–1891 (London 1891), p. 486. Baines had been imprisoned for declining to pay, at the bidding of the Arches Court of Canterbury, two shillings and six-pence in Church Rates and one hundred and twenty-five pounds and three shillings costs. The question really at issue here was whether or not the punishment was for refusing to appear in court, or disobedience to the final decree. He was released after 31 weeks of confinement. Week by week, the Nonconformist called attention to this case and praised it as a means of forcing the evil upon the public conscience.

affecting the interests of religious liberty. All parties agree in neglecting and oppressing you.[1]

Words like these aroused the support of those dissatisfied with their social position, as it did the antagonism of those loyal to the Establishment.

1. *Beginnings and Objectives*

To understand the beginnings of the Liberation Society, one must study the beginnings of the *Nonconformist* as well, for Edward Miall was the guiding mind behind them both. Each served to advance the cause of the other. Both agreed what should be the relation of the Church to the civil power.

After eight years in two Congregationalist pastorates, Miall resigned from the pulpit for the public platform in order that he might more widely set out his views. He was accused of leaving the ministry 'to scatter firebrands amidst peaceful homesteads of his brethren'. He had already contributed articles to the *Leicester Mercury* and had written a series of trenchant publications for the newly formed Leicester Anti-Church-Rate Society.

Voluntaryists in that area had been discussing since 1839 the best means of stirring the heart of English Nonconformity into aggressive action. After the series of prosecutions culminating in the imprisonment of Baines, they resolved to establish a weekly newspaper in London for airing Dissenting grievances. The *Patriot* newspaper of Josiah Conder had served somewhat in this capacity since 1832 by its defence of the principles of religious freedom, but it viewed the public conferences on the separation of Church and State as something which would effect the separation of Dissenters instead. The *Eclectic Review* (1805) of Dr Thomas Price, the *British Banner* (1843) of Dr John Campbell, and the *British Quarterly Review* (1845) of Dr Robert Vaughan, all followed the same line – that of espousing anti-State-Church principles occasionally but cautiously. A general feeling therefore prevailed among the more energetic Dissenters that the principal organs of Dissent were guilty of lamentable reserve and narrowness of view.

Miall was selected to act as the editor of the *Nonconformist* newspaper. The work was shared with his brother, Charles S. Miall, Washington Wilks, and the Rev. G. B. Bubier. Miall personally solicited funds from the various Voluntary Church Societies in the large industrial centres. On one of these visits to Manchester, on 10 August 1840, he first met Richard Cobden and John Bright, and explained the nature of the new project. Meanwhile, he wrote privately to William Baines in jail pledging to him the support of his newspaper:

I hear you have made application to the London [Dissenting] Ministers. I fear they will desert you. Let me know their answer; for I intend to put you forward in our first number. Ministerial authority has no terrors for me. I have been behind the scenes, and know that their thunder and lightning is nothing more than sheet copper and powdered resin. I hope they mean to act wisely; for if

[1] Arthur Miall, *Life of Edward Miall*, pp. 27–8.

they do not, as surely as they live I shall lift the curtain to the public and show the trick.'[1]

Accordingly, on 14 April 1841, under the sub-title, 'The dissidence of dissent and the protestantism of the protestant religion' (a phrase borrowed from Edmund Burke[2]), the first edition of the paper was issued. In this and subsequent issues the Editor featured the full story of Baines, 'a prisoner for truth's sake'.[3]

The opening appeal was for Dissenters to cease wasting their efforts in skirmishes which brought them no nearer to the attainment of their ultimate goal. Miall urged them to unite in supporting a movement, the basis of which should be national rather than sectarian. The object of their newspaper was (1) to arouse people from 'fatal apathy' concerning the evils – constitutional, philosophical, political – of an establishment of religion; (2) to motivate people to come forward and act for 'an equitable and peaceable severance of church and state'.[4]

Throughout the 40-year period during which Miall was the Editor, the *Nonconformist* gave prominence not only to ecclesiastical affairs, but also to the foreign and domestic topics of the day. Its pages included book reviews, correspondence, market reports, advertisements, metropolitan and provincial news, reports on Parliamentary debates, and selections from other newspapers on matters of current interest. As one writer later expressed it, the *Nonconformist* in fact joined the underlying aims of Dissent and Democracy.[5] This was done by making the State-Church question the controlling medium of its news.

During the first few years of its existence, the main articles of the *Nonconformist* took the form of essays upon various aspects of the Disestablishment question, which were afterwards printed separately.[6] Most of these were scathing attacks upon every agency upholding the State Church. Timid dissenting Ministers who did not wish to spoil the spirit of their brotherly love, and wavering Nonconformist laymen who hoped for union with the evangelical Churchmen received terrible rebuke. The Church of England was accused of being a species of property and not a Church. Separation of Church and State was defined as the resumption by the latter for civil purposes of all national funds appropriated to the former. The Reformation in England was viewed as a period when Parliament handed over in trust to the Anglican

[1] ibid., p. 49.

[2] First used by him in his *On Conciliation with America* (Oxford 1775) in reference to the religious denominations in the American Colonies; cf. E. A. Payne, *Free Church Tradition*, p. 113n.

[3] A. Miall, *Life of Edward Miall*, p. 48.

[4] *Nonconformist*, 14.iv.41, p. 1.

[5] Richard Masheder, *Dissent and Democracy* (London 1864), p. 136. The author was a Fellow of Magdalene College, Cambridge, and a barrister of the Inner Temple.

[6] Among these were the *Nonconformist's Sketch Book* (1842; 1845), *Views of the Voluntary Principle* (1845), *Ethics of Nonconformity and Workings of Willinghood* (1848), *The Politics of Christianity* (1863).

Church her present temporalities, which could be withdrawn whenever Parliament believed that this Church no longer truly represented national Christianity. Clerical ministrations were accused of being dependent upon the will of the aristocratic and ruling classes. State control of religion was dismissed as incompatible with spiritual freedom and independent inquiry.

Through the newspaper channel, Miall was able to mix Nonconformity with economic theory. He sought to ally the Dissenting ecclesiastical cause with the rising *laissez faire* ideals of the Industrial Revolution. The *ancien régime*, the *Nonconformist* alleged, ruled in excess, leaving nothing to voluntary and spontaneous growth. Restriction everywhere regulated markets, impeded commerce, crippled industry and paralysed religion. These conditions were due to a misconception of the true function of government and its legislative acts, which should encourage free enterprise, not limit it.

> The utmost liberty, compatible with social order, we take to be the inalienable right of all men. We ask nothing more from the state than *protection*, extending to the life and liberty, the peace and property of the governed; and to secure this to all classes of subjects, we advocate a fair and full representation of all.[1]

This theory was borne out in a series of eleven letters to the Editor of the *Nonconformist* from Herbert Spencer, the founder of evolutionary philosophy.[2] For Spencer it was the duty of government to exclude State interference with religion, commerce, charity, war, colonization, education, and public health. His main social law stated that although, in the present imperfect condition of the human race, men required protection in their dealings with one another, they required no protection in their dealings with themselves. For in seeking to protect men against the evil effects of their mistakes, the State allowed them to neglect the cultivation of faculties by which they would make themselves strong.

In his economic policy Miall envisaged his task as part of a co-operative undertaking with other reform writers and thinkers of the period. Through him the *Nonconformist* fixed upon a fundamental social bias that was in line with the Republicanism then popular in France and America. Thus, English Dissenters, who were accustomed to a familiar and comfortable theology, were thrown in touch with the 'libertine' ideas arising from 'le contrat social' and 'the age of reason'.

The doctrines of philosophical radicalism in the writings of John Stuart Mill and Edwin Chadwick, growing out of Bentham's Utilitarian formulas, were likewise apparent in the columns of the new journal.[3] For Mill, the good society was one of richest diversity, springing from the authority of human

[1] *Nonconformist*, 14.iv.41, p. 1.

[2] These were entitled 'The Proper Sphere of Government', and began to appear on 15 June 1842. At this time Spencer was an avid leader in the National Complete Suffrage Union, and an engineer on the new London and Birmingham Railway.

[3] See *Nonconformist*, 13.ix.43, pp. 627–8, for a letter of explanation on 'the beautiful principle of Bentham'. The phrase, 'the greatest happiness of the greatest number', did not originate with Bentham, it was alleged, but in Joseph Priestley's earlier works.

capacity and personality, free from artificial impediments. The good Church, according to Miall's great principle of religious radicalism, was one of rich variety, allowing the reign of the invisible hand of Providence, free from legal restraints and uniformity. To the *Nonconformist*, masses rather than classes – people rather than property – counted for most in the spheres of both Church and State. Frequently the threat of disorder from the democratic elements was necessary in order to build up enough pressure to put through an elementary reform.

2. *Role and Style*

From the very beginning Miall projected the *Nonconformist* into the Chartist agitation. A series of his articles on this subject in the paper were later reprinted as a series of tracts by the National Complete Suffrage Union. In 1848 he published a book entitled, *The Suffrage: Or, Reconciliation Between the Middle and the Working Classes*. He favoured an overhaul of the electoral and Parliamentary system as it had been left by the Whig Reform Bill of 1832. Professing to champion the cause of 'the People's Charter'[1] and its advocates, he sought to reconcile radical, physical-force Chartists with moderate, moral-force Chartists, by upholding complete suffrage. Miall was never an advocate of violence in this or any agitation. Although he was willing to frighten the upper and middle classes, he was not prepared to hurt them.[2]

With the same intention in mind, the *Nonconformist* lent aid continually to the Anti-Corn-Law movement and the work of its League. After the General Election of 1841 and the displacement of Lord Melbourne's Cabinet by that of Sir Robert Peel, the Radical-Nonconformist party was optimistic. But the declaration of policy by the new Premier gave little hope of any serious attempt being made during his ministry to reduce the duties on the importation of corn. In a series of articles in his newspaper, Miall urged the Leaguers to achieve their end by seeking first to extend the franchise. Accordingly, the League issued a declaration at Manchester in 1841 which concluded with the legal principle (taken from Sir William Blackstone's *Commentaries on the Laws of England* in 1765) that

> . . . no subject of England can be constrained to pay any aids or taxes even for the defence of the realme or the support of the government, but such as are imposed by his own consent or that of his representatives in parliament.

The forceful proclamation of the principles of this declaration by the Dissenting Editor was a contributing factor in the fusion of the more orderly

---

[1] Written and published by Francis Place and William Lovett as the political programme for the London Working Men's Association. Founded by Lovett in 1836, the Association comprised respectable and self-educated artisans. Its Charter demanded universal male suffrage, equal electoral districts, the payment of M.P.s and the removal of their property qualifications, secret ballot, and annual General Elections.

[2] His position was similar to that of a certain Scottish Chartist who vividly expressed it: 'We must shake our oppressors well over hell's mouth, but not let them drop in!' Arnold Toynbee, *The Industrial Revolution in England* (London 1884), p. 207.

workers of the Anti-Corn-Law movement with the moral-force Chartists, at a conference in Birmingham on 5–9 April 1842. Miall wrote to his friend Joseph Sturge that they were raising a power which they might be unable to control if chafed by aristocratic opposition.

The final outcome of the conference, when Miall himself was called upon to speak, was the formation of the National Complete Suffrage Union, which officially designated the *Nonconformist* as its organ.[1] This connexion continued until some months before the Anti-State-Church conference in 1844, when Miall decided that the great social issue of the future lay in Disestablishment rather than in Chartism.

Near the height of his career, Edward Miall wrote words which had always marked his style of work:

> In every department of thought or action, . . . true genius works in utter disregard of the obligations it [the code of the world, i.e. 'the thing' to do] would impose, and asserts for itself the right of transcending, if need be, any average standard.[2]

He was undoubtedly a most clever and skilful editor. Commanding a cool intellect and warm imagination, he provided the *Nonconformist* with leaders that for many were hardly surpassed by *The Times* or the *Examiner*. His viewpoint may have appeared to later generations as that of 'a Spurgeon run into a politico-ecclesiastical mould', but to his contemporaries it was more like Robert Browne speaking in an Elizabethan role. His critics contended that readers of this periodical would look in vain for an article of mystical aspiration or religious meditation. However, behind all the news lay the 'Nonconformist Ideal' that a devout life was something primarily for the individual believer and that out of this proceeded social-temporal order.

Miall's literary style was similar to his platform oratory. Frequently it exhibited qualities of grandness and power, but just as often it became harshly satirical and biting. He indulged in popular exaggeration, often becoming overwrought with the glories of 'the great and noble cause' at stake. On occasions, however, there were touching passages of Victorian romanticism, as in his letter from Inverness, 7 July 1839, to his wife:

> A host of mountains about which the light clouds of morning floated, threw up a dark blue breastwork on the horizon, and amongst them Ben Cruachan stood, like Saul amongst his companions, a head and shoulders above the rest.

As a prophet of Nonconformity, Miall made free use of commonplace

[1] A full report of the proceedings is to be found in *Nonconformist*, 13.iv.42, pp. 234–44. Mr Joseph Sturge, who presided on this occasion, said unhesitatingly that 'Mr Miall had done more by his writings to promote the great object they had in view during the last three months than any one individual had ever achieved in the same space of time' (A. Miall, *Life of Edward Miall*, p. 86n).

[2] *An Editor off the Line, or, Wayside Musings and Reminiscences* (London 1865), p. 59. This excerpt is drawn from the essay, 'Kicking over the Traces', which concludes (p. 67): 'All human judgments may be challenged by individual conviction, and it is better for the world to let the challenger take his chance of success than authoritatively to put him down.'

metaphor, palatable alike to the simple Chapel folk and the prosperous descendants of Puritan families reared on *Pilgrim's Progress*. To the Puritan of the nineteenth century as of the seventeenth century, the allegorical figure of speech, in contrast to what he thought of as the 'sophisticated language of the Cavaliers', lent itself easily to the expression of 'common truths'. Unfortunately, it sometimes led to an ugly and distorted picture as well:

> A state-church! Have they never pondered upon the practical meaning of that word? Have they never looked into that dark, polluted, inner chamber of which it is the door? Have they never caught a glimpse of the loathsome things that live, and crawl, and gender there?[1]

Miall was a versatile writer. He wrote one or two difficult books on philosophy and theology, notably, *Bases of Belief*, which seemed to be a striving after the persuasive style of Thomas Carlyle. (Élie Halévy maintains, however, that Miall's views seemed to be far more representative of the country at this time than Carlyle's.[2]) Miall made no attempt at poetry, but he tried his hand at several somewhat poetic Parliamentary 'sketches', and these showed him to be a humorous, penetrating observer of people. Of Disraeli he said: 'He carries *nonchalance* to absurd extremities. Occasionally he will adjust his neck-tie—once he positively cleaned his nails. One could hardly help suspecting that he *meant* to occupy just five hours—and that he put in practice a variety of petty arts to fill up the time.'[3]

As a journalist and essayist, he combined many of the rugged traits of Daniel Defoe and William Cobbett. But with all his satire and realism, one discovers occasional passages of unaffected response to nature. The essay entitled 'The Humorous and Grotesque in Nature' concluded: 'The prudery which sniggles and exclaims "fie", is born of conventionalism. A true response to Nature, where the higher laws and morality and religion do not prohibit it, is what no man need blush for, and invariably does him good.'[4]

C. *Preparatory Demonstrations*

The year before the formation of the British Anti-State-Church Association, there were two major circumstances which prepared the way for its programme of agitation. These appeared to confirm the view of a mass of Nonconformists that the days of the Anglican Establishment were drawing to a close.

---

[1] *The Nonconformist's Sketch Book: A Series of Views of a State-Church and its Attendant Evils* (London 1845), p. 17.

[2] *The Age of Peel and Cobden* (London 1847), p. 355.

[3] A. Miall, *Life of Edward Miall*, pp. 175–6. He described Lord Macaulay (p. 178) as 'a pet of the House of Commons. . . . His style of oratory is quite exhilarating. He is no logician, but then he makes you forget logic. . . . his imagery [is] half poetic and in exquisite taste; . . . He insinuates himself into your soul like a vernal breeze, his thoughts drop upon you like fragrant balm . . .'

[4] *An Editor off the Line*, p. 30.

1. *The Scottish Disruption*

On 18 May 1843, the Church of Scotland suffered the secession of nearly half of its Ministers, Missionaries, and lay leaders. By this act, one of the Established Churches of the British Isles was rent asunder and the Free Church of Scotland formally constituted. The advocates of the Disruption viewed it as a demonstration of fidelity to conscience, for which their country had always been proud, and following in the same spirit as that of the 1662 exodus from the Church of England. The English Free Churches drew effective parallels and pinned high hopes on what might result.

Ironically, the main leader of the Disruption, Thomas Chalmers, Professor of Theology at Edinburgh University, had on 25 April–12 May 1938 lectured in London on 'The Establishment and Extension of National Churches'.[1] Four years later, however, he wrote a letter to the Duke of Argyll vindicating his participation in the anti-patronage movement and condemning the interference of the secular courts with the spiritual independence of the Scottish Church. He warned that his followers would quit the 'Erastianized' Church and present 'an unbroken phalanx of resistance to the violence that would offer an invasion upon our liberties'.[2]

Much of the trouble centred in the question of the call of a Minister to a Church. Many Scottish people had traditionally laid great stress upon its being done through a fellowship of believers. This practice was widely cherished as a Reformation principle and a safeguard against the intrusion of unworthy persons. On the other hand, the wealthy patrons of the benefices naturally demanded non-intrusion upon their legal rights. The power of appointment should rest in their hands in order to make sure of having suitable pastors for the parishioners.

On 24 November 1842, the Scottish Convocation addressed a memorial to Sir Robert Peel, declaring the intention of a large number of its members to relinquish the Church's temporalities unless the Government granted parishioners (1) the power of vetoing the appointment of Ministers by their legal patrons, and (2) freedom in electing the representatives for their Church government. The specific grievance behind this action was the judgement in the case of the parish of Auchterarder, Perthshire, which had ruled the supremacy of civil courts over ecclesiastical courts and over the authority of the General Assembly.[3] The Cabinet was led by Lord Aberdeen to believe

[1] cf. Chalmers, *Lectures on the Establishment and Extension of National Churches* (Glasgow 1838), Lecture VI, pp. 187–8: 'we speak of the blessings of unity; and we confess how greatly more it is endeared to us, since made to perceive, that, only by an undivided church, only by the ministers of one denomination, can a community be out and out pervaded, or a territory be filled up and thoroughly overtaken with the lessons of the gospel.'
[2] William Hanna, *Memoirs of the Life and Writings of Thomas Chalmers* (Edinburgh 1849–52), iv, 274–5.
[3] According to Dr Robert Buchanan (*The Ten Years' Conflict* [Glasgow 1849], ii, 552–6) the drama of the Disruption arose from the two reforming Acts of the 1834 General Assembly – the Veto Act (on administering calls) and the Chapel Act (on dealing with Secession Kirks). The former was repudiated in the case of Auchterarder, and the latter in

that when it came to the point of surrendering their stipends or abandoning their consistency, the great body of the clergy would do the latter. The reply of Sir James Graham, the Home Secretary, confused the claims raised in the memorial, and alleged that to yield to them would lead directly to despotic power.

> Her Majesty's Ministers, now understanding that nothing less than total abroga-
> tion of the rights of the Crown, and of other patrons, will satisfy the Church,
> are bound with firmness to declare that they cannot advise her Majesty to
> consent to the grant of any such demand.[1]

Although Dr Chalmers had at first been unsympathetic to the principle of Voluntaryism, he now realized the advantage, if not the necessity, of co-operation with the Voluntaries in Scotland. The controversy originally dividing the country into Voluntaries and Establishmentarians began in 1829 when the Rev. Andrew Marshall, Minister of the United Secession Presbyterian Church at Kirkintilloch, Dunbarton, preached a sermon, 'Ecclesiastical Establishments Considered', impugning the principle of State Churches as contrary to the word of God. A reply followed in quick succession from Dr Andrew Thomson of Edinburgh. The *Voluntary Church Magazine* and Voluntary Church Associations were started on one side. They were challenged by the Established Church and the *Church of Scotland Magazine* on the other side. Both parties were almost entirely Presbyterian, held a common heritage, and accepted the same standard of faith and order.

Chalmers declared that if the voluntary principle stood the trial to which it would be put, he would welcome it even though it might demonstrate the weakness of his arguments for establishing religion in the country. The split between the Scottish Voluntaries and Freechurchmen widened as the *Nonconformist* pressed more and more for a national conference for the complete separation of Church and State. Chalmers pointed out in his letter of 31 December 1842, to W. Lennox of New York, that they all faced a common foe.

> I do hope that henceforth our friends the Voluntaries will think more generously
> of us than they have done heretofore. Not that we renounce the principle of a
> National Establishment of Christianity, for we think it quite possible to

---

that of Stewarton, thereby placing the government of the Church under civil regulation and control. In August 1834, the Earl of Kinnoul, the patron of the living, appointed Mr Robert Young of Dundee as Minister of the Church at Auchterarder. At a meeting of the congregation, only two parishioners out of 330 came forward to sign the call, while 287 indicated their dissent. The legal agents of the presentee and patron argued the case in the courts until 1839, when the decision was pronounced in their favour in the House of Lords by Lords Brougham and Cottenham. In effect this precluded the General Assembly from taking into account the reaction of a parish to its presentee, except in the matter of his professional qualifications. Hugh Watt, *Thomas Chalmers and the Disruption* (Edinburgh 1943), pp. 173–6.

[1] Torrens McCullagh Torrens, *The Life and Times of the Right Honourable Sir James R. G. Graham* (London 1863), ii, 232.

harmonize this with the principle of spiritual independence. It will be the fault of our rulers if the two are not harmonized; . . . Should this [Disruption] take place, it will be of first rate importance that we, the ejected ministers, and they, the evangelical Dissenters, should act with a common and cordial understanding together, as there is now a most formidable enemy, rising every day into greater strength, in the Puseyism of England.[1]

The Hon. Fox Maule (M.P., Perth) introduced a motion in Parliament on 7 March 1843 that the House of Commons should resolve itself into a committee to take into consideration the grievances of which the Church of Scotland complained. The motion was decisively turned down the next evening by 76 to 211 votes. The tone of the debate afforded little hope that the legislature was ready even to consider the restitution of the parishioners' former rights. This event fired the discontented parties north of the Tweed into drastic action. Chalmers had already publicly outlined his scheme for supporting the outgoing Ministers by means of weekly payments to a central sustentation fund from local associations all over the country. He wrote again to Lennox on 19 April 1843, expressing the hope that by the end of the summer there would exist about a thousand such associations.

Scotland was now in an excited state. The Church, in obvious collision with the legal authorities of the land, waited for the ensuing Assembly. The extent to which the threatened Disruption was likely to succeed became the favourite subject of betting in fashionable clubs and in the streets. A leading citizen of Edinburgh was reported to have said, 'Mark my words, not forty of them will go out.'

On the fateful day in 1843, the die was cast when Dr David Welsh, the Moderator of the General Assembly, read a brief protest against the infringement of their liberties. Before the intent audience he called for those in agreement 'to withdraw to a separate place of meeting' to form a new body for 'separating in an orderly way from the Establishment'. The son-in-law of Dr Chalmers, the Rev. William Hanna, described what followed:

Having finished the reading of this Protest, Dr. Welsh laid it upon the table [before his Grace the Lord High Commissioner, the Marquess of Bute, representing the Queen], turned and bowed respectfully to the Commissioner, left the chair and proceeded along the aisle to the door of the Church [St Andrew's]. . . . The whole audience was now standing gazing in stillness upon the scene. Man after man, row after row, moved on along the aisle, till the benches on the left lately so crowded showed scarce an occupant. More than 400 ministers, and a still larger number of elders, had withdrawn. A vast multitude of people stood congregated in George's Street, crowding in upon the church-doors. When the deed was done within, the intimation of it passed like lightning through the mass without, and when the forms of their most venerated clergymen were seen emerging from the Church, a loud and irrepressible cheer burst from their lips, and echoed through the now half empty Assembly Hall. There was no design on the part of the clergymen to form into a procession, but they were forced to it by the

[1] W. Hanna, op. cit., iv, 319–20: letter of 31.xii.42.

narrowness of the lane opened for their egress through the heart of the crowd. Falling into line, and walking three abreast, they formed into a column which extended for a quarter of a mile and more. As they moved along to the new Hall prepared for their reception, very different feelings prevailed among the numberless spectators who lined the streets, and thronged each window and door, and balcony, on either side. Some gazed in stupid wonder; the majority looked on in silent admiration.[1]

For the first time in Scottish history, two General Assemblies with identical confessions of faith convened in Edinburgh, but at the same time a new religious vitality was set to work throughout the land. The adherents to the Scottish Free Church numbered less than one-fourth of the population, yet within the first year they had raised no less than £32,000 for her various schemes of philanthropy – a sum greater by £12,000 than that raised by the whole Church in the year 1842. Before two years had elapsed the state of the building fund rendered it possible to open 500 churches, and by the end of 1848 over 700 were occupied. The years 1843–8 showed an average annual income for home and foreign wants of £300,000, approximately 600 schools opened, and 250 students training for the ministry. One of the seceding Ministers, the Rev. William Grant of Ayr, gave an account of the work swelling within his Presbytery:

> The months that followed [the Disruption] were busy months. The eleven who came out undertook to supply ordinances in thirty-three charges. It was no easy task. I find that I preached on an average twenty times a-month. My brethren were equally busy.[2]

The central Sustentation Fund for the support of the Ministers was a fine monument to Chalmers's foresight and genius in ecclesiastical finance. In the first year the Fund produced £68,000 or an equal dividend of £105 for ministerial stipends,[3] and by 1847 the common pool had reached £100,000.

In spite of these vivid testimonies to Voluntaryism, Chalmers's final verdict on the principle was unfavourable, because it could do little in face of congregational selfishness. To him, the Free Church stood ideally for the principle of a national establishment supported by the ecclesiastical endowments of its faithful members. He believed that Presbyterianism on this basis could reconcile the differences between Congregationalism and Episcopacy. Monetary considerations, however, as much as the matter of secular control, should never, in his view, bind the spiritual independence of the Church.

2. *Sir James Graham's Factory Bill*
The other public circumstance paving the way for the British Anti-State-Church Association was the Education Bill of Sir James Graham, providing for the compulsory secular and religious education of all children employed

---

[1] ibid., iv, 338–9.

[2] Thomas Brown, *Annals of the Disruption* (Edinburgh 1884), p. 202.

[3] William Addison, op. cit., p. 90, claims that this stipend was 'equal to or more than that of a Bishop of the Episcopal Church'.

in factories. Ever since the publication of the report of the Education Committee of the Privy Council in 1839,[1] which called for an overhaul in elementary instruction, this legislative struggle had been pending. Until 1843, Congregationalist leaders, who supplied the energy for the voluntary movement in education, were not opposed to state aid. But in that year they and their friends saw a subtle danger, for the educational clauses were made to appear as an incidental part of much-needed reform of factory laws. Moreover, Graham made clear his belief that the Anglican Catechism was the best medium for the religious education of the poor children.[2]

Again the Dissenters fumed against the innovation as in some way due to Puseyite tendencies. The Dissenting Deputies pictured the bill as a major legislative evil. The *Nonconformist* denounced the scheme as an attempt to create an educational establishment in which the State schoolmaster was to do the work which the State clergyman had failed to do. A satirical passage from the *Nonconformist's Sketch Book* in 1842 reflected the intensity of Miall's feeling.

> We remember being told in our youthful days, that dog-fanciers succeeded in producing the race of tiny lap-dogs by administering gin to them while puppies, and thus preventing their further growth. We shall not need to insist upon the correctness of our information. True or false it will serve to illustrate our present subject. The main end of the system of education worked by the clergy seems to be, to hinder the free development of the youthful mind, and to produce a race of intellectual dwarfs. With the miserable pittance of instruction, the coarsest rudiments of knowledge imparted in their schools, they mingle slavish maxims *usque ad nauseam*. Habits of inquiry constitute just the one thing which they labour to prevent—independence of mind, the cardinal sin which the youngsters are taught to shun.[3]

Sir James had not commended himself to the Nonconformist confidence by his handling of affairs in the Scottish Church at this time. He had in fact been blamed for the great cleavage within that Establishment. The Dissenters were most worried, therefore, that his measure would destroy the Sunday School movement and the entire system of voluntary instruction which their denominations had laboriously established in many factory districts.[4] The Home Secretary would insist upon taxation for his new schools, instruction by a

[1] The Melbourne Government in that year had created this committee, later to become the Board of Education, which was to grant £30,000 for the improvement of schools. The National Society for the Promotion of the Education of the Poor (Anglican) and the British and Foreign School Society (Dissenting) were to be the channels of State assistance. The State in turn would inspect the schools.

[2] See Francis Adams, *History of the Elementary School Contest in England* (London 1882), pp. 125 ff.

[3] *Nonconformist's Sketch Book* (London 1842), pp. 110–11.

[4] Edward Baines, as the Editor of the *Leeds Mercury*, printed his returns from parishes and townships in the manufacturing districts, comparing the Church and Chapel school accommodations. The statistics revealed that one out of every five of the population of scholars attended Sunday Schools, and that one out of every ten attended Church of England Schools. Sir Edward Baines, *Life of Edward Baines* (London 1851), pp. 316–17.

clergyman appointed by a bishop, and management by the churchwardens together with four persons chosen by J.P.s in Petty Sessions. Loss of franchise would be the penalty for those conscientiously objecting to paying a poor rate to support the scheme.

The *Patriot* began to print articles 'exposing' the terrible flaws in the provisions, and there was an outburst of Nonconformist hostility. Popular meetings were held by the hundred, in addition to lobbying, publications, and pressure upon M.P.s by their electors. Lord Brougham accused the Dissenters of undue hatred of the national establishment and of loving their sects more than education. He wished the State to train children to be morally good citizens rather than intelligent citizens. Many Anglican leaders feared that 'the supreme function of the Church as the instructress of the people' had been encroached upon by the Committee of the Council in order to disarm Dissenting opposition.

In announcing to the Commons his modifications on 1 May 1843, before going into committee, Graham complained of the religious bitterness on both sides. He submitted his olive branch, which allowed limited Dissenting instruction and moderate public control in the schools, but his opponents would not be pacified. As far as they could see, the Bill was still designed to augment the influence of the dominant religious party. In the Cabinet, even Gladstone, ardent Anglican that he was, favoured its withdrawal. Altogether, approximately 24,000 petitions with some 4,000,000 signatures went into Parliament against the original and amended educational clauses.

At last, on 15 June Sir James capitulated, 'with deep regret, and with melancholy forebodings with regard to the progress of education'.[1] Sir Robert Peel bewailed 'the sorry and lamentable triumph which Dissent had achieved'. One of Gladstone's biographers described the effect of the announcement upon the country that evening:

> . . . there were thousands of meetings held in this country for prayer and remonstrance. . . . Within the doors the people, to a man and to a woman, were on their knees in silent prayer. Suddenly the sound of carriage wheels was heard outside. A messenger had driven hard from the House of Commons with the news that Sir James had withdrawn his bill. The cheers in the street conveyed the news to the people within, and without a sign or a moment's pause they rose in mass from their knees and sang the doxology.[2]

The decision of the Government made it plain that State education in England could not become identified with Anglican education. Regulation of employment and improvement of schools remained separate considerations.

Miall now sought to turn this victory to permanent account. He hoped to do it by organizing an agency against the ecclesiastical system responsible for such legislation. The campaign of the Dissenters had revealed sources of power which they had not realized they possessed. 'We may now', he wrote, 'bid a final adieu to the system of petty warfare.'

[1] Hansard (3rd series), lxix, 1569.
[2] Thomas Archer, *William Ewart Gladstone and his Contemporaries*, i, 332.

CHAPTER 2

Political Action Methods

I do not charge the Liberation Society with the deliberate
desire to overthrow the Monarchy in this country, and to
establish a Republic in its place, but it is manifestly their
design to assimilate the Constitution of this country, in
respect of a National religion, to that of Republican
America, the historians of that country enumerating
'among the new guarantees for the public welfare peculiar
to the United States the absence of a National Church and
tithes, and the establishment of the equality of all denominations of Christians'.

THE VEN. ARCHDEACON W. H. HALE[1]

... in the old country parishes, where the Church was then
seen at her best, Miss Austen's charming clergy, though
often scholars and always gentlemen, were only the squires'
younger sons put into the family livings, in no marked way
devoted either to their sacred calling or to their humbler
parishioners. The Church had very largely lost her former
hold on the masses. Men thought that she took too much
and gave too little.

GEORGE MACAULAY TREVELYAN[2]

THE TEMPER of the times was now ready for a well-organized movement towards the separation of Church and State. There were new
achievements for greater social freedom, and there were fresh
departures from religious tradition. In 1844, the first year of the Anti-State-
Church Association, a Co-operative Movement was founded, a Factory
Reform Bill was pending, and a Dissenters' Chapel Act was passed. The Act
gave to the Chapels freedom from the stranglehold of ancient trust deeds and
from the fear of legal prosecution.

The most dogged resistance to the Liberation movement was naturally to
come from the clergy itself. Since the time of the Reform Bill in 1832, Anglican

---

[1] *The Designs and Constitution of the Society for the Liberation of Religion from State
Patronage and Control* (London 1861), pp. 37–8.
[2] *Lord Grey of the Reform Bill* (London 1920), p. 290.

divines, who had been almost unanimous in their opposition to Chartism, had felt it their bounden duty to discourage democracy and uphold the Monarchy. The dangers of such a position became apparent in 1848 when the French Monarchy fell. From the outset 'that awful word' Disestablishment was coupled in people's minds with what had been behind the revolution in France. English Liberationists using phrases such as 'liberty, equality, and fraternity' were suspected of being collaborators with the French *bourgeoisie*. This meant that most Anti-State-Church men were shut out from existing political associations, especially wherever loyal and royalist Churchmen were present.

During the early part of the nineteenth century a wide gap in political temperament had undoubtedly existed between the respectable Whigs and the radical Dissenters. As it became clear, however, that the latter were not enemies of the Throne, but ardent disciples of *laissez faire* teaching, their ecclesiastical nonconformity became an accepted political party of its own. When the Religious Freedom Society converted wealthy citizens from industrial and commercial nonconformity, this new block was accepted and the Whig party liberalized.

These Nonconformists were not entering the political arena with their eyes closed. The lessons of the past had taught them two things – or so they believed: first, that the majority of the legislators were lamentably ignorant of the principles on which religion rested; and second, that under the pretext of promoting religion, both major parties in Parliament were disposed to extend the aid of the State to all forms of religion alike, however contradictory to each other, with an evident view to using ministers of religion as tools of the government.

A. *National Conference*
A vision of how greatly different England could be with the separation of Church and State came more vividly to the mind of Edward Miall than to any other man of his time. He started his campaign with the unshakeable conviction that men with this vision (1) must labour within Parliament with political tools to put an end to all inequalities in the dealings of Parliament with loyal subjects of the realm, and (2) that they must put their trust in the force of spiritual motives and spiritual agencies to accomplish spiritual purposes. In answer to the question, 'Why not be content with your gained freedoms and seek the welfare of your own denomination rather than meddling with the affairs of a Church to which you do not belong?' he replied: 'Simply because it is the Church of England and we are Englishmen.'

In the articles in the *Nonconformist* newspaper in 1842, Miall repeatedly proposed a convention of delegates to plan steps for a vigorous movement against State religion. He was troubled by the indifference of the 'aristocracy of Dissent' that was entrenched in the metropolis. Several months after the defeat of the Factory Education scheme, he drew up an appeal, which was signed by 70 Ministers, mainly of the Midland counties, and sent it to the secretaries of the various Dissenting bodies. These latter supported the idea, although somewhat lukewarmly.

The meeting of these Ministers and others in the counties which had been called for took place in Leicester on 7 December 1843. The meeting declared itself against the principle of national establishments of religion, and called for a national conference of people so minded. Dr Francis A. Cox, Dr Thomas Price, and Edward Miall were asked to act as a temporary committee to draft the names of Ministers to constitute a provisional committee. At a later meeting in the Memorial Hall Library in London, these three men united with three others, the Rev. Charles Stovel, the Rev. James Carlile, and J. M. Hare, of the *Patriot*, who had been chosen for the same purpose.

The London Ministers were inclined to react slowly to their scheme, but the provisional committee was finally appointed, consisting of 145 Ministers and 48 laymen, and from this group an executive committee was elected. The executive committee finally included: 1 Anglican, 1 Methodist, 2 Presbyterians, 2 Baptists, and 11 Congregationalists. On 8 February 1844, the executive met to carry out detailed arrangements for a grand convocation of friends of religious freedom.

The Nonconformist press now fervently entreated Dissenters everywhere to unite. The arguments against co-operation – that the agitation (1) would cause division where union was desired, (2) would promote what was unscriptural, and (3) would involve alliances which Christians ought to avoid – were analysed and refuted. It was announced that where election of delegates by congregations was inconvenient, 'any 100 persons' were empowered to appoint two representatives by signature, and that 'females equally with males' could be represented at the approaching convention.

On 30 April, the conference, consisting of some 700 delegates, assembled at the Crown and Anchor Hotel in the Strand, 'to commence efforts for the disenthralment of religion from the secularizing influence of state control'.[1] The Conference first resolved that in no way was it to be looked upon as an official demonstration of Dissenting strength in the kingdom. It next resolved against a mere defensive policy, declaring that 'a united, earnest and scriptural effort to diffuse our sentiments should be made for the extinction of the union between Church and State'.[2]

Papers on various aspects of Disestablishment were presented during the three-day sitting. Many leading Nonconformist Churchmen would have nothing to do with the meetings. In most cases they feared the charge of

---

[1] Notable Nonconformists who were present either as delegates or in their private capacity were: the Rev. John Pye Smith D.D., F.R.S. (President of Homerton College); the Rev. Thomas Jenkyn D.D. (President of Coward College); Josiah Conder (Editor of the *Patriot*); Dr Thomas Price (Editor of the *Eclectic Review*); Dr John Campbell (Editor of the *British Banner*); Joseph Sturge; Apsley Pellatt; George Thompson; John Bright M.P.; Sharman Crawford M.P.; and Dr John Bowring M.P., Dr Andrew Marshall of Kirkintilloch, Professor N. McMichael of Dunfermline, and Dr Ralph Wardlaw of Glasgow represented the Scottish Voluntary Party.

[2] *Proceedings of the First Anti-State-Church Conference*, 1844, p. 17.

'anarchy' and the loss of what political pull Nonconformity already possessed. The Baptist Union was the only general representative group sending delegates. Other Church bodies represented by independent delegates were the Congregational Churches of London and Scotland, the 'unendowed' Presbyterian Churches of Scotland, the Friends, the Unitarians, and the Jamaica Dissenters. Several members of the Church of England were also in attendance.[1] The *Nonconformist*, reporting the proceedings in 37 columns, described it as 'the desires of many years . . . fulfilled', 'a lovely and majestic dream', and 'the greatest "fact" of the present age'. Furthermore, it reported, the differences among delegates had been negligible.

B. *Organization and Principles*
Under the heading 'Scheme of Organization to Liberate Religion in the British Empire from State Interference', the conference had approved their name as 'The British Anti-State-Church Association'. The treasurer was Dr Thomas Price; the three Secretaries Edward Miall, Dr F. A. Cox, and J. M. Hare; three Auditors; a Council of 500 and an Executive Committee of 50 members. The Council met annually, the Executive fortnightly, and both were elected at each Triennial Conference.

The first meeting of the Executive was held on 6 June 1844, at the Guildhall Coffee House. They later opened their first offices at 5 Aldine Chambers, Paternoster Row, and in 1849 these were moved to 4 Crescent, New Bridge Street, Blackfriars. Such was the suspicion which hovered over them that for a time no banker in London would accept their account. They advertised their basic principles as follows:

> That in matters of religion man is responsible to God alone; that all legislation by secular governments in affairs of religion is an encroachment upon the rights of man, and an invasion of the prerogatives of God; and that the application by law of the resources of the State to the maintenance of any form or forms of religious worship and instruction is contrary to reason, hostile to liberty, and directly opposed to the genius of Christianity.[2]

In the Annual Report for 1853 this general statement was dropped in favour of a more specific declaration of purpose: (1) the abrogation of all laws and usages which inflict disability, or confer privilege, on ecclesiastical grounds, upon any subject of the realm; (2) the discontinuance of all payments from the Consolidated Fund, and of all Parliamentary grants and compulsory exactions, for religious purposes; (3) the application to secular uses, after an equitable satisfaction of existing interest, of all national property now held in trust by the United Church of England and Ireland and the Presbyterian Church of Scotland, and concurrently with it, the liberation of those Churches from all State control.

[1] One Anglican was John Lee LL.D., D.C.L., F.R.S., a scientist and an advocate of the Arches Court, who favoured union between Dissenters and the Church of England, and became a member of the Society's Executive Committee.

[2] *Proceedings*, 1844, p. 149; quoted in A. Miall, *Life of Edward Miall*, pp. 95–6.

The subsequent agreement upon modes of action to be followed in pursuit of these objects varied somewhat from the original statement in 1844. Both assumed, however, something of a general pattern: (1) collecting and spreading evidence concerning the harmful effects of employing law in aid of religion; (2) making use of the press to further the programme of the Society; (3) holding public meetings and delivering lectures on all questions within the scope of the Society's aims; (4) organizing the friends of the Society to exert their combined influence on the public mind, and on Parliament; (5) watching the proceedings of Parliament and of other public bodies, to prevent any infringement of civil liberty on religious pretexts; (6) urging upon voters their duty to return to Parliament men of integrity who were favourable to the Society's principles and willing to advocate them.

Under the heading 'Primary Rules', it was further stated that such modes of action should be resorted to only by 'moral and constitutional means', that the Society would pursue its object without reference to sectarian or party or theological distinctions, and that the Society would not be responsible for any acts or opinions of supporters expressed without its sanction. (These second and third clauses were added to the Constitution in 1859.) In the judgement of Anglican observers, however, the members of the new Association were nothing but public enemies:

> It is not equality but only the extermination of religion from off the face of the land which would satisfy them. Some of them have shown their hands, and have not hesitated to declare that the Church as a religious body must be utterly destroyed, and no means of re-creating itself should be allowed. It has been reasonably conjectured that the residuary legatees of Disestablishment and Disendowment would be—Irreligion, Agnosticism, and Atheism.[1]

While professing that their aims must be settled by political agency, the founders of the movement firmly believed that it should have as its main-spring religious conviction. Ideally this underlying conviction was that the Christian Church had borne testimony to the native power of God's truth to maintain and extend itself. The freedom of the Church of Christ from secular thraldom, therefore, was an incomparably higher aim than any. Nevertheless, in order to avoid the weakness of religious discord within its own ranks, the leaders of the Association preferred to speak with the voice of conscience rather than with that of theology.

The Anti-State-Church body came into being just before the controversy surrounding the Dissenters' Chapel Act was settled. From the time of the Lady Sarah Hewley Charity case in 1830, orthodox Trinitarians and the unorthodox Unitarians had been struggling for the legal possession of those Presbyterian churches in which the founders had not specified that the property should be used strictly by adherents of the Westminster Confession.[2]

---

[1] A. H. Hore, *History of the Church of England* (Oxford 1891), p. 531.

[2] In 1842 the House of Lords decided in favour of the claimants that orthodox Dissenters alone were qualified to act as trustees and to share in the endowments. The entire litigation cost £30,000. A. H. Drysdale, *History of the Presbyterians in England* (London 1889),

The Irish and Scottish Presbyterians, the Wesleyans, Congregationalists, Baptists, and even the Church of England were threatened with similar doctrinal splits.

Miall deplored the division of Dissent on doctrinal or theological issues and deplored even more any loss of valuable Unitarian influence in seeking the relief of Dissenters' political grievances. He was one of eight members of the Dissenting Deputies who tried, unsuccessfully, to get that organization to drop its opposition to the proposed Act. His stand probably drew a great measure of Unitarian support away from the Dissenting Deputies and enlisted it in the work of the Anti-State-Church Association.

C. *Early Activities*

The years 1844–9 were given over mostly to indoctrination. The Association aimed to draw all Dissenting opinion to one common centre and give it coherence. But while the Association was indoctrinating the Nonconformist element, it was just as earnestly conducting propaganda among the public at large. In a single year, 1849, the Liberation leaders had delivered lectures and distributed their tracts in 167 cities in England, Scotland, Wales, and Ireland.[1]

Besides lecturing in many provincial centres, the regular lecturers presented a successful series of addresses in London, at the Literary and Scientific Institution, Aldersgate Street, in 1848. Friends of the Association on these occasions usually welcomed the speaker deputations with a special soirée and public demonstrations. In 1845 Miall made a good showing in the Southwark by-election against Sir William Molesworth, but failed at the poll.

Possibly the most colourful public discussion during this period was the debate in Liverpool, on 24 February 1847, between the Rev. Joseph Baylee of Birkenhead and Edward Miall. One month before, a meeting conducted by a deputation had been thrown into indescribable confusion by a body of local working men. Miall's biographer states that a gang of 200 ship's carpenters were hired by the Church party deliberately to disturb the meeting. The *Nonconformist* reporter referred to them as fanatical Orangemen. Miall therefore challenged his antagonists to produce their spokesman for an orderly and fair public meeting. This was promptly arranged to take place on two consecutive evenings in the municipal concert hall before an audience of 2,000 on the subject: 'Can the State Church principle for the maintenance of Christian Institutions be justified by the Word of God; and is the compulsory

---

pp. 617–20. Sir Robert Peel and his Ministry saw the plight of the Unitarians and therefore passed the Bill in 1844 securing undisturbed possession of a place of worship (and all property connected with it) to the congregation which had occupied it continuously for twenty-five years.

[1] Of the lecturers, the Rev. John H. Hinton achieved probably the greatest distinction. His books included: *The Harmony of Religious Truth and Human Reason* (1832), *A Treatise on Man's Responsibility* (1840), *A Plea for Liberty of Education* (1843), and *Individual Effort and the Active Christian* (1859).

or voluntary system in support of Christian Churches and worship most in accordance with the revealed mind of Christ?' Admission was by ticket only and platform rules were placed in the hands of committees of each side. They agreed that each disputant should have one chairman, and that a moderator chosen by both parties should decide in case of any disagreement between the chairmen. The proceedings, which proved to be both orderly and satisfactory, began by shaking of hands and ended with singing the Doxology.

A similar event took place on 29 October of that same year in the Corn Exchange at Wakefield. At the conclusion of the discussion, Miall moved a resolution that State interference with religion was a departure from the precepts of Christianity. His opponent, the Rev. J. Taylor of the Wakefield Grammar School, moved an amendment that the Established Church was neither unscriptural nor unjust but beneficial to the community. Both were carried with a large majority amid cheers.

From the start, the architects of the Association had hopes of establishing auxiliary associations for purposes of private extension and public assistance. They were aware, however, that central bodies similar to theirs could be prosecuted under the Act of 1794 against Political Corresponding Societies. Upon the legal advice of their counsel, Benjamin Boothby, the Executive Committee dropped the idea of branch associations in favour of local registrars. The Committee hoped to place them in Dissenting congregations throughout the country to act much as the collector or secretary for a missionary society. By 1847, 198 of these local agents were appointed. The fact that they were advised against keeping permanent records may account for the absence of Volume 1 of the minutes of the Executive Committee.

This scheme was, however, abandoned in 1848 because it expected too much initiative from one person and not enough from local supporters. Moreover, the central Association saw the necessity of avoiding involvement with other voluntary societies and decided upon a system of well-defined local committees. In that year these groups were formed in fifty-seven of the principal cities and towns.

The local committee existed – almost as a disguised 'electoral club' – for the purpose of banding Liberationists together, withholding their votes from unsympathetic candidates, and raising money. There was thus a thin dividing line between this system and that which the law expressly forbade. Nevertheless, after four years of activity without interference from the hand of the law, there appeared to be little cause to worry. Gross receipts of the Association increased from £967 in 1845–6 to £2,000 in 1849–50.

D. *1847 Conference and General Election*
In the months before the first Triennial Conference,[1] the Dissenters became engrossed with Lord John Russell's plan for an additional Parliamentary grant for elementary education. Despite his previous promises not to encroach

[1] See *Nonconformist*, 17.vi.80, pp. 641–3: 'The Liberation Conferences – an Historical Review'.

upon religious liberty, he now sought to assist Anglican schools by allowing a limited use of the Catechism, and limited legal administration through the clergy. The Liberation party leaders, meeting on 16 April 1847, resolved to fight the Government scheme and therefore organized a Dissenters' Parliamentary Committee, with Samuel Morley as Chairman, Charles Walker as Secretary, and a central committee composed largely of members of the Anti-State-Church Association. The committee eventually broadened into a body to secure the return to Parliament of as many representatives as possible well acquainted with Nonconformist principles. The body later became absorbed by the Liberation Society.

The Association now faced its first opportunity to combine actively its strength with other voluntary associations, and to test its electoral influence. From the conference platform in Crosby Hall on 4 May, non-State Churchmen heard biddings for them to disassociate from the Whig party – 'stoop to conquer and retreat to win'. Dissenters now determined to build the foundation of a new political party. And the most obvious means was simply to boycott any candidate unsympathetic to their aims.

In mid-August the electorate signified their preference for a continuation of reform legislation. The Whig-Liberal party remained stable and won 337 seats in the new Parliament. The Conservative party was miserably divided between 116 Peelites who had accepted the principles of *laissez faire* in the abolition of the Corn Laws, and 202 uncompromising Tories who insisted upon the traditional policy of protection.

A small but lively band of neo-Nonconformists now emerged from the bosom of the Whig party. They had been disappointed with the failures of Miall at Halifax and Sturge at Leeds, but the returns published by the *Nonconformist* showed 26 professed anti-State-Church members and 62 members 'opposed to further State endowments of religion'. These 'Radical gentlemen' had given to an English election for the first time an audible voice against the Established Church. Miall heartily congratulated their electorate:

> Well done, ay, right nobly done, fellow Nonconformists throughout the kingdom. . . . The ice is broken. The charm is dissolved. The spell which sealed the eyes and paralysed the will of the Nonconformist body is dissipated.[1]

During the period before the first Triennial Conference, the Executive had been especially anxious to defend the movement against the charge of fanaticism or revolutionary motives. But their connexions outside the country, notably in France, had caused some to mistake anti-State-Churchmen for anti-Monarchists. In 1846 Sir John Bowring (M.P., Bolton and Tower Hamlets) forwarded to the Association a letter from Count Charles de Lasteyrie of Paris, inquiring after any agency in England with which the advocates of separation of Church and State in France might correspond. Another French Voluntaryist, Dr Merle d'Aubigné, whose writings on Disestablishment were published by the Association, had been invited the

[1] Arthur Miall, *Life of Edward Miall*, p. 128.

same year to a 'Liberation Breakfast'. In the violent year of 1848 Miall and Sturge and other English Chartists formed a special deputation congratulating M. de Lamartine (the Minister of Foreign Affairs) upon the success of the provisional Republican Government.

The Anti-State-Church confederacy, admittedly, could not pretend to be innocent of extreme ideals. The negative sound of its title, together with its avowed aim to reapportion the wealth of the National Church, was certain to antagonize many ordinary and peace-loving citizens. Dr Thomas Price, of the *Eclectic Review*, wrote to the *Nonconformist* voicing the uneasiness of many earnest Evangelicals:

> The Association, it is frequently alleged, is not lovely; it does not promote Christian brotherhood; it tends to separate rather than unite . . .

As Treasurer, he invited his readers to a 'sifting investigation of the Society' with a view to smoothing over its organization at the forthcoming Conference.

At that time the constitution was revised to the satisfaction of the vast majority of delegates. But in reply to those who disapproved of enforcing spiritual conviction by political means, Miall left no doubt as to where he stood:

> Do something for the sake of consistency—for your own character's sake—for the sake of the Church of Christ; do *something* to show you are in earnest— something that will tell more effectively in checking ecclesiastical encroachments, and settling religion upon its true basis, than is likely to be done by denouncing every movement of your own friends. Don't stand stock-still year after year merely to be shot at! Take up some position, at least, which will not lay you open to these successive assaults.[1]

[1] *Nonconformist*, 13.i.47, p. 17.

CHAPTER 3

Dissenters' Grants and Religious Education

We want not to overbear the conscience of dissenters; but, if possible, disarm their hostility to an institute, of which we honestly believe that its overthrow were tantamount to the surrender, in its great bulk and body, of the Christianity of our nation.

THOMAS CHALMERS[1]

. . . on our principles, all civil disabilities on account of religious opinions are indefensible. For all such disabilities make government less efficient for its main end: they limit its choice of able men for the administration and defence of the state; they alienate from it the hearts of the sufferers; they deprive it of a part of its effective strength in all contests with foreign nations. . . .

LORD MACAULAY[2]

THE MORE GENTLE, idealistic Nonconformists thought the constant plea for Parliamentary action on the 'Church of England question' unnecessary. The social boycott of Dissent by Anglicanism would be ended 'if it was God's will'. Moreover, it appeared to them that the national Establishment was suffering from an internal dissension which would eventually bring about its own readjustment.

They had substantial evidence for this. Several months after the formal alliance of anti-State-Churchmen in 1844, a petition went to the Primate, Dr William Howley, from several peers of the realm, seeking a revision of the parochial system and the participation of the laity in religious functions. The petitioners included the Duke of Sutherland, Viscount Sandon M.P., the Earl of Denbigh, and the Earl of Gainsborough, Viscount Morpeth, Lord Calthorpe, Lord Francis Egerton M.P., Lord Robert Grosvenor M.P., and Lord Ashley M.P. Less than a year later they saw the Established Church shaken by Newman's conversion. In 1846 the 'more peaceful' Nonconformists

---

[1] *Lectures*, p. 188.
[2] 'Gladstone on Church and State', *Edinburgh Review*, April 1839, p. 64.

participated in the founding of the Evangelical Alliance to unite all English Protestants, Episcopalian and non-Episcopalian alike, in common resistance to Roman Catholicism. In 1849 they witnessed two clergymen, the Rev. Thomas Spencer and the Rev. G. H. Stoddart, mount the platform of the Anti-State-Church Association, and another, the Rev. and Hon. Baptist Wriothesley Noel, secede to their ranks after faithfully serving in the Anglican priesthood for twenty-one years.[1]

The other class of Nonconformist, who liked to be thought of as more practical, usually pointed to the past. They were not deceived by these surface tensions in the Anglican Church. Their fathers had fully known its rigidity and they had learned how unalterable it could be under duress. The one place where their arguments were likely to carry weight was the House of Commons.

Those who upheld the Establishment could hardly be blamed for believing the worst of those who had refused to conform. Nonconformity was obviously envious of their religious privilege and aimed to make England like America – 'that Paradise of sects'. But Dissent had no official recognition in the law of the land; if it had, the State would be bound to promote it. This was maintained by J. S. Brewer thirty years later:

> *Salus populi suprema lex;* and if that safety and well-being consisted in dissent, or were more highly advanced by it than by any other means, the supreme and over-ruling law of all government, to which all other laws, all other considerations, must be subordinate, would constrain the State to tender, strengthen, promote, and regulate dissent.[2]

Such was the quasi-Erastian theory upon which Sir Robert Peel and Lord John Russell often worked. In the 'State of England question' neither Prime Minister had much faith in the conscience of the individual, and even less in the voluntary principle. But faced by the spectacle of starving people during the 'hungry 'forties', the Liberal-conservative and the Conservative-liberal combined forces and repealed the Corn Laws in 1846. The result was a victory for the Free-traders with Bright who spoke for manufacturers and labour, and a defeat for the Protectionists with Disraeli who spoke for landlords and clergy. The Tory party fell in twain when Peel turned away from the policy of the 'squirearchy-hierarchy' which that particular Parliament had been elected to carry.[3] In 1834 his Tamworth Manifesto, touching on Dissenting grievances, had shown which way he was leaning. In this electoral address he

---

[1] C. Silvester Horne, *Nonconformity in the XIXth Century* (London 1905), p. 123, claims that this secession caused 'almost as great a sensation as Newman's accession to Rome'. See also B. W. Noel, *Essay on the Union of Church and State* (London 1848), p. 262.

[2] J. S. Brewer, op. cit., p. 176.

[3] In his *Disraeli: A Picture of the Victorian Scene* (London 1927), p. 129, André Maurois maintains that Sir Robert's heart was in his opponents' camp all the while. 'By his birth Peel was much nearer to the factory than to the manor or the cottage, much more of a Puritan than a Cavalier.' The bitter rivalry between Gladstone and Disraeli started in 1841 when Peel chose the former for his Cabinet and ignored the latter. 'Gladstone was a man after his own heart, like him "Oxford on the surface, and Liverpool below".'

suggested removing all abuses which impaired the efficiency of the Establishment, and promised to carry on with legislation in the spirit of the Reform Bill. However, Russell stepped in and the Whigs were to hold power until 1858.

With the old opposition routed, Dissenting leaders saw brighter prospects. In 1836 Lord John's Bill for the Registration of Births, Deaths and Marriages, together with the Bill for the Solemnization of Marriages (which appointed civil registrars to do the registering and to be present for 'solemnizing' in licensed non-Anglican Chapels), became law without a division. The powerful Manor-house and Parish-house combination in the Commons was disrupted for the time being.

But the time of combined effort by the new radical forces, with grave consequences to the Established Church, had not yet come. Ironically, the question in which the Nonconformists were now chiefly interested were minor State grants to Roman Catholics, Anglican schools, and themselves. Because Dissenting opinion was divided on each question, the Association had to speak cautiously. Their political comprehension was still in its infancy.

A. *Maynooth College Grant*

During the first half of the nineteenth century, Roman Catholics in Britain had been freed from three of their post-Reformation restrictions. In 1817 they were allowed into the national Army and Navy, in 1829 they were permitted to enter the British Parliament, and in 1845 they received what amounted to State recognition of one of their Colleges. The last of these events occasioned the formation of another 'anti-' society in Victorian politics – this time against the government sponsorship of 'Popery'. Many Englishmen feared Roman Catholicism and its consequences more than they did extreme Anglicanism or any other religious creed.

As part of his policy of pacifying the Irish, Peel agreed in 1845 to the suggestion of the Vatican to improve and renovate their training College for Priests at Maynooth, Co. Kildare. The First Lord of the Treasury proposed, therefore, (1) to allow the trustees to hold Crown lands to the value of £3,000 per year; (2) to grant £30,000 alone for the fabric; and (3) to increase the general endowment from £9,000 to £27,000, charging it to the Consolidated Fund. The *Nonconformist* retorted that this was part of an attempt by the Premier to live down the name 'Orange Peel'.

In his book on *The State in its Relations with the Church*, Gladstone could not see the value of this grant, which had been made annually since the Act of Union in 1800. He believed that it was contrary to the conscience of the State. To the surprise of the Prime Minister and his friends, he therefore resigned as President of the Board of Trade to maintain his self-consistency on the matter.[1]

[1] Philip Magnus, *Gladstone: A Biography* (London 1954), says (p. 68) that Gladstone 'was inclined to regard' this 'as the silliest action of his life'. In his letter of resignation to Peel, Gladstone suggested that, if diplomatic relations were renewed with the Papal Court, he would like to be appointed British Minister to Rome!

An anti-Maynooth Committee, representing all Evangelical denominations, was swiftly set up to stop the Government measure. The chairman, Sir Culling Eardley Smith, summoned a general council of Protestants to voice their objections at Exeter Hall on 30 April 1845. When the 1,000-odd delegates decided not to object on the ground of ecclesiastical endowments, the Liberation group headed by the Rev. J. P. Mursell and Dr F. A. Cox left the conference. A committee of thirty-five with the Rev. John Burnet as chairman convened a new conference on 21 May at Finsbury Chapel, adopting the platform of the British Anti-State-Church Association. With nearly the same number of people present as before, speeches were made denouncing any desire of the Evangelicals to protect the Irish Anglican Establishment, its endowments, or its exclusive claims upon 'the truth'.

The Association then despatched to Sir John Bowring LL.D. (M.P., Bolton), one of the leading Voluntaryist spokesmen in the House, two resolutions: first, in matters of religion man was responsible to God alone, and the legislation of the State in such matters interfered with that vital communion; second, this endowment of Roman Catholic institutions was impolitic, and 'inimical to the civil and religious interests of the Empire'. The Association tried to make clear that no offence was intended against Roman Catholics as such, but against the principle of ecclesiastical endowments.

Protestations meanwhile were sent from practically every Orange sector of the nation. Petitions with 1,120,000 signatures were carried into the Commons. The Dissenting Deputies composed an elaborate appeal to the young Queen, as 'the benign ruler of the House of Brunswick', to dissolve Parliament and to allow her subjects time to judge on the issue.

Peel's Bill, however, passed its second reading by 323 to 176 votes on 18 April after six nights of weary debating. On coming out of Committee on 5 May, Sharman Crawford (M.P., Rochdale) moved an amendment against the report being accepted and against any subsidies (tithes, rents, taxes, cesses, *regium donum*'s) to 'any particular religious denominations'. It lost by 141 to 2 votes – his vote and that of Charles Hindley (M.P., Ashton-under-Lyne), both cast on behalf of the Association. The scheme became law and the College received the money.

The Association wrote to Sir John Bowring, placing the blame for the trouble upon 'the ignorance of the legislators'. He replied politely and sympathetically that he was fully aware of his serious responsibility as a legislator but that 'something must at times be conceded to invincible prejudices and interest'.[1]

Catholic Emancipation in 1829 would not have been possible without the backing of the Nonconformists already in Parliament. The friendly spirit resulting from this co-operation was illustrated when Daniel O'Connell appeared on the platform of the Protestant Society in 1829 and thanked 'our Protestant Dissenting brethren'.

[1] Annual Report, 1846, p. 9. Nine years later Bowring became Governor of Hong Kong. He wrote the hymn, 'In the Cross of Christ I glory'.

But the decision on Maynooth in 1845 proved embarrassing to those anti-State-Churchmen who had hoped to use Catholic Ireland as the first main springboard against the Church of England. By this successful manœuvre on the part of the Peel ministry, the Irish Radicals and English Dissenters were split.

In the summer of 1844, the year before the Maynooth question broke out, Miall with his friend J. M. Webb had visited Ireland and its 'uncrowned king' O'Connell, who was then in prison. Miall wrote that the confinement of the Irish Liberator by the Peelite Government would turn out to be its most fateful mistake in dealing with the Irish crisis. The English Liberationist at first admired O'Connell as one who sought 'great political ends', and paid tribute to his energies:

> ... I observed no impatience—no symptoms of repining—no tacit expression of feeling that he had made a mistake. On the contrary, he appeared thoroughly satisfied; and when I congratulated him on the quiet demeanour of the Irish people, I shall not soon forget the sudden gleam of joy which lighted up his countenance as he asked, 'Isn't it beautiful!'[1]

This good opinion had to be revised later. Greatly to Miall's disappointment O'Connell abandoned not only his stand in favour of the repeal of the Union for Irish self-government, but also the principle of Voluntaryism in religion in favour of State endowments to Maynooth. He bitterly reviled Miall and his Voluntaryist 'knaves' because of their opposition to the Maynooth money. The fiery Irishman spoke of Miall as 'a vagabond who once bothered me . . . who is just as ugly as his name'. Miall tossed off the remarks as coming from one drunk with his own ambition.

Doubtless the ill fortunes of the Irish Catholic leader and his people gave him good grounds for seeking more drastic remedies. His mistake lay in his failure to see that all of his friends were not on one side of the Irish Sea. Many English Nonconformists said Amen to the judgement of Lord Palmerston in support of the College grant.

> Our only choice is between leaving six millions of men in comparative ignorance, and in consequent bigotry and superstition, or endeavouring to enlighten them, and at least to make them good Catholics if we cannot make them Protestants; and in making this choice we must not forget, as some men in their zeal seem to do, that Roman Catholics are Christians.[2]

B. *The Regium Donum*

A comparatively small item in British Parliamentary history, the *Regium Donum* was to be nevertheless no small embarrassment to non-State-Churchmen. In an endeavour to discourage Dissenters from making awkward demands, but also to show appreciation of their loyalty, Sir Robert Walpole

---

[1] *Nonconformist*, 31.vii.44, p. 550; quoting letter of 25 July, from the 'Vale of Avoca'.

[2] Evelyn Ashley, *The Life and Correspondence of Henry John Temple Viscount Palmerston* (London 1879), i, 486.

had arranged in 1723 that a half-yearly gift should be made from the Royal Purse for the relief of Dissenters. The amount at first was fixed at £500 for poor widows of Dissenting ministers, but it later fluctuated to nearly £2,000 for the Ministers as well. Although no conditions were imposed, the grant seemed to be an effective instrument of control in the hands of successive Governments. It was rumoured in Parliamentary circles that it did not cost the administration half so much to manage the Dissenters as to purchase a paltry borough.

The grant had mischievous consequences in another respect. During the Georgian period the names of the distributors and beneficiaries were not generally known. The secrecy inevitably provoked distrust, and the means of allocation gradually created petty jealousy. It was referred to as 'Achan's wedge'[1] in the camp of the Dissenters.

In 1804, at the outset of William Pitt's second Ministry, the grant was directed to be made in the future by an annual vote of Parliament. The sum was entrusted to nine trustees – three each from the Presbyterian, Independent, and Baptist denominations. But when it became identified as a Parliamentary grant rather than a charitable donation from the Sovereign's personal bounty, the reaction against it grew worse.

In 1836 H. Aglionby (M.P., Cockermouth) obtained a return of the names of the committee by whom the *Regium Donum* had been distributed and the mode in which the money was apportioned. In 1837 the March issue of the *Congregational Magazine* contained a strong article which held 'the mammon' responsible for their dampened political ardour. Four years earlier the Dissenting Deputies had openly condemned 'the compact' as a direct violation of the sacred principles of Dissenters. But it was not until 1845 that the Ministers of the three denominations sought to find an alternative scheme for avoiding the hardships to grantees.

It was then that the Anti-State-Church Association became involved in the controversy. A special committee published an 'Address to the Distributors and Recipients of the Parliamentary Grant for Poor Dissenting Ministers in England and Wales'. Signed by Dr F. A. Cox (formerly a distributor), J. M. Hare and Edward Miall, it appealed to their fellow Dissenters 'to remove this foul blot from the fair fame of their consistency'. As long as they enjoyed these grants they could not with a free conscience object generally to the national endowments of religion. The *Nonconformist*, using the words of Horace's *Odes*, doubted whether these small sums went invariably to the poorest of their Ministers:

> *Virtute me involvo, probamque*
> *Pauperiem sine dote quaero.*[2]

The appeal was answered shortly afterwards in similar tones by the Rev.

---

[1] cf. Joshua 7: 19–25.
[2] *Nonconformist*, 9.vii.45, p. 480; quoting Horace, *Odes* III, xxix, 54–6.

John Clayton M.A. and the Rev. A. Rees D.D.,[1] two of the distributors. Another exhortation came from the Association in a paper by the Rev. Daniel Katterns of Portobello. The entire matter was then aired by another distributor, the learned Dissenting divine, the Rev. John Pye Smith, D.D., F.R.S. He showed that the *Regium Donum* was not derived from compulsory taxation of the public, but was a private Royal charity permanently charged on the Royal Estates.[2] As such, therefore, it could not be open to the same objections urged against the levying of taxes for the support of religion. Finally, Dr Pye Smith invited members of the Executive Committee to meet him in debate, but they did not accept. Instead they printed their rebuttal, and subsequently he relinquished his connexion with the Association.

The Maynooth question meant dragging into the general controversy on ecclesiastical grants the question of the Irish *Regium Donum* as well. The Dissenting Deputies in 1753 had actually helped to obtain this additional money for Dissenting ministers in Northern Ireland. The question here was made more serious because a portion of the participators were reputed to hold anti-Trinitarian doctrines. However, it was maintained that abolition would be certain to bring considerable hardship to the pensioners.

The Association said that what was good for the Irish Roman Catholics would have to be good also for the Irish Presbyterians. The Executive Committee therefore pressed for a division in the House of Commons against 'both donums'. But Charles Hindley's motion on 13 June 1845 received only 3 votes.

A succession of divisions followed at the instigation of the leaders of the Association. In 1846 Bright presented petitions against the English and Irish 'indulgences'. In 1847 when George Matthews of Dublin Castle submitted his Commissioner's Report to Her Majesty, opponents claimed that it upheld the grant as part of a system of State favouritism. In 1848 and 1849, Charles Lushington moved that the vote on the money be struck from the Miscellaneous Estimates. Notwithstanding the support in debate of eight anti-State-Churchmen, he succeeded in gaining only 28 votes against 60, and 33 against 52.

Lord John Russell indicated that his Ministry would certainly not give up these grants unless he was guaranteed that the charity would be perpetuated in another form. The grants were kept, anti-State-Churchmen said, merely to extend the circle of petty patronage surrounding the Government.

C. *Elementary Education*

Lord Macaulay stated in 1847 that of 130,000 couples married in 1844, one-third of the bridegrooms and nearly one-half of their spouses were unable to

---

[1] Not to be confused with Thomas Rees LL.D., F.S.A., author of *A Sketch of the History of the Regium Donum, and Parliamentary Grant, to Poor Dissenting Ministers of England and Wales* (London 1834).

[2] *A Vindication of the Royal Bounty to Poor Protestant Dissenting Ministers* (London 1849), p. 4.

sign their names. The illiteracy and ignorance among the growing industrial population of Britain was indeed a serious problem. Soon after the Reform legislation of 1832, many voices were raised in Parliament against the idea that education was for the privileged few. But in the nineteenth century, as always, to enter upon the problem of educating the humblest classes was, according to George Kitson Clark, '. . . like entering among those rocks in India which are tenanted by many millions of vigilant and irascible hornets.'[1]

During Lord Melbourne's administration, beginning in 1834, most Non-conformists were on the side of the Government on the question of national education. Parliament had just begun voting £20,000 annually for the erection of school buildings, and the amount was being divided between the British and Foreign School Society (undenominational) and the National Society (Anglican).[2] By 1839 the same Government sought (1) to increase the annual grant to £30,000 in order to establish a Normal College for training teachers of all faiths, and (2) to place the supervision of all future Parliamentary grants for education in the hands of a committee of the Privy Council. Lord Brougham remarked that the increase to £30,000 would hardly be exorbitant, for in that same year £70,000 was voted for building Royal Stables.

The 'tocsin of alarm' over the new plan came this time from the Church of England. The first proposal, which would make for combined secular and separate religious instruction, was eventually surrendered by the Government. Distinctive religious instruction (under the superintendence of a special Rector) was to be given at special times by various Ministers of religion who would not hold position on the College staff. The second proposal, although barely passed in the Commons and badly treated in the House of Lords, was upheld by the Crown. An address by leading Peers asking the Queen to disallow this provision was carried in procession directly to Buckingham Palace. In reply, she said that she saw no harm in her Privy Council committee superintending the grants. 'I trust', she added, 'that the sums placed at my disposal will be found to have been strictly applied to the objects for which they were granted, with due respect to the rights of conscience, and with a faithful attention to the security of the established church.'[3]

The Anglican leaders made the best of the situation by obtaining control of the appointment of inspectors set up under the committee. The Government declined, however, to give the British and Foreign School Society a voice in appointing these 'itinerant curates' for their schools.

The dissatisfaction of the Established Church made it easier for the Tories to wreck the Melbourne Ministry in 1841. Wishing to avoid a similar fate,

---

[1] *Peel and the Conservative Party* (London 1929), p. 435.

[2] The latter group was started in 1811, after the model of Dr Andrew Bell, for 'the Education of the Poor in the Principles of the Church of England'. The former was founded in 1808 by the Quaker, Joseph Lancaster, for the instruction of children in general Christian principles.

[3] *Annual Register 1839*, lxxxi (London 1840), 140 ff.

5

Peel reversed his predecessor's policy by showing more partiality to the Established Clergy in national education. This became evident in the factory education scheme put forward in 1843 by his Home Secretary, Sir James Graham. This stubborn Scotsman evidently had a premonition of what was ahead, for in 1841 he wrote to Lord Brougham: 'Religion, the keystone to education, is in this country the bar to its progress.'

With the return of the Whig ministry in 1846 there was a disposition to leave the matter of popular education alone, and to avoid the anger of both Anglicanism and Dissent. Moreover, the presence of Peelite Conservatives and Bright Radicals made this imperative, if the Russell Government wished to stay in office for long.

> The new Whig policy, like Walpole's of old, was not to rouse the sleeping ecclesiastical Cerberus, chained at present at the entrance of the House of Lords.[1]

Lord John Russell believed that if any move had to be made in the direction of improved popular education, the safest thing would be to extend State aid through as many channels as possible. Accordingly, the Minutes of the Council, framed by the Secretary, Sir James Kay-Shuttleworth, and dated August and December 1846, were laid before the Commons in April 1847 for approval. These innocently called for (1) assistance in maintenance and salaries of the teaching staffs, (2) additional building allowances to schools endorsing the Government management plan, and (3) support for plans respecting the apprenticeship of pupil-teachers. In receipt of the portions from the lump sum of £100,000, the Anglican, Wesleyan, Roman Catholic, and undenominational schools were to be treated alike. This all sounded highly satisfactory, but Russell now had to contend with an organized movement against any State assistance for purposes of religion. Miall rebuked the Prime Minister for his 'game of levelling up'.

The Voluntaryists and the Anglo-Catholics were the most outspoken opponents – for vastly different reasons. The latter rejected any departure from the centuries-old tradition that all worthy education was religious and the responsibility of devout men of the Church. To them the management clause of the Government denied that fact.

> I believe that their principle is vicious—the principle of entrusting the effective control of a Church School to a Committee of Management, however such Committee may be composed, instead of to the parish Clergyman—and that, so long as this principle is retained, these Clauses cannot be made *safe* by any process.[2]

The former disowned any system which was not fundamentally self-reliant. They rejected religious instruction that ignored the inherent power within the Christian faith to regulate itself.

> Though all the machinery of government should be swept away to-morrow

[1] G. M. Trevelyan, *History of England* (London 1947), p. 648.
[2] George A. Denison, *Church Education* (London 1849), p. 13.

nothing which exists of real Christianity would die. In those minds wherein it now exists, it would continue to exist; . . .[1]

Russell was accused of preferring the Established to the Voluntary principle because the new appropriation under the Minutes of the Council would mainly benefit Anglican Churches. This was understandable inasmuch as their schools were the most numerous. But to Nonconformist educators the denominational character of a State-aided school did not always depend upon the beliefs of the benefactor by whom a school was built, but upon the preference of the parents for whose children it was provided. Dr Dale observed a generation later in his *History of English Congregationalism* that the children of a district were sold to the Church which was willing and able to find the funds to buy them.

Several months before the Parliamentary elections in mid-1847, the Dissenters' Parliamentary Committee was whipped up expressly to oppose Liberals who had voted for the Minutes.[2] Edward Baines met the partisans of the Privy Council proposals in a public debate before an audience of 15,000 in Cloth Hall, Leeds. He wrote to the Marquess of Lansdowne, the President of the Education Committee of the Council, showing that the plan in full operation would cost the country £1,742,500 each year and that it would bring 88,000 persons into receipt of State pay. This, he believed, was not the rightful responsibility of the State.

But again the Dissenters could not achieve unanimity. The majority of Anglicans were joined by the Roman Catholics, Unitarians, Scottish Presbyterians, and Wesleyan Methodists. This left scattered religious minorities, the Baptists, and the Congregationalists to stand by themselves. After three nights of debating, the Prime Minister obtained the sanction of the House for the crucial Minutes. A motion for a clause exempting children of Dissenters from religious instruction in Anglican schools was lost, and the Independents complained that the steps taken by the Government were in full collaboration with 'the dominant sect'.

In all these proceedings, the Anti-State-Church Association had to remain relatively quiet because many of its supporters did not regard the Government action as an intrusion into the sacred realm of conscience. Some believed that the ignorance of the country could never be overtaken without some assistance from the State. The Executive, therefore, could at best warn that the new scheme would lead to 'a juvenile establishment', comprehending all sects, with all the inherent evils of the State Church Establishment.

---

[1] E. Miall, *Views of the Voluntary Principle*, p. 20.

[2] F. Adams, *History of the Elementary School Contest in England*, pp. 130–6. The Committee took credit for the defeat of Benjamin Hawes at Lambeth and of T. B. Macaulay at Edinburgh.

PART TWO

Expansion and Growth
1850 – 1861

CHAPTER 4

Introductory

'There are many symptoms apparent which indicate a *weakening* of the Establishment principle. It is distinctly observable in Parliament, and in the country, and especially so within the Established Church itself, and from this you will draw encouragement, and gather fresh strength for the future stages of the conflict.'

JOHN BRIGHT: from letter to J. Carvell Williams on the Society's Triennial Conference in 1853.[1]

THE RELIGIOUS CENSUS in 1851 was a true testimony of the remarkable spread of the voluntary principle throughout the country. On Sunday, 30 March of that year, the total Church of England attendance at the morning, afternoon, and evening services was 5,292,551, and that in non-Anglican churches was 5,603,515.[2]

During the next decade the British Anti-State-Church Association grew in popularity, adopted a wider policy, and expanded its organization. The Free Church movement became definitely linked with the general movement toward a more democratic society. At the third Triennial Conference in 1853 the Association broadened its name to 'The Society for the Liberation of Religion from State-Patronage and Control'.

During the Palmerstonian 'fifties, equalitarian principles reached the foundation of the Liberal-Whig governments. Within the space of a few years a succession of Bills granting wider social and religious freedoms became law – the Oxford University Act in 1854, the Liberty of Worship Act in 1855, the Cambridge University Act in 1856, the Divorce and Matrimonial Act in 1857, the Admission of Jews to Parliament in 1858, and the opening of Grammar Schools to Dissenters in 1860. Apart from the Crimean War (1854–6), it was for Britain a period of comfortable peace and world leadership – if one forgot the turbulent but remote foreign events such as the Indian Mutiny and the Chinese War. Nevertheless, amid this Victorian

---

[1] *Nonconformist*, 11.v.53, p. 371.

[2] *Report on the Religious Worship in England and Wales*, by Mr Horace Mann to Mr George Graham (Registrar-General), p. clxxxii (and see p. xli).

complacency and proud industrial prosperity epitomized by the Great Exhibition of 1851, the radicalism of Charles Kingsley and Frederick Denison Maurice in their Christian social economics filled a significant place.

The areas in which the Liberation Society moved would bring it in touch with a multitude of sympathizers. In 1850 and for a few years afterward, the Society was feeling its way. By 1861 it had become a pressure group to be seriously reckoned with in national political circles. During this eleven-year period it became clear that the methods of the Society must be radical. The cautious efforts of the earlier years, to contain within the Society both the progressive and conservative wings of Nonconformity, were set aside.

This was also a period of mounting optimism for the Society and the Voluntaryists. They saw in the successful termination of the struggle for Free Trade in 1846 the prospect of a successful legislative struggle for free religion. There was an eagerness to test in the ecclesiastical arena the practical effects of the new licence already working in the spheres of capital and industry. The British were showing greater moral responsibility for man's secular needs.

A. *Parochial Disputes*

For the Church of England this decade brought a mood of growing depression, due mainly to crucial disputes in doctrine. Chief of these was the case of *Gorham v. The Bishop of Exeter*, in which the former contended that spiritual regeneration did not always follow the administration of the sacrament of Baptism. Gladstone believed that nothing less than 'the death of the Church of England is among the alternative issues of the Gorham case'.[1]

Dr Henry Phillpotts refused in 1849 to allow into his Diocese the Rev. Charles Gorham because of his heretical views. At first, in the Court of Arches under Sir H. Jenner Fust, the Bishop's decision was upheld, but on 8 March 1850 the Judicial Committee of the Privy Council (in the judgement delivered by Lord Langdale) reversed the decision of the ecclesiastical court. The Judicial Committee had been formed in 1834 by Lord Brougham and therefore it was still regarded by many clerics as a strange innovation.

The Bishop of London (Dr Charles Blomfield) maintained that questions of doctrine should not be determined by a court composed chiefly of laymen. The Prime Minister, Lord John Russell, however, explained to the Primate, Dr John Sumner, that the decision did not oblige any member of the Church to accept the opinions of Gorham; it only pronounced that such opinions did not disqualify him from holding a benefice in the Church. As to the competence of the new court, the Premier believed that justice was more secure under the State than the Church:

> ... If for ... the present constitution of the Judicial Committee of Privy Council we were to substitute the Upper House of Convocation with the addition of some learned judges, I fear we should subject the rights and privileges of the clergy,

[1] John Morley, *Life of Gladstone*, i, 283: letter of 9.iv.50, 'to a clerical friend'. See also *The Great Gorham Case: A History in five books, including expositions of the rival baptismal theories, by A Looker-On* (London 1850).

and the patrons of livings, to an ecclesiastical body more intent on theology than on law and liberty. . . .[1]

Another blow was struck at Tractarianism in the Bath Judgement (*Ditcher v. Denison*) later in 1856. Archdeacon Denison of Taunton was then judged by the Primate, through his assessor Dr Stephen Lushington, to have violated the Thirty-Nine Articles by his teaching on the Eucharist that the body and blood of Christ was received by the faithful and unfaithful alike. A group of Churchmen appealed against the decision and called for a 'free and lawful' synod of Bishops of the province of Canterbury to review the case and to safeguard the creeds of the Church.

When the Dean of the Arches, Sir John Dodson, declined to entertain his appeal, the Archdeacon next went before the Queen's Bench which granted a mandamus and ordered Sir John to hear the appeal. In May 1857, the Dean avoided this order by ruling that the proceedings against the Archdeacon 'were bad in law', as not having commenced within the statutable period. The Judicial Committee of the Privy Council simply confirmed Dodson's dictum and there the matter ended. Dr Blomfield brought in a Bill in the Lords to create a new tribunal for ecclesiastical appeals – a Court of Bishops in place of the Judicial Committee. It was dropped, principally on the ground that it interfered with the Royal Supremacy.

At the same time, in spite of the turmoil over doctrinal differences, there were indications that a greater degree of democracy was finding its way into Anglican circles. In the summer of 1857, several leading Churchmen began holding services for twelve consecutive Sunday evenings in Exeter Hall, London. Bishops Tait (London) and Villiers (Carlisle), Canons Miller and Cadman, and the Rev. Hugh Allen were among the Evangelical clergy who took part. Lord Shaftesbury, Lord Panmure and Dr Hugh McNeile were the chief lay leaders serving on the Committee. These services were arranged mainly for the working classes who 'were not habitual church or chapel goers', and were conducted without Prayer-book (except for the Litany), surplices, organ-music, reserved seats or collections. Each week thousands were attracted, other public halls were opened, and services in this style were on the verge of becoming a national movement.

With the commencement of another series of such meetings the following November, however, the committee in charge neglected to ask permission afresh from the incumbent of the Parish Church (St Michael's, Burleigh St), the Rev. A. G. Edouart. He exercised his legal authority under the parochial system and issued an inhibition. Public reaction from *The Times* to *Punch* condemned as folly the circumstances that permitted such blocking. In the House of Lords, the Earl of Shaftesbury pronounced shame upon the High Church party and warmly commended the group of Nonconformist Ministers who stepped in and carried on with the services.

To rectify the awkward position of the law, Shaftesbury introduced a

[1] Spencer Walpole, *The Life of Lord John Russell* (London 1889), ii, 118.

Religious Worship Bill on 8 December 1857. This would extend the effects of the Liberty of Worship Act of 1855 by permitting occasional worship in any building 'not usually appropriated to religious worship'. In debate on the second reading on 8 February, it was withdrawn because of opposition from the Episcopal Bench and the highly successful meetings for working classes under High Church auspices at Westminster Abbey and St Paul's Cathedral. An attempt by Dr Sumner, the Archbishop of Canterbury, to meet the problem in a Special Services Bill failed for similar reasons; after having passed all stages in the Lords, it was mysteriously dropped in the Commons.

Also in 1857, Dr Sumner invited to the Guardroom at Lambeth Palace Dr E. Steane (Baptist) and Dr Jabez Bunting (Wesleyan) as a mark of the unity of the Church and the tolerance of the Primate. When it was learned that, at the request of His Grace, an extempore prayer had been offered by the latter Nonconformist Minister in the presence of four Anglican Bishops, some Anglo-Catholics regarded it as 'Spurgeonism creeping into the Church'.

The Liberation Society experienced growing impatience with feeble attempts by the National Church to become freer. To Liberationists the Establishment seemed predestined for a long while yet to remain under upper class ideals and controls. Where others had failed with the middle and working classes, the Society was determined to succeed by banding together political and religious Nonconformity into a forceful electoral movement. Generally speaking, the Whig statesmen were not Dissenters, but they relied heavily on the Nonconformist-Radical vote. The Liberation Society was devoted therefore to the task of making sure that this vote was used where it would add the most to its power.

B. *Literary Activities*

The literary activities of the Society were greatly extended during this period. A constant stream of popular tracts came from the press of the Society, and at first they were more widely used than any other kind of publication. The literary standard of these writings may be judged by the title given to an early series, 'Tracts for the Million', some of which were translated into Welsh. In 1850 the Rev. Charles Williams, who had been formerly Superintendent of the Religious Tract Society, was appointed as full-time Editor; shortly after he took office the Executive Committee decided to raise £1,500–2,000 for extending the publication department.

However, by 1851 the committee recommended the suspension of Williams and his first volume of *The Church of England in the Reigns of the Tudors* on the ground that it contained questionable views and was not suitable for inclusion in the collection of works known as 'The Library for the Times'. This action may have been simply a matter of expediency, owing to heavy expenses incurred by the Society in moving to new offices. But the publication department during this time had become the best source of income.

Williams was replaced in June 1851 by Cyrus R. Edmonds, who previously had written a biography of John Milton for the 'Library of the Times' collection. The literary sub-committee, however, again criticized the Editor, this time for his somewhat highbrow publications, and called for more popular tracts and pamphlets. His reluctance to agree led to his suspension also, and that of the entire 'Library for the Times' as well.

It was clear that the Society was divided between two literary policies – to gain quick results with popular, easily understood literature for the masses, or to show the educated elements that Liberation principles had worthy historical and cultural grounds. When Edmonds went, a recommendation was passed that another £1,500 be raised for the publication fund and literary expansion, using large quantities of cheap tracts and easily understood pamphlets. A good example of this kind of publication was Miall's *What is the Separation of Church and State?*:

> (1) . . . the repeal of all laws or portions of laws which inflict penalty, or civil disability, on account of religious profession. (2) . . . the abolition of all preferences and privileges conferred by law, in favour of any form or forms of religious faith or profession. (3) . . . the resumption by the Legislature, for strictly secular purposes, of all national property now devoted to the maintenance of religion.

The project of 'The Library for the Times' was designed to appeal more to the better-read Nonconformists and Churchmen.[1] The idea had been pursued by Williams, but more seriously followed up by Edmonds. Edmonds had also recommended adapting a series of reprints with annotations or biographical sketches by the Editor: Milton's *Considerations Touching the Likeliest Means to Remove Hirelings out of the Church*, Locke's *Letter on Toleration*, and Cobbett's *Legacy to Parsons*. In a booklet on *Sydney Smith and the Bishops*, Williams violated the copyright of certain extracts from Lord Macaulay's work. Edmonds sent an apology and the learned historian replied promising to use his influence to prevent the publisher, Longmans, suppressing the work.[2]

The Executive Committee turned to its advantage the newspapers and journals that were 'organs of the rising Liberalism'. Of these, the *Nonconformist*, because of the prominent position which its Editor occupied in the decisions of the Executive Committee, was the channel most easily and frequently used. In it were reported the proceedings of public meetings and resolutions of the Committee. These full reports were usually in the *Patriot*,

---

[1] This Library series consisted of: *The Martyrs, Heroes, and Bards of the Scottish Covenant*, by George Gilfillan; *Footsteps of Our Forefathers*, by J. G. Miall; *The Life of Roger Williams*, by the Rev. Romeo Elton D.D.; *The Life of Constantine the Great*, by Joseph Fletcher; *The Life and Times of John Penry, M.A., Martyr*, by John Waddington; *The Church of England in the Reigns of the Tudors* and *The Church of England in the Reigns of the Stuarts*, by the Rev. Charles Williams; *The Test of Experience; or the Voluntary Principle in the United States*, by the Rev. J. H. Hinton M.A.; *Classical Selections from British Prose Writers* (Illustrative of the Principles of Intellectual, Civil, and Religious Freedom); *John Milton: A Biography*, by Cyrus R. Edmonds; *The Treasure-Seeker's Daughter: A Tale of the Days of Religious Persecution*, by Hannah Lawrance; *The Hallowed Spots of Ancient London*, by Eliza Meteyard.

[2] Minute 672: 15.i.52.

and the *British Banner* as well; abridged reports usually appeared in the *Wesleyan Times*, the *Christian Times*, the *Freeman*, the *Daily News*, and the *Morning Star* journals. Before the third Triennial Conference in 1853, notices and advertisements of the proceedings were carried in forty English and Scottish newspapers.

In June 1855, the monthly journal called the *Liberator* was founded as the official organ of the Liberation Society. Thenceforward the *Liberator* was the principal medium of the Society's popular propaganda. The first issue, amounting to 1,440 copies, was sent out to subscribers of £1 and upwards, to Members of Parliament, newspaper and magazine Editors, mechanics' institutes, colleges, and advertising agencies.

A 'Press (or Printing) sub-committee' came into being early in 1854, with the responsibility of supplying articles, paragraphs, and information to newspapers and periodicals, also purchasing literature to be distributed by the Society's executive members. This sub-committee proposed: (1) forming a reference library and a register of ecclesiastical data for the Society's speakers or writers, and (2) appointing a research expert to comb through printed sources and to file the useful information.

Herbert S. Skeats, author of *A History of the Free Churches of England from A.D. 1688–A.D. 1851*, was secured for this research role on the Society's staff. By 24 May 1861, he had taken on the supervision of the publication department as well. Under the scholarly Skeats the literary quality of many publications again became distinctly better, but because of the desire of some of the Committee for the literature of the Society to remain 'popular', his suggestions were not always heeded.

C. *Finances, Meetings, and Related Groups*

The sub-committee in charge of the finances of the Society consisted of businessmen who believed that the best way to fight 'vested interests' was with money. There were frequent changes of policy, economy measures, and the means for accumulating funds were continually explored with the result that the net income of the Society steadily increased. In the year 1849–50, receipts and expenditure amounted to £1,732; in the year 1860–1, they amounted to £4,413, but not without times of uncertainty during this decade. The Society often found itself in a vicious circle – increase of finances in order to increase activities, and increase of activities in order to increase financial strength.

Early in 1850 the Executive recommended that there be appointed a financial agent, one of whose duties was to canvass for and collect subscriptions in town and country. Later, the appointment of a collector for the London area alone was considered more practicable. The position was advertised, thirty-one applications were received, and Peter William Claydon of Bath, who later wrote widely on political history, was finally selected. He held this employment for eighteen months only and was released because his travelling expenses were felt to be excessive.

Meanwhile, with a view to increasing the subscription lists, and achieving the aim set at the 1854 Annual Meeting for an annual income of £5,000, local secretaries in the large cities were urged to hold large public soirées. Edward S. Pryce was next chosen to fill the office of travelling agent and to promote this scheme for collecting finances. He struggled with the budget for three years, and resigned in 1857 because he felt the expenditure on staff (£1,300 per annum) to be out of all proportion. Toward the latter part of this period the financial crisis eased enough to permit an increase in the salary of Dr Foster (Chairman of the Parliamentary Committee) to £500 per annum plus £50 expenses, and an allocation of £1,000 to carry the Church Rate Abolition Bill through the 1861 Parliamentary Session.

By a new system of collecting money, started in 1859, the country was divided into districts, each to be supervised by a collector or agent residing in that area. These 'district' or 'financial' agents were selected for Yorkshire, Somerset, Gloucestershire, Lancashire, Eastern Counties, Midland Counties, South Wales, and London. Two years of operation showed this system to be highly successful.

Among the notable names that appeared in the subscription lists, surprising to the Society's opponents, was that of T. Milner Gibson, a Privy Councillor and President of the Board of Trade in Lord Palmerston's Cabinet. Through Gibson and another donor, Charles Gilpin, the Secretary of the Poor Law Commissioners, it was feared that the Liberation Society had access to private Government information. Other subscribers included: Sir Samuel Morton Peto, Bt, M.P., the wealthy London builder and railway contractor; Apsley Pellatt M.P., glass manufacturer; John Remington Mills M.P., silk millionaire; and Sir William Clay, an Anglican, prominent merchant, and leader of Church Rates Abolition.

The Society chose not to limit the scope of its organization to the London metropolitan area, as had been the case with the Dissenting Deputies and other kindred societies. Through the activities of its Deputation sub-committee, many people who were not reached ordinarily through the Society's publications, accepted Disestablishment principles. The peculiar task of this particular committee was commonly referred to by its leaders as 'outdoor agitation'. It was responsible for arranging public meetings and lectures throughout England, Scotland, and Wales, conducted by the representatives of the Society either from the local area, or from the central offices. The results of these meetings were frequently reported at the sittings of the Executive Committee in London. In addition, passages were often read from the private diary of John Kingsley, one of the most active of the deputation speakers, giving detailed accounts of his tours.

The meetings and lectures were not always favourably received. On 26 March 1850, at Bishop's Stortford, a meeting conducted by the Rev. John Burnet, and J. Carvell Williams was broken up by an organized body of antagonists. Violent opposition to a public meeting held by Edward Miall was reported in one instance, and open resistance by the local clergy at Romford recorded in another. At a public gathering in his own parish of Islington in

1851, Mr Miall upon rising to speak was hurled bodily from the platform.

During the years 1850–3 the Deputation sub-committee organized a series of public rallies in London that were held in conjunction with the annual Council meeting of the Society. Full advantage was taken of these visits of some 500–600 council members together with hundreds of friends and guests, from all parts of the British Isles, to stimulate them with the ideals of the movement. This tremendous enthusiasm in the large metropolis remained with those from small communities long after the wording of the elaborate resolutions had been forgotten. The Liberation leaders saw the value of emotional appeals and lofty exhortations to Victorian audiences:

> Gather you, gather you, angels of God
>   Chivalry, justice, and truth;
> Come, for the earth is grown coward and old,
>   Come down and renew us her youth.
> Freedom, self-sacrifice, daring, and love,
> Haste to the battle-field, stoop from above,
>   To the day of the Lord at hand.[1]

The plan for rallies in London prevailed over another for separate conferences in the counties at large. The policy for the time being was to concentrate on 'a few telling meetings', which would be under the close control of the central office. Accordingly, in November 1852, the London Literary Institution was booked for four monthly meetings with special public addresses.

John Bright, in reply to an invitation to speak at the public meeting on 2 May 1853, which he was unable to accept, cautioned against making the meetings occasions for rabid attacks upon the Church of England.

> . . . I need not tell you how heartily I sympathise with every honest effort to free Christianity from the mischiefs which are inseparable from its connexion, under any form, with the State. . . . In the course of your great movement, I should recommend strongly that it should not appear to be an attack upon the Established Church, so much as upon the false principle upon which all established churches are founded; that you should rather labour to free all churches from the fetters of the civil power, than to overturn a particular church. In the one case you will probably find your labours and arguments appreciated more and more; in the other, you will raise hostile feelings, which make argument useless, and convictions impossible. . . .
>
> I wish you every success at your annual meeting, and in the noble undertaking to which you have committed yourselves.
>
> Believe me, yours sincerely,
John Bright.[2]

In 1853 a branch office was opened in Manchester with John Kingsley as secretary. The 'Manchester School' of Cobden and Bright, which had long taught the precepts of Free Trade, peace, and good will to all people, was the

---

[1] Written by Charles Kingsley and quoted at a Liberation rally on 6 May 1857 in St Martin's Hall, Long Acre.

[2] *Nonconformist*, 11.v.53, pp. 370–1.

natural breeding ground for Liberation principles. Kingsley was familiar with the 'political potential' of this entire North of England industrial area, and saw it as a centre of Nonconformist support. At the time of his report to the Society, seventy gentlemen connected with congregations, churches, Sunday schools, and other educational institutions in Manchester, had united together for a thorough study of the Society's principles and to consider means of spreading them. 'The real spirit of the plan', he wrote, 'consists in our purpose to organize a body of young men, of superior intelligence and Christian character, who shall stand in closer relation to the principles we cherish.' This body of vigorous exponents was to be backed by a group of Ministers and influential laymen. Soon after its formation, Sir Elkanah Armitage gave an inaugural address on behalf of the local constituency, and a finance committee went into operation. Kingsley carried on with his reports to the Society's Executive Committee.

The Society sought from the first to establish friendly relations with the Protestant Dissenting Deputies. Although operating mainly within the London area, this was an effective organization that had existed since 1732 for the protection of Dissenters' rights.[1] John Remington Mills M.P., Chairman of the Deputies from 1844 to 1853, served as a member of the Society's Executive Committee for three years, 1858–61, and was a liberal contributor to its funds. The Rev. Henry Richard, later M.P. for Merthyr Tydfil and also Chairman of the Deputies in 1874, was on the Executive Committee of the Liberation Society in 1851. The other Chairmen during this period, Sir Samuel Morton Peto M.P., and Apsley Pellatt M.P., were likewise members of the Society's Executive. The latter had been an Auditor for the Society since its beginning and joined the central committee in 1853, but the former remained on it for only one year, 1859. The Rev. Francis A. Cox D.D., LL.D., Honorary Secretary to the Anti-State-Church Association, had been actively interested in strengthening Nonconformist political witness by proposing, together with Professor C. J. Foster LL.D., a merger with the Protestant Dissenting Deputies. This idea was officially dropped on 23 March 1853, because the Association 'refused to narrow its basis'.

Again, after the formation of the Parliamentary Committee of the Society in 1854, it was recommended that the Deputies be approached on the possibility of a union or at least a 'working co-operation' with that body. A meeting of M.P.s was held at the invitation of Hull Terrell, Secretary of the Deputies, when it was resolved that their own Parliamentary Committee be formed. Dr Foster was appointed to this committee to represent the Society, but the proposal for closer union with the Deputies was not welcomed by them though they were prepared for joint action in particular cases.

Why the Dissenting Deputies declined to unite with the Liberation Society's Parliamentary Committee is open to speculation. It is known that the Deputies disdained the Society's publicity methods. This aloofness may have incited the Society to even greater aggressiveness. There was evidence of a

[1] See B. L. Manning, *The Protestant Dissenting Deputies* (Cambridge 1952).

mild spirit of competition between the two bodies as to which better represented the 'official voice' of Dissent.

Throughout the years 1850–61, the Society extended its agitation overseas indirectly, by establishing links with similar Dissenting bodies in several of the British colonies. Many Nonconformists and not a few Liberal politicians were pressing for relaxation of controls by the Imperial Government in the religious affairs of their respective colonies.

Especially on the question of support of the clergy from local revenues, colonial Liberation leaders requested the Society to act on their behalf in the Houses of Parliament. When Bills involving this question were sent before the home Government, letters stating the case for separation of Church and State were received from Canada in 1854, Victoria (Australia) and Ceylon in 1855, and Jamaica in 1856.

A sub-committee was appointed in 1857 to consider steps for promoting the principles of the Society in the reorganization of the Government of India. Special minutes were approved which stated that it should refrain from officially identifying itself with any particular Christian society.[1]

> . . . neither by contributions from public funds, by grants of public land, by appointment to ecclesiastical office, nor by the establishment of ecclesiastical law, should it give countenance to the idea, that to convert the natives to the Christian religion, or to control the efforts of those who within the proper limits of the law seek their conversion, is any part of the business of the State.[2]

A letter was received from the Tasmanian Anti-State-Aid Association, in January 1860, telling of a Bill passed by the Legislature in that colony for the abolition of existing ecclesiastical grants and of the mode in which it had been passed. The Liberation Society was asked to exert its influence to induce the Crown to withhold assent until the colonists had the opportunity of fuller expression of opinion on the matter. Accordingly, the Parliamentary Committee decided that a deputation should wait on the Duke of Newcastle, the Colonial Secretary. He later stated in Parliament that Royal Assent would be withheld from the Bill because it did not sufficiently respect the vested rights of the clergy.

D. *Parliamentary and Electoral Committees*

Since the General Election in 1847 the Society had been holding a knife over the Whig elements in the Liberal party. Without the support of the Liberation bloc of twenty-six members in the Commons, the Liberals had a precarious majority of one or two votes. On the rare occasions when the Peelites and Protectionists did act together, their combined number was still insufficient to bring about a Conservative victory. The Tories therefore occasionally wooed the Radicals, hoping that such an addition, although peculiar, would bring down the Russell Ministry. For this reason the Prime Minister had to walk carefully on religious questions.

[1] Minute 758: 30.x.57.
[2] Special Minute: 18. xi. 57.

At the time of the 1852 General Election the Society was thinking of ways of continuing its unique Parliamentary influence. For the Third Triennial Conference Edward Miall prepared a paper, 'The Prospects and Duties of the Society in relation to the House of Commons and to its Constituent Bodies'. This set forth a plan to constitute two additional committees for Parliamentary and electoral purposes.

At the Annual Meeting in 1852,[1] a 'Blue Paper' was issued by the Society with practical suggestions for selecting the right candidates on the ballot in the pending national election. This paper was accompanied by a message to the electorate by J. Carvell Williams, on the duty to back anti-State-Church principles. A General Election sub-committee had already been formed and as a result of its efforts in Rochdale, helped by Bright's recommendations, Miall was elected in 1852 to that seat. A total of forty Protestant Nonconformists were also returned.

At a special public soirée early in 1854, Miall announced the formation of both the Parliamentary Committee and the Electoral Committee. The duties of the first were

... to watch over Parliamentary business in all its forms, with a distinct view to the Society's object—to keep up a constant communication with Members of the House of Commons likely to be influenced by their representations—to supply information, and endeavour to promote such well-chosen and concerted action as would turn to the best account whatever Parliamentary strength Dissenters may possess.[2]

The responsibilities of the Electoral Committee were described as

... that of inquiry into the state of the constituencies, to ascertain where attempts might properly be made to obtain the return of representatives holding the Society's principles, to suggest suitable candidates, and in other ways to work electoral machinery as far as possible for anti-state-church purposes.[3]

The work of the Electoral Committee eventually became much less essential than the Parliamentary Committee to the life of the Society. This may have been due to the fact that the first chairman, Samuel Morley, was more of a philanthropist than an organizer. The secretary, Edward S. Pryce, could not give his undivided attention to his duties because of his acceptance earlier of a post as one of the Society's travelling agents. The principal function of the Electoral Committee became increasingly that of augmenting the income of the Society, and instructing the Nonconformist electorate in local constituencies. In 1857 the two Committees merged. Circulars entitled 'Hints to the Electors' were issued by the combined Committee for the elections of 1857 and 1858.

[1] Richard Masheder, *Dissent and Democracy*, p. 144, reports Miall as stressing also at this meeting: 'Help forward the Suffrage whenever you can – help forward the separation of Church and State whenever you can: but if you cannot do both, help forward the Suffrage, and the other will be secure.'

[2] Patriot: 6.ii.54.

[3] ibid.

The Parliamentary Committee was anxious to keep before the public the results of Parliamentary voting on the various bills. In 1854 and again in 1857, an 'Occasional Paper' was prepared, furnishing a sketch of ecclesiastical business during the previous Parliamentary session, together with the division lists on certain debates.[1] This was forwarded to a selected list of M.P.s, to the press, and to a number of the Society's influential friends. In 1861, the Parliamentary Committee was authorized to act as an Electoral Committee in order to obtain required information and to prepare for a General Election. Morley having resigned as chairman of the Electoral Committee, Dr Foster became personally responsible for the introduction to the constituencies of candidates acceptable to the Society.

1. *Dr Foster and other Leaders*

The growing influence and prestige of the Parliamentary and Electoral Committees in the private operations of the Society during this period was due in no small measure to the guidance of Charles James Foster LL.D., who joined the Executive Committee in 1854. In 1856 he replaced Edward Pryce as manager of all Parliamentary business.

Dr Foster was one of the figures prominent in the foundation of London University, being a Professor of Jurisprudence there from 1850 to 1858. He had worked to obtain for London University a representative in the House of Commons. He laboured for Parliamentary measures which would bring equal educational opportunities in endowed grammar schools for children of Nonconformist parents. Through his experience as a Common Law and Parliamentary Counsel, and through his wide circle of friends in the legal profession, he was able to bring valuable resources to the strategy of the Parliamentary Committee. He exerted qualities of daring leadership in his office. It was he who established contact with agents in Ireland pledged to one object, 'the destruction of the Irish Establishment', and he who drew up the basis of agreement on their plans of action: 'secularization of the national property and simultaneous withdrawal of grants to other religious bodies'.[2]

According to the Society's Minutes on 16 February 1857, Dr Foster personally effected a private union of 10–20 M.P.s on one occasion for the purpose of defeating the Government on 'the next party vote'. He assiduously undertook schemes to increase the number of the Society's friends on local Parliamentary registers, and thereby contributed to many of the Liberal successes in the 1857 General Election.

A good example of the tenacity with which he pursued Liberation aims was his handling of the 1861 Census controversy. He first organized a deputation of the Executive Committee, in company with deputations from three other Dissenting bodies, to see Lord Palmerston on certain provisions of the Government Bill. The same deputation later co-operated in the formation of

---

[1] *Liberator*, supplement, Nov. 1856, pp. 221–32: 'Votes of Members on Ecclesiastical Questions in the Session of 1856'.
[2] Minute 674: 16.ii.57.

a Census Amendment Committee, composed of representatives of various denominations including the Church of England. The Census Bill for 1861 provided that

> . . . every householder should, under penalty, make a return of the 'religious profession' of 'every living person' sleeping in his house on the night of the 7th of April, 1861; and that it was understood that the statistics of the amount of religious accommodation, and of the attendance, would not be again obtained.[1]

It was resolved by this Committee that strenuous efforts should be made by the Society to expunge the words 'religious profession' from the Bill. Nonconformists, without exception, complained that in the case of 'nominal or uncertain' Christians the Church of England, as the denomination with the most wealth and political influence, would naturally benefit most. The Anglican hierarchy, they said, would regard the result as a question not so much of statistics as of dominance. Dr Foster finally helped to draw up the memorial, with the names of 171 Liberal M.P.s, which was presented to the Prime Minister in protest. The combined actions brought the withdrawal of the offensive words, and the Liberationists hailed it as another propaganda victory. Lord Palmerston and his Home Secretary, Sir George Cornewall Lewis, eventually gave way 'in deference to the feelings of Nonconformists, rather than assent to their reasoning'.

The Parliamentary Committee pursued a line of tactics different from those hitherto commonly employed by the Society at large. For the most part, Dr Foster avoided sensationalism and the shibboleths of the public platform, rather furthering the Society's aims through useful contacts in Parliamentary circles. He preferred to build up the Society by quietly cultivating the friendship of the 'right people', rather than noisily appealing to the masses. Foster had a basically different approach to the work of Liberation from that of the forceful and relentless Miall. Sooner or later one of these contrasting styles of leadership had to give way, and it was eventually that of Foster, who resigned on 26 June 1863, to take up an appointment in New Zealand.

The Society was always eager to identify its reputation with that of well-known Dissenters in Church and State. From 1854 onwards there was a series of private meetings to win important converts to the principles of Voluntaryism and to induce them into active participation. Some of these became moderate and some ardent Liberation supporters, who later stood out in the history of English Nonconformity. A number of the moderates, however, severed official connexion with the Society as its programme became more radical.

Additions to the Society between the years 1850 and 1861 included ten M.P.s elected to the Executive Committee. These members were: Apsley Pellatt of Staines, R. Gardener of London, James Bell of London, James L. Heywood of Liverpool, W. Biggs of Leicester, Thomas Barnes of Farnworth, Edward Miall of London, Sir S. Morton Peto of London, John R. Mills of

---

[1] Minute 1063: 27.iv.60.

London, and H. Pease of Darlington. The Rev. Joseph Angus D.D., Principal of Regent's Park College, joined the Executive early in 1857, for two years. The Rev. R. W. Dale D.D., accepted a place on the Committee in 1860 and occupied it until 1889. Herbert S. Skeats, formerly connected with the Voluntary School Association, was employed late in 1860 as press correspondent, librarian, and head of the publication department. Upon Miall's recommendation, William Edwards became Treasurer in 1850, and four years later Chairman of the Executive Committee with authority over all departments.

There was some unrest and disagreement on the method of achieving specific goals. It seemed, moreover, that some members of the Executive felt that, through Edwards, Miall was able to exercise too freely his will upon the course of deliberations.

Besides Dr Foster, there were seven other major resignations from the Society during this period. First, the Rev. Dr Ralph Wardlaw left in 1850, followed by Dr Thomas Price and Mr Albert Cockshaw in 1852. The Rev. William Forster of London (father of the Rt Hon. W. E. Forster), active in the Society from the beginning, resigned in 1852 because of certain 'unfair allegations' in the *Nonconformist*. John Kingsley, who had been one of the outstanding lecturers and secretary of the Manchester committee of the Society, broke off from the London Executive in 1855. The work had grown to such proportions in Manchester that the Committee there evidently felt independent of the control of the central office, and resented its attempts to regulate their programme. The prominent Dissenter, the Rev. John Howard Hinton, withdrew his name from all Committees in 1855. John Remington Mills M.P. cut his connexion with the Liberation Society late in 1861, in preference for the more 'cautious' methods of the Dissenting Deputies.

Before the General Election in 1859, Edward S. Pryce resigned as Treasurer, deputation organizer, and secretary to the Electoral Committee and Parliamentary Reform Committee, to avoid entangling the machinery of these organizations, which 'although not rivals, are quite distinct'. Shortly afterwards Samuel Morley withdrew as chairman of the Electoral Committee, which later united with the Parliamentary Committee under Dr Foster. These Committee adjustments were in part due to a dissatisfaction with the support given to Miall by the Nonconformist and Liberal electorate at Tavistock, where at the by-election in February 1859 he was narrowly defeated by only forty-four votes.

2. *The 1861 Party Manifesto*
A significant paper was prepared by a special sub-committee which contained a plan of operations for the 1861–2 Parliamentary season. This was to be the 'Society Manifesto' or statement of political strategy for several years afterwards.

The gains of the Society in the expansion of its organization was not matched by gains in the Parliamentary votes. The Manifesto attempted to set forth explanations for this failure. The moral force which constituents exerted upon their elected representatives to further the views of the Society was ineffective. The consensus of the Commons was prejudiced against all measures 'looking in the direction of religious equality', even when it was known that the Society was not responsible for them.

The Society was determined to make the most of the fact that the Tories were not agreed among themselves. According to the Manifesto, if the Conservatives were released from the fear of the immediate abolition of Church Rates, they would soon forget the threat they had made to divide the 'religious equality' party. Liberationists were strong enough to block every form of legislative compromise. They were therefore content 'to abide their time', and to concentrate their energies upon the formation of a Parliament more in unison with their wishes.

Certain steps were suggested for carrying this Parliamentary policy into effect: (1) a series of public lectures conducted by 12–20 competent spokesmen residing in various parts of the country, and public meetings in selected towns where the friends of the Society were numerous; (2) observances of the bicentenary of St Bartholomew's Day 1662 and making the most of its connexion with the principles of the Society; (3) skilful use of the Liberal newspapers, and bringing the editors into personal contact with the members of the staff and Executive of the Society; (4) concentration upon plans for the next General Election and a carefully devised effort to make the most of the predominantly Nonconformist population in Wales.

This entire statement of political action was summarized in words which read much like a party creed for religious equality:

'No State favouritism' may be put forward as the true political meaning of our movement. Ecclesiastical differences ought not to be regarded by the Legislature as the proper measure of our legal and social rights. Law should not, and shall not place us, under social disadvantages on account of our religious faith and practice. We decline to be dealt with as inferiors. We stand upon equality of citizenship. We refuse to be taxed for a class, or to be excluded as a class from any benefits which ought to be common to all. We have the same right in justice, though not in law, to unpledged municipal action, to participate in national educational and charitable resources, to the use of parochial burial grounds, etc., etc., as Churchmen. These things are as much ours as theirs. We claim to be on an equal footing with them. We will tolerate no monopoly.[1]

---

[1] Manifesto, Minute 1206: 27.ix.61

CHAPTER 5

Church Rates

The indignation on one side encountered obstinacy on the other, and in many cases the clergy and their adherents fought with tenacity, not so much for the rate, as for supremacy; while the vestries became training schools of religious freedom. At a calm distance from these excitements it is now easy to see that the mass of Nonconformists, and of many more outside of them, learned from these object-lessons the injustice and intolerance of a State Church, and soon came to regard the Liberation Society as a protector.

HERBERT S. SKEATS[1]

'Gibbon declared that nothing "was so dangerous as the virtue of priests". . . . I will venture to paraphrase that sentence by saying that nothing is so dangerous as the orthodoxy of Radicals.'

LORD ROBERT CECIL[2]

N O LEGISLATIVE undertaking during this period occupied the Liberation Society more than that of Church Rates. It appointed a Church Rate sub-committee which resolved to spend its entire force to end the 'obnoxious ecclesiastical tax'.

Liberation leaders led Nonconformist-Radicals in a great offensive, but they provoked Churchmen to consolidate their ground with the utmost tenacity. Parish priests swore never to give in, and Nonconformist parishioners never to give up. An animosity grew up between them which perpetuated itself long afterwards, not excluding modern times. Both sides lost the good will of many enlightened statesmen of the day, the Anglicans becoming increasingly indignant and the Dissenters progressively bitter.

An example of the heat engendered by this Church Rate controversy is found in a letter by Mr Edward Miall in 1851 to the Rev. Daniel Wilson, Vicar of St Mary's Church, Islington.[3]

[1] Skeats & Miall, op. cit., p. 541.
[2] Speech in House of Commons on the Third Reading of the Church Rate Abolition Bill, 19.vi.61. Hansard (3rd series), clxiii, 1294.
[3] *Nonconformist*, 3.xii.51, p. 957.

Reverend Sir,

The law of the land, I believe, justifies you in regarding yourself as my spiritual pastor. Why it should be so, I attempt in vain to conjecture. I derive no benefit from your ministration, and I know not that I have ever been within the walls of the same building with you but once, when, as Chairman of a public meeting, you witnessed the perpetration, by two clergymen, of a gross outrage upon my person, without interference or protest.

This day, for the second time since I have resided in your parish, two silver spoons were taken from my house, by a rate-collector, acting under a legal warrant, for the payment of the sum of two shillings and threepence, charged to me on a "rate for annuitants on chapel of ease, and interest on loan for building the new churches.". . .

You will probably absolve yourself from blame, in this matter, by attempting to throw it upon the law. Let me undeceive you—if, indeed, you are under any such delusion. The law is but an instrument. They who agree to put it in force are the responsible agents. . . . And this you have done in the venerable name of Christianity!

I shall doubtless be reminded, Reverend Sir, that this is a debt for church-building, incurred by the parishioners of St. Mary's, Islington, the interest on which common honesty binds them to pay. . . . I repudiate the moral right of your congregations to render me liable for debts contracted for their comfort. Honesty, no doubt, prescribes the repayment of the loan. Decency points out that they who enjoy the benefits of it should take upon themselves the just responsibility. When *we*, Sir, the despised Nonconformists among your parishioners, erect places of worship, in which we may assemble to pay our homage to the common God and Father of us all, we feel ourselves bound, not only to make good our pecuniary obligations, but to do so without thrusting our hands into the pockets of our neighbours. . . .

I am, reverend Sir,
Your most obedient servant,
Edward Miall.

To devotees of the Church of England, rate payment was not a legal requirement but a religious responsibility and service, and as such was equally binding. To the *Liberator* this was like saying, 'There's no compulsion, my dear – only you must!' Lord Macaulay declared in his last speech before the House of Commons (19 July 1853, on the Clergy Annuity Tax Bill) that ecclesiastical taxation could only cause the Church to be hated – and with this loss of love he felt that it was better for the Church 'not to exist at all'.

Inside Parliament each party was strong enough to block passage of schemes which were workable, but not suitable to their respective interests. In 1868 the Voluntaryists eventually claimed a victory, but a costly one. Episcopalians thereafter became more determined than ever to resist all other such encroachments upon their property rights.

A. *Preliminary Court Cases*

There were almost no legal precedents to show that Church Rates had been seriously opposed in principle before the 1830s. Until then the question had always been one of amount, but in 1837 a case arose which brought a thorough examination of the law on Church Rates and the extent to which they might be enforced. A majority of the vestry in the parish of Braintree, Essex, had voted to postpone a Rate for one year, but the Churchwardens in defiance of the vestry proceeded to levy it on their own authority. The legality of the Rate (2s. to the £) was therefore contested, and the dispute eventually went to the House of Lords.

The case of the parishioner *Bruder v. Veley* the Churchwarden started in the Consistory Court on 15 November 1837. Dr Stephen Lushington delivered a judgement supporting the warden, stating that the obligation of parishioners to repair the parish church was imperative – the vestry could only decide how the obligation should be best carried into effect. However, on appeal at the Court of the Queen's Bench in February 1841, Lord Denman declared that the action of the Churchwardens was 'illegal and void', and that the Ecclesiastical Court might be prohibited by a Court of Common Law from enforcing payment of the Rate. On a writ of error brought before the Court of the Exchequer Chamber, Lord Chief Justice Tindal confirmed the decision of the Queen's Bench. He intimated that possibly the Churchwardens and a minority of the vestry might make a Rate legally, as the majority had thrown away their votes in refusing to perform their legal duty.

This latter suggestion of the Chief Justice led to another and more complex case from Braintree. Also in the Consistory Court of London in January 1842, John Gosling, an occupier of lands within the parish, was cited by Veley for avoiding payment of Church Rates. Whereupon another vestry was convened and the Rate was refused by the majority of the parishioners present. When the Churchwardens with the minority voted the Rate, it was likewise resisted and the matter was again brought before Dr Lushington, the Vicar-General. He had previously upheld the legality of a Church Rate levied by the Church-wardens 'on their own authority', but now decided that a rate levied by the Churchwardens *and* a minority could not be upheld. Yet on appeal to the Arches Court of Canterbury, Sir H. Jenner Fust, the Dean of Arches, declared that the Rate was lawful and asserted the Ecclesiastical Court's right of jurisdiction in the matter.[1]

There followed a series of unsuccessful attempts to overrule the Arches Judgement – first tried in the Court of the Queen's Bench in 1847, and next argued from 1848 to 1850 in the Court of the Exchequer. The latter pronounced that the action of the Churchwardens was 'valid', but that the only means of enforcing payment of Rates was ecclesiastical censure.

The unhappy parishioners finally took their grievance to the House of Lords. The hearing on 12 August 1853 was marked by a lengthy and scholarly exposition of related cases by Lord Truro. No textbook or authority on ecclesiastical law, he maintained, showed any exception to the rule that the power for making a Church Rate belonged with the majority of the vestry. Soon afterward, the Lord Chancellor (Lord Cranworth) declared the con-

[1] Phillimore, *The Ecclesiastical Law of the Church of England* (London 1895), pp. 1445–6.

sensus of the Justices that a valid Rate must be made with the approval of the majority. It was therefore ruled by the Crown that in the proceedings of the Exchequer Chamber and of the Queen's Bench there had been a 'manifest error'. It was also ordered that the plaintiff 'be restored to all things which he has lost by occasion of the said judgement'.

By 1859 refusals to make Church Rates had occurred in 1,525 parishes all over the country. The man largely responsible for bringing about this state of affairs was Samuel Courtauld of Braintree. He had been the original proposer of an amendment in the vestry meeting of his parish protesting against the irregularity of the Churchwarden's action. He had supported the litigation through its complicated stages to its successful end. In 1855 at a public dinner he received a handsome testimonial from thousands of opponents of Church Rates throughout the United Kingdom.

> Presented, by friends of civil and religious liberty, to Samuel Courtauld, Esq., in commemoration of the wisdom, courage, and public spirit with which he conducted the Braintree Church-rate contest, through sixteen years of litigation, from 1837 to 1852, and finally established the necessity of a vote in vestry to legalize a rate, and the right of a majority to negative its imposition.[1]

B. *Experimental Legislative Attempts*

A Select Committee was appointed in 1851 by the House of Commons to consider the differences of practice throughout the country in assessing and levying these Rates. Carvell Williams, the Secretary of the Liberation Society, soon afterward drew up a circular asking all Nonconformist supporters for evidence on Church Rates which would be submitted to the Select Committee. A circular whip, also issued by Williams, was addressed to all Liberal M.P.s, reminding them well in advance that the question of Church Rates was arising on 26 May 1853, and urging them to support the proposition of Sir William Clay.

The lively debate in 1853 was started by Robert J. Phillimore (M.P., Tavistock), who cited numerous historical grounds vindicating the power of the State to exact such money in the name of the Church. He did admit the necessity for an alteration of the law in view of the growing strength of Dissent. He moved, therefore, that persons signifying their Dissent should forfeit their right to appear at the Church vestry meetings, and their right to vote on Church Rate issues or any question relating to the management of Church property. The Church fabrics should be subject to the direction of the Rate-payers and not under the control of the Clergy and Churchwardens. The reason for such changes, he explained, was that the maintenance of the present system of Church Rates might cause that which they sought to avert – the separation of Church and State. Rate contests in the courts were the surest means at the disposal of the Dissenter to advance the deeper question upon which they hinged – that of Disestablishment. The law of the land should be so fixed that these litigations could not take place to achieve such an end.

[1] *Liberator*, Oct. 1855, pp. 54–5.

Sir William Clay (M.P., Tower Hamlets) answered by sharply describing Church Rates as

> spoliation in disguise . . . a direct act of injustice to our Nonconformist fellow citizens as clearly as if we took the money out of their pockets by an Act of Parliament.

He believed the Church of England had already shown itself capable of thriving on voluntary means of support. His amendment to Phillimore's motion asked that the House resolve itself into a Committee to consider the abolition of Rates, to replace this Church money from pew rents, or to increase the valuation of Church lands and property.

Sir William had been sustained in debate by Sir Samuel Morton Peto, Edward Miall, and Apsley Pellatt. Both Sir George Grey and Lord John Russell deprecated religious establishments for religious purposes, but opposed the motion and amendment because of the 'vagueness' of the remedies. Sir Robert Inglis, representing as usual the Tory and High Church policies of 'No surrender', regarded both the motion and amendment as equally impossible. In the division the motion was lost by 172 to 220 votes, notwithstanding the support of Lord Stanley and the followers of Sir Robert Peel.

Near the time of this debate Lord Stanley, whose father (Lord Derby) had been Prime Minister for a few months in 1852, had published his views, suggesting a new definition of Church membership

> . . . which might supersede the highly constitutional, exceedingly ancient, but practically quite obsolete assumption that every individual composing the nation, is in connection with the national Church.[1]

The vestry, he thought, should be limited in future only to Churchmen who were Rate-payers. A much wider range of subjects would then come under the jurisdiction of a vestry meeting thus constituted. Furthermore, in this way a significant step would be taken towards granting the laity a fuller share in managing ecclesiastical affairs.

Next, on 9 May 1954, Mr C. W. Packe (M.P., Leicestershire) proposed (and later withdrew) a Bill by which two distinct Rates – one for repair of the churches, and the other for furniture and services – could be levied respectively. All parishioners were liable to the first, and all but members of Nonconformist Churches who made declaration of such membership, were liable to the second.

Gladstone (then M.P., Oxford University, and Chancellor of the Exchequer), speaking on 21 June, admitted the justice of relieving Dissenters from the Rate, but rejected the idea of Church property being placed in the hands of the Rate-payers as financially unsound. Lord John Russell (M.P., City of London) already had in mind a scheme to give just compensation to the Anglican Church for the loss of revenue brought about by any alteration of

---

[1] *The Church-Rate Question Considered* (London 1853), p. 40.

the law on Church Rates. Such a scheme he promised to bring forward in the following session.

In 1855, Russell could not make good his promise. Clay's clauses, on the other hand, had lost much of their vagueness: (1) the entire abolition of Church Rates; (2) continuance of Rates for the liquidation of Church debts contracted with reference to Rates; (3) giving Churchwardens, as before, full authority to provide for the repairs and maintenance of the Church, and to defray the charges connected with the conduct of divine service. On 26 July the Bill was counted out and withdrawn by Clay.

Shortly after the failure of these proposals in the Commons, the Society's leaders sent out an address to residents where Rates had hitherto not been opposed, urging them to express their dissatisfaction, 'which they were sure existed'. At the same time the Executive Committee was prepared to furnish legal advice and information to enable such parties to fight the battles in the vestry.

This address had been sent out largely to lessen the effect of Lord Robert Cecil's measure, approved in the 1855 Session, calling for a return of the number of parishes where Church Rates had been granted or refused. It was shown that, in 408 out of 9,672 parishes making replies, Rates had not been granted – Lord Robert maintained, therefore, that 95 per cent of the parishes had no trouble with the Rate.[1] These statistical claims tended to increase the intervention of Liberationists in the untroubled parishes.

C. *Conditional Government Support*

Up to 1855 abolition was unreservedly resisted from the Treasury Bench. In the next year, however, it became an open question with the members of the Government. On 5 March Sir William Clay received the conditional support of the Cabinet.

In his Bill, backed by Edward Miall, he endeavoured to show the fallacy of the argument that Churches would fall into decay if Rates were no longer levied. The Conservatives represented by Lord John Manners (M.P., Colchester) and Sir Stafford Northcote (M.P., Dudley) were still adamant. They first denounced Clay's measure as one of 'spoliation and confiscation', and secondly, accused it of denationalizing the Church by taking management from parishioners and placing it in the hands of 'a remote corporation'.

In more moderate tones, the Home Secretary, Sir George Grey (M.P., Morpeth) maintained his opposition to total abolition, but said that in cases where the law could not be enforced in levying this tax, the Government regarded the abolition of Church Rates as an accomplished fact. He favoured certain amendments to soften the law.

Lord John Russell felt that it was better to leave the law in its present state, because of there being no fair compensation to the Church for its loss in any

---

[1] The Society contested the accuracy of these figures and brought out its own return with 'the real truth' which showed 1,130 parishes where rates were not levied. *Liberator*, Nov. 1857, pp. 186–7.

scheme of alteration. Lord Palmerston agreed that Church Rates were the ancient property of the Church; but it was now a problem of how to appropriate this property for its rightful purpose. The Government would therefore propose:

> . . . where a Rate has not been levied, or where it shall not be levied, there it shall be voluntary in one sense of the word—that is to say, those not regarding themselves as members of the Church of England shall not be liable to have the Rate forced upon them; but on the other hand we provide for an organization for the proper application of those sums which, either by voluntary contributions or payment of a rate, shall be available for repair of the fabric of the church and maintenance of divine worship.

Just before the division, Miall (M.P., Rochdale) reminded the House that Churches were national property, but as Episcopalians used them rent-free, they ought to keep them in repair. The second reading passed by 221 to 178 votes, and the Government then introduced amendments to which the Liberation Society agreed; (1) Persons declaring they are not members of the Church of England were to be exempt from Church Rates; (2) Rents were to be charged on sittings for defraying expenses then payable out of Church Rates; (3) Rent charges were to be given to defray expenses then chargeable on Church Rates; (4) The Incumbent and Churchwardens were to be a corporation. When, however, the Government failed to set a date for debate on these amendments, Sir William abandoned his Bill with keen disapointment.

Lord Palmerston later revealed the intention of the Government to introduce a Church Rate Bill in the 1857–8 session, somewhat along the lines he had suggested in 1856. This was encouraging news to the Nonconformists. Therefore, a deputation of 140 of their leaders, including eleven members of Parliament, visited the Prime Minister at his residence on 27 January 1858. His replies to their questions were thought to be unduly evasive and light-hearted. Whereupon they later drew up resolutions declaring their determination to press for total abolition without delay, and recommending all friends of religious liberty to contest the levying of Rates in all parishes.

D. *Deadlock and Defeat*

The dissolution of Parliament took place in March 1857, and the Abolitionists suffered an unexpected set-back when Sir William Clay failed to retain his seat for Tower Hamlets. Sir John Trelawny (M.P., Tavistock), however, consented in 1858 to take charge of the desired Bill. Meanwhile, on 19 April another deputation from the Committee of Anglican Laymen, with the Duke of Marlborough acting as spokesman, waited upon Lord Derby in protest. One year before, the Marquess of Blandford had presented a similar deputation of this Committee to Palmerston, when it was maintained that the abolition of Church Rates would deprive the Church of England of approximately £350,000 in annual revenue.

The second reading passed easily by 214 to 160 votes, and the amendments went through committee without serious difficulty. The third reading passed in the Commons for the first time on 3 June, and to the anxious Dissenters it afforded a much-needed feeling of triumph. Sir John wrote a letter to the Liberation Society stating, 'The truth is, the cause was ripe, and our case irresistible.'[1] The principal issues at stake were now generally understood, and some kind of adjustment in the law was bound to come eventually.

The controversy was now no longer to redress a grievance, but to assert an impossible principle, said the Committee of Laymen. This was not borne out, however, by the lurid accounts of Church Rate exactions on the early pages of the *Liberator*. Quarrels in the parishes continued unabated and the disputants began pleading with a torrent of petitions to the Houses of Parliament.

On 2 July 1858, for the first time the Church Rate Bill went to the House of Lords where it was severely defeated. How long, asked the Society, will you carry on a struggle in which you are sure to be beaten at last?

During the twenty-one months following, a deadlock ensued, in spite of honest attempts to design a working formula from the plans already debated. Strongly opposed by Sir John Trelawny and the Liberation Society, another Government Bill was defeated on 9 March 1859. Six days later a Bill of the Society fared no better and likewise became defunct.

In this latter debate the speeches of Darby Griffiths (M.P., Devizes) and A. J. Beresford Hope (M.P., Maidstone) particularly denounced the Liberation Society, its leaders, and publications. Hope quoted from a tract entitled 'The Doctrine of Voluntaryism' in which its author, the Rev. Dr Ralph Wardlaw, had justified 'pulling down the Church'.

Upon a motion of the Duke of Marlborough, a Committee of the Lords on Rates was formed in 1859 to try to break the deadlock; Dr C. J. Foster and Mr Samuel Morley were summoned, among others, to give evidence. Confronted with specimens of the Society's literature, Foster and Morley were examined concerning the ultimate objects of the Liberation movement. These they frankly admitted to go considerably beyond the extinction of Church Rates – something which had never been concealed by Disestablishers. The Committee treated this as a great discovery, said the *Nonconformist*, in order 'to spur all parsondom into alarm and activity'[2] against the power of the Liberation Society.

Early in 1860, the second reading of Trelawny's Bill again passed, but with an alarming increase in the minority vote. The Society took this as a sign to open a grand petitioning campaign, in hopes of pushing the Bill through that year.[3] Their hopes seemed within reach when late in March the Bill came out of Committee unaltered. A week before the third reading, 5,281 petitions with

---

[1] Minute 827: 25.vi.58.

[2] *Nonconformist*, 26.vi.61, p. 501.

[3] The Society had asked for an inundation of a quarter of a million signatures. *Liberator*, March 1860, p. 44. Petitions were placed in shops, advertisements placed in the London daily (Radical) newspapers, and 10,000 circulars were sent out by the Society asking for petitions to the Commons. The Congregational and Baptist Unions likewise issued circulars; the Dissenting Deputies circulated petitions among 107 congregations.

582,836 signatures had been presented to the House of Commons in favour of abolition, but these did not enable the abolitionists to muster more than a majority of nine votes.

Petitions were then poured into the Upper House – eventually 150 petitions for each day the Lords sat in Session. This did not stop another crushing defeat, but the results of the debate there on 19 June did bring encouraging signs. Lord Lyveden had been secured, after some difficulty, to take charge of the Bill, and he gave it a lively defence. The Duke of Marlborough revived the testimony of Dr Foster and Mr Morley before the Select Committee, but treated it more calmly than before. The Archbishop of Canterbury (Dr Sumner) modified his opposition and expressed his earnest desire for a measure that would 'annihilate the plausible objection' of the Dissenters.

Although it had now become apparent to the leaders of the anti-Church-Rate party in the Commons that only a compromise could bring reasonable legislation, the Society still persisted with a policy of total abolition. To the Society, compromise meant that Protestant Episcopalians would be permitted to use the machinery of public law to defray the cost of their own religious worship – an arrangement 'the State would never think of conceding to any other denomination'. The Parliamentary Committee, however, recommended on 21 December 1860 that petitioning of Parliament for abolition should cease 'for the time being'. In lieu of these petitions, memorials were to be addressed by electors to their representatives urging them to vote on every division of the Bill. Furthermore, £1,000 was to be expended for carrying the Bill in the coming Session.

Throughout the 1860–1 Session, the Parliamentary Committee concentrated upon bringing pressure to bear upon 'border-line M.P.s'. Special agents were designated, instructed in practical means of resisting Rates in the vestries and before the magistrates, and sent to the 'crucial' districts.[1] In addition, the Society's Church Rate sub-committee devoted much planning and advertisement toward a massive Church Rate conference. This was presided over by W. Schofield (M.P., Birmingham), at Freemasons' Hall on 12 February, was attended by 800 people, and was liberally supported by the Society.

A fortnight after this conference, the second reading of the Abolition Bill passed by 281 to 266 votes. It was then clear that a split had developed in the pro-Rate party between the backers of Sir William Heathcote's policy of sensible concession and Disraeli's policy of 'No surrender'.

On 27 February, Sir John Trelawny opened debate on his Bill (having dissociated himself from the evidence of the Society before the Lords' Committee) by pointing to the evidence of Dr Stephen Lushington before that Committee concerning the glaring inadequacy of the law. He closed by saying that those who stood for their extreme rights were the worst enemies of the institution which they were supposed to defend. Sir William Heathcote (M.P.,

---

[1] The Rev. H. M. White, curate of Andover and former Fellow of New College, Oxford, but not a member of the Society, preached a sermon before the University on 10 February against Church Rates. *Liberator*, June 1861, pp. 100–1.

Oxford University) said that he would not stand for extreme rights and he would vote for abolition in order that the Government might propose an arrangement which the whole House might accept. Gladstone (Chancellor of the Exchequer and M.P., Oxford) claimed that he was bound to vote against the Bill as a member for a clerical constituency. John Bright (M.P., Birmingham) warned that the Nonconformists, like the Puritans before them, would never abandon the cause of freedom until complete victory was won. In more pacific tones than usual, Disraeli (M.P., Buckinghamshire) deplored taking from his Dissenting countrymen 'the privilege of self taxation'.

> We have heard a great deal of Dissenters in this and previous debates on this subject, and one would almost suppose from the manner in which the Dissenter was mentioned that he was some stranger in the country, or some wild animal. Why, Sir, a Dissenter is our friend, our neighbour, our tenant, our tradesman; he is an Englishman, animated by all the feelings and principles of Englishmen.

The existence and prosperity of the Church of England did not depend on Church Rates, said Lord Russell (M.P., City of London), and therefore the sooner they were abolished the better it would be for the Church. The M.P. for Cambridge University, Spencer Walpole, asked whether it was not reasonable to expect the nation to maintain its national places of worship – voluntary effort could work only for temporary projects, but never for that which was nationally permanent in character.

The weakness of the Conservatives proved, however, to be illusory at the time of the third reading, which was postponed for a fortnight. When it came, on 19 June 1861, its rejection was sought by the Conservative opposition as a trial of party strength. In the extra time they had gained extra strength, and the Radical measure was lost by the casting vote of the Speaker, J. Evelyn Denison (Viscount Ossington).

The debate on this reading was conducted by thirteen M.P.s, each of whom had compromise suggestions to make. Everybody agreed that Dissenters were entitled to some relief, but nobody had strong confidence in any one particular solution. Trelawny insisted that dislike of the Liberation Society was not a good reason for rejecting the Bill. He deplored any 'ticketing system' which would require registration of Dissenters and those who objected to Church Rates. He threatened that if the Bill did not pass that year, it might fall into the hands of someone less moderate than he. Sotheron Estcourt (M.P., Wiltshire N.) would allow every man to exempt himself personally from an obligation to support a Church of which he was not a member. R. A. Cross (M.P., Preston), however, felt that the only safe course was to depart from the old system as little as possible.[1]

Sir George Lewis (M.P., Radnor and Home Secretary) believed that pew rents should be fixed upon those only who were members of the parish churches. To do this, said C. N. Newdegate (M.P., Warwickshire N.), would

[1] Cross's Church Rate Laws Amendment Bill embodied this 'principle of personal exemption'. It was brought into the Commons on 24 July 1861 with some novel features, and withdrawn the same day.

uproot the parochial system which lay at the root of the country's culture. John Bright, eager to restore peace in the parishes, urged the abolition of summonses, magistrates, bailiffs, and the leaving of all else in the law as it was. A Rate, he agreed, could be made by those spending it, but its payment should be optional.

The reasons for the narrow defeat were: (1) the weak character of debating by the advocates of the Bill, (2) the association of the Liberation Society with the designs of the Bill, (3) the increased activity of the Church Defence Association and the anti-Abolition party, and (4) the feeling M.P.s had of 'getting tired' of the subject.

In view of the imposing array of schemes, drastic revision in the strategy of the Society was now clearly necessary. Embarrassed but far from disheartened, the Executive Committee expressed in several resolutions its regret at the failure of Trelawny's Bill. One of these was a hopeful sign for a more charitable and less rigid policy in a future settlement in a new Parliament:

> . . . this Committee believes that the opponents of Church Rates will cheerfully concede to Episcopalians any legal arrangements deemed necessary to render a transition from the compulsory to the voluntary system of providing for the repair of the Church of England edifices, and for the due celebration of Divine worship therein, as easy and as little offensive to their feelings as possible.[1]

---

[1] Minute 1187: 21.vi.61.

CHAPTER 6

Irish Church Affairs

With respect to State endowments and Establishments of religion, I am no great lover of them; the good they do is never unmixed, and it may sometimes, even when the religion so endowed is most true, be problematical whether they do more harm or good. It is, however, one thing not to *create*, and another thing to destroy.

SIR ROUNDELL PALMER[1]

Every man ought to be interested in putting error out of the world as speedily as possible—the mistake is in supposing that the quickest and seemliest way of doing so, is by hunting down all who harbour it.

EDWARD MIALL[2]

LORD MACAULAY had once said that the only end of teaching was that man might learn, and that it was idle to talk of teaching truth in ways which would only cause men to cling more firmly to falsehood. In Ireland, as elsewhere, the first requirement in learning the steps toward national independence was the removal of religious inequalities.

Liberationists had no wish to encourage sedition, although their role was suspected by many on both sides of the Irish Sea as part of an effort to throw off the 'yoke' of English rule. The Society was ready to take full advantage of the dissatisfaction of Roman Catholics with the claims of the Anglicans to be the 'recognized' Church in Ireland. Ireland was under an Imperial rule which officially sanctioned no other religious body, but there was no love for it on the part of the majority of the citizens. In the year 1856, 13 per cent of the population were members of the Established Church and 77 per cent were members of 'other Dissenting Churches'. For these reasons Whig and Liberal statesmen now asserted that the state of affairs in Ireland demanded serious revision.

Before the union Ireland was governed by the British cabinet, through the Irish

---

[1] Afterwards Earl of Selborne, *Memorials: Part I Family and Personal 1766–1865* (London 1896), ii, 298: letter to Arthur Gordon, 12.x.56.
[2] *Nonconformist*, 27.viii.56, 'Wanted, A Positive Theology', p. 633.

landed gentry, according to their views, and in their interests. After the union it was just the same. She was treated as a turbulent and infected province within the larger island; never as a community with an internal economy peculiarly her own, with special sentiments, history, recollections, points of view, and necessities all her own.[1]

A. *Minor Disturbances*

A great deal of the anti-Irish agitation stemmed from the anti-Papal agitation caused by the 'Apostolic Letter' of the Holy See in 1850. Referring to the mission of St Augustine under Gregory the Great, and to the great solicitude of the Pontiffs for the Catholic Church in England ever since the 'commencement of the schism', the letter announced the re-establishment of a hierarchy of Bishops throughout the Kingdom. According to the common laws of the Church of Rome these Clergy would derive their titles from their own Sees which were constituted by decree of Pope Pius IX.

In a letter to his brother (Sir William Temple) on 27 January 1851 Lord Palmerston acknowledged the right of the Catholics to organize their Church as they wished, 'if it had been done quietly and kept in the bosom of the Church'. But what offended the country was the Pope's published allocation and Cardinal Wiseman's public announcement (as the Archbishop of Westminster) of his new dignities. The first represented England as a land of benighted heathen, and the second proclaimed that the Vatican had parcelled out England and Wales into twelve territorial dioceses. Both sought the restoration of Catholic England 'to its orbit in the ecclesiastical firmament'.

Dr Wiseman defended his Pastoral by pointing out that Roman Catholics in the country were already ruled by Bishops (Vicars Apostolic), and claiming that there was no law forbidding the title of Bishop.[2] The Pope himself had been preoccupied with the matter since 1847, when he had appealed to the British Government that what had been permitted in their Colonies would hopefully be tolerated at home. The pronouncements were not an act of rivalry to the Established Church.

It was not long, however, before Parliament retaliated with Ecclesiastical Titles Assumption legislation to protect the prerogatives of the Crown. The Prime Minister, Lord John Russell, affirmed in his letter to the Bishop of Durham (Dr Maltby) that 'my alarm is not equal to my indignation'. What he disliked most was the grandiloquent language of the Bull. He emphasized that the real 'danger within the gates' lay in the Roman liturgical practices introduced by 'the unworthy sons of the Church of England'. The Papal claim of supremacy over the realm of England was inconsistent with the Queen's supremacy and with the Protestant tradition of the nation. He

---

[1] Morley, *Life of Gladstone*, i, 688–9.

[2] Nicholas Wiseman, *An Appeal to the Reason and Good Feeling of the English People on the subject of the Catholic Hierarchy* (London 1850).

therefore heatedly proposed a Bill to forbid the new titles and thus reduce 'the mummeries of superstition'.[1]

In one of his great orations, Gladstone opposed the Bill's second reading on 25 March 1851, and was sustained by Sir James Graham and Lord Aberdeen. The latter regarded the Pope's action as foolish and offensive, but insufficient ground for penal enactment. He pointed out the close parallel between the position of the Bishops of the Episcopal Church of Scotland and that of the Roman Catholic Bishops in England. It was folly to suppose that any object was gained by banning the use of names which had no real legal significance. John Bright sternly rebuked the first Minister of the Queen for offending eight millions of her subjects and creating fresh discords between the Irish and English countries.

The House voted overwhelmingly (438–95) against 'the papal aggression', giving an element of confidence to a shaky Government. The Act, however, was ignored by the Roman Church, was not enforced by the English State, and was repealed twenty years later in Mr Gladstone's own administration.

Unlike the excitement of both the Protestant and Evangelical Alliances and the Protestant Dissenting Deputies in their crusades, the Liberation Society leaders refrained from expressing strong anti-Catholic sentiments. They looked upon such an indulgence instead as 'a quarrel between rival hier-archies, in presence of the great prizes provided by the State'. The aim of the Society was to strike at the heart of the trouble – the union between Church and State – and to call people to see that as the real enemy.

This climate of feeling naturally led people to re-examine the advisability of the Government grant to the Roman Catholic College of Maynooth in Ireland. The question had been stirring criticism ever since 1845 when an Act of Parliament placed the grant on the Consolidated Fund. The appearance of the report of the Commissioners of Inquiry into the state of Maynooth College in 1855 revived hostilities.

Outside Parliament a demonstration of eager Protestants was called in April of that year by Mr R. Spooner (M.P., Warwickshire N.) to protest and proclaim, 'Delenda est Maynooth!' The conference resolved:

> That the endowment of the College at Maynooth, for the training of Romish priests, is contrary alike to the dictates of Holy Scripture and to sound public policy; and that the Papal system—by its recent aggressions in England, Holland, Piedmont, Germany, and America, its persecutions in Tuscany, its repressive efforts in Spain, and the late addition to its unscriptural dogmas—manifests itself to be still dangerous to our institutions, incompatible with freedom of conscience, and subversive of religious truth.[2]

In these matters the Society adhered to a policy of neutrality. It simply

---

[1] Spencer Walpole, *Life of Lord John Russell*, ii, 120–1. About this time *Punch* came out with a cartoon showing little Johnny Russell chalking 'No Popery' on Cardinal Wiseman's door and running away. The Premier had also been ridiculed by High Churchmen for his 'Broad' Episcopal appointments. A. Wyatt Tilby, *Lord John Russell*, p. 118.

[2] *Nonconformist*, 25.iv.55, p. 321.

expressed the hope that Irish Roman Catholics would not accuse it of intolerance, for the loss of their endowment was a blow aimed 'to shake the ecclesiastical system from which they had been the severest sufferers'. Like the Government, members of the Society did not wish to lose the confidence of the Irish Liberal party.

The above conference formed an anti-Maynooth Committee and appointed a special deputation. Sir Culling Eardley,[1] one of its Anglican leaders, requested Lord Palmerston to receive it. The Whig Premier responded unsympathetically:[2]

> My dear Sir Culling,
>
> I was sorry to be unable to write to you at the time when your servant brought me your letter. I regret that I cannot receive the deputation which you mention either to-morrow or Thursday, as my whole time is engaged on both of these days.
>
> It seems, however, to be of less consequence, because I can easily imagine what the deputation would have to say to me, and while, on the one hand, I could not hope to change their opinion, I am quite sure they would not alter mine.
>
> Yours sincerely,
> Palmerston.

In spite of stalling tactics by the Opposition, on 15 April 1856, Spooner pressed successfully for a Committee to look into the College endowment, with a view to stopping it from the Consolidated Fund. Support came from a 'curious combination' of the upholders of the Protestant Establishment and the advocates of the voluntary principle.

Two months later a Bill was brought in to place the grant on the Annual Estimates, and thus subject the amount to regular review. Describing the Maynooth money as a 'national sin', Mr Spooner bitterly attacked as well the doctrines and practices of the Catholic Church. Henry Herbert (M.P., Kerry) therefore obstructed division on the second reading by speaking up to the time when, according to House rules, all proceedings on opposed motions were suspended. This was the closest the anti-Maynooth campaign came to success in Parliament, before it was finally settled as part of the Irish Church Act in 1869.

Of more immediate interest to the Society was the matter of the Royal Purse to Protestant Dissenting Ministers. Here was another irksome monetary issue which became a beam in the eyes of those who had been campaigning against the Parliamentary grant to the Roman Catholic College at Maynooth.

Known as the English *Regium Donum*, it was abandoned on 18 July 1851, when the Chancellor of the Exchequer, Sir C. Wood (M.P., Halifax), announced that the Government would not place the grant on the votes, and therefore it would be dropped from the Estimates. John Bright (M.P.,

---

[1] i.e. Sir Culling Eardley Smith, mentioned on p. 37 above; he had taken the surname of Eardley in 1847.

[2] *Nonconformist*, 25.iv.55, p. 322.

Manchester) under the instructions of the Liberation Society, took the lead in opposing this grant as 'secret service money'. He saw in the Royal Purse the means of making Dissenters dependent upon the State and deterring the congregations from liberality in their contributions. The nine distributors, representing the three major Nonconformist denominations in England and Wales, were suspected by some of their colleagues of keeping secret the names of the 300 recipients of the money. Lord John Russell was suspected of defending the grant with the idea of weakening the arguments of the Voluntaryists and Liberationists.

The reasons for and against the Irish *Regium Donum*[1] were much the same as in the case of its English counterpart. Bright was again its antagonist and the spokesman of Liberation principles. Having failed in 1850, he resumed his plea in 1854 for reduction of the 'hush money', as he now called it. On what grounds, he asked, could Irish Presbyterians claim State support, in the absence of which other Dissenting bodies maintained a more vigorous existence? His motion was lost, but his speech was published by the Liberation Society for circulation in Ireland. Letters from Dr Wilson, of Presbyterian College, Belfast, to the Society, challenged the accuracy of the speech.

The Irish Presbyterian Society favoured the preservation of the grant to prevent cases of hardship. The Liberation Society maintained that there were other groups in favour of it for purely selfish reasons: (1) Irish nationalists were for it because it brought £40,000 of public money each year into Ireland. (2) The Roman Catholics were for it as an apology for the Maynooth grant. (3) The Government was for it because most governments liked to have a hold of this kind upon sectarian bodies. (4) Members of the Established Church were for it, because they regarded little outworks of this type as 'extra-mural fortresses of the great hierarchical citadel'.

During this period many of the Unitarians, representing the more prosperous families among the Presbyterians of Ireland, scorned the Society. They naturally urged the Government not to cease this support so that an added financial burden would not fall back on them. In 1860, Mr W. E. Baxter (M.P., Montrose) moved that this Crown gift 'cease and be extinguished', but the attempt was easily defeated when the Government whipped against his motion.

The third financial dispute to arise out of the Irish Church legislation in the House of Commons during this period was the question of Ministers' Money. This had been a tax of one shilling in the pound, imposed upon the houses in certain Irish towns (many of them occupied by Roman Catholic families) for the support of the Protestant incumbents of the parish churches.

Dating back to the Act of Settlement in the reign of Charles II, Ministers' Money was not strenuously opposed until the action of the Aberdeen

---

[1] Sir Roundell Palmer estimated that during the years 1690–1870 the total sum voted by Parliament through this channel was £1,868,480. Compensation for discontinuance of grants amounted to £768,929. *Defence of the Church of England against Disestablishment*, pp. 215–16.

Government in 1854. In that year the Secretary for Ireland, Sir John Young (M.P., Co. Cavan), introduced a Bill specifying a new means of collection (by Town Councils), which became law and made this taxation more vexing. The opponents put the issue in the same category as Church Rates, holding that many residents were obliged to support a Church of which they did not approve.

In face of the fact that there were sufficient funds to supply the needs of Protestants in the country by other Church revenues, Lord John Russell called for a Bill to amend the situation. The following year the Government supported a measure of Mr W. T. Fagan (M.P., Cork) that the £12,500 per annum be paid out of the surplus of the funds of the Ecclesiastical Commissioners instead of being imposed upon the eight towns then subject to the burden. Sir George Grey and Lord Palmerston admitted that the system of collection was 'onerous, odious, and impossible'.

The Bill passed quickly through the final stages in both Houses, and the third reading was approved on 1 July 1857. The Liberationists and Nonconformists regarded this as a 'consolation prize' and as an omen of what lay ahead in the Church Rate controversy.

B. *The Society and Irish Agents*

A great part of the success of the campaign against the Church of England in Ireland was due to close co-operation between the Liberation Society and 'agents' in that country. The Editor of the *Nonconformist* newspaper had established a number of valuable contacts for the Society in his visit to Ireland in 1844, including a personal interview with Daniel O'Connell, the ardent Irish nationalist.

Edward Miall reported to the Executive concerning an important public meeting held in Clonakilty, County Cork, on 15 August 1856, and attended by approximately 15,000 persons. William O'Neill Daunt, one of the prominent patriots organizing the function, expressed their desire to work with the Society in carrying out systematic agitation in Ireland. They disclaimed any idea of restoring any part of the Church property of Ireland to the Catholic Church. An address was delivered to Miall, thanking him for his Disestablishment motion in the Commons and entreating him 'to persevere in his noble efforts'.[1]

Dr C. J. Foster was promptly dispatched to interview personally three of the Irish sympathizers, Henry Decie of Phale, A. C. Sayers of Fernhill, and Daunt of Kilcascan. As Chairman of the Parliamentary Committee he submitted a paper suggesting a basis of operations between them and the Liberation Society. The Maynooth question presented some difficulties for full agreement, and it was therefore decided that each side should follow its own course independently. On the policy for the next Parliamentary Session,

---

[1] John Francis Maguire sent a letter expressing regret for his absence and praising Miall as the right kind of Liberal, who in 'devotion to the voluntary principle' did not 'gratify hatred of the Catholic Church' (*Nonconformist*, 27.viii.56, p. 634).

the Society would press for a Select Committee of inquiry into the Irish Church. In this undertaking Irish agents would be relied upon for evidence on (1) the history, origin and extent of endowments, (2) the mode of distribution, (3) their social and political effects, and (4) the working of the voluntary principle in both Protestant and Roman Catholic Churches. In conclusion, the object of the Liberationist party was affirmed:

> . . . entire secularization of national property of Irish Establishment and sim-ultaneous withdrawal of Grants to other religious bodies.[1]

Daunt, formerly private secretary to O'Connell, endorsed Dr Foster's plan and assured him that other public meetings would follow that of Clonakilty toward a *bona fide* Disestablishment movement. After these consultations Daunt recorded in his diary:

> Arrived here, C. J. Foster, LL.D., from London, deputed by the Liberation Society to confer with me respecting the best mode of making an effective and combined battle against the anti-Irish State Church. Mr Miall, the member for Rochdale, desires me to consider Dr Foster as his *alter ego*. I find that our Clonakilty meeting has excited an interest in England that I had not dared to hope for. . . . They expect 200 votes in support of Mr Miall's next motion in the House of Commons.[2]

This understanding between Irish Catholics and English Voluntaryists required cautious moves on both sides. The defenders of the predominantly Evangelical Church of Ireland were fervently appealing to all within the Reformed tradition not to desert this 'bulwark of Protestantism'.

C. *Disestablishment Motions*

The Society first took action in the matter on 10 January 1850. Mr Miall then revealed to the Executive that he had been in consultation with Mr J. A. Roebuck (M.P., Sheffield) who had agreed to introduce a Bill on the Irish Church, based on the principles of the Liberation Society. A definite motion on the subject was made the responsibility of a special sub-committee, which soon put forward strong recommendations for an Irish Church Disestablish-ment Bill.[3] John Bright was asked to present petitions in support and to move that their number be printed with the votes of the House of Commons. When Roebuck became rather evasive, a motion was shaped more in line with his moderate wishes, but discussion on it was prevented by the counting out of the House.

The next official move in this direction did not come until November 1855. The Parliamentary Committee then asked Miall, now M.P. for Rochdale, to present a motion in the coming Session which would set forth the views of the

---

[1] Minute 643: 17.xi.56.

[2] W. J. O'Neill Daunt, *A Life Spent for Ireland: being Selections from his Journals edited by his Daughter* (London 1896), p. 134.

[3] Minute 674 (articles 2, 3): 16.ii.57.

Society on the Irish *Regium Donum*, Maynooth Grant, and Ministers' Money. His motion first read:

> That this House do resolve itself into a Committee, to consider the temporal provisions made by law for religious teaching and worship in Ireland.

Its introduction, fixed for 22 April 1856, was not made, because of an unexpected adjournment of the House on the occasion of the great Naval Review at Spithead marking the cessation of the Crimean War. Another date was secured, 27 May, when Miall submitted a stronger motion:

> That this House do resolve itself into a Committee, to consider the Temporalities of the Irish Church, and other pecuniary provisions made by Law for Religious Teaching and Worship in Ireland.[1]

At the commencement of the sitting on that day there was a large attendance. Two hours were taken up by a discussion on an eviction case in Ireland, and a member who deplored the battleground of the temporalities of the Irish Church moved that the House adjourn. Lord Palmerston rose and answered that Mr Miall had experienced difficulty in obtaining a day, and it would be discourteous to expose him to any further delays.

Thus the question of an ecclesiastical Disestablishment and Disendowment was again allowed to enter the British Parliament, this time launched by the Liberation Society. Its spokesman charged that the Irish Church before the Reformation was indigenous, but afterwards was an importation. The three ways in which the principle of Church Establishment had been manifest in Ireland – persecution, ascendancy, and indiscriminate endowment – had all failed. The Protestant Church had taken possession of the property which had formerly been Catholic, and thereby created the social devastation of religious discord. This kind of religious inequality Miall eloquently condemned:

> We have seen how, wherever it fairly gets head, it withers as with a cleaving curse all a nation's better capabilities; how it loosens all the ties by which society is held together; how it dries up the kindly feelings which spring out of the common relationships of life; how it weakens mutual confidence; discourages enterprise; checks industrial development; and substitutes for the glow of a healthy national activity, the wasting fever of popular excitement. It is among the greatest calamities which can befall a nation.[2]

All the changes, he continued, undertaken to solve the Irish problem had been negative ones. In the Maynooth Endowment Act of 1845 the English Parliament meant to recognize the principle of equity as necessary in all future ecclesiastical policy for Ireland. That was a step in the right direction, which should now be followed by the more effective move of impartial Disendowment. Miall then denied the stock objections: that it would impair the Act of Union between England and Ireland and bring wholesale confiscation; that it would endanger the English Church and disown Irish Protestants.

[1] Hansard (3rd series), cxlii, 737.
[2] ibid., 718.

To carry out Disendowment, he suggested constituting a special Court of Equity having the powers of an Executive Commission. He would put at the disposal of that Court the fee-simple of all State ecclesiastical endowments in Ireland, the fund under the Ecclesiastical Commissioners in Ireland, the grant to Maynooth College charged annually upon the Consolidated Fund, and the Parliamentary grants for the Belfast Professors and Nonconformist Ministers. He finally asked for a Bill to carry out two major proposals:

> 1.   That it is expedient to make provision for the application to other than ecclesiastical uses, of all sites, glebes, tithes, rent-charges, and estates, at present enjoyed or received by any clerical person of the Protestant Episcopal Communion in Ireland, for the support of Divine worship according to the rites of the said communion—but so as not to affect in any manner existing life-interests, and to pay due regard to any equitable claims which may arise out of the secularisation of such property.
>
> 2.   That it is expedient to exclude from the estimates annually presented to this House on account of the grant commonly called the *Regium Donum*, all sums on account of new congregations—and also to reduce the said grant, and the grant now annually made for the professorships of the Belfast College, according as the lives fall in of any persons at present in the receipt of any monies out of either of such grants.[1]

The Liberation leader had delivered his first major Parliamentary speech in one and three-quarter hours, and in a temperate tone which surprised those who expected a radical tirade. Without attempting to do justice to the arguments presented, Mr C. N. Newdegate (M.P., Warwickshire N.) asserted that Mr Miall was a disguised Jesuit pretending to be a friend of Protestant Dissenters. After stating his dislike of this kind of 'religious discussion', Lord Palmerston (M.P., Tiverton) replied briefly that the Irish Church temporalities were secured by a formal Act of Union and could not be diverted from their original purpose without violating the pledge then entered into by the Imperial Government.[2] He saw the union of Church and State as a proper part of the organization of a civilized country. Miall had made the mistake, said the Prime Minister, of not contenting himself with what he was objecting to, but was proposing schemes for converting the sacred lights of the Church into secular lighthouses. The motion was lost by 93 to 163 votes, the Liberationists lacking the Whig support which had been present on a similar vote twenty years before.

Supporters of Mr Miall, however, were satisfied that he had stated the case in a lucid and unanswerable manner. He had demonstrated that the temporal condition of the Irish Establishment was, in the words of the *Daily Telegraph*,

---

[1] ibid., 736.

[2] ibid., 765–70. The Fifth Article of the Act of Union declared: 'That the Church of England and Ireland, as now by law established, shall be united into one Protestant Episcopal Church, to be called the United Church of England and Ireland, and that the doctrine, discipline, worship, and government of the said united Church, shall be, and shall remain, in full force, for ever, as the same are now by law established.'

'a national disgrace, which it has become wholly impossible to defend, even upon the low plea of expediency'.[1] *The Times* had a different summary:

> The House, then, while it sympathized with Mr Miall's facts, did not go along with his or his school's theories. We are practical people, and our bias, moreover, is in favour of existing rights and institutions. We do not like wholesale confiscation, total overthrows, or volcanic disturbances of any kind.[2]

[1] 30.v.56.
[2] 29.v.56, p. 8.

Oxford and Cambridge Reforms

> Untie our hands and open our gates, and let us at least try
> if we can attract here, and can usefully deal with, that
> larger circle of youth whom we are told we ought to have
> here.
>
> THE REV. MARK PATTISON M.A.[1]

> What does it signify that you seem to open a door for the
> admission of Dissenters, if, when it is opened, you find a
> Cerberus that stands ready to devour the man when he
> enters? The honourable Gentleman argues as if there was
> nothing in the world but the matriculation test which
> interferes with the admission of Dissenters.

> W. E. GLADSTONE (M.P., OXFORD UNIVERSITY)[2]

ONE OF THE SPHERES in which Dissenters felt religious discrimination most keenly was in University and College education. Traditionally the Anglican Church in England had been the guardian of
the highest seats of learning. Higher education had long gone hand-in-hand
with high religion and high society, and aspiring Dissenters saw that there
was little chance of separating education from the control of the other two.

Again, legislation provided the best hope of solving the difficulty. But the
initiative lay largely in the hands of the reform educationists rather than with
the Liberationists. University education seemed to be a matter in which the
Liberation Society was more of an interested supporter than an active origi-
nator. Yet each party had the backing of the other in Parliament – the
Liberationists contending that the abuse in education was but another
manifestation of the evils of too much State religion, and the national
educationists maintaining that its deadness was due to the intrusion of too
much religion.

In their endeavour to win the minds of Englishmen, Nonconformists could
hope to compete with the well-trained leaders of the Church of England only

---

[1] Giving evidence before the Oxford University Commission, 1852. James Heywood,
The Recommendations of the Oxford University Commissioners (London 1853), p. 43.

[2] Speech in the House of Commons, 22.vi.54, on the Oxford University Bill. Hansard
(3rd series), cxxxiv, 549–50.

if each side had the same intellectual and educational advantages. This was not possible so long as Oxford and Cambridge, which still held their monopoly in the English academic world, insisted that Nonconformists must first subscribe upon matriculation to the Thirty-Nine Articles of the Church of England. To the enlightened Nonconformist, this was the worst kind of intellectual dishonesty and was contrary to the spirit of the day with its emphasis upon non-classical and scientific subjects. Many observers felt that Oxford and Cambridge were nurseries of Anglican manners and social graces, failing to match the practical achievements of an age of emancipation from the old and invention of the new. In the chapter, 'I Decide Against Holy Orders', rejecting weak and artificial University education, Frederic Harrison reflected upon his acceptance of a radical political philosophy at Oxford:

> . . . those who turn to what was being stated in the Palmerstonian 'fifties by Carlyle, Kingsley, Goldwin Smith, Mill, Bright, and the disestablishment orators and organs need not be surprised at the heat of a young student thrown into that world.[1]

Early in 1854, the Liberation Society sent a circular to Dissenting Colleges and Institutions and influential educationists, urging them to undertake practical steps toward promoting the principle of religious liberty in the two shrines of scholarship. Dr C. J. Foster, the Society's chief legal advisor and Professor of Law at London University, advertised in the press and leading weekly journals the resolution of the Parliamentary sub-committee that

> . . . this principle is violated in the exclusion of all but Members of the Church of England from the University of Oxford, and from the honorary and pecuniary rewards of learning at the University of Cambridge—these Institutions being national in their character, and being so regarded by the Legislature.[2]

This grievance, in the words of a modern historian, 'touched the whole reformist philosophy of the new era'.[3] A broad theory of national education affecting administration, examinations, fellowships, professorships, and the extent of speculative or scientific inquiry, was all tied up with the question of limitations. Dogmatic ecclesiasticism had long been recognized by liberal educators and humanitarians as the cardinal cause of the stagnation of these ancient corporations.

The complaint was not a new one, for it had been brought before Parliament in 1772, when a petition was presented by a large number of Clergymen on the subject of alteration in clerical oaths. In 1834 a Bill was brought in by Earl Grey's Ministry for the relaxation of Statutes relating to subscription and the admission of Dissenters to degrees in Arts, Law, and Medicine. It passed the Commons by a large majority but was lost in the Lords when Lord Melbourne, who had just then replaced Earl Grey as Prime Minister, expressed his disapproval. The practical effect of the defeat of this Bill was the establishment in

[1] *Autobiographic Memoirs* (London 1911), i, 147.
[2] Minute 123: 6.iii.54.
[3] Addison, *Religious Equality in Modern England 1714–1914*, p. 68.

1836 of London University, whose degrees were open to students of all creeds. Again in 1843 the question was brought forward, when it was insisted by non-subscribers that the Thirty-Nine Articles were not an absolute body of doctrines.

In the departments of Biblical Criticism, the Greek and Hebrew languages, and Systematic Theology, Nonconformist Ministers in their training were often ahead of the Anglican Priests. Dr John Angell James of Spring Hill College, Birmingham, scorned anyone who believed that the oracles of wisdom were only for those within the Apostolic Succession:

> Let him impeach our argument and not our style of writing, lest we should ask the question, so little to the credit of Episcopalian charity, who is it that excludes us from the seats of learning and then mocks our ignorance?[1]

A. *Oxford Remedies*

To the surprise of many in 1850 the Prime Minister, Lord John Russell, announced the appointment of a Royal Commission to inquire into the state, discipline, studies, and revenue of the two Universities. The Oxford group consisted of the chairman, Samuel Hinds (Bishop of Norwich), Archibald Tait (Dean of Carlisle), Francis Jeune (Master of Pembroke College), Henry Liddell (Headmaster of Westminster), John Dampier (lawyer), Baden Powell (mathematician), and George Sacheverell Johnson (philosopher). The secretaries were Arthur Penrhyn Stanley (Canon of Canterbury) and Goldwin Smith (Tutor at University College, Oxford). The Cambridge committee included John Graham (Bishop of Chester), Adam Sedgwick (Professor of Geology), and Sir John Herschel (author of *Discourses on the Study of Natural Philosophy*). Attempts by Tractarian theologians to thwart the operations of the committees by challenging their 'constitutionality' failed, and the reports were presented for Oxford in July 1852, and for Cambridge in August of the same year.

The high and 'unanswerable' merit of the former report was attributed to the reformist enthusiasm of Canon Stanley and the sagacious liberality of Dean Tait. Stanley described its tone as 'propitiating the Radicals'. Tait unofficially denounced some of the oaths as 'relics of a barbarous and irreligious state of society'.[2] The report made no specific references to religious tests, but rather hinted at the desirability of bringing the Universities alongside the State in removing civil disabilities for religious reasons.

Lord Aberdeen's Coalition Government brought in, on 22 June 1854, a Bill 'to make further provision for the good Government and Extension of the University of Oxford, and of the Colleges therein . . .' This measure, which was drafted by Gladstone and Robert Lowe (M.P., Kidderminster), was meant to be the model for Cambridge as well. It provided for a new

---

[1] *Dissent and the Church of England* (London 1830), p. 117; quoted by R. W. Dale, *History of English Congregationalism*, p. 628.

[2] Randall T. Davidson & W. Benham, *Life of Archibald Campbell Tait* (London 1891), i, 169.

Hebdomadal Council, it permitted the establishment of private Halls, it suggested opening one-fourth of College fellowships to laymen, and it made provision for the establishment and endowment of new professorships.

On the thorny topic of entrance requirements for Nonconformists this reform Bill was silent. James Heywood (M.P., Lancashire North), a member of the Liberation Society, therefore promptly moved the clause:

> From and after the first day of Michaelmas Term, 1854, it shall not be necessary for any person, upon matriculation at the University of Oxford, to make or subscribe any declaration, or take any oath, save the oath of allegiance, or an equivalent declaration of allegiance, any law or statute to the contrary notwithstanding.[1]

The debate which ensued set the stage for all later legislation on University reform.

The opposition claimed that the adoption of this clause would mean the defeat of the entire measure in the Lords, and would lead to 'heathenism' in the University. The Chancellor of the Exchequer, Gladstone, who was also a member for Oxford University, said that if Dissenters were admitted, so would the Roman Catholics be, and this would impair the working of the Anglican faith. Lord John Russell (M.P., London) said that if Dissenters were admitted to Oxford and to the enjoyment of its emoluments and privileges, they should not become part of the governing body. Sir Roundell Palmer (M.P., Plymouth) said that if Dissenters claimed that no institution was national unless all members of the nation had access to it, they must consistently pursue that principle either by abolishing every national institution which did not comply, or by revolutionizing such institutions until that principle was satisfied. Later he wrote:

> I had myself no love for the particular test of the Thirty-nine Articles, as applied to lads of eighteen or nineteen, fresh from school, or indeed as applied to anybody; nor did I undertake its defence. But I could not help knowing, that on the part of the very young it meant, practically, not assent to dogma, but submission to authority; and that in all cases its effect was to place under restraint in the University tendencies of opinion which might otherwise have been at open war with the Church, not to say with Christianity.[2]

For the supporters, Heywood pointed out that he wished to benefit not only Dissenters, but Churchmen who also objected to their sons signing the Articles and who also favoured the right of private judgement in doctrine upon which many in their own Church were divided. The most telling argument was advanced by the son of the Earl of Derby (the Chancellor of Oxford University), Lord Stanley (M.P., King's Lynn), speaking from the Conservative benches. The strongest reason for continuing religious tests, namely, the fact that Oxford was primarily a school of theology, was actually the strongest argument in favour of the amendment clause. It was a complete

[1] Hansard (3rd series), cxxxiv, 512.
[2] *Memorials: Part I*, ii, 203.

reversal of the usual educational process to require a student to accept conclusions before he could employ the assistance of the University to examine views upon which those conclusions were based. The vote for the motion was 252 and 161 against.

Heywood then moved a second clause:

> From and after the first day of Michaelmas Term, 1854, it shall not be necessary for any person, upon taking any of the degrees in arts, law, or medicine, usually conferred by the said University of Oxford, to make or subscribe any declaration, or to take any oath, save the oath of allegiance, or an equivalent declaration of allegiance, any law or statute to the contrary notwithstanding.[1]

Lord John strongly opposed this provision on the ground that granting Nonconformists degrees would lead to their voting in Convocation and sharing in University government. Upon the third reading of the Bill, Heywood modified his clause to extend only to the B.A. degree in all fields except Divinity. Lord John thereupon declared that 'if Dissenters were allowed to run the race, they should not be excluded from all the prizes'. Gladstone declared his support, convinced that he was thus 'doing his best for the interest of the University of Oxford'.[2] The clause passed overwhelmingly by 233 to 79 votes, and the third reading got through by 139 to 129 votes.[3]

The Bill was brought into the Upper House on 6 July by Viscount Canning, strongly supported by the Dukes of Argyll and Buccleuch. Its successful course was due largely to the attitude of the previous Premier, the Earl of Derby, who regarded it as 'far less dangerous' than it first appeared. He was opposed to the abolition of oaths, but this difficulty could be overcome by a declaration on the part of the Government that the connexion between the Church and the University should be preserved, its system of Collegiate discipline enforced, and the wills of the founders kept inviolate.[4] Despite solid opposition by the Bishops, the third reading passed without difficulty, and on 7 August the Bill received the Royal Assent. After the passing of this Bill, the University passed a statute making B.A. examinations in theology optional to those Nonconformists exempted by the head of their college. No such provision, however, was made for Anglican students who did not agree with the Thirty-Nine Articles.[5]

The Lords had put into the new Act a proviso of the Bishop of Oxford (Samuel Wilberforce) enforcing subscription wherever it had been previously

[1] Hansard (3rd series), cxxxiv, 588.

[2] ibid., 891.

[3] ibid., 909.

[4] ibid., 1238–40. He strongly opposed, however, the establishment of private Halls (clause 27), which he regarded as an undesirable innovation in the Constitution. Lord Carlisle defended it as the only means of providing 'retreats' for Dissenters to enjoy their privileges with comfort and dignity. This clause passed by 109 to 76 votes.

[5] cf. correspondence between Dr Hawkins, Provost of Oriel College, Oxford, and Sir Culling Eardley, who sought to have his name reinstated on the College books after the passage of the 1854 Act; see James L. Heywood, *The Recommendations of the Oxford University Commissioners* (London 1853), pp. 188–91.

required as a qualification for office, and thereby continuing the exclusion of Dissenters from the Masterships of Grammar and other Public Schools. The Liberation Society was annoyed by this and disappointed that Heywood had yielded to the suggestion of the Government that the subject of public schools should be dealt with by means of a new Bill.

Later, with a view to introducing such a Bill, Heywood proposed the consideration by a Select Committee of such clauses of the Act of Uniformity as imposed limitations upon the advantages of academical, grammar, or free education. That Act required any schoolmaster keeping any public or private school to declare that he would conform to the liturgy as by law established, and also to obtain a teaching licence from the Bishop of the diocese.[1] Palmerston admitted the expediency of removing such obsolete regulations, but he did not like the idea of tampering with the new settlements of the Oxford University Act of 1854. Disraeli did not like tampering with the old settlements of the Act of Uniformity. Heywood lessened the scope of his motion, but to no avail.

B. *Cambridge Aftermath*

The Chief Commissioner of the Poor Laws, Mr E. P. Bouverie (M.P., Kilmarnock), was granted leave, on 31 March 1856, to bring in a Cambridge University Reform Bill which was to be backed by Lord Palmerston. The Liberation Society had asked that the liberality of its provisions should be bound by the enactments of the Oxford Bill. But because the doors were already open to Dissenters at Cambridge, the provisions in the first clause proved to be more liberal:

> From and after the first day of Michaelmas Term, 1856, it shall not be necessary for any person on obtaining any exhibition, scholarship, or other college emolument available for the assistance of an undergraduate student in his academical education to make or subscribe any declaration, or to take any oath, any law or statute to the contrary notwithstanding.[2]

When attempts to amend this clause were easily defeated, Heywood went further with additional clauses: a second, that Dissenters receiving the M.A. degree be allowed to vote for members of Parliament and hold membership in the Senate at Cambridge; and a third that Dissenters be permitted to occupy University offices (excluding Divinity) without subscribing to the Articles. Despite assurances from Heywood that Dissenters rarely retained their Dissent for more than two generations, and from Lord Monteagle that their full admission to the University would eventually mean their full absorption, the third clause was withdrawn in the Commons and the second

---

[1] Irene Parker, *Dissenting Academies in England* (Cambridge 1914), pp. 46–8. Many of the ejected teachers at Oxford and Cambridge who would not accept the rulings of the Uniformity legislation in 1662 gave their services to Dissenting Academies. Thus in many cases they elevated the educational standards of these Academies beyond the Church grammar schools.

[2] Hansard (3rd series), cxxxvii, 1733–4.

was narrowly defeated in the Lords. The final Bill passed with the first clause intact, and called for eight Commissioners to frame new statutes,

> . . . with a view to the promotion of useful learning and religious education in the Colleges and the University, as well as to the advancement of the main designs of the founders and donors, so far as such designs had been consistent with the purposes of useful learning and religious education in the different academical institutions of Cambridge and Eton.[1]

---

[1] James Heywood, *Academic Reform and University Representation* (London 1860), p. 248.

CHAPTER 8

Religious Equality in the Colonies

> The country is told that British subjects abroad must not
> look to their own country for protection, but must trust to
> that indifferent justice which they may happen to receive
> at the hands of the government and tribunals of the country
> in which they may be. . . . Now, I deny that proposition;
> and I say it is the doctrine on which no British minister
> ever yet acted, and on which the people of England will
> never suffer any British Minister to act.
>
> VISCOUNT PALMERSTON[1]

> An opportunity had been given me of largely benefiting
> mankind. I accepted it. An end was put to closing the lands
> against the poor, and established churches, with numerous
> endowments, were got rid of. Because of the cruel system of
> land laws which prevailed being broken down in one part
> of the Empire, all other places would necessarily follow;
> and indeed they did.
>
> SIR GEORGE GREY[2]

ONE OF THE great facts in the events of this period was what Spencer Walpole called the 'prodigious increase in the number of English-speaking people'. In his *History of England* he asserted that this was 'not merely the chief fact in the history of the nineteenth century, it is the most important circumstance in the history of the world'.[3] Rapid growth of population at home naturally meant considerable overflow to colonies throughout the British Empire.

During this period, therefore, the spread of the Liberation Society's principles could not be confined to England; they travelled with many British

---

[1] Speech as Foreign Secretary in the Commons, 24 June 1850, during the Don Pacifico debate – the debate which set the foreign policy for the following decade. W. Baring Pemberton, *Lord Palmerston* (London 1954), p. 178.

[2] Speech as Governor of New Zealand before the Legislative Council, 18 June 1851, concerning sale of the waste lands of the Crown. Wm. Lee Rees & L. Rees, *The Life and Times of Sir George Grey, K.C.B.* (London 1892), i, 160.

[3] *A History of England from the Conclusion of the Great War in 1815* (London 1890), vi, 381. The increase in Britons at home was from 19 million persons in 1816 to 29 million in 1861.

emigrants to numerous foreign parts. Nothing more clearly demonstrated the vitality of Voluntaryism than the agitation against the State-Church system which grew up in the various Colonies. The Liberation leaders, in their campaign at home, realized the propaganda value of colonial ecclesiastical reforms. They not only urged and aided Nonconformists to protest against favours granted to the Church of England in the Colonies, but 'drew lessons' from these actions to illustrate the force of their principles. They corresponded frequently with Nonconformists abroad who were anxious to have somebody speaking for them in the Imperial Parliament.

The political ideals exported by the Society were those which had long been operative in colonial communities. Equality of opportunity for all was naturally attractive to those in the new world who had sought freedom from the control of the old privileged classes. The Colonists had built their homes and established their businesses largely through private industry and initiative. The less the State interfered in such pursuits, the more practical good, they believed, would come from their individual abilities. Many of them were therefore suspicious of any enterprise which was strongly dependent upon any kind of State subsidy or assistance. As stated in a leading article in *The Times*,

> Wherever our colonial empire spreads, the voluntary principle will go with it. It is part and parcel of our Imperial policy. . . . There is a risk in everything, but we do not see what greater risk there can be in trusting to this natural working of things in religion than in trusting to the principle of credit in trade.[1]

A. *Canadian Clergy Reserves*

The control of the Clergy Reserve lands in Canada by the Imperial Parliament had been hotly disputed by that Colony during the twenty-five years before the settlement in the Bill of 1853. The majority of the two million citizens, led by the Roman Catholics, wanted this control placed in the hands of the Canadian people. The Church of England Clergy and 'a few loyal subjects', fearful of their loss, desired the jurisdiction of the British Parliament to remain as final in such matters.

Before 1791 (when Canada was divided by William Pitt into Upper and Lower Provinces) the Clergy Reserve lands were the property of the Crown by right of conquest. Approximately $1\frac{1}{2}$ million acres of unsold land (some estimates went as high as 3 million acres) had been appropriated by George IV for the maintenance of the Protestant Clergy, and a limited power of dealing with these 'waste lands' was given to the Legislature of Canada in the Constitutional Act of 1791. By 1827 the French representative assembly of Lower Canada, which consisted of strong Roman Catholic elements, was granted control of these lands for the Catholic Church there.

In the Upper, or English, representative Assembly, however, the Reserve lands were a source of contention among the various denominations, and it

---

[1] 16.x.56; similar articles appeared on 22.xi.56, 4.ix.57.

was therefore proposed to apply the revenues of the property there to secular purposes. This Assembly passed at different times no fewer than sixteen resolutions, addresses, or Bills, all of which were rejected by the Legislative Council of that Colony. By 1831, in response to these repeated appeals, the Imperial Government was ready to return these lands to the general demesne and control of the Crown.

The storm first broke under the Colonial Secretaryship of Lord Ripon when he authorized the retention of £3,000 from the sale of these lands for the salary of the Anglican Bishop of Quebec, Dr C. J. Stewart. The French Catholics immediately denounced the home Government for diverting money which should have been at their disposal, to subsidize instead a Church to which only one-fifth of the Protestants and one-twenty-fifth of the entire population of Canada belonged. The French Assembly stoutly refused to pass a civil list for the payment of official salaries in 1833, and in 1836 the Assembly in Upper Canada followed suit. Both Provinces demanded control over their own finances and appointment of their own Legislative Council. This the home Government refused and rebellion broke out under Louis Papineau in 1837.

At the beginning of the 1838 Parliamentary session at home, Lord John Russell, as Prime Minister, brought in a Bill which suspended the Canadian Constitution and appointed Lord Durham as Lord High Commissioner and Governor General with extraordinary powers to deal with the troublesome state of affairs in both Provinces. Numerous reformers on both sides of the Atlantic felt that the catastrophe had come through 'the perversity of a foolish King and weakness and disunion among his Whig ministers'. But Sir William Molesworth's vote of censure on the Colonial Minister, Lord Glenelg, was thrown out by a majority of twenty-nine.

The Durham Report of 1839, which advised that the colonial leaders should in future be chosen from the ranks of the majority in the elected Assembly, became the substance of Russell's Canada Union Act of 1840. Parliament quickly endorsed proposals for converting the Clergy Reserve Lands to the purpose of religious instruction, without limiting it to either Roman Catholic or Protestant Churches.[1] Furthermore, a guarantee was obtained from the Consolidated Fund of £7,090 per annum for the Church of England and £1,580 for the Church of Scotland (both in Canada); in the event the sale of the lands did not realize a sufficient sum. The guarantee was never put into effect, because the sale of the lands always produced a surplus.

As the movement toward self-government in the colony became stronger, and as the proceeds of the Clergy lands mounted, the Imperial Parliament was again forced to modify its position. The more Canada became a deposi-

[1] Mr Gladstone, while Chancellor of the Exchequer in 1853, showed that returns of the funds given to Roman Catholics out of the Reserved lands amounted to more than to all the other religious denominations – the Church of England and the Church of Scotland excepted. Those advocating the Act of 1840, he said, were helping indirectly to endow the Church of Rome in Canada. *Nonconformist*, 9.iii.53, p. 203.

tory for the victims of the economic revolution going on in Great Britain, the more unsettling was the law which kept out of cultivation this vast acreage of rich lands. Many Canadians therefore renewed their pleas for the application of all the revenues of the Reserves to secular rather than religious uses – or, in the language of the Dissenters, for Disestablishment.

The Bill of 1853 was intended by Russell's Ministry to grant to the Canadian Legislature the power of disposing the Protestant Clergy Reserves in the same way that they had already granted authority to deal with Roman Catholic endowments. Parliament was now asked to decide whether such a question affecting exclusively local interests of a Colony should be dealt with by the colonial Legislature.

The opposition came from traditional Tories such as Sir John Pakington, Spencer Walpole, Sir Robert Inglis, and Lord John Manners. They were against Government action on the grounds of incompatibility with the Constitutional Act of 1791, rejection of the 1840 guarantee, breach of national faith and trust, and spoliation of sacred property.

The supporters of the Bill came from two groups – those promoting the peace of the colony, and those promoting the principle of religious liberty. In the first group were Russell, Derby, Gladstone, and the Bishop of Oxford. In the second group were the Radicals united under Sir William Molesworth, Miall, and Bright. Several weeks before the introduction of the Government measure on 4 March, the Society sent to all Liberal M.P.s a report by Miall that the legislation was a further example of 'the global trend' toward complete religious equality.

Because the Colonial Secretary, Newcastle, was in the House of Lords, the burden of Ministerial defence fell on Sir William Molesworth (M.P., Southwark) as the First Commissioner of Works. He was known as a firm believer in the old Radical creed of the Manchester School – 'Peace, Retrenchment, Reform'. He also accepted the ideal set out in Bentham's pamphlet, 'Emancipate Your Colonies' – the complete separation of the Colonies from the mother country. Sir William maintained in his major speech that 'the State ought not to entail any portion of the public estate in perpetuity'.[1] Complete self-government and self-determination on these matters in the Colonies would bind them even closer to Great Britain in language, custom and political ideas.

Gladstone urged the House to 'be just and fear not',[2] even though the Colony might use the powers of the Bill to depart from the wishes of friends at home. By rejecting the Bill they would render the Church of England odious in the eyes of many people of Canada. The second reading was approved by 275 to 192 votes.

[1] Hugh E. Egerton (ed.), *Selected Speeches of Sir William Molesworth, Bart., P.C., M.P., on Questions relating to Colonial Policy* (London 1903), p. 437. In 1845 at the election for the Southwark constituency Molesworth and Miall were rival candidates.

[2] quoting Dr G. J. Mountain, Bishop of Quebec, in a letter to Lord John Russell. Hansard (3rd series), cxxiv, 1152.

On going into committee, Russell sought to continue the guarantee arrangement of the Act of 1840, which would make it possible to take money from the Consolidated Fund for the Scottish and Anglican Churches in Canada, if needed. The guarantee would not be in perpetuity but would stand merely as collateral security to cover a possible loss on sales.

Miall thought the guarantee would jeopardize the voluntary principle. He vindicated that principle by citing statistics to show how successfully it had fared in the American Colonies. He deplored the idea of Englishmen at home being 'saddled' with a financial responsibility to support the Church in Canada when it was now ready to trust its own energies. When Gladstone said the guarantee should not be terminated without hearing from the parties concerned, Bright accused him of having a 'peculiar interest' in the Society for the Propagation of the Gospel in Foreign Parts. After a stormy debate, the vote for the omission of the crucial third clause (permitting the guarantee to remain) was carried by 176 to 108.

The Radical-Liberation bloc, however, came to the Ministerial side on the third reading when the Prime Minister asserted that, in the event of the Clergy Reserves being secularized by the Legislature of Canada and of such an Act receiving the Royal Assent, there would be no claim or guarantee for any payment from the Consolidated Fund. The real issue at stake, Russell said, was one of true self-government for this Colony. He was not prepared to comment on the merits of the voluntary principle in England, but if the Canadian Legislature were to accept that principle of their own free will, he would not shrink from the consequences. Cheers greeted his pronouncement that all future dealings with the Colonies should be founded upon 'liberal and generous principles'.

After a third-reading victory of 288 to 208 votes, the Bill was sent to the Upper House. To some of the opponents in the Lords it was purely a case of the rights of the Established Church being envied by the sectarians and Roman Catholics in Canada. Newcastle, however, rejected this idea and defended the proposals.[1] Derby, on the other hand, proposed a 'compromise amendment' to protect the rights of property already affirmed by Parliament, and those funds (from interest and dividends and rents from the Reserves) which had already been invested with trustees.

The Episcopal Bench was divided on this compromise. The Bishop of Exeter, Henry Phillpotts, contended that religion could not be adequately maintained without temporal provision. The Bishop of Oxford, Samuel Wilberforce, favoured holding on to half of the Church property as provided by Derby, but not at the expense of losing the Colony. The Bishop believed,

---

[1] He wrote, in a letter of 29 November 1862, to Lord Monck, Governor of Canada, who had complained of 'small jealousies' among the Ministers in Canada: 'The Governor of a constitutional Colony should endeavour to imitate the conduct in this respect of our good Queen, who has never throughout her reign allowed any whisper to be raised that she was sovereign of a Party.' John Martineau, *The Life of Henry Pelham, Fifth Duke of Newcastle 1811–1864* (London 1908), p. 311.

in the words of Burke, that 'the fierce spirit of liberty is stronger in the English Colonists than in any other people of the earth'. When the amendment was defeated by 77 to 117 votes, the Bill quickly passed, and soon became law.

The last action upon Clergy Reserves by the Liberation Society during this period occurred early in 1854. At a meeting of the Executive Committee on 9 February, a letter was read from their agent in Toronto, stating that

the Local Executive declined bringing in a Bill for their secularization without appealing to the country and there was reason to fear that yielding to home and other influences they will endeavour to obtain the return of a Parliament favourable to a redistribution of the Reserves among all denominations.[1]

Such a plan, promoted by High Churchmen and Reserve stipendiaries of the Society for the Propagation of the Gospel, solicited the support of those Roman Catholics who were generally interested in State recognition. On 12 July the Liberation Society recorded with pleasure the withdrawal of the Bill for Redistribution.

The year following, the Secularization Act was passed, and the Reserves of the Church realized altogether about one million pounds. The life claims of the incumbents were commuted, and the claimants paid off in a round sum all at once. The remainder went to various municipal corporations in proportion to the number of inhabitants under their jurisdiction.

B. *Australian Government Grants*

The Act 13 & 14 Victoria, cap. 59 (known as Earl Grey's Bill), providing a Constitution for the South Australian Colonies in 1850, not only made allowances for ecclesiastical grants but enacted that these could not be discounted by the colonial Legislature without the consent of the Imperial Parliament. A large number of Colonists, particularly the Dissenters, considered this to be a denial of the freedom which they had eagerly sought in emigration, and a perpetuation of the unhappy alliance between Church and State which they had left behind in England. The Act for the 'better Government of Her Majesty's Australian Colonies' ruled, however, that £6,000 per annum for religious worship should be raised from local revenues. Again, those who were not members of the Church of England foresaw the beginning of a much dreaded 'endowed religion'.

Before the introduction of the Bill into the British Parliament, communications were dispatched from Australia to the Liberation Society, objecting both to the grant for religious worship and to the final control which the home Government would exercise in the matter. The Executive Committee issued circulars to Liberal M.P.s urging them to oppose the legislation and requested Charles Lushington (M.P., Westminster) to propose the deletion of the offensive clauses of the Bill.

As a pioneer of radical Imperial policy, who was destined later to become Colonial Secretary, Molesworth felt sufficiently disturbed by the measure to make three outstanding speeches against it. Pakington stated that he and his

[1] Minute 93: 9.ii.54.

fellow Conservatives would assent to the Constitutions for South Australia, if the existing provision for public worship were continued. Elaborating upon a Constitution drafted by himself, the Radical statesman proposed that there should be no national nor Established Church in the Colonies. The hereditary Monarchy of Britain could retain all the rightful powers of Government with the exception of taxation. To prevent Australians from imitating their brethren in America,

> I propose that the Colonial Office shall cease to interfere with the management of the local affairs of these Colonies, and that they shall possess the greatest amount of self-government that is not inconsistent with the unity and well being of the British Empire.[1]

The issue arose again in 1854 when a new Constituent Act for Victoria was sent to England for the confirmation of Parliament and the assent of the Sovereign. One of the clauses of this Bill permitted an increased appropriation of £50,000 per annum out of the provincial revenue for ecclesiastical purposes. Liberation leaders at home were shocked at the size of the figure. The unmistakable hostility of the Colonists was expressed to Queen Victoria in a memorial with 11,221 signatures. In it they complained that the clause represented the feelings of Government appointees to the Legislative Council, and not the will of the majority of the people of Victoria. They prayed that the question be reviewed by the newly elected legislative bodies being provided under the Constituent Act.

The Imperial Parliament was now faced with a rising spirit of self-reliance from Independents, Baptists, a majority of Wesleyans, two-thirds of the Presbyterians, numerous Roman Catholics, and not a few Episcopalians – among them the Bishops of Tasmania (Dr Nixon) and Melbourne (Dr Perry). The 1860 Census for South Australia showed 117,967 church members, of which but 43,487 were attached to the Church of England. Of these various denominations, the Independents had voluntarily raised £24,000, the Presbyterians £17,000, the Baptists £7,500 and the Wesleyans £6,000, each for the support of their own institutions and Ministry. The former Governor, Sir George Grey, had encouraged such self-help and had declared that 'those who preach the Gospel should live by the Gospel'.[2]

A deputation from the Dissenting Deputies waited upon Sir George Grey on 15 December 1854; and on 7 June 1855 a larger one consisting of delegates from the Deputies, the Liberation Society, the Congregational Union, and the Colonial Missionary Society, waited on the Prime Minister, Lord John Russell.[3] In both instances the deputations maintained that (1) such a taxation was unfair, particularly upon the large number of Church leaders who had refused State financial aid, and (2) the measure should have been decided in

---

[1] Hugh E. Egerton (ed.), op. cit., pp. 392–401: 'Constitution for New South Wales, and, with the requisite alterations, for all the other Australian Colonies and New Zealand', pp. 291–392: Speeches on Australian affairs.

[2] W. L. & L. Rees, *Life and Times of Sir George Grey*, ii, 598.

[3] B. L. Manning, *Protestant Dissenting Deputies*, pp. 438–9.

the Lower House elected by the suffrages of the people. Sir George Grey assured them 'that there would be an opportunity for full discussion in Parliament' while Russell 'declined to omit the clause authorizing the £50,000 appropriation', but told the Nonconformist spokesmen that they could introduce amendments to the measure in the House of Commons.

Accordingly, amendments were attempted by Edward Miall on the second reading and the Committee consideration of the Bill. He charged that the State scheme for supporting public worship was an unfair practice, because three-fourths of the denominations had repudiated it and further because it excluded Jews. In Committee on the Bill, Russell replied that nothing equalled the tyranny of the Voluntaryists when their doctrines were not assented to – he could not sanction taking away the money already voted by the Colony. Miall believed that the tyranny belonged to the colonial Legislature, and if it had done what was under consideration in a proper manner, Parliament would not then be asked to condone it.

Miall's motion was defeated decisively. The Victoria Government Bill together with the New South Wales Government Bill, and the Waste Lands (Australia) Acts Repeal Bill, passed by comfortable margins and received the Royal Assent on 16 July 1855. Consequently, the aggrieved Colonists had to live with their ecclesiastical grants until 2 June 1857, when legislation was passed in Victoria to abolish State aid to religion after 31 December 1859.

Tasmania was one of the South Australian Colonies once described by the Colonial Office as 'a place to which convicts used to be sent, and which now supplied gold and wool'.[1] This Colony, however, was another which did not want portions of its wealth allocated by the State for public worship. Late in 1859, the Liberation Society received a letter from the Chairman of the Southern Tasmanian Anti-State-Aid Association, informing the Committee of a Bill passed by the Tasmanian Legislature for the abolition of existing ecclesiastical grants 'upon certain terms', and requesting the Society to exert its influence to induce the Crown to withhold Assent to the measure.[2]

The preamble to this Bill, 18 Victoria, cap. 12, stated that the £15,000 reserved *sine qua non* for public worship under the 1857 Constitutional Act of the Colony should cease. Of this amount, £9,000 had been available to the Church of England, and £6,000 to other denominations. In place of this annual appropriation, £100,000 was to be issued in debentures chargeable on general revenue. The sum distributed among the several Churches then receiving State assistance was to be in proportion to their members as shown by the last census of the population of Tasmania. This would mean amounts of £62,017 to the United Church of England and Ireland, £21,903 to the Church of Rome, £9,384 to the Church of Scotland, £6,136 to the Wesleyan Methodist Church and £557 to the Jewish denomination.[3]

[1] Martineau, op. cit., p. 287.

[2] *Nonconformist*, 28.xii.59, pp. 1035–6.

[3] James Fenton, *A History of Tasmania from its discovery in 1642 to the present time* (London 1884), p. 306.

The Nonconformist bodies of the Colony which were opposed to Government support combined efforts with the Anti-State-Aid Association to make vigorous protests. They argued that State-endowed Churches had been merely substituted for a State-aided Church. The endorsement of the scheme by the Governor, Sir Henry Young, and the Bishop of the Colony, Dr F. R. Nixon, was harshly criticized as favouritism toward one section of the community. The Liberationists capitalized on the strong feeling against increasing the public debt and the popular demand for economy in expenditure of public resources. But the Bill swept through the Legislative Council in a single day in a House from which many members were absent.

The Parliamentary Committee of the Society therefore sent a deputation to the Colonial Secretary requesting that the Royal Assent be withheld from this Bill until an opportunity had been given to the Tasmanian voters for a fuller expression, by placing the subject before their own constituencies. Whereupon, backed by Derby and Grey, Newcastle announced in the House of Lords that the Royal Assent would not be given to this Tasmanian measure. Grey reminded him that it was the duty of the Colonial Secretary to see that there was no invasion of vested rights, and the duty of the Crown to protect those who had accepted employment under a different colonial régime.

C. *The Indian Mutiny*

The great rebellion in India in 1857 gave the Liberation Society another opportunity to implement its views on religious equality and on separation between the Christian faith and the temporal power. The Society drew a parallel between the evils of social caste in India and those of religious classes in England.

The Government saw matters in quite a different light. The uprising placed in jeopardy not only the Indian Empire, but Britain's prestige among nations. Palmerston therefore refused help from Prussia and Belgium, believing his own country should deal with the mutiny by its own means. Accounts in the public press concerning the disastrous consequences gave rise to an indignant demand throughout Britain for inquiries and explanations.[1]

The true causes were as much religious as they were military and commercial. The clash between native and imported ways of worship had to be taken into consideration. In India, as in other possessions, nothing acted so dangerously upon the conduct of the native as the belief that the authority of the Crown was exercised to induce him to abandon the religion he professed.[2] The Radical-Liberation party at home believed that the Legislative Council

---

[1] Lord Aberdeen attributed the 'bloodthirsty spirit' which took possession of the press and people to the frustration felt at the end of the war with Russia without any 'signal or specially glorious triumph'. Lord Stanmore, *The Earl of Aberdeen*, 3rd ed. (London 1905), p. 305.

[2] H. H. Dodwell (ed.), *The Cambridge History of India* (Delhi 1958), states that 'Certain British officers preached the Gospel to their men with the enthusiasm of Cromwell's Ironsides, . . .' (vol. vi, chapter x, 'The Mutiny', p. 173).

of the Colony had often been guilty of this and of meddling with the Hindu faith.

The latter indictment was based on at least two grounds. First, a system of colonial land laws stated that no man should lose his property on account of his change in religion. This was directly contrary to native tradition, since a great deal of property was held hereditarily by Hindus as trustees for the maintenance of the Hindu faith. Secondly, a great 'national system' of education was established in 1854 by the Legislative Council. The use of the King James version of the Bible in these schools aroused the suspicion that the missionary teachers were proselytes of the British Government working against Brahmanism.

Many of the Nonconformist Missionaries themselves were objecting to certain features of the Government policy. After the insurrection was ended, at a missionary conference in Calcutta on 15 September 1858, a petition was addressed 'to the Honourable the Legislative Council of India', stating

> that your petitioners have long lamented that the regulations of the British Government, alike in the Bengal and the Madras code [1810], have for many years contained, and do still contain, a formal recognition of endowments 'for the support of mosques, Hindoo temples, and colleges,' as endowments 'for pious and beneficial purposes,' and have declared, and do still declare, that 'it is an important duty of Government to provide that all such endowments should be applied according to the real intent and will of the granters.[1]

The Missionaries objected that the East India Company had taken guardianship of all such endowments and thereby was connected with the management of 'heathen shrines'. Since the Government did not extend guardianship to trusts for Christian purposes, Hindu and Mohammedan endowments should be free of control in the same way.

At the bottom of the trouble were many other dissatisfied people whose animosities had long been smouldering. Those offended by the domination of an 'alien and infidel' race; those profiting through diversities of rank, status, and religion; those incensed by the relaxation of marriage laws and family taboos; aggrieved chiefs, dispossessed landholders, and villagers objecting to taxation – all combined to produce a dangerous threat.

The spark which touched off the explosion was a rumour that, under army specifications, the rifle cartridges bitten by the Mohammedan and Hindu troops had been greased with the fat of the abhorred pig and sacred cow. Before the truth could be told, the enraged troops mutinied against their officers and destroyed several English garrisons.

The immediate intervention of the Governor of the Cape Colony, Sir George Grey, undoubtedly saved India. He sent £60,000 out of his colonial treasury to Calcutta together with two regiments and a force of artillery. On his own authority he instructed Sir Colin Campbell, who happened to be passing through the Cape on his way to contend with trouble in China, to relieve instead Sir Henry Havelock at Lucknow.

[1] *Nonconformist*, 10.xi.58, p. 890.

On 24 August 1857, Richard Cobden wrote to John Bright: 'The entire scheme of our Indian rule is based upon the assumption that the natives will be the willing instruments of their own humiliation.'[1] He doubted that Britain could govern India well or continue to hold it permanently.[2]

Palmerston, however, was not so pessimistic, and promptly set his Ministry to the task of remodelling 'the obsolete machinery' for ruling India. The East India Company, which all political parties agreed was to blame, was abolished, and India was to be ruled in the name of the Queen. The Royal proclamation decreed, 'firmly relying upon the truth of Christianity', that the Sovereign did not seek to impose her convictions on any of her subjects; that everyone, regardless of religious beliefs, should have freedom of worship and impartial protection of the law; and that her subjects should be fairly admitted to offices 'in our service' according to ability and qualification.

At the same time the Liberation Society, 'with powerful and unlooked for allies', released the following resolutions on the future government of the vast Colony:

1. The Government and those in authority should respect the civil laws of the country, recognise the spiritual and temporal needs of the natives, and put the Christian religion in as favourable light as possible.
2. The Government, however, should not identify itself with any one Christian denomination, neither by contributions from nor grants of public lands, nor by any establishment of ecclesiastical law.
3. The Government should guarantee all natives of the Colony the fullest freedom to worship, teach, celebrate, and persuade others, whatever faith they may possess.
4. The Government should not unjustly support the interests of European residents by permitting the natives to be deprived in court of their property on religious grounds.[3]

Shortly afterwards, at a meeting of the Society for the Propagation of the Gospel in Foreign Parts, chaired by the Archbishop of Canterbury (Dr Sumner), resolutions of a very different kind were adopted:

1. To double (at least) the number of the Society's European missionaries in India, and to promote by every available means the education, training and ordination of the more advanced native converts for the work of the Christian ministry among their own countrymen.
2. To found new and strengthen existing missions in the Presidential and other principal cities of India, wherever there may appear to be the best opening, with a view to bring the truths of Christianity before the minds of the upper as well as of the lower classes in those great centres of population.
3. To press again upon the attention of the Indian Government the urgent necessity of a subdivision of the enormous dioceses of Calcutta and Madras, and especially to insist upon the desirableness of establishing a bishopric for

[1] John Morley, *The Life of Richard Cobden* (London 1881), ii, 209.
[2] ibid., ii, 207.
[3] Special Minute: 18.xi.57.

the Punjaub, another for the North-Western Provinces, and a third for the province of Tinnevelly.[1]

Only time could tell which of the two approaches would work for the greater benefit of India. Many Christian leaders believed that India had been brought under the British Crown by the Providence of God 'to conquer and convert the darkness' which had prevailed in that country for centuries. Some political thinkers, however, doubted the distinction between this kind of conquest and that which world history often had condemned.

An interesting encounter on Degree Day at Cambridge in 1859 was indicative of what lay ahead in the relations between Church and State throughout the Empire. Sir George Grey, who had just been recalled from the Governorship of Cape Colony, was the recipient, together with Gladstone, of an honorary degree at the University. Gladstone, as Chancellor of the Exchequer, dwelt 'upon the inadvisability of expending so much strength and money in foreign missions, and urged that their efforts should be concentrated on the great centres of population in Great Britain, where millions of English people were growing up in practical heathenism'. Sir George expressed strong disagreement with such an outlook, and won the applause of the audience. 'To centralise and restrict missionary efforts would be to stunt the Christian growth of the Church. In commerce, in science, in philanthropy, expansion ensured health and strength'.[2]

---

[1] *Nonconformist*, 2.xii.57, p. 942.
[2] W. L. & L. Rees, *Life and Times of Sir George Grey*, ii, 309–11.

CHAPTER 9

Endowed Schools, Burials, Oaths

> I am not afraid of the effects of reform, and I have no doubt the abuses are sufficiently great to justify those who seek for change. But I much doubt the probability of any great improvement. Influence, intimidation, and corruption are inseparable from any representative system, and, with all our professions, the English are as venal as any people in Europe.
>
> THE EARL OF ABERDEEN[1]

> We are no levellers. We do not confound all classes of society, but we say that, in whatever class of society a man is, his religious opinions should not exclude him from its benefits.
>
> JOHN REMINGTON MILLS[2]

A. *Endowed Schools and Charities*

THE QUESTION of national education was not normally within the range of the Liberation Society, except as a testimony to the power of Voluntaryism – the ability to provide public education through voluntary and private means rather than through State support. The Society was not as yet an agitator in the controversy concerning reform in elementary and secondary education. Only where it was related to the appointment of Dissenters to boards of trustees in Endowed Schools did the Society feel that its cause was at stake.

This did not imply, however, a general absence of Nonconformist interest. A Royal Commission on Education was appointed in June 1858 by Lord Salisbury, the President of the Council in Lord Derby's Ministry. Of the seven Commissioners, two were Nonconformists, Mr Edward Miall and Mr Goldwin Smith. The Commission was asked to inquire into the state of popular education in England, and to report on measures necessary for extending good and inexpensive elementary instruction to children of all classes. The full report was released in March 1861, and recommended a national system of education with county and borough boards. It also advised

---

[1] Stanmore, *The Earl of Aberdeen*, pp. 210–11: letter to Gladstone.
[2] *Liberator*, March 1857, p. 34. Mills was proposing the principal toast, as chairman of the 'Religious Liberty Dinner' at the London Tavern, on 18 February 1857.

that Government Inspectors make no examinations in religious knowledge. As a member of the Voluntary School Association, Miall maintained in a minority report that State education would mean education by the State Church.

A few years before this, the feeling of Nonconformists and Dissenters on endowed elementary education came to a head in the complicated Ilminster Grammar School Case. What the Braintree Case was to Church Rates in attracting public attention, the Ilminster Case was to the issues related to Endowed Schools. By this dispute in the courts, said the *Nonconformist*, 'they have made a capital opening for our guns, and put our forces on their mettle'. Church Defenders now visualized trustee meetings, like vestry meetings on Church Rates, becoming arenas for testing the strength of Nonconformist principles.

For 150 years the Ilminster Trust (which was an endowment not only for the School but apparently also for roads and other matters connected with education) had been administered by inhabitants of the town irrespective of their Churchmanship or Dissent. Eventually the full board of twenty trustees was reduced to five – three Dissenters and two Churchmen. Upon the reappointment of trustees by the Master of the Rolls, Sir John Romilly, to fill up the vacancies, the total became fourteen Churchmen and six Dissenters. In 1857 the newly appointed Vicar of the parish raised objection to the administration of the trust and sought the removal of the Dissenters.

To the Churchmen concerned the decision rested upon a question of fact, whether or not the repair of roads and bridges was, as deemed by the Dissenters, a principal and substantial part of the charity. To the Dissenters the decision depended upon the interpretation of the wording in the deed which simply specified that students should receive instruction 'in godly learning and knowledge' under a master (or trustee) who was 'an honest and discreet person'.[1] Under such a proviso, they held, the trust could not be exclusively Episcopalian. But in the Court of Chancery on 25 June 1858, Sir George Turner and Sir James Knight Bruce ruled in favour of the Vicar and declared that the trust did not necessarily entitle Dissenters to hold the office of trustee.[2]

The law of the land had already declared that (1) where religion was to be taught in an endowed school, it was presumed to be the religion of the Church of England, and (2) where charters were silent on the point, religion must be taught according to the creed of the Establishment – to which the schoolmaster must belong. Added to these was the judgement of the Justices in the Ilminster Case disqualifying Dissenters even in 'open trust deeds' – where the conditions for holding office were expressed in general terms. The Liberation Society loudly complained that the position of Dissenting trustees everywhere was thereby called into question, not excepting those boards where 'their fathers had sat for centuries undisturbed'.

The Dissenters said that the 690 Endowed Grammar Schools, many of

[1] James Heywood, *Academic Reform and University Representation*, p. 242.
[2] Skeats & Miall, op. cit., p. 540n.

which dated back to the reign of Edward VI, had been founded at the time of the Protestant Reformation out of the spoils of the suppressed Catholic monasteries and chantries. Those founded before that time were not exclusively for the use of the Church of England. Dissenters believed that the founders of the charities during this period had the general object of embracing everybody, so far as was possible, and not excluding from benefits all who did not belong to the Church of England. These endowments had been established at a time when the entire population was supposed to be attached to the Church of England, and since that was now not the case, some alteration in the law was imperative. The steady growth of Protestant Nonconformity, and the great increase of the number of students seeking admission to these schools, had forced the authorities to be unduly particular as to whom they admitted.

The Churchmen said that any attempts 'to neutralize an injustice' amounted to snatching these endowments from the Established Church and forfeiting them to whatever denomination the majority of trustees might determine. This kind of dealing on the part of the Dissenters could hardly be consistent with their declaration that they did not mean to touch the rightful property of the Church. The Anglicans believed that their title to the property of the Church of England was confirmed by the Acts of Parliament which created the legal severance from the Church of Rome.[1] Next to an Act of Parliament there could be no better title to property than a tenure of 300 years. This tenure had been repeatedly traced back to the will of the founders, and well arbitrated upon the principles of reason and common sense by a long line of competent judges. The schools of Henry VIII and Edward VI and Elizabeth I, originating after the break with the Roman Church, were thus clearly intended to be schools of the Anglican Church and of none other.

Altogether, four measures were devised in 1858 to cope with these problems concerning Endowed Schools: Bills of Lord Stanley of Alderley (supported by the School Trusts Committee), L. L. Dillwyn (supported by the Liberation Society), Sir Hugh Cairns, and Lord Cranworth. The first stipulated that no one should be ineligible as a trustee of any school or charity on account of his religious opinions, unless there be provision for such exclusion in the charter or deed. The second, the scheme of the Society, provided:

> In all cases in which the founders of any educational charity have not expressly provided that the teaching of some particular religious doctrine shall form part of the instruction to be provided by such charity, persons of all religious denominations, who shall otherwise be fit objects, shall be entitled to participate alike in the benefits thereof.

The third recommended that where twenty-five years' usage could be shown in the appointment of Dissenters, they should be named as proper trustees, notwithstanding any doubt as to the construction of the 'original instrument'.

[1] Sir Lewis Dibdin, *Establishment in England: being Essays on Church and State* (London 1932), p. 36.

Lord Stanley's Bill was first to go down to defeat, on 19 July, largely on the strength of the argument of the Lord Chancellor Chelmsford. He pointed out that there were many instruments of foundation in which Dissenters were excluded by express terms, and yet all schools with such foundations were embraced in this Bill. The effect of this measure, he said, would be undue interference with Church schools and foundations, and mischievous consequences. Both Lord Cranworth and the Duke of Somerset thought that the whole law on the subject was 'at sea' and ought to be reconsidered. The Lords therefore waited a year while the Commons grappled with the questions.

In 1859 Dillwyn (M.P., Swansea), member of the Society's Executive Committee, failed with his more comprehensive measure, despite support by the Attorney-General, Sir Richard Bethell, and the Vice-President of the Committee of the Privy Council for Education, Robert Lowe. The form of the Bill was so drastically altered by a Select Committee of the Commons that it was withdrawn. The third Bill, that of Sir Hugh Cairns (M.P., Belfast), aroused no interest and was therefore quietly dropped. Soon after, on the Society's platform at the national Triennial Conference on 7–8 June 1859, the Chairman of the Parliamentary Committee, Dr C. J. Foster, retorted that 'it ought not to be the law . . . that a Dissenter is a person who cannot be deemed in law to be an honest and discreet man, competent to teach godly learning'.[1]

By 1860, hope on the issue rested primarily with the proposal before the Lords in the hands of Lord Cranworth. Unless some satisfactory legislation were passed, he asked, what would prevent anybody from instituting a suit to oust Lord Aberdeen, Lord Panmure, and himself as governors of the Charterhouse School? Lord Chancellor Campbell reckoned that donors of the endowments in question would have made provision for the admission of children of Dissenters, had they foreseen the state of affairs facing the Legislature. When Cranworth promised that the substance of his Bill would not embrace national schools or effect the status of trustees, it was resolved in the affirmative. Dillwyn stated in the pages of the *Nonconformist* that at this stage the Bill was worth neither opposing nor accepting.

In Committee, one week later, the Archbishop of Canterbury (Dr Sumner) said that more power should be vested in the trustees of the Endowed Schools to make the rules for admission of Dissenting children, in accordance, of course, with the religious instruction afforded under the endowment. Lords Stanley of Alderley, Brougham, and Cranworth dissented from this view. The first argued that it would make all present Dissenting trustees liable to suspicion; the second, that it would excite great discontent among a numerous, powerful and wealthy body of citizens; the third, that it would render exceedingly difficult the question of who was a Dissenter. Was a person a Dissenter who had never taken the sacrament of Communion according to the Church of England rites? Or was he one who went occasionally to a Dissenting place

---

[1] *Liberator*, Aug. 1859, pp. 127–32: in the course of a research paper in which Foster summarized the series of decisions by which the Chancery judges had 'built up the legal doctrine excluding Dissenters from the management of public education charities'.

of worship? He hoped not, and because no final answers could be given, it was inadvisable to legislate on these matters. The Archbishop's amendment was accordingly thrown out.

Lord Cranworth's Bill was eventually put in a form suitable to the Upper House and on 31 March 1860 it was placed on the Statutes as the 'Act to Amend the Law Relating to the Administration of Endowed Charities'. The precise change effected by this measure was that parents could object to their children learning any particular doctrines or formularies, but only in cases of 'open trusts' or where such teaching was not expressly laid down by the founders. Clause 7, which declared Dissenting trustees 'not to be ineligible', was struck out with great reluctance by Cranworth. When Lord Chelmsford remarked that it would be unwise for Dissenters to become trustees 'under any circumstances', Lord Brougham sharply reprimanded him:

> . . . his noble and learned Friend indulged in the habit not uncommon with alarmists at reform and every kind of progress of using his telescope at both ends; and, having seen at one look a remote object magnified and brought near, he next applied the other end to the near objects, and thus made them appear remote and insignificant. . . . It was well for him that he had not taken the same liberties with his glass while he was the ornament of another profession.[1]

The fervid and forensic Welsh Liberal, Dillwyn, made a further effort to salvage the full rights of Dissenting trustees. This Bill, introduced early in 1861, was based on the principle already accepted in Cranworth's Act – that the Commissioners should not, unless so required by the founders, exclude persons from being trustees of charities merely on the ground of their belief. That Act, however, had referred only to Commissioners and therefore was not binding on Chancery judges. It was also open to the construction that religious belief might be one objection among others. Dillwyn assured the House that this Bill met these defects, and the second reading passed by 164 to 157 votes.

Supporters had attempted to show the simple aim of the Bill to be allowance for Dissenters to act as trustees of charitable schools, but under the supervision of the Courts of Equity. The opposition had cautioned that the effects of the Bill went far beyond schools, and warned that Mr Dillwyn, on the basis of his past record in legislation, would build further demands upon these concessions. Mr Lowe ridiculed Dillwyn for saying that he had no reason to feel ashamed of his connexion with the Liberation Society. Lord Robert Cecil (M.P., Stamford, and later Lord Salisbury) then struck out at the Liberation Society itself:

> The Liberation Society takes advantage of every loophole. . . . Let the House pass the present Bill . . . and it will throw a firebrand into every parish where there is an endowed school to be contested. . . . The Liberation Society will issue its mandates, its professional agitators will be set in motion, no money will be spared, and every conceivable legal quirk and quibble will be employed in order

---

[1] Hansard (3rd series), clvi, 1225.

to give the keenest possible edge to the weapon which Parliament is now asked to provide; and the result—the inevitable result—will be the destruction of pure religious teaching in every endowed school throughout the country.[1]

After this attack, an amendment not to go into Committee passed, and the Bill was therefore rejected. Mr Miall lost no time in making a rollicking reply in the columns of the *Nonconformist*:

Let the Cecils have their turn while they may; the day of the Cecils, happily, is not everlasting. We can bear their taunts as they look over the wall of their fortress; for we know though the siege be protracted, it will have an end, and that, too, very humbling to Cecil pride. . . . The moon will come to its full, though every dog in the universe should howl its dissatisfaction.[2]

B. *Nonconformist Burials*

Before the burial legislation during this period, the only public burial places in England were the graveyards of the Established Church. There were comparatively few graveyards belonging to Dissenting chapels and cemeteries formed by private companies. The parish churchyard was the common burial place and one in which the Common Law of the realm granted to every parishioner the right to burial.

But as property of the parish church, the churchyard was under the control of the incumbent, who received the fees for interment and who was the only person authorized to read the recognized Burial Service. He or any other clergyman substituting for him could refuse to conduct the Service in the case of infants or adults unbaptized according to the rites of the Church of England. In this contingency he was simply acting in harmony with the doctrines of his Church and the law imposed upon him by Parliament.

The Liberation Society and other Dissenting bodies were determined to abolish the distress and disgrace imposed upon their people by these discriminating practices. In the burial of their loved ones, Dissenters felt they were treated as 'freakish Christians who were to be put in watertight compartments' marking them off from the normal life of the nation. The defence of Dissenters before the law in these disputes was left largely in the hands of the Dissenting Deputies, mainly because the Society had assumed leadership in the agitation against Church Rates. Both Committees, however, united against the inclination of many in Church and State to perpetuate the petty distinctions of the living among the dead.

In 1850 the Metropolitan Interments Bill engaged the attention of the Liberation Society's Second Triennial Conference. This measure proposed to create a public Board of Health with authority to close and open cemeteries, to divide and supervise them, and to allot fees and rates. The Executive Committee lost no time in convening a public meeting, issuing circulars to Liberal M.P.s, and generally exposing the objectionable character of the ecclesiastical provisions. Mr C. Lushington (M.P., Westminster) agreed with

[1] Hansard (3rd series), clxii, 680.
[2] *Nonconformist*, 24.iv.61, p. 321.

the Society to press for amendments against the payment of fees to the clergyman in cases where his services had not been rendered. Despite these efforts, the Bill passed the Commons without serious division.

A petition to Parliament was placed in the hands of Lord Monteagle, lamenting that the measure (1) kept up the invidious distinctions in the burial of the honoured dead, (2) gave to the Bishop of London and Anglican chaplains exclusive privileges, (3) secured compensation in perpetuity to incumbents of parishes who would be no longer required to perform the Burial Service, (4) appropriated any surplus in the compensation fund as additional income to incumbents of new Metropolitan parishes. Notwithstanding the cry of the Society against this 'unblushing cupidity of the State-Church system', the Lords let the Bill become law, because of the public outcry against cholera epidemics.

Owing to the impracticable features of the new Act, the Government of Lord Derby passed another Metropolitan Bill in 1852 – its operations extended to the rest of the country in 1853 – which became the foundation of all controversial legislation on funerals during the remainder of the nineteenth century. Its greatest drawback was the division of the new cemeteries into consecrated and unconsecrated ground. Nonconformist Ministers were forbidden to enter and officiate in the former part. By this exclusion Nonconformist bodies were aroused to attempt countermeasures. These would insist that, where there was no public cemetery containing unconsecrated ground, non-Anglican Ministers should function in the parochial churchyards at the interment of their dead.

In 1855, after repeated attempts by Apsley Pellatt (M.P., Southwark) to obtain the appointment of a Select Committee to inquire into the working of the Burial Acts, Sir William Molesworth (M.P., also Southwark) for the Government introduced and carried the 'Burials Beyond Metropolis Act'. The object of this enactment was to meet the case of parishes where, Dissenters being few in number, there was no desire to have the Burial ground divided into two parts; it was also to prevent Dissenters from being victimized with heavier charges.

Surprisingly, on 17 August 1857, a Burial Acts Amendment Bill, brought in by the Under-Secretary for the Home Department, Mr W. Massey, passed through the Lords substantially unimpaired and received the Royal Assent. Its provisions settled the more important points which during this period had been the cause of Burial Board feuds. (1) Burial Boards might, instead of having cemeteries divided into two parts, provide distinct unconsecrated burial grounds. (2) If a burial ground provided under the Church Building Acts was transferred to a Board, such a Board might, if the vestry thought fit, add to it unconsecrated ground. (3) No wall or fence was to be required between the consecrated and unconsecrated ground, a boundary mark of stone or iron being sufficient. (4) If a Bishop refused to consecrate, the Archbishop could be appealed to, and he could license the ground; prior to the decisions of either, interments according to the Book of Common Prayer should take place. (5) The Board fees would be alike in both sections of the ground – the sums received by the undertaker in the consecrated ground for incumbents, clerks, and sextons, being extra charges.

In debate, the Bishops of London (Dr Tait) and Oxford (Dr Wilberforce) had insisted that fees should be the same for burial in consecrated and unconsecrated ground, in order to avoid any 'huckstering and cheapening' of the occasion by inducing relatives of the dead to bury them as Dissenters. The form of the clause finally settled upon prevented any such practice and was similar to the clause suggested by Mr Dillwyn on behalf of the Liberation Society.

Sir Samuel Morton Peto (M.P., Finsbury), a former member of the Society's Executive, came forward with a Bill in 1861 to allow unbaptized parishioners burial with the rites of the denomination chosen by the relatives. Only riotous, irreligious, and indecent behaviour at the graveside should be punishable. The second reading, however, was easily defeated. The Liberation Society now concluded that Peto's policies were too bold, and planned therefore to launch a moderate measure of their own through Dillwyn. This shift was undoubtedly due to his seeming disavowal on the floor of the House of any official connexion with the Society.[1]

C. Qualification for Offices

Lord John Russell succeeded in 1858 with his Act for an alteration in the Oaths of Allegiance, Supremacy, and Abjuration, in order to admit Jews to Parliament. This marked the third phase, so Gladstone said, of an irresistible movement. The Tory party had fought first for an Anglican Parliament; second, they fought for a Protestant Parliament; now they had lost the fight for a Christian Parliament. Many wondered how much further this struggle would go.

Toward the end of this period the Radical-Liberation party, with George Hadfield (M.P., Sheffield) as spokesman, pressed with a Bill against unnecessary religious qualifications for public offices. He denied that the proposals had emanated from the Liberation Society; they were twice carried through the Commons, but twice rejected by the Lords. The Bill had proposed that no person – (1) chosen as Mayor, Alderman, or Common Councilman, (2) appointed a Magistrate or admitted to any civic office of employment, or (3) accepting any grant or commission from the Crown – should be obliged to subscribe to the declaration required by the Acts repealing the Test and Corporation Acts. This declaration stated that the party taking the above oaths

> . . . will not exercise the power, authority or influence of his office to injure or weaken the Established Church or its Bishops and Clergy in the possession of the rights and privileges to which they are by law entitled.[2]

In the principal supporting speech, the Home Secretary, Sir George Lewis

---

[1] *Liberator*, Aug. 1861, p. 133, on which is given his explanation of the misconstruction of these words.

[2] 9 Geo. IV, cap. 17; 1 & 2 Vict., caps 5, 15, 52.

(M.P., Radnor) declared that the protection which the declaration afforded the Church was absolutely useless, there being no punishment assigned to its violation. Hadfield and his associates wanted to revoke also the clauses which forbade any member of the Corporation from attending Dissenting chapels with their insignia of office. This qualification was particularly galling to those Dissenters suffering from a sense of social inferiority.

Thus the holders of municipal posts, who possessed comparatively little power to do injury to the Establishment, were not able to fill the positions to which they had been elected without first swearing 'solemnly and in the presence of God'· that they had no ulterior designs upon the Church of England. A number of Ministers of the Crown, however, who could exercise comparatively greater influence on the destinies of the Church, had avoided the declaration and immuned themselves from the consequences by means of an annual Indemnity Act.[1] Clearly this anomalous absurdity could not continue indefinitely.

Church Defenders insisted upon this declaration, because it acknowledged the predominance of the Anglican Church, and it acted as 'a bridle on the hostility of Dissenters' in their quest 'to destroy' the nationality of the Church. Opposition to Hadfield's Bill was therefore bitter in the Upper House, notwithstanding the support of the Lord Chancellor (Campbell). Just because the Dissenters wanted the measure, said Lord Chelmsford, they should not have it. He was not prepared to sacrifice the declaration to their 'sickly consciences' and 'unreasonable scruples'. To prove the great danger he proceeded to 'unmask' the activities of the Liberation Society, the writings of the *Nonconformist's Sketch Book*, and the utterances of Samuel Morley, Thomas Binney, and John Bright.

In answer to these quotations and the 'bugbear' of the Liberation Society, Earl de Grey and Ripon responded with a reactionary quotation from one of the meetings of the Church Defence Association:

> The English Clergy are very much in the position of the Duke of Wellington's Guards at Waterloo. They have been lying down while the shot of the enemy was flying over them. The critical moment has arrived. It must be now or never and the watchword is 'Up Guards, and at 'em!'[2]

[1] This annual Act, originating in the time of George II (1 Geo. II, stat. 1, cap. 5), gave relief to any who 'through ignorance of the law, absence, or unavoidable accident' had failed to carry out the provisions of the Corporation and Test Acts. E. A. Payne, *Free Church Tradition*, p. 76.

[2] Hansard (3rd series), clxii, 10: spoken originally by Mr Henry Hoare, the Treasurer of the Church Defence Association (an Association of Clergy and Laity for Defensive and General Purposes) at Fenny Stratford, Bucks. As a prominent London banker and Churchwarden of St Dunstan-in-the-West Church, Mr Hoare helped considerably to bring about the revival of Convocation in 1854. His books included: *The Defence of a Refusal to Profane the Order for Burial of the Dead* (1850), and *A Catechism of the Church* (1867). One of his aims in organizing the Defence Institution in 1859 was to combat the work of the Liberation Society. The names of the members of the first Executive Committee, and the Rules and Objects of that Association are to be found in James Bradby Sweet's *A Memoir of the late Henry Hoare* (London 1869), pp. 446–51.

He believed that the Church of England rested upon a very different foundation from 'the declaration' in question. Really, the Church depended more upon the affection and respect of her people, on the beauty of her services, on the truth of her doctrines, and on the piety of her Ministers.

PART THREE

Achievement and Award
1862 – 1869

CHAPTER 10

Introductory

Above all, the suggested line of action must, if adopted, be adopted with our whole soul. Retreat will be out of the question. Everything must lead to the object to be achieved. It must be the fly-wheel of our whole machinery. *Aut Caesar, aut nullus*, should be our maxim; or, to adopt words of more solemn import, we should resolve, with the apostle, 'This one thing will we do'.

> EDWARD MIALL: from paper on the electoral policy of the Society, Free Trade Hall, Manchester, 18 November 1863.[1]

IN THE YEARS 1862 to 1869 the country saw the Liberation Society continuing to grow and approaching the peak of its progress. The efforts of the leaders were to gain the Society several Parliamentary victories, but none so notable as the abolition of compulsory Church Rates in 1868 and the Disestablishment of the Irish Church in 1869.

Compared with the Church Rate Bill finally agreed upon, Mr Gladstone's Irish Church Bill was achieved with surprising rapidity. In the Minutes of the Society in this period one detects a note of eagerness to have the Rates issue settled quickly in order to concentrate on the more basic Irish issue. With the minds of both Nonconformists and Churchmen diverted to the larger question, Gladstone succeeded with a legislative problem which had baffled politicians for more than forty years. Whether he planned both Bills as concessions to pacify Dissenters, to save the English Establishment, or to unite Liberals, was open to much speculation.

Undoubtedly, the success of these Bills would have been further delayed had it not been for Gladstone's astuteness and his understanding of these Nonconformist grievances. He had progressed beyond his earlier Conservative creed laid down in *The State in its Relations with the Church* (1838), and *Church Principles* (1840),[2] to make room for the Liberal *laissez faire* doctrine

---

[1] *Liberator*, Dec. 1863, p. 189.

[2] In these works he set forth the following 'norms': '(a) the State is intended by God to be a "moral person"; (b) the State is capable of acknowledging, and is therefore morally bound

of the State. As expounded by J. S. Mill, Locke, and Bentham, the State had no direct concern with the ultimate truth of ethical or theological doctrines; its only concern was with their civic usefulness or harmfulness. The traditional theory of the union between Church and State could no longer be nationally held, as Gladstone expressed in 1868 in *A Chapter of Autobiography*:

> There are two causes, the combined operation of which, upon reaching a certain point of development, relaxes or dissolves [the] union [of State and Church] by a process as normal . . . as that by which the union was originally brought about. One of these is the establishment of the principle of popular self-government as the basis of political constitutions. The other is the disintegration of Christendom from one into many communions.[1]

On this basis he courageously committed himself to specific politico-ecclesiastical tenets of the general Liberal party policy. He revealed more than a passing sympathy with the Nonconformist ideal of a 'free Church within a free State'.

In return for this more kindly attitude on the part of the head of the Government of the State, the Liberationists were willing to act more moderately in Parliament. The first of the letters from Gladstone to the Liberation Society, commending its fine conduct in the settlement on Church Rates, represented more than mere political expediency on his part.

Penmaenmawr
Aug. 14th, 1868

My dear Sir,

I thank you for sending me a copy of the Minute of your Committee, which I have read with much pleasure. We may not be quite certain that we have heard the last of Church Rates in Parliament, but the teeth and claws of the controversy are drawn.

Your tribute to Mr Hardcastle was well deserved. I should myself have offered him a public acknowledgement, had I not been driven to dispose of the Bill at half past two in the morning.

I must add that nothing could be more loyal and considerate than the conduct of the Abolitionists in and out of Parliament throughout the proceedings on this

---

to acknowledge, truth, when adequately presented to it; and (c) a marriage between Church and State is the best possible ideal, which therefore Christians should always have in view.' Alec R. Vidler, *The Orb and the Cross* (London 1945), p. 136. Mr Vidler suggests that inwardly Gladstone never believed differently on these matters, but outwardly he changed because of the consequences of the Tractarian Movement, and the expediency of his political career. As the traditional union between Church and State became weaker, so there became apparent a separation between Gladstone's creed and career; cf. Chapter 7, 'Gladstone's Creed and Career'.

[1] (London 1868), pp. 59–60.

Bill from 1866 to the final close. And I have seen enough to know that no small share of this acknowledgement belongs to you.

I am, my dear Sir,
Faithfully yours,
W. E. Gladstone.[1]

J. C. Williams, Esq.

A great deal of the success in reaching these legislative aims was due to the adoption by the Society of a new 'Electoral Policy' in 1863. It forged a bond of union among Liberationists at a time when the Church of England was beginning to shake with serious doctrinal and liturgical divisions. The policy called upon the Nonconformist electorate and the supporters of the Society to withhold their votes from candidates who would not pledge themselves in favour of the doctrines of absolute religious equality. By this means the Society figured prominently in the triumph of the political ambitions of the Liberal party in the General Election of 1865. Such an alliance with the party gave the Society greater confidence for the work which lay ahead. The special Parliamentary Paper reflecting upon the session of 1867 expressed great optimism in the fact that

> . . . in the House of Commons at least, the friends of Religious Equality have been successful in almost every occasion of importance . . . they have had in nearly every instance, the united support of the Liberal party and the expectation that the extension of the franchise will increase their political influence.[2]

The ascendance of a Liberal majority coincided with other liberal movements in other areas of society. The victory of the North in the American Civil War and the death of Palmerston paved the way for the second Reform Bill of 1867. Fashioned by Bright, Disraeli, and Gladstone, it extended voting power to the whole of the middle and working classes of the towns, and gave labour a voice in the Commons as influential as that of trade or land. By the Act, leaders of religious equality, educational opportunity, and free enterprise now had an effective means of achieving their democratic goals.

Into this historical scene the principles of the Liberation Society fitted better than at any previous period. Its spokesmen found many champions in other fields speaking a similar language, and therefore attempted to render a common interpretation for them all. Anti-State-Churchism as a philosophy of politics and economics was foremost in the minds of many leading thinkers in the countries of Europe. The movement in England, which was liberationist though not revolutionary, was carefully calculated to enlist equalitarians with Nonconformists in a campaign against 'clerical monopoly'.

A. *Miall's Leadership*

The activities of the Society during this period were still closely associated with the 'Christian politics' and personal ambitions of Edward Miall. The

---

[1] Minute 165: 11.ix.68 (an unpublished letter).
[2] Minute 536a: 30.viii.67.

Rev. Christopher Nevile, who resigned from his Anglican benefices to join the Liberation cause, spoke of the Society's leader as 'a man honestly endeavouring to bring the policy of his country into greater harmony with the Gospel'. In 1862 Miall published for the Society his critical work on *Title Deeds of the Church of England to Her Parochial Endowments*.[1] In 1869, the Society's political strategy became a more serious threat in his return to the House of Commons as a member for Bradford.

In this provocative book, Miall compiled statements of authorities and historical source material, to call into question the claims of the Church of England to her endowments. He did so by tracing the successive laws, extending over a period of three centuries, by which these endowments were created – laws which were sharply enforced, and not very willingly obeyed. It was a scholarly attempt to which the supporters of the Society referred for many years in substantiating the justice of their claims. By it Miall gave the arguments in favour of Disestablishment a strong legal basis, largely because this was the ground upon which they were to be finally decided. He believed, however, that beyond the question of the rightful ownership of Church property in England was the question of how it might be best applied to the service of man.

Miall first defined the Church of England as the whole body of the people of England as 'religiously organised', just as the State or Commonwealth of England meant the whole body of the people of England as 'politically organised'. He denied that the endowments of the Church of England rested upon the same foundation as those in the possession of Dissenting denominations: the property of the first was national, that of the second was not. He proposed to treat State-Church endowments with the same rightful freedom as other national property, and denied that this amounted to 'spoliation and confiscation'.

His general thesis concerning parochial tithes – which, he claimed, constituted the great bulk of the Church endowments – was that they were the property of the country for public religious uses. Tithes were the result exclusively of public law, he said, and did not originate in private liberality. To describe them as 'endowments' was simply a figure of speech. More accurately they were an 'ancient tax' prescribed by public authority, operated by public authority, and upheld by public authority.[2]

The highly controversial conclusions to which Mr Miall came were as follows:[3]

First, the British Constitution knows nothing of the Church of England as distinguishable from the whole people of England. It does recognize what

[1] John Pulman, a barrister of the Middle Temple, claimed to expose this work in his book, *The Anti-State Church Association and the Anti-Church Rate League, Unmasked* (London 1864).

[2] *Title Deeds of the Church of England to Her Parochial Endowments* (London 1862), pp. 1–6.

[3] ibid., pp. 96–102. These are similar to those of Sir James Mackintosh in his *Vindiciae Gallicae: Defence of the French Revolution and its English Admirers . . .* (Dublin 1791).

Parliament has created: a body of laws regulating the ecclesiastical affairs of the nation, and ecclesiastical officers to whom it assigns the carrying out of these laws.

Second, the Church of England is no more a corporate body than the Army of England. It has no corporate rights or claims, and therefore can own no property, nor be despoiled of any.

Third, although a particular religious polity, discipline and liturgy have been ordained by law, the Church was framed by Parliament for the whole people, absenters and dissenters included, not for the part of them called Protestant Episcopalians.

Fourth, the Protestant Episcopalians cannot make any special or independent claim to the use of Church property. They did not come to the State with endowments of their own. It was King, Lords, and Commons which begat Protestant Episcopalianism in place of Roman Catholicism.

Fifth, because the State has never allowed the fee-simple of Church property to pass from under its control, Church property can only be national property ecclesiastically applied. The State has itself prescribed all the conditions of usufruct, and, even in the case of the landed estates of the Bishops, it has required homage to the Crown as feudal Sovereign of their possessions.

Sixth, parochial endowments are nothing more or less than the peculiar possession made by the State to give effect to its ecclesiastical policy for the time. This policy the State has changed as frequently as it has seen fit, and this it is entitled to do as public opinion shall authorize and require by law.

The majority of Tory Churchmen dismissed these views as simply impossible. The Ven. Archdeacon George Denison, writing in his *Church and State Review*, urged readers to be on their guard against the 'clever heads' in Miall's organization and its revolutionary doctrine of religious equality all round.[1] The country was warned to beware of the 'Serjeants' Inn clique' as a sinister foe bent on plunder. Religious folk were cautioned that Liberationists were creeping into Sunday Schools and Day Schools, the press and the pulpit, libraries and lecture halls, the parish vestries and Parliament itself in order to disseminate their anti-State-Church dogmas. Staunch Anglicans were marshalled to fight on all fronts.

> And if the masses favour such nostrums as those of the Liberation Society, it is because other and sounder views have not been laid before them. Here, indeed, a great omission, a grievous oversight, has to be redeemed. It is the bounden duty of Churchmen and Constitutionalists to meet the Liberation Society on this arena; . . .[2]

Miall was asked to give an inaugural address at the seventh Triennial

---

[1] *Church and State Review*, Aug. 1864, p. 38.

[2] Masheder, *Dissent and Democracy*, p. 349. The *modus operandi* of Dissent was described by this writer (p. 4) in the words of the old rhyme:
'The good old law, the simple plan,
'That they should take, who have the power,
'And they should keep who can.'

Conference in 1865, marking the twenty-first anniversary of the founding of the Society. He went before 742 delegates from thirty public bodies, described as the Parliament of Nonconformity, representing 'the intelligence and resolve of the religious middle classes'. Two eloquent and popular Nonconformist preachers, the Rev. J. Guinness Rogers (Congregationalist) and the Rev. Charles H. Spurgeon (Baptist) came forward on this occasion as supporters of the Society and friends of Mr Miall.

Miall spoke at length of the founders and leading men present at the first Triennial Conference in 1844. The framework of their Constitution through-out the years, he observed, had remained substantially the same. To his mind, the movement would never tend toward narrow and sectarian issues, but always toward a broad and national principle. He believed that the power of the Society and its principles was demonstrated by (1) the Clergy bitterly denouncing the Liberation Society and organizing the Church Defence Institution,[1] (2) the Conservative party making the question of Church Establishment the principal concern of that party organization and policy, (3) ecclesiastical issues being carried to the hustings, in a manner hitherto unknown.

Miall was sensitive, however, to the accusation of friends and foes that the Liberation Society was fostering free religion, and that he was forsaking sacred for secular principles. He therefore made clear his position that a Disestablishment which allowed the widest diversity of belief and laxity of practice would be 'injurious to religion and demoralising to the nation'.[2]

B. *Finances and Young Men's Conferences*

In 1859, the financial statement at the Triennial Conference showed an increase in £500 in the subscription list; in 1862, a further addition of £1,000; and in 1865, an improvement to the extent of £700. The Seventh Triennial Conference in 1865 inaugurated a Special Fund of £25,000. The raising and expenditure of this money was to be spread over the ensuing five years. The Manchester Nonconformist Defence Association, formed in 1864, declined to amalgamate their Special Fund with that of the Society and thereby ended a hope of raising a combined total of £50,000.

In 1869 the Treasurer was able to report the largest annual income since the beginning of the Society – £8,913. This was doubtless due to the fact that there were more subscribers in 1869 than in any previous year of its history –

---

[1] In 1863 this Institution announced that in 394 out of 710 rural deaneries affiliated Associations had been formed. These often worked in conjunction with another organiza-tion called the Committee of Laymen (of which John M. Knott of Harrow-on-the-Hill was Secretary). On 6 February 1867 the Council of the Church Defence Institution insti-tuted a newspaper, the *Orb*, as the official organ. At the same time it appointed lay corres-pondents, under an organizing Secretary, for Parliamentary boroughs and in towns of a population of 5,000. Occasionally the Liberation Society sent 'under-cover' reporters to important Church Defence Association meetings. The reverse was also true; cf. *Noncon-formist*, 20.x.66, p. 996.

[2] *Liberator*, May 1867, pp. 70–1.

approximately 10,000. Also in that year there were numerous payments into the Special Fund of amounts promised within the above five-year period, totalling £19,387. Finances for the future were greatly improved by a reversionary legacy willed to the Society in 1869 by one of its wealthy supporters, Mr W. J. Etches of Derby, leaving £10,000.

The work of the Society assumed an even more energetic character when it projected a movement among the young Nonconformists of the country. The older the Society became, the more necessary it became to win the minds of those who could pursue the aims in later years.[1]

For this reason, the Executive Committee called a Conference of Young Men on 9 January 1867, at Radley's Hotel, London, to organize their support in the programme of the Society in the Metropolis. Nearly 1,000 invitation cards and explanatory circulars were addressed to younger Ministers, students of Nonconformist Colleges, Young Men's Christian Associations, and young laymen engaged in active Christian service in the Nonconformist Churches.

At these proceedings, the broad principle of 'the liberation of religion from State patronage and control' was often linked with 'the spirituality of religion'. The young men were urged to examine thoroughly the principles upon which all State Churches were based, and then to identify themselves with the Liberation Society. Further, it was suggested that small societies be formed in the Churches for reading of essays, circulation of the Society's publications, and discussion of State-Church questions. Finally, a Committee of Young Men was appointed to act in conjunction with the Executive Committee.

In the opening address, the Rev. Alexander Hannay of Croydon spoke against 'the idea of comprehension' in the Church of England which gave to all creeds within its pale the comfort and aid of national patronage. While the State still held its theory of uniformity, it had permitted in practice a Church of growing contradictions. Therefore it was wrong to say that, because the forces of dissolution were already at work, Dissenters should stand back and allow them to work. In the closing speech, Edward Miall called for self-sacrifice and warned that there would be no quick and attractive success:

> This is not going to be a popular agitation for a long time to come; on the contrary, depend upon it, all the respectable influences of the world will frown upon this movement. It has been so hitherto; it will be so, in spite of your joining it, for a long time to come. . . . You will come down rapidly in the estimation of many of your friends.[2]

Some of the speeches before impressionable youths at these rallies bordered on demagogy. Before a crowd in Manchester on 14 March 1867, the Rev. Alexander McLaren exclaimed, to the accompaniment of loud applause, that instead of allowing the free and natural growth of the love of God in the

---

[1] *Punch* (11.xii.69) joked about the Society's advertisement offering a prize of £50 for a book, historical and biographical, written for young people, which would illustrate the principles of the Liberation Society.

[2] *Nonconformist*, 16.i.65, pp. 45–6.

world, the Established Church 'poked its clumsy hand' in the ground, dragged the seed to the surface, and 'set policemen to watch over' it to prescribe the fragrance of the flower.[1]

For the students in this movement the debate throughout the country on University Tests was an effective point of reference. Oxford Radicals such as Charles Roundell (Fellow of Merton College), Albert Rutson, Frederic Harrison, and Goldwin Smith addressed young Liberation audiences on this subject with telling results.

By 1868 the Society was congratulating itself on the popularity of the Conferences. These had been conducted that year in twenty-four major cities where local youth committees or Young Men's Associations worked on instructions from the Central Committee in London.

C. *Parliamentary and Electoral Action*

The style of political action in which the Society engaged during this period is best seen in the special papers setting forth recommendations on Parliamentary issues. All these documents expressed a high degree of confidence, in spite of legislative setbacks in 1861.

The Parliamentary Paper of 1862, largely the work of Dr C. J. Foster, was prepared for the Sixth Triennial Conference that year. The strategy agreed upon was to regard such measures as Hadfield's Qualification for Offices Repeal Bill, Sir Morton Peto's Burial Bill, and Dillwyn's Endowed Schools Charities Bill as platforms for agitation on the Church Rate question. This latter question was to be withheld till the most propitious time for division. In the meantime, outdoor agitation by public meetings and distribution of publications were to be fully utilized in building up sympathetic public opinion. It was proposed 'to excite, collect, and concentrate' political movements in Ireland, Wales, and Scotland in support of the separation of Church and State. The Bicentenary of the ejectment of the Nonconforming Clergy on St Bartholomew's Day 1662 was to be marked as 'a blight' upon the conscience of the national Church.

On 26 June 1863, Dr Foster gave notice of his intention to resume his legal practice in New Zealand, and his resignation as Chairman of the Society's Parliamentary Committee. This serious loss called for a reconsideration of the reasons for which his office had been created, and a review of the range of the Committee's work. Accordingly, a new 'Electoral Policy' was announced, based upon the rule of mutual political assistance:

> ... we should act with the Liberal party in future Elections on the well understood but indispensable condition, that up to the measure of our strength in the local register the objects about which we are interested shall be advanced by the Election—that as a part of the Liberal force in each constituency, and in due proportion to that part, we should be recognized in the political programme of the candidate who wishes to receive our assistance—and, if this measure of justice be denied us, that we resolutely withhold our cooperation—our vote and

Nonconformist, 13.iii.67, p. 207.

influence—whatever may be the consequences of our abstention to the Liberal party.[1]

There were several motives behind the formulation of this rule: (1) to give primary loyalty to principles rather than party; (2) to place responsibility for division upon those who ignored the aims of the Society; (3) to lay the foundation for a new political party based upon the principles of religious equality.

This radical electoral policy was formally approved by a special conference of leading Liberationists convened for that purpose on 11 November 1863 at Radley's Hotel. In May 1864, the Council of the Society expressed confidence that the policy would not lead to a separation between Nonconformists and the Liberal party. The Annual Report of the Executive Committee for 1864 stated that district conferences had been held at Bristol, Norwich, Halifax, Manchester, Leicester and Plymouth, where the objects of the policy had been fully defined and sanctioned.

In the General Election of 1865 the questions in which the Churches were deeply concerned became the battlefield of political parties. The Church of England faced a dilemma, for the lower forms of political warfare were neither edifying nor attractive. Should she avail herself of the vast political power placed at her disposal to resist Dissenters? Or would the conflict of politics so mar her mission and injure her character, that she ought not to revile her enemies?

Nonconformists and Radicals led by the Liberation Society had their own answer. J. M. Hare, of Forest Hill, London, was appointed Electoral Agent in 1864 to 'make contacts' throughout the country. The Parliamentary and Electoral Committee canvassed for precise information concerning the mood of each constituency, the names of influential Liberal electors, and the probable outcome on the all-important day. Circulars and letters were sent to each borough and county, seeking similar information. Election promises made by M.P.s and views expressed by candidates on ecclesiastical questions were published in the *Nonconformist*. Advertisements were placed in public journals giving the qualifications of voters, informing them how to make claims for voting privileges, and urging friends of religious equality to register in time. The Committee prepared a complete electoral history of each constituency, and a tabulated chronicle listing the votes of M.P.s on all religious questions during the previous Session.[2] Herbert S. Skeats, the sub-Editor of the *Liberator*, published a volume with the results of every Election in every constituency of the country over the previous thirty years.

The Parliamentary and Electoral Committee gave first consideration to those constituencies held by Tory members where it seemed probable that a

---

[1] Minute 286: 23.x.63.

[2] These records of votes on the various Parliamentary divisions were greatly in demand. Some 1,500 extracts from this chronicle were sent out. In some cases these extracts were printed in local newspapers, and in others they were printed on bills and circulated among the electors.

Liberal could be elected, and second to those constituencies held by 'luke-warm' Liberals where a man more friendly to the Society might be elected. The 1863 Electoral policy of the Society was pressed to its limit, thus making it necessary for candidates of both parties to address themselves to the Dissenters.

The result of the Election was caught in the words of the *Liberator*: 'Many an old bark this year has been wrecked.'[1] Mr Gladstone, rather than Lord Palmerston, was the personality which commanded the spotlight. Gladstone's rejection at Oxford University and his election at Lancashire naturally brought him into closer identification with the religious freedom platform.

The returns of the Election showed 288 Conservatives, and 371 Liberals including 87 Dissenters. The new Parliament included 3 members of the Liberation Society Executive – Samuel Morley, Duncan McLaren, and Thomas Barnes – in addition to 15 subscribers, and 22 other Protestant Nonconformists. Of the various shades of Liberals all but 10 were in favour of the abolition of Church Rates, the most conspicuous exceptions being Sir Roundell Palmer and Lord Stanley.

Most of the Liberals losing their seats had been loyal upholders of Lord Palmerston's Whig old guard. Although his spirit was still present in Lord John Russell as the respectable 'Whig Liberal' Prime Minister, the latter was now the leader of a party of change. Lord John Russell had used the adage: 'Those, who oppose improvement because it is innovation, may one day have to submit to innovation which is not improvement.'[2]

Among the Conservatives, one-fourth were pledged to a moderate measure of reform, and were willing to entrust to the 'intelligent portion' of the labouring classes an adequate share in Parliamentary representation. There were also in their ranks forty-one gentlemen who called themselves 'Liberal-Conservatives'.

The new Liberal majority in Parliament, pledged to radical reforms, contained 4 Irish peers, 2 Viscounts, 4 Earls, 32 Lords, 1 Marquess, 67 Baronets, 8 Knights and 312 graduates of national Universities. No longer could the term 'Radical' be connected solely with Nottingham stocking-frames and Lancashire hand-looms.

In preparation for the following General Election in 1868, the Committee of the Society followed much the same procedure as in the previous one. There was, however, a newly enfranchised electorate which afforded them an added opportunity for further gains. Liberationists again canvassed ceaselessly among their electors in the constituencies. Party candidates, voters, and campaigners all found the Society to be an even greater asset than before in their electioneering.

The paramount issue to be decided was that of the Irish Church and Mr Gladstone's readiness to sacrifice it. The Society again freely supplied information concerning proper legal registration of electors, the past votes of

[1] *Liberator*, Aug. 1865, p. 138.
[2] Spencer Walpole, *Life of Lord John Russell*, ii, 428.

M.P.s on ecclesiastical measures, and special facts relating to the Irish Establishment. From December 1867 to November 1868, the total number of addresses or lectures given by the Society's twenty-seven paid lecturers on the Irish Church question amounted to 515. The principal lecturer of the Society, Mr Mason Jones, delivered stimulating addresses on this question in each of the Metropolitan boroughs.

In the publishing department the pamphlets, tracts, and leaflets on the Irish Church totalled 44 separate publications, of which 1,060,000 copies were distributed. Orders were made for 57,000 placards and bills, and 1,000 copies of Skeats's pamphlets on Irish Church statistics. Circulars were sent to 62 county and 104 borough constituencies asking for electoral information, and urging electors to secure pledges from candidates to support Gladstone's ecclesiastical policy. The Society declined the request of Irish supporters to send lecturers there, having agreed to confine all activities, except publications, to England.

The result of the voting amounted to a strong and certain expression throughout the country in favour of Disestablishment and Disendowment in Ireland. The principles of religious equality had not in any way lost their place in the public mind. The Society now had five members of its Executive Committee – Duncan McLaren (Edinburgh), Henry Richard (Merthyr Tydfil), Alfred Illingworth (Knaresborough), Samuel Morley (Bristol), and Edward Miall (Bradford)[1] – as well as twenty other active supporters in the new House of Commons. A total of 222 Conservatives were returned against 386 Liberals. Of the latter number only six were for no radical alteration in the Church of England in Ireland. Separate Liberal majorities of 29 in England, 13 in Wales, 45 in Scotland, and 27 in Ireland comprised the party's sweeping majority of 114.

Since it was in the three last-named sections of the nation that the exercise of Nonconformity had been most concentrated, such a result was interpreted by many observers as a sign of the declining power of the Church of England. With the cause in Ireland practically a foregone conclusion, the Society began to think earnestly in terms of Disestablishment in Scotland and Wales.

The appointment of J. Carvell Williams in September 1865, as chairman of the Parliamentary Committee, was a wise one. Although he lacked the legal experience of his predecessor, the office of Recording Secretary had equipped Williams to understand the strength and weakness of the Society better than any other person, except Miall himself. Before joining the executive in 1848 Williams had been secretary of the Religious Freedom Society. In his new role of leadership, he concentrated more upon winning friends than attacking enemies.

Early in 1866, under Williams's guidance, a sub-committee of the Society studied prospects of better representation of Wales in Parliament. In particular they sought to improve the electoral register in Cardiganshire to secure the

[1] Miall was returned in 1869, the victorious candidate of 1868 having been unseated on petition for 'bribery and corruption'.

return of their friend Henry Richard, and to promote a conference for the formation of a Liberal Association of South Wales. This conference took place at Swansea later in 1867, with strong backing from the Society. Williams stressed the importance of the fact that Nonconformists there represented 79 per cent of the worshipping population. Richard called upon his hearers to stand firm to their principles, to endure 'the frown of Squire this or Lady Bountiful that', and to elect more men to follow in Mr Dillwyn's loyal band of 'Welsh reserves'.[1]

Also in 1866, when it was discovered that the Dissenting Deputies had arranged to hold a Parliamentary Breakfast on the same date as that of the Society, Williams proposed that the two bodies have a joint breakfast meeting. This was done at the Grosvenor Hotel on 12 April, John Remington Mills presiding, with seventy-two in attendance. The gathering became a regular occasion for publicly announcing Nonconformist policy before the opening of each new Parliamentary Session.

A Parliamentary Paper for the 1865–6 season, calling for more money, more meetings, and more organization – mainly for the extension of the franchise and for legal assistance to those resisting Church Rates in the Courts – was deferred by Williams. Instead, he devised a plan of action expressed in more moderate terms. It called attention to the fact that the General Election was remarkably free from deprecatory references to the Society on the part of candidates. The Election had demonstrated that fidelity to principle was indeed expedient, and that promotion of progressive ecclesiastical views was certainly not unpatriotic. Concerning future strategy in Parliament, the new Parliamentary Committee chairman believed,

> . . . it might be premature, for a political organization like our own, to lay down beforehand a fixed and absolute programme of Parliamentary action. It is much better that its first advance should be of the nature of a *reconnaissance*. In reference to that our efforts for some time to come must necessarily be in the main of an educational character[2] . . . we have to teach abstract truths through the medium of practical measures.[3]

---

[1] L. L. Dillwyn (M.P., Swansea) was then leader of the 'religious equality' party in the Commons. C. S. Miall, *Henry Richard, M.P.: A Biography* (London 1889), pp. 119–24.

[2] See Minute 604: 10.xi.65. Mr James Bryce, Fellow of Oriel College, Oxford, was asked (p. 317) if he would write a history of State Churchism. The Rev. R. W. Dale agreed (p. 323) that a series of lectures ought to be given 'of the highest class' and 'bearing expressly on the philosophical and political aspect of the Society's principles'. In the *Patriot* magazine for the first quarter of 1863, Dale contributed a series of articles discussing some of the theories of advocates of the union of Church and State; these included the views of Hooker, Warburton, Paley, Chalmers and Gladstone.

[3] Minute 610: 17.xi.65.

CHAPTER 11

St Bartholomew's Day Commemoration

> . . . should the existing establishment at last come down, its ruin will be still a monument. History will say: 'There lies the institution which understood neither how to retain its friends, nor how to shut out its enemies. There lies the house in which the martyrs lived and which Bartholomew's Day left desolate. There lies the Church which expelled the Puritans, and kept them out so long that they would not come in again . . .
>
> THE REV. JAMES HAMILTON, D.D.[1]

> The religious settlement of the restoration was not conceived in the spirit of compromise which marked the political and social settlement. . . . The arrangement actually made, under which the Church of England and the various Puritan Churches followed each its own lines of development, rendered toleration inevitable ere long, and led to the variety and competition of religious bodies characteristic of modern England.
>
> GEORGE MACAULAY TREVELYAN[2]

THE MOVEMENT to commemorate the great Puritan exodus in 1662 originated in the minds of a few earnest leaders of the Congregational Union of England and Wales (the Rev. J. Guinness Rogers, the Rev. Samuel Martin, and Samuel Morley) who were also members of the Liberation Society. They were most anxious that the Bicentenary year should not pass without a decided act of remembrance. Nonconformists who reflected much upon their heritage were not slow to assent.

Accordingly, these Congregationalists formed the nucleus of a committee for planning the appropriate activities. It resolved to raise a Bicentenary Nonconformist Fund to be devoted to: (1) the erection of Congregational Chapels in England and Wales, (2) the building of a Memorial Hall in London and a Congregational Church in Paris, (3) and the founding of College endowments, scholarships, and Pastors' Retiring Funds. The occasion

---

[1] From the sermon preached by this London Presbyterian Minister on St Bartholomew's Day, 1862 (Skeats & Miall, op. cit., p. 574).

[2] Master of Trinity College, Cambridge. *History of England*, p. 450.

was also to be a time of prayerful thanksgiving for the privileges enjoyed by Victorian Nonconformists in contrast to those denied their Elizabethan predecessors.

Shortly afterwards the Baptist Union convened a similar committee which called for a wider and more united observance by the whole Nonconformist body of Britain.[1] Miall and many colleagues were not in favour of mere denominational extension being a basis of the commemoration. The larger Central United Committee was thus formed at a meeting at the Baptist Library on 9 December 1861, to work also in co-operation with the original Congregational committee. Offices were taken at No. 10 Broad Street Buildings and the officers elected were: Mr Edward Swaine as Chairman, Sir Samuel Morton Peto as Treasurer, and the Rev. Samuel Cox as Secretary.

The Committee issued an address bearing on what had been called 'the second Protestant Reformation in England', and 'the revolt against the sacerdotalism of Laud and Rome'. A body of 2,000 Clergy of the Church of England had been unable with good conscience to make the declaration imposed by the Act of Uniformity, of 'unfeigned assent and consent' *ex animo* to all and everything contained in the Book of Common Prayer then revised by Convocation. These men, by the provisions of the Act, were thus deprived of their livings and turned adrift with their families into the world. The radical division in English religious life was thereby established between Church and Dissent.

One of the results of the commemoration was generally a revived interest in the history of the period of the Protectorate. Royalist-minded Anglicans pointed with amusement to the stern Hebrew-like laws and austere religious zeal which bred notorious hypocrites. Independent-minded Dissenters pointed to fidelity to conscience and loyalty to their spiritual King. Individual thinkers and interpreters such as David Hume regarded the country as rising to dignity and greatness under the Commonwealth:

> The bold and restless genius of the protector led him to extend his alliances and enterprises to every part of Christendom; and partly from the ascendant of his magnanimous spirit, partly from the situation of foreign kingdoms, the weight of England, even under its most legal and bravest princes, was never more sensibly felt than under this unjust and violent usurpation.[2]

The Liberation Society purchased outstanding historical works of reference for those wishing to prepare special lectures. Many lecturers were arranged, notably Dr T. McCrie (Presbyterian), the Rev. Alexander McLaren (Baptist), and the Rev. R. W. Dale (Congregationalist). The Society urged its sup-

---

[1] *Nonconformist*, 29.i.62, p. 104. Beginning on 22 January, the *Nonconformist* listed each week the names of the ejected clergymen, and also printed thirteen consecutive papers on the history of the event.

[2] *History of England* (London 1791), VII, lxi, 245–6; cf. B. M. Cordery & J. S. Phillpotts *King and Commonwealth: a History of the Great Rebellion* (London 1875), pp. 343, 352, 359, 376, 378.

porters to imitate the bold action rather than the theological opinions of their brethren of 1662.

Hostilities over the Bicentenary began in Birmingham Town Hall when the Rev. Canon J. C. Miller made the first attack in an address under the auspices of the local Church Defence Association. Coming from one of the eminent ecclesiastical gladiators of the city, the arguments of the Canon were in the main those also put forward by the Evangelical Alliance. He distinguished between the 'conscientious' and the 'political' Dissenters. He ridiculed the voluntary system as being nothing more than 'the commercial system'.[1] He condemned the Act of Uniformity, denounced King Charles as 'that wretched and perfidious profligate', and venerated the honesty and sacrifice of the unfortunate Clergymen. Nevertheless, he regretted the Bicentenary celebration as ruinous to the cause of Christian unity and love. He threatened to end his co-operation with Evangelical Dissenters in the work of the Birmingham Bible Society (of which he was Chairman) if they did not desist from this campaign against the Church of England.

A fortnight later Robert W. Dale was ready to speak in the same place on the same subject and to answer the charges of Dr Miller.[2] It was to be the occasion which launched Dale into his career of public service. The Hall was crowded to capacity and many hundreds were necessarily refused tickets. The Chairman, the Rev. R. D. Wilson, and the lecturer, on making their entrance on the platform, were greeted with hearty applause, which, 'increasing as it lengthened, culminated in loud cheers'.

The eloquent young preacher opened with an historical review, which in no way condoned the intolerance and severity of the Presbyterians. He dealt then with the objection so often raised that the ejectment of the Puritan party was an act of retaliation for the injustice that they themselves had committed in the expulsion of 2,000 Episcopalian Clergy when the country was in the throes of civil war. The Puritans were ejected when there was no threat from them to the peace of the country, whereas the Episcopalians expelled were at that time the avowed enemies of the existing Government.

It was true that little continuity of theological faith remained between the forced Nonconformists of 1662 and the willing Nonconformists of 1862. But the main objections of 'the dispossessed' were still valid. According to Mr Dale, these were the doctrines of Baptismal Regeneration, the language used in the Confirmation service, the Absolution in the service for Visitation of the Sick, and the form of the Burial Service. Broadly speaking, the old Puritans objected to the idea behind the revised Prayer Book of 1662 which connected human salvation with the sacraments. Modern Puritans were justified in

[1] The 'Offertory Movement' in the Church of England approved of the voluntary system. The National Association for Promoting Freedom of Public Worship in the Church of England issued an 'Address to Church Builders' in 1862, objecting to 'the pew system' and recommending the Free Churches' system of 'Weekly Offerings'. *Liberator*, Oct. 1862, p. 165.

[2] 'Churchmen and Dissenters: their relations as affected by the Proposed Bicentenary Commemoration of St Bartholomew's Day, 1662', in A. W. W. Dale, *Life of R. W. Dale*, pp. 167–74.

taking the opportunity afforded by this commemoration for reviewing the whole history of the Established Church, to test the harmony of its principles with the New Testament, to investigate its constitution, and to inquire into its influence on the religious welfare of the English people.

> I have no doubt that there are vast numbers of men in the Church belonging to the three great parties represented by Dr. Newman, Mr. Wilson and Dr. Vaughan, who conscientiously believe that it is a right thing to play fast and loose with language (of the Prayer Book) on behalf of their several theories, . . . We wish to remind the clergy belonging to these three sections of the Church in our day, of the incomparable fidelity of the two thousand men who never dreamt of sophistries like these.[1]

Present-day Nonconformity, Dale continued, had not shifted its ground, for it was still seeking the religious liberty which the deprived Ministers found dear. He ended magnanimously with an unexpected tribute to the Church of England that brought the audience to its feet.

One point was frequently overlooked at these meetings when Nonconformist enthusiasm ran high. It was the fact that the 2,000 were divided among the Presbyterians who believed in the alliance of Church and State, and the Independents who rejected it.[2] This being so, it could legitimately be urged that it was unfair to take the ejectment of all 2,000 as the text from which to argue for the principles of the Liberation Society.

Congregationalists, or old Independents, proudly claimed to be the true descendants of that tradition which repudiated the interference of court and magistrate in matters of religion. On this point they were at one with the Liberation doctrine opposing a State-controlled Church. For them, one of the great lessons drawn from the events of the Restoration was that to place legislative authority at the control of the Church was to arm it with the sword of the persecutor.

After Dale's lecture, the newspapers of the country were crowded with discussion of the related issues. Anglicans took offence to one particular passage which called upon the Evangelical Clergy to secede from the Church of England, or in other words, to reject conformity to the Liturgy and subscription to the Articles.[3] Clergymen who were willing to do this in principle but not in practice were accused by Liberationists of constituting an 'invertebrate priesthood'.[4] Canon Miller resigned soon afterwards from the Birming-

---

[1] *Nonconformist*, 12.iii.62, p. 223.

[2] cf. R. W. Dale, *History of English Congregationalism*, pp. 418 ff.

[3] Mr E. P. Bouverie's Clergy Relief Bill in 1862, which had this problem in view, was rejected on the third Reading. It sought to make allowances for Clergymen who came to opinions different from or inconsistent with the subscription they had made at Ordination. Sir William Heathcote, for the Opposition, denounced it as a measure to encourage and facilitate secession from Holy Orders.

[4] See *A Few Words on the Clamour for a Revision of the Liturgy in a letter to the Archbishop of York* [Dr William Thomson] (London 1862), by the Rev. Christopher Nevile, who left the Anglican Church to join the Liberation Society. The cases in 1862 of *Gorham v. The Bishop of Exeter* (Dr Henry Phillpotts), *Bruder v. Heath* and *Wilson and Williams v.*

ham Bible Society. Sir Culling Eardley, the Chairman of the Evangelical Alliance, visited the city but failed to restore peace between the belligerents. Lord Shaftesbury, in the following May at St James's Hall, speaking before the Pastoral Aid Society, answered Dale with similarly strong sentiments:

> 'Sir, I believe you are very ignorant; to say the truth, you are a very saucy fellow, and if you think you represent the great and good Nonconformists of former days, the Howes, the Bunyans, the Flavels, the Wattses, or even that you have anything akin to the good, sound, and true religious Nonconformists of the present day, you are just as much mistaken as you would be if you thought you were well versed in history, or had ever been initiated in the first elements of good breeding or Christian charity.'[1]

Black Bartholomew's Day (24 August) fell on a Sunday, and it brought with it one of the most widely observed religious demonstrations ever known in English history. No part of the country was silent. The smallest villages kept it as fittingly as the large towns and the Metropolis. The Congregational Committee brought out the memorial volume of Dr Robert Vaughan (Editor of the *British Quarterly Review*), entitled *English Nonconformity*. The columns of the *Patriot*, the *Freeman*, and the *Nonconformist* contained comment on nearly 1,000 sermons. The Liberation Society spent £155 on sending 100,000 copies of the address of the Bicentenary Committee (prepared by Edward Miall) to Dissenters throughout the United Kingdom. An additional 36,300 copies of the address were stitched in ten periodicals, in two London and seven Provincial daily newspapers, and in most Dissenting journals.

Summing up all the proceedings, the *Liberator* said that its doctrines had never been more aptly upheld by so many people who had never been identified with the Liberation Society. In contrasting tone, *The Church Review* on 15 August published a 'Hymn for the Patronal Festival of St Bartholomew':

> Thee, not least, today our Patron
> We would hold in honour due,
> As thy festival we welcome
> Guileless Saint Bartholomew.
> May thy holy prayers, uplifted,
> Where thou seest, face to face,
> Gain for us, by earth yet trammel'd,
> Blessings of celestial grace.

Dr Arthur Stanley, the Regius Professor of Ecclesiastical History at Oxford, made an effective allusion to the real problem in his pamphlet on 'State Subscription'.[2] He seriously advocated the abolition of subscription to

---

Phillimore all served to remind the public of the binding effect of the doctrines upheld in the Act of Uniformity.

[1] *Nonconformist*, 14.v.62, p. 418.

[2] cf. *Liberator*, June 1863, pp. 89–90, for (i) reference to this pamphlet, (ii) a letter with similar emphasis by the Rev. F. D. Maurice, and (iii) Lord Ebury's Bill for the abolition of the declaration of 'unfeigned assent and consent' in the Act of Uniformity.

both the Articles and the Prayer Book in their literal and grammatical sense, for it closed the door against the entrance of many conscientious persons into the Church.[1] The Oracle at Delphi, the learned man concluded, commanded the reverence of Greece without any walls of defence, for the grandeur of its natural position was sufficient.

---

[1] By the year 1865 there had come into existence an Association for Promoting a Revision of the Book of Common Prayer and a Review of the Acts of Uniformity; the Secretary was the Rev. R. Bingham M.A.

CHAPTER 12

Irish Church Disestablishment

> If anything could make us believe, in spite of all evidence,
> that Mr Miall is right, that establishments demoralise the
> souls of their supporters, it would be to see the soldiers
> of the Church placing its earthly interests so high above
> its spiritual character, and on its behalf using weapons from
> which the children of Voltaire turn with contemptuous
> loathing.
>
> *Spectator*[1]

> We who did our lineage high
> Draw from beyond the starry sky,
> Are yet upon the other side
> To earth and to its dust allied.
>
> W. E. GLADSTONE[2]

IN CONTRAST to the prolonged quarrel on Church Rates, it seemed ironical that the Church of England in Ireland should be disestablished and disendowed in but two years of concentrated agitation. The fate of the Church in Ireland in 1869 was due primarily to changes working within that country, rather than to those at work in England.

Because of discontent and unrest among the Irish Nationalists, most of whom were devout Catholics, settlement of this problem was imperative. And to all parties concerned it was as much a religious as a political problem. The Irish Catholics scorned the Established Church of their country as a badge of conquest and a garrison of the English. The English Catholics also mistrusted the Imperial Government for perennially pointing to instances of 'Papal aggression', and shutting their eyes to the gross anomaly of the Protestant Church in Ireland.

The Society had fewer subscribers in Ireland than anywhere else, but since the debate on Miall's motion in 1856 calling for the secularization of Irish Church property, they had viewed the discontent there as a powerful ally to their cause in England. Although the Society could not be considered in any

---

[1] quoted in *Liberator*, May 1869, p. 71.

[2] In the Commons, 30 March 1868, quoting the Archbishop of Dublin, Dr Richard C. Trench. Hansard (3rd series), cxci, 494.

way the instigator of unrest in Ireland, it did profit greatly by introducing the issues into the Disestablishment controversy in England. This caused the Society to become an even more lively topic of conversation on the floors of both Houses.

Lord Palmerston and his Whig régime had admitted in 1856 that the fifth Article of the Act of Union between the two countries could not prevent Parliament from dealing with the problem. Wealthy Churchmen grumbled that Disendowment meant bankruptcy. Radical Nonconformists argued that it meant peace to the country. Goldwin Smith, the Professor of Modern History at Oxford, and others like him frankly and openly referred to the Irish Church as 'a blunder and a fraud – though a pious one'.

The 1861 Census for Ireland revealed that of a population of 5,764,543 there were 4,490,583 Roman Catholics, 678,661 members of the Established Church, and 528,992 Presbyterians. The only State support received by Irish Non-conformist bodies was the Maynooth grant of £26,000 for the Roman Catholics, and a similar annual sum – the *Regium Donum* – for the Presbyterians. The Established Church, however, in order to maintain two Arch-bishops and ten Bishops in Ireland, was granted from national revenues £80,000 in yearly incomes alone. Statistically, there was one Bishop in England to 410 benefices, comprising 1,500,000 souls. In Ireland the figures amounted to one Bishop for 118 benefices, comprising 5,000 souls. In England a parish of this size was usually looked after by an Incumbent and probably two Curates. In Ireland it was looked after by a Bishop who had numerous Deans, Chapters, Archdeacons, and parochial Clergy under his supervision for religious services.

Thorough as this ecclesiastical organism was, the Church was not growing, but rather becoming 'small by degrees and beautifully less'. Irish Catholics and English Voluntaryists used such facts to show the glaring contradiction of the Establishment.

A. *Preparatory Movements*

Early in 1863 the Liberation Society fully resolved to bring these matters before the House of Commons, and requested R. B. Osborne (M.P., Liskeard) to put forward the Irish question. It was found that L. L. Dillwyn (M.P., Swansea) had a similar intention. The Welsh leader called for a Select Committee to inquire how far the distribution of endowments for religious purposes throughout Ireland could be altered for the general welfare of all Irishmen. After several speeches in support and an amendment calling for a Royal Commission to this end, Dillwyn withdrew in favour of a motion by Osborne simply 'that a Select Committee be appointed to inquire into the present Ecclesiastical settlement of Ireland'.

On 26 June, Bernal Osborne opened the attack with a clever speech. At one point he set before the House the reduction plan of Archbishop Richard Whately which had been included in a Bill brought in by Sir George Lewis and had been opposed by Lord John Russell! It sought to place all the tithes in one common fund, to make the Church congregational in government, and to redistribute the money to Protestants, Presbyterians, and Roman Catholics according to the number of their respective congregations. It further called for a concordat with the Pope, and satisfactory agreement with the Roman Catholics. The motion was dropped by 67 to 228 votes.

This was merely the beginning, so far as the Society was concerned. The question was not yet a bond of party, a rallying cry for the hustings, nor a 'living germ' of Liberal progress. At this stage it was the debate itself and the direction to which it pointed that was important in the eyes of the Society. The voices of statesmen and pens of writers would gain in momentum.

Meanwhile, the Liberation Society was kept informed concerning developments in Ireland through Mr W. J. O'Neill Daunt, one of the leaders of the Irish National movement.[1] In a letter placed in the Minutes on 21 October 1862, he urged the Society to abandon opposition to the Maynooth College endowment and thereby to obtain clear support of Irish Catholics. Dr C. J. Foster replied that the Society would neither openly oppose it, nor would they support the continuance of the grant.

Although the Society did remain silent concerning Maynooth, they were loudly opposed to the Irish *Regium Donum*. Early in 1864 a deputation consisting of fifteen Ministers and seven M.P.s from the General Assembly of the Presbyterian Church in Ulster was received by the Lord Lieutenant. They sought an additional £16,000 for a total of £41,000 per annum, and wished the *Regium Donum* like the Maynooth Grant to become a charge on the Consolidated Fund, instead of depending on an annual vote of Parliament. The Royal Gift, they claimed, was in accordance with a practice long established from the time when James I had induced some Scottish families and their Ministers to emigrate to Ireland. The vote for the increase was lost in the Commons by 21 to 127 votes.

The Society kept up its pressure by sending money for lectures to Presbyterians opposing this policy of State aid,[2] and by enlisting their help for an organized petitioning movement throughout Ireland. By the end of the 1864 Session petitions signed by 30,000 persons had been sent to the Commons requesting that the State-Church be abolished in Ireland. Two years later the number of signatories to petitions for Disendowment had been increased to 202,632.

The formation of the Irish National Association, at the Rotunda in Dublin

---

[1] Daunt received an invitation to become a member of the Executive Committee, but he declined because of poor health and the inconvenience of attending their meetings in London. He added in his private journal: 'I have found some of our Catholics unwilling to join forces with men so full of anti-Catholic bigotry as the English nonconformists, but I think I have tolerably well removed that unwillingness. . . .' His great hope was to get both the Catholic prelates and the Liberation Society working together 'in the same harness'. He was twice again asked to accept position in the Society in 1865 and in 1870. *A Life Spent for Ireland*, pp. 192, 261.

[2] Parl. Com. Min., 6.i.65. The Rev. S. Rodgers, Presbyterian Minister of Belfast, was granted £100 for the publication of his lecture on the adverse effects of the *Regium Donum*.

on 29 December 1864, was watched with great interest by the Liberation Society. The Association represented the feelings of Catholic Clergy, educators, politicians, and land reformers. John Bright sent a letter expressing his sympathy and that of many English Liberals with its objects: (1) to reform the law of landlord and tenant, securing to the latter full compensation for his improvements of the land; (2) to abolish the Irish Establishment, bringing a 'Free Church with Free Land'; (3) to establish free education, allowing denominational teaching in all branches; (4) to re-establish the Irish Constitution of 1782 with the exclusive government of the Irish by the Queen, Lords, and Commons of Ireland.

Among the speeches on this occasion, O'Neill Daunt maintained that the Fifth Article of the Union said nothing binding about the revenues of the Church of England in Ireland. He denounced what Lord Castlereagh had said at the time of the Union, that its leading features were 'one State, one Legislature, one Church'. Daunt declared that there could never be one loyalty, one conscience, and one religious belief in Ireland. The Society promptly decided to publish this fiery speech. The Secretary, Carvell Williams, wrote inquiring of the future plans of the Association, and in his reply[1] Daunt confirmed that a large part of its activities would be anti-State-Church. After hearing the news of Mr Miall's return to Parliament for Bradford, the Irish Liberation leader wrote in his journal on 18 March 1869:[2] 'Surely the best thing I ever did for Ireland was to effect that alliance with the English Liberation people, which at last bids fair to result in the overthrow of State Churchism among us.'

At a subsequent conference of the Association in Dublin on 12 May 1868, under the presidency of Daunt, a brief résumé of the extent of its co-operation with the Liberation Society was presented. A resolution, expressing the gratitude of the Association to the English Voluntaryists and the Society, was carried with loud acclamation.

In 1865 a Bill of Mr W. Monsell (M.P., Limerick Co.) was brought in for altering the oath required of Roman Catholic members of Parliament, and was linked with the Irish Church question. The oath was originally prescribed by the tenth statute of George IV, cap. 7, sec. 2:

> I do swear that I will defend to the utmost of my power the settlement of property within this realm, as established by the laws; and I do hereby disclaim, disavow, and solemnly abjure any intention to subvert the present Church Establishment, as settled by law within this realm, and I do solemnly swear that I never will exercise any privilege to which I am or may become entitled to disturb or weaken the Protestant religion or Protestant Government in the United Kingdom.

In debate it was argued that the safety of the Church Establishment was not threatened by disloyalty of Roman Catholics, but by attacks of those with no religion. Moreover, theological differences should never separate countrymen

---

[1] Minute 479: 3.ii.65.
[2] Daunt, *A Life Spent for Ireland*, p. 257.

in the discharge of their duties in the Legislature. Sir George Grey believed that the oath ought to be made uniform for all M.P.s, inasmuch as none wished to disturb the Act of Settlement. After a successful second and third reading it passed to the Lords, where it was defeated. Lord Derby declared that the so-called disability was imaginary – the oath did not deprive any Catholic of any political privilege to which he already had a right.

The year following, the Bill was brought in by the authority of Her Majesty's Government, and had the support of Mr Disraeli for substituting a uniform Parliamentary oath. It went through the necessary stages in the House of Lords on 15 April, but only after it had been agreed that the oath should contain expressions of (1) allegiance to the reigning monarch, (2) recognition of the Protestant succession to the throne, (3) and acknowledgement of the supremacy of the Crown. The Parliamentary Committee reported on 9 May that it had received the Royal Assent.

Three minor Bills, early in 1867, extended new privileges to the Roman Catholics. The first, the Catholic Oaths Bill, was (1) to allow all persons without reference to religious belief to fill the offices of Lord Chancellor and Lord Lieutenant of Ireland, (2) to permit judicial and corporate functionaries to attend Dissenting or Roman Catholic places of worship with the insignia of office, (3) to substitute the new Parliamentary oaths for the oaths then required from office-holders. The second Catholic Oaths Bill was to abolish the declaration against Transubstantiation, against the adoration of the Virgin Mary, and against the sacrifice of the Mass – all of which were required to be taken by certain Protestant office-holders. The third Bill, introduced with these other two, aimed at opening certain professorships (of Anatomy, Surgery, Chemistry and Botany) in Trinity College, Dublin University, to all persons irrespective of religious creed. All were read a second time – the first two without opposition, the last by a large majority – and all easily gained the Royal Assent by mid-1867. The office of Lord Lieutenant was barely excluded from the Bill in both Houses.

Henry Fawcett (M.P., Brighton) moved, on 24 July 1867, that Scholarships and Fellowships of Trinity College, Dublin, should not be limited to members of the Established Church. An amendment to alter the Constitution to include Dissenting Colleges and their students in the University was withdrawn, and the motion resulting in a tie was lost by the Speaker's vote.

Irish M.P.s inquired of the Society what course it would take in the event of the Government proposing, as it was rumoured it would do, to endow the Roman Catholic University in Ireland. Because of sharp differences of opinion expressed on the subject at the Parliamentary breakfast with the Dissenting Deputies on 15 February 1866, no clearly defined position could be put forward.

In the special paper on 'Parliamentary Action for 1865 and 1866' the Society reaffirmed that the Church question lay at the root of the Irish difficulties, and that 'full consideration of the Disendowment of the Irish Establishment could not be long postponed'. Dillwyn presented his motion again, calling for the

11

attention of the Government to the unsatisfactory position of the Irish Church. The debate was without great effect and was soon adjourned.

Earl Grey laid before the House of Lords, in March 1866, a plan for proportionate distribution, by Commissioners, of the State ecclesiastical funds among the Clergy of the three principal religious divisions of Ireland. His plan was for giving two-fifths of the revenues to the Roman Catholics, two-fifths to the Anglicans, and one-fifth to the Presbyterians. The Upper Chamber believed that his scheme went too deep, and was likely to be the seed of further jealousies. The motion was negatived without a division. Grey warned that sooner or later the unjust state of affairs in Ireland would force a remedy.

His words were fulfilled sooner, for the crusade of the fanatical Fenian Brotherhood against the 'tyranny of the Protestant landlords' and the 'yoke of British rule' became very serious in 1866–7. The spectacle of poor Irish peasants and rash youths in pitched battles with forces of the Crown, parades in the streets and speeches by agitators in the public squares, shocked the conservative sensibilities of many British people.

The revolting bloodshed in Ireland and the wild demonstrations in England clearly had the markings of another Civil War in the British Isles. The executions of Fenian 'martyr' conspirators in Manchester and Dublin brought a wave of public outcry against a nervous Tory Government. The grievances of Irishmen, whether in England, America, or their own country, could hardly now be described as 'imaginary'. In his book *Ireland and Her Agitators*,[1] Daunt explained that 'the Fenian exhibition' was not simply an internal conspiracy by isolated extremists, but a disease of national discontent flowing from the consequences of the Articles of Union.

The remedy, said the *Nonconformist*, must be 'radical enough to grapple with the disease and to expel it from the body politic'. Undoubtedly, a surge of patriotism – the want of national institutions, a national capital, and anything deserving to be called national life – was at the heart of the insurrection. The best solution in the eyes of the Liberationists was simply to disestablish the Church of England as the national Church of Ireland, and thereby to institute absolute religious and social equality. The immediate answer of the Government was to increase law enforcements, to punish conspirators severely and to suspend the Habeas Corpus Act.

The forces of Conservatism were now under severe pressure to make adjustments, and changes of political leadership were bound to come. 'What I fear in Gladstone', said Archbishop Tait on one occasion, 'is his levity'.[2] But when the promising aristocrat decided to become a Liberal statesman, he could not have been more serious.

In two very earnest speeches on private motions for a Parliamentary inquiry into the position and possessions of the Irish Church, Mr Gladstone first gained the unreserved confidence of the Nonconformists, and made clear his break with the Conservative party. In his role as Chancellor of the

---

[1] (Dublin 1845), pp. 250–5.
[2] Goldwin Smith, *My Memory of Gladstone* (London 1904), p. 18.

Exchequer he declared himself in favour of a readjustment of the Establishment because the Irish public demanded it.

> The first responsibility of every Legislature in every age must be to adapt the laws and institutions of the country to the wants of the country which it governs, and it would indeed be a miserable excuse . . . if we were to say that, although we did not think an institution was beneficial, we thought it ought to be maintained, and we would maintain it because it was made by a Parliament of men now dead, . . .[1]

Six weeks later, Sir John Grey, the leader of the Irish Liberal party, introduced his motion, in accordance with the wishes of the Liberation Society, that the House resolve itself into a Committee to consider the temporalities and privileges of the Established Church in Ireland. The Society's whip was disregarded and the motion lost, but in his speech on this occasion Gladstone laid down the fundamental bases of ecclesiastical statesmanship from which he never departed. There were three grounds, he said, on which a Church Establishment might be maintained: (1) on the ground of truth – this was difficult to claim in Ireland where a predominant priesthood taught that truth was not found in the Established Church; (2) on the ground that it is the Church of the bulk of the population; (3) on the ground that it is the Church of the mass of the poorer portion of the population. Would Anglicans, he asked, tolerate the same situation if the Roman Catholic Church were the Established Church of England?[2]

After expressing himself in this manner, Gladstone could not remain in the seat for the University of Oxford. Nonconformists of all classes were now ready and anxious to support his candidacy in South Lancashire, and he was ready to accept the leadership of the Liberal party.

The Lords sensed what was in the offing and decided to delay no longer in dealing with the trouble across the Irish Sea. On 24 June 1867, they agreed to a resolution for which Earl Russell was responsible, calling for a Royal Commission to determine

> the nature and amount of the property and revenues of the Established Church in Ireland, with a view to their more productive management, and to their more equitable application for the benefit of the Irish people.[3]

Formerly, Lord John Russell had approved secularization of the Church revenues for education or other public utility, and a fair application of the voluntary principle. He now announced a plan for dividing up the revenues which would leave the Church of England in possession of one-eighth of her endowments, giving over one-eighth of them to the Presbyterian Church, and assigning six-eighths to the Roman Catholic Church. The last-named body

---

[1] Hansard (3rd series), clxxviii, 425: 28.iii.65.

[2] Hansard (3rd series), clxxxvii, 129–30.

[3] Hansard (3rd series), clxxxviii, 421–2. The Commission consisted of the Earl of Stanhope, the Earl of Meath, Viscount de Vesci, Sir Joseph Napier, R. S. Adair Esq. M.P., Dr Ball, M. E. P. Shirley Esq., Mr George Clive M.P. and Mr Edward Howes M.P.

would use such funds (1) to rebuild or repair Catholic churches, (2) to furnish glebe houses and glebe lands to Parish Priests, and (3) to begin an increase in incomes for Priests. He favoured disestablishing the Irish Church to the extent of depriving her dignitaries of their legal right to precedence, and excluding her Bishops from seats in the House of Lords. He objected, however, to the full application of the principles of the Liberation Society. The *Nonconformist* described Russell's scheme as affording 'ingenious directions for cooking the hare, but omitting to say how the hare ought to be caught'.

In debate Earl Russell defended his plan as similar to the workable schemes of other European states that had been encumbered with Catholic–Protestant divisions. In a 'No surrender' speech, Lord Cairns revealed that the Liberation Society had united with those in Ireland seeking alteration of laws affecting the tenure of land, in order to form a strong party for sinister Parliamentary action. They would use Disestablishment in Ireland as a precedent for its occurrence in England, and a Royal Commission would encourage that precedent. On the contrary, Lord Kimberley, former Lord-Lieutenant of Ireland, thought that the Commission was the best way of defeating the objects of the Liberation Society. The Duke of Argyll vindicated the Society's principle that Churches should be free from alliance with political injustice. In the case of Ireland, Church revenues might be part of that political injustice – especially the tithes, which were not private property, but a rent upon the land at the disposal of the Parliament. Attempts by the Irish Episcopate failed to limit the resolution, and the motion simply praying for a Royal Commission was agreed to without further ado.

The much awaited document appeared on 21 September 1868. It consisted of a Report proper filling fifteen folio pages, a series of summary tables extending over ten pages, and comprehensive statistics covering 600 pages. The general idea behind the Report seemed to be one of improvement in the internal arrangements of the existing Establishment – in effect, a partial Disestablishment.

The Parliamentary Committee of the Society promptly denounced this 'tripartite plan' of Earl Russell and Earl Grey, as only modifying the nature of the Establishment, as failing to solve sectarian bitterness, and as overlooking the fact that the Roman Catholics themselves did not wish such endowment. The policy for which the Society unwaveringly stood was, 'the disestablishment of the Church of England in Ireland, the impartial disendowment of all religious bodies in that country, and the application of the ecclesiastical property of the nation to national and unsectarian purposes'.[1] This was advertised in forty-five newspapers throughout England, Scotland, and Ireland. At the suggestion of Miall, the Executive Committee approved the formation of a special Irish Church Committee which was to plan strategy on the Irish question. It was decided that Carvell Williams should go to Ireland in the autumn of 1867 and gain first-hand information.

On his return he reported visiting Roman Catholic Clergy, journalists,

[1] Minute 507a: 5.vii.67.

M.P.s, co-operating Dissenters, and the Committee of the Irish National Association. He had given assurance of the interest of the Liberal party, particularly at the forthcoming General Election, and had urged the Irish people to impress the mind of the English people with the importance of dealing promptly with the question. His impression was that the Irish Establishment was definitely doomed, but that Presbyterians were politically passive, and that the Catholic Dissenters were hopelessly divided. Irish friends would certainly assist, but ultimate Disestablishment itself could be achieved only through a powerful influence in the Liberal party in England.

Accordingly, the Society's Irish Committee asked the Committee of the National Association in Ireland to issue an address to English Liberals urging them to come to their aid. Furthermore, it was decided that the Society's publications on the Irish problem should be circulated throughout Ireland, and that a private conference of key politicians should be called in England to develop future agitation.

The Conference on the Irish Church was convened on 11 December 1867 at the City Terminus Hotel in London, by means of private invitations issued by the Executive Committee. Among the ninety-five gentlemen present were Edward Miall as chairman, Carvell Williams, Charles Roundell, Sir Patrick O'Brien M.P., Boyd Kinnear, Albert Rutson, the Rev. Alexander Hannay, and Henry Richard. The views represented were various, but resolutions were passed endorsing the Society's policy of impartial Disendowment supported by more petitioning at large, more sympathetic M.P.s, and more information to electors. Despite the unanimity of feeling on the basic question of Disendowment, some difference of opinion was expressed on 'what was to be *done* with the money'.

At the Parliamentary Breakfast of the Liberation Society and the Dissenting Deputies on 10 March 1868, the latter desired that Mr Gladstone be confronted by a strong Nonconformist deputation. Instead, the Society advised that the Prime Minister be informed that, should he desire support in advocating a policy of impartial Disendowment, the Nonconformists would arrange a great demonstration in his favour. This proved to be the wiser means toward their end.

B. *Gladstone's Liberal Resolutions*
On 23 March 1868, having declared several weeks previously that the hour had struck when the Irish Church must cease to be established and the question settled by means of Disendowment, Mr Gladstone gave notice of three resolutions. Two days later, Bishop Wilberforce of Oxford wrote concerning them:

It is altogether a bad business, and I am afraid Gladstone has been drawn into it from the unconscious influence of his restlessness at being out of office.[1]

The declaration of the Premier, however, which followed somewhat the line

[1] G. W. E. Russell, *William Ewart Gladstone* (London 1913), p. 199.

of Mr Miall in 1856, practically assured the Government of the united support of the Irish Nationalists, Liberal economists, Nonconformists, and members of the Liberation Society. These resolutions were a necessary fulfilment of the election pledges which he had made to these groups:

1. That, in the opinion of this House, it is necessary that the Established Church of Ireland should cease to exist as an Establishment, due regard being had to all personal interests and all individual rights of property.
2. That, subject to the foregoing considerations, it is expedient to prevent the creation of new personal interests by the exercise of any public patronage, and to confine the operations of the Ecclesiastical Commissioners of Ireland to objects of immediate necessity, or involving individual rights, pending the final decision of Parliament.
3. That a humble address be presented to Her Majesty, praying her, with a view to the purposes aforesaid, to place at the disposal of Parliament her interest in the temporalities of the Archbishoprics, Bishoprics, and other Ecclesiastical Dignities and Benefices of the Church of Ireland, and in the custody thereof.[1]

The effect upon Nonconformists throughout the country after the release of these words was almost magical. The Irish Committee of the Society increased the number of paid lecturers to twenty-four, among them the Rev. Mason Jones of the National Reform Union, to uphold Mr Gladstone's resolutions 'of crowning merit'. Tens of thousands of pamphlets were distributed in London and sent throughout the country. Thousands attended a meeting at St James's Hall on 6 April addressed by Messrs Jones and Miall with Earl Russell presiding, also at the Metropolitan Tabernacle on 22 April with John Bright presiding. The London Working Men's Association organized similar meetings.

In the Commons debate, John Bright's response to Disraeli for his 'parting shot' at Gladstone's resolutions was unforgettable. According to Bright's biographer the House listened 'in an electrical condition' and responded with cheering laughter as the powerful Quaker hammered against the arch-Conservative's contention that the Establishment was a protector of freedom of religion and toleration.

'Mr. Disraeli seems to read a different history from anybody else, or else he makes his own history, and like Voltaire, makes it better without facts than with them.'[2]

Disraeli never made a more angry and excited retort upon a political opponent, and threw down the gauntlet for the crucial Disestablishment debates to follow. The country waited expectantly while the leaders of the participating parties prepared feverishly, not at all sure of what lay ahead.

[1] Minute 61: 27.iii.68.
[2] George B. Smith, *Life of the Right Honourable John Bright, M.P.* (London 1889), pp. 286–90.

In September 1868, just before the General Election, Gladstone released his *Chapter of Autobiography*. The publication traced in detail the history of his opinions on the Irish Church and took the public into his full confidence. It pacified those who were anxious about his intentions on the separation of Church and State.

> When ... the community itself is split and severed into opinions and communions, which, whatever their concurrence in the basis of Christian belief, are hostile in regard to the point at issue, so that what was meant for the nation dwindles into the private estate as it were of a comparative handful, then the attempt to maintain an Established Church becomes an error fatal to the peace, dangerous perhaps even to the life, of civil society. Such a Church then becomes (to use a figure I think of John Foster's) no longer the temple, but the mere cemetery of a great idea.[1]

As the world became Christian, Gladstone here maintained, Christianity became worldly. And of all the Churches in the world the Irish Church had the most pay and the least work. The English State at the Reformation had transferred to the use of a small section of the Irish population large resources which formerly had been employed for the benefit of all the people.

Gladstone's plan, of which his three resolutions were but seedlings, was to withdraw from all religious parties in Ireland that which was the ground of envy among them. To withdraw State support would not weaken Protestantism and strengthen Roman Catholicism, for the strength of any religion did not depend upon its material possessions. His plan was put forward not by enemies of the Church, but by friends of religious equality who wished it to leave as little soreness behind as possible. His plan answered the question of what was just and good for Ireland, rather than what was expedient for 700,000 Protestant Episcopalians there.

The few Whigs led by Earl Russell eventually came under Gladstone's banner. In his third letter to Chichester Fortescue, the Irish Secretary, Earl Russell dropped his stand on 'proportionate endowment' and accepted 'impartial disendowment'. This shift seemed to be in line with the Whiggish temperament which extended back to William III, Burke, and Fox – reconciling popular aspirations with aristocratic institutions. Although the Whigs were often looked upon as political middlemen on the Irish Church issue they stood nearer the Liberals than the Tories.

During his election campaign Mr Gladstone claimed that he had lost his seat for Oxford University for refusing to condone the Irish Church, but this did not mean his wishing to approve the principles of the Liberation Society as they applied to the English Church. Thus he said in a speech on 22 October 1868, to his electors in South Lancashire:

> I know that, even if I were a member of the Liberation Society, which I am not, and if I agreed with the principles of the Liberation Society, which I do

[1] pp. 60–1; see also Thomas Archer, *William Ewart Gladstone and his Contemporaries*, iv, 292.

not, I should still look two or three times at the business of disestablishing the Church of England, before I set about it.[1]

Gladstone warned Disraeli, however, not to press Conservative arguments too far or Liberals would be forced to apply theirs to consequences they at first never intended. He was in favour of removing a Church to which the majority of the people were hostile, but he was not so minded with a Church loved and respected by the people. In the latter case, Priest and people were bound closely together, making for a strong Church. In the other, Priest and money were closely bound together, making for a weak Church.

1. *Disraeli and the Tories*

Benjamin Disraeli was prepared to endanger the solidarity and popularity of his Government and party in resisting a plan of secularization for the Irish Church. He would consent either to economizing on the money which it spent, or dividing it among the other Churches, but he would never consent to divert from religious uses any property that had been once consecrated thereto. Thus he contended that Gladstone's proposals were 'vast and violent'.

Other Conservatives contended that the problem was the regrettable out-come of Catholic Emancipation. The Liberal chief, they feared, would use 'the ruins of the Irish Protestant Church' to remain in office. Disraeli was bothered not so much by the 'No Popery' cry from many in his own party as by the idea of 'No Protestantism' implied by many Liberals. After all, en-dowments, even as Dissenters understood them, were not unjust sources of income. Protestant Episcopalians were able to show in any court of Equity that they had done nothing to forfeit the exclusive use of property rightfully entrusted to them.

The Tories in general were convinced that any solution to the problem must be found in a process of 'levelling up' rather than 'levelling down', for it was better to create than destroy. They answered the Liberal charge that the Government was to blame for failing to provide a solution, by pointing out that the present House had not been elected to decide on the Irish Church. They realized too well that the party which passed a suitable Bill on the Irish Church would be governing for many years.

To Disraeli it seemed that certain Ritualists in England were in 'con-federacy' with the Irish Catholics, and were using the Liberation Society for the destruction of the union between Church and State. He was asked by one of his constituents, the Rev. Arthur Baker (the Rector of Addington), to explain this assertion. In a reply on Maundy Thursday 1868, signed 'your faithful member and servant', he wrote of his highest respect for, and the country's long indebtedness to, the High-Church party – and 'the other great party'. To him the existence of parties in 'our Church' was a necessity, not a

[1] *Nonconformist*, 28.x.68, p. 1051. The *Nonconformist* had already denied that Miall was in any kind of league with Gladstone. They had met personally on but two occasions – once at a deputation to the Government, and again at the funeral of Cobden.

calamity; they were the natural consequences of 'the varying and opposite elements of the human mind and character'.

> When I spoke I referred to an extreme faction in the Church, of very modern date, that does not conceal its ambition to destroy the connection between Church and State, and which I have reason to believe has been for some time in secret combination, and is now in open confederacy, with the Irish Romanists for the purpose.
>
> The Liberation Society, with its shallow and short-sighted fanaticism, is a mere instrument in the hands of this confederacy, and will probably be the first victim of the spiritual despotism the Liberation Society is now blindly working to establish.
>
> As I hold that the dissolution of the union between Church and State will cause permanently a greater revolution in this country than foreign conquest, I shall use my utmost energies to defeat these fatal machinations.[1]

Disraeli distrusted the Liberationists also because of their connexion with the philosophers and intellectuals.[2] Moreover, they identified themselves with the poor man who bargained with the rich man when he had given up the idea of becoming wealthy. For the Tories there was no escaping the testimonies of the past. Any attempt to ignore its verdicts, to reverse its decisions, and to undo what it had done, would result in considerably more than the destruction of the Church Establishment. In the appointment of Bishop Tait to the Primacy in 1868, the worried Conservatives were given a greater protector not only of the Church of England, but of the 'constitution of England' as well.

In the Disestablishment question Disraeli and his disciples felt the crisis of England was fast arriving, and that the solutions of the Opposition were dangerously affecting the tenure of the Crown. Although there was no longer the 'divine right of Kings', there was still, very much embodied in the national Establishment, the divine right of government.

2. Bright and the Radicals

Liberationists and Nonconformists believed that the 'earthquake' in Ireland had been caused, in the words of John Bright, by 'an absolute aristocracy and an alien Church'. Nevertheless, he assailed as 'high crime' Disraeli's insinuation that they were marshalled against the Queen who really held the flag of religious justice. A Jewish Crown Minister who so deceived his Sovereign, said the Quaker orator, was as guilty as a conspirator who would dethrone her.

---

[1] *Liberator*, May 1868, p. 73; *Nonconformist*, 15.iv.68, p. 367.

[2] At a Diocesan Conference in Oxford on 25 November 1864, he expressed strong feeling against the evolutionary and rationalistic trend of the Broad Church movement. He asked: 'Is man an ape or an angel? My lord, I am on the side of the angels. . . . When we are told that the teachings of the Church are not consistent with the discoveries of science, . . . I totally deny the proposition. . . . It is between these two contending interpretations of the nature of man and their consequences that society will have to decide.' T. A. Kebbell, *Selected Speeches by the Earl of Beaconsfield* (London 1882), ii, 611–12. Shortly after this, cartoons appeared throughout the country picturing Disraeli with angel's wings and Gladstone with devil's horns.

Those following Bright believed as Gladstone did in this matter, but they often said it in more radical terms. Their most telling argument they described as common sense, namely, that it was not possible to justify the Church of the minority as the Church of the nation. They could not be accused of weakening Protestantism, for far more converts were going over to Rome from the Church of England than from Nonconformist Chapels.

Episcopalians, the Radicals said, placed too much faith in tithes and glebe lands, and not enough faith in the Church's missionary zeal. The Voluntary principle opened up wider financial resources than the 'cash down' principle. It made possible a new life and energy which sprung from self-dependence. The example of the Irish Roman Catholic Church itself attested to the strength of Voluntaryism.

Bright softened the radical attitude somewhat by urging kind and peaceful dealings with the Irish Churches which were to undergo the serious operation. The actions of the Government should be moved by Christian leniency, and should be respectful to the interests of groups in Ireland, for all were basically part of the same Christian body. In order that no ecclesiastical body might be thrown 'cold and naked' upon the world, he favoured granting from the disestablished property £1,000,000 apiece to the Roman, Anglican, and Presbyterian Churches.

He differed from the Liberation Society on the disposal of the *Regium Donum* and Maynooth Grant after Disestablishment. In order to protect the life interests of Presbyterian Ministers as would be done with Anglican Clergy, property or trusts should be given in lieu of the special gift and grant. But it must be property which Parliament could never regulate, and having consented to their absolute ownership on that condition, the three Churches of Ireland should be supported as voluntary Churches.

> There have been great objections to the plan, and among those who have objected to it, as might possibly have been expected, were gentlemen of the Liberation Society. Now, I know many of the leading members of that society, and they are very good men. Even those who may think they are mistaken, if they knew them would join with me in that opinion. One of them, at least, who was once a Member of this House, and in all probability will be here again—Mr. Miall—is not only a good man, but he is a great man. I judge him by the nobleness of his principles, and by the grand devotion which he has manifested to the teaching of what he believes to be a great truth.[1]

During this crisis Gladstone proposed to Bright that he enter the Cabinet as President of the Board of Trade. At first Bright was fearful of departing from his lofty independence of character which had been admired by his electors and lowly countrymen. But he realized at length that the new Government wished thereby to keep the confidence of Nonconformists, and therefore he accepted.

---

[1] Hansard (3rd series), cxc, 1657.

3. Broad Church Position

Dr Frederick Temple, later Archbishop of Canterbury, fairly and concisely expressed the feeling of Liberal Anglicans concerning the temporal and spiritual claims of the Church of England and Ireland when he said on one occasion, 'It must be tried by its work, and I will accept no other title.' Broad Churchmen, like High Churchmen, had never greatly admired the Irish Church because of its Evangelical and anti-Roman colour. J. A. Froude felt that the Church in Ireland was militant in the spirit of Luther, but as a missionary institution it had not been a success.

The parties in the Church of England were divided as to whether or not the breaking off of the Church in Ireland meant affecting the sanctity of the Coronation Oath. If a change in the Church effected a change in one of its religious services, Liberal Churchmen believed that Parliament rather than the Church was the best medium for deciding what was right. Parliament could withdraw whatever it was convinced was no longer useful to the whole people of the country. It had withdrawn itself from the rule of Monarchs, and so it could rightfully withdraw itself from the control of the Church.

Lord Lyveden presented to the House of Lords, on 23 June 1868, a petition signed by Liberal Churchmen who were convinced that the Irish Establishment was an injustice, and prayed the House to remove the cause of offence. Among the 261 names were Professors Maurice, Kingsley, Jowett, and Plumptre; Deans Alford of Canterbury and Elliot of Bristol; Archdeacon Sandford; Doctor Butler and Doctor Temple, Headmasters of Harrow and Rugby, respectively; W. H. Bateson, the Master of St John's, Cambridge; Edwin A. Abbott, the Headmaster of City of London School; and George Ridding, the Headmaster of Winchester.

4. Roman Catholic View

Irish Catholics had always believed that the Church of England as the Established Church in Ireland was a 'mocking misnomer'. To many it was the symbol of a suspicion which the English appeared to hold toward the Irish and their national institutions. Other Catholic minorities in Britain could readily sympathize with the Irish.

The Roman Catholic hierarchy were naturally the most outspoken of leaders against the non-native Church. They voted at a meeting in Dublin, in October 1867, not to accept any endowment from the State out of the property and revenues now held by the Protestant Establishment. This declaration left standing three possible solutions from which Parliament must choose – to make Roman Catholic Clergy a stipendiary Clergy, to establish the Roman Catholic Church as the State Church, or to abolish the existing Establishment.

Not only were there complex questions concerning the Church and land to be settled, but education in Ireland presented its problems as well. In higher education Roman Catholics saw several possibilities: (1) unlimited access to the educational privileges of Trinity College and other Anglican foundations in Dublin University, (2) alteration of the Constitution of the Queen's

University to include 'dissenting' with the other four 'secular' Colleges, (3) endowment by the State of a Roman Catholic University and charter of incorporation. Most Catholics were strongly in favour of a denominational system of education and therefore preferred the third possibility. Because of the varieties of religious belief and the differences among religious orders, State aid made for continuous competition and jealousy. At any rate this was their view at this stage in Irish history.

The Catholics of Ireland objected to the indiscriminate application of the revenues to ecclesiastical uses, but not to their application for the general good of the country. They did not approve of the idea of 'assistance by concurrent endowment', nor of any kind of financial aid to other Church communions. Specifically, they wished to use the Church temporalities for educational purposes. For this reason the Liberation doctrine of complete self-reliance created a serious point of difference between the Radicals and the Romanists. Earl Grey maintained in his *Letter to John Bright, Esq., M.P.*, that a purely voluntary association could rightfully possess an endowment.

> I regard it as a palpable and dangerous fallacy to affirm, that those who require religious instruction and consolation ought to pay for it, . . . Those who stand most in need of religious instruction are precisely those who are the least willing to pay for it.[1]

Although the Roman Catholic Church did not approve of Fenianism, the movement had religious collaborators sprinkled throughout the country. The social revolt would cease only when small peasant farmers were released from the foreign control of Protestant landlords, were given tenant rights, and were permitted a more democratic representation in Parliament.

C. *Disestablishment Debates in 1868*

The House of Commons on 30 March commenced one of the great debates of the Victorian age. 'Never was our political system more severely tested,' wrote John Morley, 'and never did it achieve a completer victory.' Both sides were eager and waiting. Disraeli and Gladstone engaged in a brilliant duel of oratory – one claiming that he held his position by favour of the Crown, and the other by favour of the people.

More public interest was centred upon the debates than usual, because of the attempt by a presumed Fenian upon the life of the Duke of Edinburgh while on a Royal visit to Ireland. From the galleries several relatives of the Royal Family witnessed various stages of the proceedings – Prince Christian, Prince Louis of Hesse, and Prince Arthur.

The final verdict of the House was caught in the opening speech of Mr Gladstone, describing the Establishment as the 'kingly ghost' of Hamlet:

> We do it wrong, being so majestical,
> To offer it the show of violence;

[1] *Letter to John Bright Esq., M.P. respecting the Irish Church* (London 1868) p. 6; the letter was written on 26 March 1868.

> For it is, as the air, invulnerable,
> And our vain blows malicious mockery.

but declaring with equal fervour:

> *Venit summa dies et ineluctabile fatum.*[1]

One of the most successful speeches, as far as the Liberation Society was concerned, came from Sir John Coleridge (M.P., Exeter). He approached the question from the lawyer's point of view, showing that the Statutes of Mortmain were 'from the earliest times, notices to all mankind that the Statutes of England, and the Parliament of England, claimed to have this matter of endowments in their own hands'. He proceeded to argue that ecclesiastical property was subject to public law, that there was no principle of special immunity for Church Establishments, and that 'the union between the Irish and the English Church, in so far as it existed at all, existed in virtue of the fifth section of the Act of Union, and that "what an Act of Parliament had done, an Act of Parliament could undo".'[2]

After five days of exhausting speech-making and voluminous rhetoric, the House rejected by 330 votes to 270 an amendment of the Foreign Secretary, Lord Stanley (M.P., Lynn Regis), to wait for the new Parliament, and thus allow more time for airing the conflicting schemes. Gladstone's Disestablishment motion passed 328 votes to 272, and from this point onwards, his proposals moved quickly. In a week the three resolutions passed through Committee unopposed; also a fourth, calling for the discontinuance of the Maynooth Grant and the *Regium Donum*.

Gladstone next swiftly introduced and passed through Committee what he considered the 'natural sequel' to his resolutions – his Suspensory Established Church (Ireland) Bill, curtailing patronage and new ecclesiastical appointments. Throughout these debates on Gladstone's resolutions and Suspensory Bill, there were more frequent references to the Liberation Society than ever before.[3] The principles of the Society and the person of Mr Miall were disputed almost as keenly as the terms of the motions. Mr Bright alleged that the Church of England was not really suffering from the assaults of the Liberation Society, but from its own internal party division.[4] When Lord Elcho (M.P., Haddingtonshire) asked Bright directly to answer whether or not he was a member of the Liberation Society, he denied that he was. His Lordship then 'unmasked' the Society's programme and warned the House that it would advance considerably beyond Ireland.

Gladstone replied that among those dissatisfied with the Church of England,

[1] Hansard (3rd series), cxci, 494.

[2] E. H. Coleridge, *Life & Correspondence of John Duke, Lord Coleridge, Lord Chief Justice of England* (London 1904), ii, 72. This speech was later published by the Liberation Society.

[3] cf. Hansard (3rd series), cxci, 1649–71; cxcii, 743.

[4] J. H. Muirhead, *Nine Famous Birmingham Men* (Birmingham 1909), describes John Bright's speeches on the disestablishment of the Irish Church as 'among the noblest in the language' (p. 285).

the Liberation Society was following a perfectly open method of assault, whereas the Ritualistic and Liberal Churchmen were not. When Viscount Galway (M.P., Retford, East) challenged his claim that Miall's proposals showed understanding liberality, Gladstone answered that they were more liberal in dealing with the English Church than his own for the Irish Church. The Church of England would in effect be free to go into the world with eighty to ninety million pounds in their pockets. Personally he did not favour this idea, but he was convinced that to remove a bad Establishment was to strengthen a good one.

Disraeli followed, flatly rejected Gladstone's defence of the Society, and produced a copy of the April 8th issue of the *Nonconformist* from which he read:

> As it has been with one Establishment, so probably it will be with the others. Their time is fixed. . . . An impulse will come suddenly, and from an unanticipated quarter.[1]

In similar vein, in debate on Gladstone's Suspensory Bill, the Home Secretary, Gathorne Hardy (M.P., Oxford University) had contended that the men of the Liberation Society were 'planting their batteries on the vantage ground of this Bill with the certainty that they would ensure the fall of the Church'.

> The idea that this so called religious equality can be confined to one point of the Empire is perfectly absurd, and the men who have theories on this subject, and who have agitated them honestly, uprightly, and in a manly manner, as Mr. Miall has always done—these men, though they do not prominently put forward on all occasions their ulterior views, yet they would, if pressed, admit that what they have at heart is the destruction of all religious Establishments, and the absolute separation, or, as they call it, the liberation of religion from the control of the State.[2]

Then came the dreaded debate of the Established Church (Ireland) Bill on 26 June in the 'citadel of privilege'. Reports in the press described large crowds waiting outside the House of Lords, additional police forces on duty to prevent intrusion of unauthorized persons, and arrival of distinguished leaders of State.

The debate in the Commons had been disdained by several peers as a 'Parliamentary field day'. But the opening speech of Lord Granville depicted it rather as an 'ordered review' of serious portent. Lord Clarendon told the nobles that it would never do for the House of Lords 'to jog along by the Parliamentary train while the House of Commons travelled by express'. Lord Derby quoted the same excerpt from the *Nonconformist* used by Disraeli in debate on 1 May, but with the addition of a closing sentence which the Prime Minister had omitted:

> He [Gladstone] knows not yet whither his convictions will ultimately impel

[1] *Nonconformist*, 8.iv.68, p. 337.
[2] Hansard (3rd series), cxcii, 743.

him. . . . He may be regarded as raised up and qualified by Divine Providence for great and beneficent purposes.[1]

The Earl of Carnarvon regarded the Bill as dangerous because it would further 'ultramontane tendencies'. The Duke of Somerset ridiculed it as promoting a most confusing state of affairs – if an Established Church Bishop would be permitted to remain in his diocese under existing arrangements until his death, there would be some Prelates under the State and some living under private voluntary means. The Marquess of Salisbury asked his colleagues not to depart from the tradition in the Upper Chamber of tempering harsh legislation. The Irish, he maintained, were being offered what they did not ask for, and what would not pacify them. It was land and not Church reform for which the country's agitators were craving. Of all the monuments of conquest, the landlord, and not the Clergyman, had been foremost and most despised.

On the third night of debate, the proceedings were witnessed by several members of the Royal Family, including the Heir Apparent, and the Duke of Edinburgh, who had narrowly escaped assassination in Ireland. The Bishop of Oxford (Dr Samuel Wilberforce) was not unmindful of the Duke's presence when he urged rejection of this measure as an attempt to 'buy off assassins'. The Scottish Presbyterian Duke of Argyll maintained that the Irish Church property was 'not the property of God'. The Archbishop of York (Dr William Thomson) asserted that the consequences of such an Act would hinder the work of the blessed Gospel. Earl Russell placed over these words of his brethren the failure of the Church to promote true religion and morality in Ireland.

The Lord Chancellor, Lord Chelmsford, then spoke with great nobility for three hours. He referred to Mr Miall not unkindly, and concluded by pleading with the House to reject the Bill as an attack on sacred property, on the supremacy of the Crown, and on the interests of the Protestant Faith. According to the *Nonconformist* reporter, after the noble Lord had resumed his seat, genteel decorum gave way to prolonged Ministerial cheers and applause on the floor, accompanied by 'the action of boot-heels and umbrellas' in the galleries.

The Bill lost by 192 to 97 votes, but many felt that it had been rejected on the ground that legislation on the matter should be deferred until the country could examine the Report of the Royal Commission, and pronounce judgement at the General Election. The Report of some 600 pages was issued on 27 July 1868, and recommended economizing rather than Disestablishment. The major changes suggested were: one Archbishop instead of two; eight Bishops instead of twelve; the Primate to receive £6,000 per annum, Bishops £3,000 per annum, with £500 extra when attending Parliament; the thirty Deans and Chapters reduced to eight; two Archdeacons allotted to each Diocese instead of the existing thirty-three; suspension of appointments to benefices in the patronage of the Crown or the Episcopate where services had not been

---

[1] *Nonconformist*, 8.iv.68, p. 349.

performed within twelve months and where the membership was under forty; where Church members were fewer than 100, an additional *ad valorem* tax to be made on benefices of more than £300 per annum. The proceeds of this economy were to be placed in the hands of the Ecclesiastical Commissioners for strengthening benefices inadequately endowed.

D. *The General Election and 'Practical Suggestions'*

The Election on 16 November 1868 was a triumph for the resolutions of the new Prime Minister and the cause of a reformed Church in England. Liberationists had strained every nerve and pressed every man into service. The *Liberator* in December of that year frankly said, 'This is the Lord's doing, and it is marvellous in our eyes.'[1]

The outcome of the Election turned entirely on religious equality and the Irish Church. The great debate on whether or not Protestantism was in danger, was carefully weighed. A total of 222 Conservatives and 386 Liberals were returned, and of the latter number all but three were pledged to Irish Disestablishment. The national verdict could no longer be open to question, and even the freshly appointed Archbishop of Canterbury (Dr Archibald Tait) yielded to it.

The controversy brought in by the old Parliament had raised some difficult questions on the major operation which the new Parliament had to perform: (1) What part of the Church endowments was to be absorbed by the State, and what part left to the Church? (2) In what cases were parsonages to be handed over to the State and how much of their glebe lands was to be given up? Were Churchyards to remain the property of the nation or of the disestablished Church? (3) How long a period of time must pass before the will of the individual donor became merged in the will of the nation? (4) Who was to superintend the dividing and handing of the property over to private hands – the Imperial Government, a 'constituent Congress', or a board of Commissioners of the Irish Church? (5) What was to be done with the money given to the State? Was it to be used for educational, civil, or charitable purposes? (6) Were the liturgy and creeds and government of the Church of the past to remain that of the future?

The Liberation Society drew up a private paper with 'Practical Suggestions' bearing on these questions, which was eventually sent to the Prime Minister.[2] These undoubtedly had not a little influence upon the content of the Government Bill when it was finally framed. The first main section of the document had to do with the details of Disestablishment and the future government of the Irish Church:

First, gradual Disestablishment over a lengthened period (until the death of existing Bishops, Clergy, and functionaries) would keep the Church in a hybrid condition, partly voluntary and partly established. The political results

[1] *Liberator*, Dec. 1868, p. 205.
[2] Minutes of Executive Committee, 22.i.69.

of this would be objectionable, for if an Establishment was acknowledged to be wrong, it should be continued no longer than absolutely necessary.

Secondly, care should be taken to prevent the creation of new vested interests which would mean setting up additional claims to compensation. The operations of the Ecclesiastical Commissioners concerning the union or severance of parishes, and the re-appropriation of ecclesiastical revenues, should be suspended.

Thirdly, Disestablishment should take place at a fixed period, when the provisions of the Act would take full effect. The Crown should then cease to appoint Bishops, and the existing Bishops should no longer have seats in Parliament. The coercive powers vested in the Ecclesiastical Courts should be withdrawn. The legal rights and privileges, as also the legal disabilities of the Clergy, should be withdrawn. Everything in the shape of legal and political ascendance should come to an end, and the Irish Church should be in the position of the Church of England in the Colonies, where Churches were not established by law,

> in the same situation with any other religious body, in no better, but in no worse position, and the members may adopt, as the members of any other communion may adopt, rules for enforcing discipline within their body, which will be binding on those who expressly or by implication have assented to them.[1]

Fourthly, the fullest liberty should be given the members of the Church to determine its future organization, discipline, and administration. Individual congregations or bodies of communicants should be free to accept doctrine, articles, and canons unfettered by legislation.

The second main section of 'Practical Suggestions' concerned Disendowment and compensation:

First, two bodies of Commissioners should carry out the principles of Disendowment. One would determine the compensation to be awarded to the Clergy and the amount of property to be retained by individual incumbencies. The other body could act as the financial agent of the State, (1) by paying compensatory claims, (2) transferring to the proper parties such property as it might be agreed to hand over to the members of the Church, (3) giving requisite titles, and (4) holding the surplus property for the purposes to be determined by Parliament. In lieu of these Commissions, a special Court might be instituted – similar to the Encumbered Estates Court – to discharge both of these judicial and administrative functions.

Secondly, existing legal obligations on the Clergy should cease. Compensation should be paid to them without reference to future discharge of clerical duties, and fixed accordingly. They might then enter into fresh contract with the new Church government.

Thirdly, where there were sufficient members to render it needful, Church

---

[1] Judgement of the Judicial Committee of the Privy Council in the case of *Long v. The Bishop of Capetown*, 24 June 1863; cf. Charles Gray, *Life of Robert Gray, Bishop of Cape Town and Metropolitan of Africa* (London 1876), i, 514. See also the Society's document, 'Practical Suggestions', p. 227 below.

12

edifices should be retained by them. Churchyards should be vested in the parishioners and placed under the government of some local authority.

Fourthly, the Episcopalians of Ireland should not be entitled to retain possession of the parsonages and glebe lands, except where they had originated in private beneficence. But to avoid conflicting claims upon property created by public taxation or by individual donors, the money value of the parsonages and glebes should be given to the Church *in all cases* instead of giving the parsonages and glebes themselves.

Fifthly, compensation to Episcopalians should not involve the necessity of granting endowments to Roman Catholic and Presbyterian communities, further than the satisfaction of existing life interests.

Sixthly, the Presbyterian Minister might be compensated by converting the share of the *Regium Donum* received by him into an annuity, fixed without requiring the continued discharge of ministerial duties. The grant to Maynooth College annually paid out of the Consolidated Fund should be commuted by way of compensation for cessation of the grant.

Seventhly, no Act of Parliament bearing on the Disendowment of the Church should constitute a precedent for any future legislation interfering with the doctrine, organization, discipline, or administration of the Church. The disendowed Church should hold property subject to the jurisdiction of the ordinary courts of law, in the same way as other religious bodies.

Along with these suggestions, Miall sent a letter to the Prime Minister:

(Confidential)   Willand House, Forest Hill.
                                         Jan. 23, 1869.

Dear Mr. Gladstone,

Those with whom I have been in the habit of acting in connexion with politico-ecclesiastical questions are naturally anxious that the measure, or measures, about to be proposed to Parliament for the disestablishment of the Irish Church should be of a character which will enable them to give to the government their heartiest support. They would regard it as a great misfortune to find themselves in a position which would compel them to assume an attitude of antagonism to Her Majesty's Ministers in regard to any material portion of the scheme framed by them to give effect to the will of the nation, as expressed at the recent General Election.

Their recollections of the frankness and sincerity with which you received their representations having reference to your Bill for the Abolition of Compulsory Church Rates, and of the advantageous results of the co-operation thereby secured, encourage them to believe that you will be willing to receive in the same spirit their suggestion on a subject in which they are still more deeply interested.

They have, therefore, ventured to submit for your perusal the accompanying statement of the conclusions at which they have arrived after careful and repeated deliberations, and which have been drawn up for confidential use alone, and not with any view to publication.

Altho' they have endeavoured to express themselves with the utmost explicitness, it is possible that, in regard to certain points, you may desire further explanations, and, if it should be consistent with your sense of public duty to see two or three of us, in an informal way, and, of course, confidentially, we should have great pleasure in acquiescing in any arrangement which you may suggest for that purpose. This, however, is a matter entirely for your own consideration.

> I am, dear Mr. Gladstone,
> Your's very faithfully,
> Edward Miall.

To this he received the following reply:

(*Private*)   10 Downing St., Whitehall
                                                             Jany. 27, '69.

Dear Mr. Miall—

I thank you for your letter and for the enclosure, which I have read with much interest. I will forthwith bring it under the notice of my colleagues.

In a field so wide, it would be unwise to hazard any over-comprehensive prediction; but, after perusing this able statement, I retain the cheerful view of our relative positions which I entertained upon receiving it.

Should there be occasion, I will not fail to avail myself of your kind offer, and you will, I conceive, probably be in communication with one or more of the other Ministers. But I do not expect to have to ask more of you, or of any others, than this—that they will give their main heed to the general bases, spirit and scope of an extended legislative measure, and will not sacrifice the whole to parts, if those parts be of comparative insignificance. Even this I say, not at all in the prospect of any special disagreement, even on particulars, but simply because it is the only principle on which very large and complex measures can be justly, or successfully, dealt with.

> Believe me to be,
> Very faithfully your's,
> W. E. Gladstone.[1]

The Government was ready to deal as liberally as possible where individual interests were concerned, but less willing where institutional interests were concerned. 'Give as much as you can to persons, and not more than you must to corporations', was the guiding principle. They appeared not to wish a greater amount of pain to the Irish Anglicans than was necessary for their healing.

E. *Disestablishment Debates in 1869*

The great debate on the Irish Church Act of 1869 absorbed the attention of electors everywhere across the nation. The transaction, however, presented serious dilemmas. Earl Granville, the Liberal go-between in the Upper House, wrote on 14 February to General Grey: 'Mr Gladstone will probably show the Queen that we are between two fires',[2] i.e. the Bishops and the Radicals. The age of toleration and the age of religious equality were heading for a 'show-down' on the national political scene.

---

[1] These unpublished letters are found in Minute 228: 5.ii.69.

[2] Lord Edmond Fitzmaurice, *The Life of Granville George Leveson Gower, Second Earl Granville, K.G., 1815–1891* (London 1905), ii, 9.

The *Daily News* gave the following account of the preliminaries:[1]

When the Clerk read the title of 'The Irish Church Bill', a whole covey of members rose from the Opposition benches to present petitions against the second reading. One after another came the representatives of English and Irish constituencies – principally the latter – until the black bag that hangs at the side of the table for their reception first gaped, and was then choked, and ultimately had to be carried out by an over-weighted messenger, and replaced by an empty sack. The performance of this prelude, which passed amidst the cheers of the Conservatives, and at last excited the laughter of their opponents, occupied some time, and it was about ten minutes past five when Mr. Gladstone formally moved the second reading of the bill.

The provisions of the Irish Church Act were set forth by the Prime Minister in a speech which, as an exposition of a great legislative scheme, had never been surpassed.[2] By this Bill Gladstone inaugurated a beneficent revolution, with perhaps the most severe institutional change since the Repeal of the Test and Corporation Acts. To the Nonconformist leader, John Bright, the demands on Disendowment were at last satisfied.

. . . if I were particular on the point as to the sacred nature of the endowments, I should even then be satisfied with the propositions in this bill—for, after all, I hope it is not far from Christianity to charity; and we know that the Divine Founder of our faith has left much more of the doings of a compassionate and loving heart than He has of dogma.[3]

Free Churchmen everywhere gave unqualified support to Gladstone's proposals, rejoicing in their just and comprehensive character. The Roman Catholic *Tablet* characterized the Bill as the complement to the 1829 Emancipation Act. The *Church Times* spoke of it as the State seizing property of a corporation for the benefit of the national exchequer. The Irish Clergy put forward their 'No surrender' resolution.

The Irish Church Reform question had taken precedence over the Land Reform question, and for this Gladstone was sharply criticized. Many Irishmen had a stronger craving for attachment to their native soil than they had for removal of a foreign Church. Land had been, nevertheless, the great bulwark of the alien Establishment, enabling some landlords to keep their tenantry in subjection and their M.P.s in Parliament. Disestablishment and removal of the Protestant ascendancy would therefore weaken the motives for maintaining such a land system.

The Conservatives hoped that the Nonconformists would find cause for dissent within the Liberal majority. They knew that the point where this was

[1] quoted in *Nonconformist*, 24.iii.69, p. 271.

[2] His speech filled 55 columns in Hansard, occupied three hours and a half, and contained an inexhaustible wealth of argument. Previously, at Queen Victoria's request, Gladstone had called upon Dr Tait, the Archbishop of Canterbury, on 19 February, to discuss the forthcoming policy of the Government – 'the virtual rehearsal of his great speech'. Davidson & Benham, *Life of Tait*, ii, 11–17.

[3] William Robertson, *Life and Times of the Right Hon. John Bright* (London 1883), p. 462.

most likely to occur was in the issue centring on the Maynooth Grant and the Regium Donum. Rather than take away the grants from the Presbyterians and Roman Catholics, should not some endowment be given to place them in perfect equality with those Episcopalian priests who should be allowed to keep their parsonages and glebes? Would the corporation created to manage the Maynooth trust be dissolved, and if so, would Belfast Theological College be treated in the same way? These questions subtly played on sectarian feeling and the Conservatives prayed that Gladstone would throw an 'apple of discord' among his own followers.[1]

The Opposition did not intend giving up meekly. On the second reading on 18 March, Disraeli startled the Liberals by claiming that the Established Church was not limited to those who were in it, but that the union between Church and State was a guarantee of religious liberty and toleration to all citizens alike. Sir Roundell Palmer (M.P., Richmond) spoke of the pain he felt in crossing party lines by favouring simple Disestablishment only (abolition of political privileges), but not Disendowment (taking away property). To Spencer Walpole (M.P., Cambridge University) Disendowment was contrary to all rights of sacred property and the laws of human society. Gathorne Hardy (M.P., Oxford University) irately called the Bill the result of the Fenian movement and Roman Catholic envy.

For the Government, John Bright saw the measure giving tranquillity to the people and adding new lustre to the Throne. Edward Miall (now M.P. for Bradford) likened the wild calumnies against Mr Gladstone to those he had himself experienced. In his maiden speech, Henry Richard (M.P., Merthyr Tydfil) declared that many of the poor people of Wales had never experienced freedom from the Anglican Establishment, and he referred to Gladstone as 'the great Liberator'. The Solicitor-General, Sir John Coleridge (M.P., Exeter), reminded the House that the property of the Church was not inviolable, and that Bishop Butler himself had declared that every gift to a Christian Church was a human donation, not a divine right, and must be subject to human laws. The Chancellor of the Exchequer, Robert Lowe (M.P., London University), asserted that Disestablishment without Disendowment was impossible. If the Church were left in possession of its vast wealth without any control of the State, it would be the beginnings of a new theocracy and a return to the medieval struggle for power.

After four nights of weary debating, the second reading passed at 2.30 o'clock in the morning of 23 March, by 368 to 250 votes. Mr Gladstone wrote to Earl Granville that the majority in the division had exceeded his expectations and would 'powerfully propel the Bill'.

---

[1] When told that the Presbyterians of Scotland favoured this compensation measure of the Bill, C. N. Newdegate (M.P., Warwickshire, N.) answered that he 'could see under the gown of John Knox nothing but the spectre of the Pope of Rome'. When the Bill passed into Committee in the Lords, the Duke of Cleveland proposed a radical plan of indiscriminate endowment which would provide Roman Catholic priests and Presbyterian ministers with parsonages and ten acres of ground out of the surplus. It was not accepted.

In Committee on 16 April, the first clause of the Bill became the most hotly
disputed because it involved the question of Royal Supremacy. Disraeli
claimed that its effect was to separate religion from the Crown, and to deprive
the Church of Ireland and the Church of England of their identity under the
same Sovereign. This clause, explained Gladstone, would make the laws of the
Church still the law of the land, would thereby 're-establish' the Church in
Ireland, and place it on the same legal footing with all other Christian bodies
with freedom of organization. The Government easily defeated amendments
to overrule the working of the 39th clause which provided for equitable
compensation to Maynooth and Belfast Colleges.

Thus on 28 May the Bill with its sixty-three clauses 'glided off the stocks
without once losing its equilibrium'. Nothing depended on the third reading,
and every speech showed signs of intellectual exhaustion. After being in the
Commons from 16 April to 31 May, occupying twelve sittings, and involving
twenty divisions, the Bill went up to the Lords with the moral force of the
House of Commons behind it.

The Liberation Society rested confident that Mr Gladstone would 'not
retire in face of patrician violence'. Writing to the Birmingham Liberal
Association, John Bright threatened to introduce legislation revising the
constitution of the Upper House if it rejected the Bill. Earl Granville pacified
the angry Peers by explaining this as 'merely a display of a pugnacious
"John-Bullism" '.[1]

1. *Amendments in the Lords*

To the disciples of Liberalism this debate in the Lords was the most memorable
event since that of the Reform Bill of 1832. Disraeli in a letter to Archbishop Tait called the majority in the Commons 'mechanical' and urged his
Grace to lead the Lords in an unfaltering stand. A head-on collision between
the Houses of Parliament therefore seemed imminent.

A group of 150 Conservative lay peers assembled on 5 June at the residence
of the Duke of Marlborough for the purpose of affirming their determination
to resist the Bill. Lords Derby, Cairns, and Harrowby pressed for thorough
and obstinate resistance. A minority led by Lords Stanhope, Salisbury, and
Carnarvon favoured an allowance of the second reading, but serious alteration
in Committee. Another private meeting was called at Lambeth Palace shortly
before the debate to seek out the mind of the spiritual Peers of the realm.
Under the sober advice of the Archbishop of Canterbury, who had consulted
with the Queen, the second strategy prevailed[2] in spite of painful appeals from
his friends 'in Christ's holy name to spare our feelings, and to save us from the
taunts of the wicked, by abstaining from sanctioning this ungodly measure'.

---

[1] Fitzmaurice, op. cit., ii, 12.

[2] cf. letter to Gladstone from Granville, who spoke of the good fortune to have at this
time an archbishop 'as little prejudiced as Dr Tait. With either Sumner or Longley [his
predecessors] we should have been shipwrecked, for without the consent of the English
prelates the Lords would not have given way' (Fitzmaurice, op. cit., ii, 14–15).

Another friend wrote: 'It fills our hearts with utter dismay to think of the possibility that the Prelates of the English branch of the Church should at once desert their Irish brethren.'[1]

Earl Granville calmly presented the measure to the Lords as unquestionably for the good of the nation. All through the various stages of this Bill in the Commons there had been few derogatory references to the Liberation Society. But in the Upper Chamber, still smarting under the burning words of Bright in his public letter, the familiar denunciations were renewed. The Earl of Harrowby suspected the mission of the Liberation Society to Ireland of subversive designs, as the compact made with the Irish National Association under the guidance of O'Neill Daunt clearly showed. The Foreign Secretary, Lord Clarendon, replied that there was no direct understanding with the Liberation Society in formulating the Bill. The Earl of Derby hoped that in the Upper House there were none 'with whom the cry of justice to Ireland was accompanied by some whistle to the Liberation Society over the hedge'. He was sure, however, that the Government had capitulated to the wishes of the members of the Liberation Society because of their support in the recent General Election. He called Mr Bright the *alter ego* of Mr Miall, and through the former the Society had connexion with the Cabinet. Again the Earl of Clarendon denied that there had been any close relationship between the private counsels of the Government and the Liberation Society. Unconvinced, Lord Westbury attacked the Bill as 'the fortuitous concurrence of intellectual atoms, being the joint production of Her Majesty's Government and the Liberation Society'.

The division took place on 19 June after four consecutive nights of debating, and until the last moment the result remained quite uncertain. At three o'clock in the morning before a packed House the vote was read: 179, content with the second reading; 146, non-content. Lords Salisbury and Dufferin, the Duke of Argyll, and the Marquess of Lansdowne were among those voting for the Bill. Bishop Thirlwall of St David's was the only prelate supporting the act of Disestablishment. The Archbishops of Canterbury and York (Tait and Thomson) did not vote, retiring behind the bar.

When the Bill went into Committee, the pivotal question for the Church was, Can we save the endowments, and if not all, how many? As expected, the Lords aimed at recovering for the Disestablished Church, from the Established, a greater part of the property which the Bill devoted to national purposes. Many of the Churchmen were prepared to bear the ordeal of Disestablishment, but not the humiliation of relying upon the voluntary principle. The Archbishop of Canterbury wrote to the Queen that unless the new Church could have £3,000,000 'to float' itself upon, it meant to throw over the Bill. The amendments, however, asked for much more than that:

1. The bill as passed by the House of Commons deprived the Church of all political privileges not enjoyed by the members of other religious bodies.

[1] Davidson & Benham, op. cit., ii, 28-9.

The Lords resolved that the existing Irish Bishops should continue to sit in Parliament, though they would no longer represent an Established Church.

2. The Bill secured to the Bishops and Clergy fixed annuities equal to their present incomes, but allowed them to commute the amounts, according to the value of each life interest, with a view to the payment of the commutation to the representative body of the Church. The Lords provided that all the Annuities should be commuted, and at fourteen years' purchase. This change, it was estimated, would endow the Church with an additional £1,200,000.

3. The Bill provided that, in calculating the value of the Annuities to be received by the Clergy, the salaries paid to their Curates, and the payments which lessened their present incomes, should all be deducted. The Lords determined that the Clergy should have compensation for the salaries which they paid to their Curates, and the Curates should receive compensation for the same sums. The Clergy were also to be compensated for taxes and payments which were then deducted from their incomes. This change, it was estimated, would give an additional £1,000,000 to the Church.

4. The Bill not only gave to the Church all Church edifices, but all the parsonages with the gardens attached, on repayment to the State of either the amount of money borrowed for building, or of ten times the value of the sites, whichever sum might be smaller. The Lords gave the parsonages and glebes to the Roman Catholic and Presbyterian Clergy. This was estimated to be a grant of an additional £152,000 to the Church.

5. The Bill allowed the Church to retain all the private endowments which had come into its possession since 1660. The Lords added all the endowments dating one hundred years further back, together with the Royal grants, or Ulster glebes. These changes, it was estimated, gave more than an additional £1,000,000 to the Church.

6. That the Irish Church controversy might be finally closed, the Bill provided that the surplus property should be applied 'for the advantage of the Irish people', and 'for the relief of unavoidable calamity and suffering', but 'not for the maintenance of any Church or Clergy, or other ministry, nor for the teaching of religion'. The Lords struck out these words of the preamble and enacted that Parliament should determine thereafter on the appropriation of such surplus. And they did this, among other reasons, 'in the hope that the surplus may ultimately be applied to the endowment of various religious denominations in Ireland'.

7. Gladstone estimated the total proceeds of the Church property at approximately sixteen millions, and the amount of compensation given by the Bill at £8,650,000, and the surplus at £7,350,000. The Lords, it was calculated, gave between four and five millions additional to the Church, and thereby reduced the surplus to about three millions. This surplus, they suggested, should also be applied to ecclesiastical purposes.[1]

In spite of this 'bountiful softening of the blow', the third reading was heatedly contested and passed by only 121 to 114 votes. Protests were signed by sixty peers stating their reasons for dissent, and were officially registered in the annals of the Upper House.

[1] Statements from a special white paper in the files of the Liberation Society: 'How the Lords have amended the Irish Church Bill'.

Gladstone declared that the mutilating amendments of the Lords meant 'war to the knife'. The Society went into a fury of protest against 'the manœuvres to create a wealthy ecclesiastical corporation', and urged meetings at every possible level to register disapproval. At a joint meeting with the Dissenting Deputies, strong objections were made to the amendments as (1) provoking religious inequality, (2) unjust to the Irish people, and (3) substituting a system of 'glebing all round'.

The Lords temporal and spiritual now faced the danger of flouting the will of the nation in the General Election and starting a far worse campaign against the Church of England. Many Peers, however, defended their action on the ground of the infinite value in the union of Church and State as (1) affording an eminent platform for spreading moral principles in a society of luxury and decadence, and (2) opening the way for the influence of Christianity upon the higher thought of modern nations. The Archbishop of Canterbury prayed that in the anxious time before them their minds might be kept calm.

2. *Final Settlement*

After five nights in Committee in 'the place of the peers', the Bill came back to the Commons. In a single sitting on 15 and 16 July it was restored to its former state by large majorities. The preamble, which would distribute the £16,000,000 of property 'not for the maintenance of any Church or Clergy, nor for the teaching of religion, but mainly for the relief of unavoidable calamity and suffering', was restored by 346 to 222 votes. The postponement of the surplus was rejected by 256 to 164 votes. Gladstone's uncompromising speech to the accompaniment of lusty Radical cheers showed the unbending temper of the Commons. The Lords, he snapped, had been as far out of touch with the feeling of the country as if they were 'living in a balloon'.

They were not moved. By a vote of 173 to 95 on 22 July, they insisted on their alteration of the preamble. Suffering from illness, and under severe strain over these events, the Prime Minister was now disposed to throw up the Bill. He was, however, outvoted in his Cabinet, and Lord Granville threatened to resign from leadership of the party in the House of Lords if he did surrender.

When it seemed most likely that the measure would be shipwrecked, a way out was found. On learning that the Government was prepared to concede something, the Opposition was found to be willing to yield considerably more – so much more that many in the Irish Church declared that they had been betrayed. The final bargaining was settled privately between Lord Cairns and Earl Granville on 4 August in the Colonial Office.

The Government agreed to allow the preamble to stand as the Lords wished.[1] The date of Disestablishment fixed by the Commons was adopted. The additional private endowments, the Ulster glebes, and the Clerical tax were quietly given up by the Lords. The Government modified the provisions

---

[1] But words were inserted in the 68th clause, prohibiting the use of the surplus for other than secular purposes ('the relief of unavoidable calamity and suffering'). See Morley, *Life of Gladstone*, i, 681–2.

as to commutation and the Curates. The claims insisted upon by the Lords for concurrent endowment and for ecclesiastical residence to the Clergy free of charge, were surrendered. The net result of the amending action of the Lords was an additional £1,000,000 more than the original Commons estimate for the new Church, and the assertion of the power of the Upper House by postponing legislation in regard to the surplus. The remainder of the Commons' re-amendments were accepted.

At the very end, the Archbishop of Canterbury praised a sober religion supported by endowments and denounced the voluntary principle as 'pandering to the passions of the people'. The House of Commons had heard enough. On 23 July it wearily agreed to the Bill, which on 26 July received the Royal Assent. Peace returned to Parliament and the country sighed with relief. The final motion was complex:

> Resolved, That this House doth not insist upon its disagreement to the Amendments insisted upon by the Lords; and doth agree to the Amendments made by the Lords to the Amendments made by the Commons to the Amendments made by the Lords, and to the consequential Amendment to the said Bill.[1]

Briefly, the major effects of the compromises were:

1. On 1 January 1871, the Irish Church would 'cease to be established by law'.
2. The offensive words in the preamble were struck out.
3. The glebe-houses with their curtilages would be purchased, as the Bill originally provided, not given.
4. The conditions on which the Annuities were given to the Clergy in compensation for their vested interests would be commuted.
5. The salaries of Curates would be deducted from the Annuities of incumbents only in cases in which income tax had been paid upon that basis of calculation for the five preceding years.
6. The Ulster glebes would be retained by the Nation.[2]

So the impossible was done. For a while, some swan-songs of 'The Church is gone' were heard. But the majority of Churchpeople regarded the whole affair as another milestone in the march of democratic principles. The Liberation Society leaders acknowledged in a special minute that it had not been their doing alone:

---

[1] Hansard (3rd series), cxcviii, 592.

[2] cf. *Nonconformist*, 28.vii.69, p. 705, giving the following summary: '. . . the whole property of that Church has already become vested in the Commissioners appointed by the Act, subject to compensatory annuities to the Episcopal and Presbyterian clergy whose life interests it guarantees, to the grant of all Church edifices and furniture, of all the parsonages and their appurtenances, of 500,000*l*. in lieu of private endowments, and of twelve per cent. upon the commutation of three-fourths of clerical annuities in each diocese, whenever that commutation shall have been effected, to the Church Body hereafter to be constituted; subject also to payment of fourteen years' purchase in the place of the endowment granted to Maynooth College. Over the appropriation of the surplus which the Act mainly devotes to charitable purposes ["to the relief of unavoidable calamity and suffering"] Parliament will exercise direct supervision.'

The Committee desire to express their strong and lasting sense of obligation to the Right Honourable William Ewart Gladstone, M.P., for the courage and decision with which he undertook the settlement of this great controversy; the distinguished ability, and the conscientious consideration, with which he has grappled with its difficulties, and the unswerving adherence to right principles which has marked his conduct of the measure which has now become law. They have also regarded with admiration the efficient aid afforded to the Prime Minister by his colleagues in both Houses of Parliament, as well as the ardour and fidelity with which the Government has been supported by the Liberal party in the House of Commons.[1]

To this the Prime Minister responded:

11 Carlton House Terrace,
Aug. 6, 1869.

My dear Sir—

I am much indebted to you and to the Committee on behalf of which you act, both for the frank and firm support you have afforded to the Government and myself, and for the more than kind acknowledgement of our exertions which you have forwarded.

We and the Committee may not be, and we are not, at one in our abstract or general views of Church Establishments, but we have acted cordially together on broad and intelligent grounds where we agreed, and we shall, I am sure, continue to respect each other when we may differ.

I remain, my dear Sir;
Faithfully your's,
W. E. Gladstone.[2]

---

[1] Parl. Com. Min., 4.viii.69.

[2] For this unpublished letter, together with those of John Bright and Earl Granville, see Minute 351: 17.ix.69.

CHAPTER 13

Church Taxes

> Do not let us deny the good and the happiness which they
> [the modern Puritans] have accomplished; but do not let
> us fail to see clearly that their idea of human perfection is
> narrow and inadequate, and that the dissidence of Dissent
> and the Protestantism of the Protestant religion will never
> bring humanity to its true goal.
>
> MATTHEW ARNOLD[1]

> It is true that . . . our fathers did not build places of worship
> with graceful spires, and columns crowned with clustering
> beauty, and windows rich with purple and gold; they did
> not feel secure enough in their liberties to invest their
> money in buildings, of which new political convulsions
> might deprive them.
>
> ROBERT W. DALE[2]

AT THE BEGINNING of this period, the opponents of the Liberation Society were able to maintain the existing law on Church Rates. As the law stood and as time passed, however, it operated confessedly more to the detriment of the Establishment. Therefore in this matter, far better than in others, the Society was now willing to await the pleasure of Parliament.

To Liberationists there was no better arena for the discussion of their principles than the Parish vestries, and no greater source of strength than the continuance of parochial contests in the law courts. To Churchmen, apart from open violence and sedition, there was no lower form of political action.

The principle of Voluntaryism, despite its vindication, presented a problem to non-established Clergy, for it often meant reliance upon the support of wealthy individuals in the congregation. This sometimes led to a subtle form of patronage and control. A Pastor who wished to admonish his people strongly had to face the possibility that those who supported him could force him out of office.

---

[1] *The Cornhill Magazine*, July 1867, p. 46: from 'Culture and its Enemies', Arnold's lecture in the Chair of Poetry at Oxford, being mainly a reply to Frederic Harrison.

[2] From his lecture, 'Churchmen and Dissenters . . .', in A. W. W. Dale, *Life of R. W. Dale*, p. 170.

The pulpit's laws the pulpit's patrons give
And those who live to preach must preach to live.[1]

A. *Revised Strategies*

Because of the rejection of the third reading of the Abolition Bill in 1861 by the margin of the Speaker's vote, and because of growing impatience in the House with the behaviour of the Abolitionists, the Society's Executive Committee called for a change of strategy at the opening of the 1862 session.[2] Instead of pressing for an early division as expected, the Bill would be introduced but the second reading delayed. This would force its opponents either to come forward with their own reform measure, or to demonstrate the futility of further resistance to Abolition.

Throughout the 1862 session, the chief object of the Society in Parliament was to avoid the risk of 'mischievous defeats', but at the same time to elicit more facts and to prompt more meetings, and the national Bicentenary commemoration of the ejectment on St Bartholomew's Day was to afford a 'strong talking point'. A maximum effort was to be made with publications, slanted to the Anglicans, which should deal with the success of Voluntaryism in the Church, the 'Offertory Movement', and the testimonials of several well-known Churchmen. The hope was to convert active opposition into neutrality, and neutrality into support.

The Church Rate Abolition Committee of the Dissenting Deputies and the Society endorsed the above strategy, and furiously rallied the support of the bodies represented to it. Abolitionists and Liberationists were determined to erase the humiliating defeat of the previous division in the Commons.

On the eve of the expected victory, 8 May, a large number of leading Nonconformists gathered in Freemasons' Hall, where a testimonial of £5,000 inscribed with 1,500 names, together with a handsome silver and coffee service, was presented to Edward Miall. After refreshments the guests listened to speeches acknowledging his labours towards the relief of this grievance and his leadership of Nonconformity.

Church Rates had now become the great political puzzle of the day. Many wondered whether the Bicentenary marking the rejection of religious uniformity in 1662 would finally lead to an end of the compulsory ecclesiastical tax in 1862. But six more years were to pass before a successful solution was reached. During that time large Houses were on hand for full dress debates on the issue.

One of these, on 14 May 1862,[3] had some particularly dramatic moments. Introducing his Bill, Sir John Trelawny (M.P., Tavistock) assured the opponents that its supporters were not enemies, but friends anxious to see the

[1] S. N. Kingdon, *A Lecture on the Voluntary System as a Means for Supporting the Christian Church* (London 1868), p. 8.

[2] Special paper, 'Parliamentary Action in 1862', contained in special minutes, 5.ii.62; cf. also *British Quarterly Review*, January 1862: 'Distinctive claims of the Dissenters upon the Liberal Party'.

[3] Hansard (3rd series), clxvi, 1674–1727: cf. *Nonconformist*, 21.v.62.

Church on a stable, self-supporting foundation. Sir George Lewis (M.P., Radnor), the Secretary of State for War, although preferring a system of pew rents, accepted the voluntary alternative. The principal speech came from John Bright (M.P., Birmingham) who received rapt attention as usual from both sides of the House. 'The apostle of Nonconformity' asked the Conservatives if they were afraid that Churchmen would not maintain their places of worship, 'wash surplices, keep their churches clean, and do everything which the most humble congregations of the Primitive Methodists in this country do for their chapels'. There was little tolerance in the Toleration Act if it only amounted to saying, 'Walk out of our Church if you like; go to what chapel you like, but still you shall contribute to the support of a form of worship which you do not approve.' Concerning the Liberation Society, which had been an object of scorn in several opposing speeches, he said that it was

> . . . a frightful object—I do not know whether in the nightly dreams, but, at all events, in the waking visions, of honourable gentlemen opposite. It has been greatly abused in this House—most undeservedly and unjustly so. It is an honest society, with earnest men, working for what they believe to be good, and therefore, however much you may abuse it, it is not to be despised.

For the Opposition, Sotheron Estcourt (M.P., Wiltshire N.) reviewed the major measures that had been proposed, believing they might be combined in one to transfer liability for the Church Rate from occupiers to owners, and to repeal the existing legal process for a compulsory rate in favour of a voluntary one. In a 'crescendo' speech with a vengeance, Disraeli (M.P., Buckinghamshire) hit at Bright indirectly by accusing the Government of betraying Cabinet secrets through certain of its members to the Liberation Society. Sir John Pakington (M.P., Droitwich) believed that although Lord Russell had changed his vote in favour of Abolition on the previous division, he had not changed his principles. To Sir John, the Liberation Society sought not relief from payment of a rate, but destruction of the Church, which he sought to prove by quoting a passage from Miall's pen:

> The Church of England is an image carved with marvellous cunning, tricked out in solemn vestments, a part woven by human fancy, a part stolen from the chest of truth. . . . An attention to rites for the performance of which fees may be exacted – heartless formality – a blind, unreasoning, ignorant superstitious obedience to the priesthood – payment of tithes and Easter-offerings and Church-rates – these are the great objects of our Establishment. To shatter this image, and give the dust of it to the four winds of heaven . . . is the sacred mission of Protestant Dissenting Ministers.

No one in the House rose to defend these bitter sentiments. The report of what followed was graphically written by the correspondent of the *Nonconformist*.

> The question was then put. Clearly the lungs of Liberal members must have improved if we may judge from the Speaker's decision that the 'Ayes' had it.

'Strangers must withdraw' was the signal for clearing out the seats below the Speaker's gallery; and the outgoing and incoming tide struggled for a moment or two in the lobby. The bells tingled furiously, as though the Palace of Westminster were on fire, and the stream of members poured from all sides into the lobby. Some time before the doors were banged to, the current had ceased to flow. There were no stragglers – not even an Irishman clamouring for admittance. . . .

Hastening to the reporters' gallery for a view of the division scene, we found the floor and benches of the House deserted, with the exception of the tellers and officials, though not a seat was vacant in the Speaker's or Strangers' gallery. The tellers soon left on their exciting errand. . . . 'We shall poll 285, and have a majority of from three to five', we heard a Conservative member complacently remark about five o'clock, and the downcast face of Sir Charles Douglas corroborated the surmise. Slowly the members returned to their seats, blocked up the bar, filled the lobby beyond, and overflowed into the side galleries. Lord Palmerston, as he emerged from the 'Aye' lobby, and walked firmly but unconcernedly to his seat, attracted special attention. Anon there was a buzz of excitement, then audible whispers of 'Another tie', and at last a ringing Opposition cheer as the paper was handed to Colonel Taylor, and the tellers advanced with many bows to the table. For some moments the Tory whipper-in essayed in vain to speak amid the prolonged shouts of triumph from his friends. At length silence was restored, and he read out the numbers – Noes, 287. Ayes, 286.[1]

It was a galling moment for Sir John Trelawny and Sir Charles Douglas who had laboured together hopefully. The Society had gained little by refraining from their usual custom of pressing M.P.s to fulfil this election pledge. Nevertheless, even in defeat Abolitionists were congratulating themselves that there had been a larger number of votes favouring the measure than in any previous division.

The next year on 29 April, the majority against the Abolitionists was more decisive – 275 to 285 votes – and there was no longer a mood for congratulation. Instead certain Liberationists were accused of having become 'waverers and trimmers'. The Church Rate debate again became the debate of the session and the Liberation Society again became one of its foremost themes. The Liberal Ministry was accused of not desiring a settlement of this question, in order to have a red flag to wave before the constituencies at the next General Election. The Conservative opposition was accused of preventing the solution in order 'to sting and inflame Dissenters like moral mosquitoes'. The *Liberator* for May 1863 contained reports of nearly forty Church Rate contests and law suits handled by Liberation lawyers during the previous month.[2]

In his speech of introduction, Sir Charles Douglas (M.P., Banbury) asserted that his was not a Bill of the Liberation Society, but a remedy based on the Voluntary principle. He explained that the majorities for Abolition had

[1] *Nonconformist*, 21.v.62, p. 462.

[2] The Executive Committee decided to furnish legal assistance to parties threatened with criminal proceedings for non-payment of Church Rates. John Bennett had been hired in the previous year as the Society's chief legal adviser in this matter. Minutes 297: 13.xi.63; 307: 11.xii.63; 417: 9.ix.64.

decreased, because it was no longer an 'open question' – since 1860, when the Liberal Cabinet had been divided on the question, the Conservatives had made it a party issue. Again, when the votes had been declared, a deafening burst of cheers from the Opposition benches announced the defeat of the Bill. Sir John Trelawny soon afterwards served notice of relinquishing co-sponsorship of the proposals, and Dr C. J. Foster, chairman of the Parliamentary Committee, tendered his resignation from the Society. Whether the Society liked it or not, these incidents were a worrying blow to the *morale* of its supporters, and so the Abolition Bill was not introduced in the Commons again until 1866.

To safeguard against further legislative defeats until the disposition of the Commons was more favourable, the Society introduced to the country an 'Electoral Policy' with a new mode of political action. It urged an attitude of 'passive resistance' to the designs of the Palmerston-Russell Government. It called upon Liberation Electors throughout the country to get pledges of support from candidates, or not to vote for them at Election time. The effect of this policy was (1) to force the Liberal party to accept Church Rates and Liberation grievances as official party questions, and (2) to transfer the brunt of attack from Parliament to the parishes.

The advances of the Conservatives in the divisions of 1861, 1862 and 1863 led many of them to boast that abolition was doomed and that compromise was inevitable. In that spirit, the Attorney-General, Sir Roundell Palmer (M.P., Richmond), introduced in 1864 a Church Building Acts Consolidation Bill, making inhabitants of new parishes liable to the repair costs of the churches. It succeeded in drawing the Nonconformists back into the heat of debate on the sore topic.

In protest against the Bill, a joint Committee was convened with representation from the Dissenting Deputies, the Church Rate Abolition Committee, and the Liberation Society. They considered plans for obtaining in the Select Committee the insertion of a clause prohibiting the levy of rates for churches in new parishes. An interdenominational meeting denouncing the new form of 'the darling tax' was held at Fendall's Hotel in Westminster. Shortly after, on 31 May, a deputation consisting of twenty-eight M.P.s and twenty other representatives of nine Dissenting bodies waited upon Lord Palmerston (having previously waited on the Attorney-General), acquainting him with the feelings of the Joint Committee. The result was the withdrawal of the Bill by the Attorney-General, Sir Roundell Palmer, on 9 June.

One other event in 1864 aroused the Church Rate question out of its temporary dormancy. Mr (later Sir) John Coleridge, the Liberal candidate for Exeter, was rejected in the by-election by the abstention of Nonconformists because he would not support total Abolition. The defeat created a considerable impression in high party circles.

B. *Moderation Moves*

Then came the General Election of 1865 and the awaited change in Government. On 17 November 1865, Carvell Williams wrote that the Parliamentary initiative of the Society during the first session of the newly elected House would be limited to the abolition of Rates, 'to which we are morally bound'. It was thus decided to move slowly, partly in order to find a leader for the Bill in place of Sir Charles Douglas who had lost his seat for Banbury. After several unsuccessful attempts, Mr J. A. Hardcastle, a Churchman and M.P. for Bury St Edmunds, accepted the responsibility.

The sting of the Church Rate system had always been its authorization of an ultimate resort to compulsion in making provision for divine worship in the Established Church. In the debate of 1866, it was clear to those who were offended that Hardcastle's measure was a sure remedy. Neither commutation nor exemption were any longer serious alternatives. On this occasion Mr Gladstone, who was eventually to cut the knot, first voted for Abolition.

Previous to the introduction of Hardcastle's Bill, a total of thirty-six attempts had been made to settle the question, and twenty divisions had taken place – the smallest number of members voting had been 395, and the largest 577. Hardcastle believed it was now time that Parliament came to a solution, and that such could be found by abolishing compulsory rates and substituting voluntary subscription.[1]

During the course of this debate 'the ghostly spectre of the Liberation Society' ceased to appal the minds of the Opposition, with one exception. Mr C. DuCane (M.P., North Essex) described it as an agency impatiently awaiting the downward extension of the suffrage – soon to be proposed – in order to renew its attacks on the Church and effect more drastic changes. He believed that if these Rates were abolished the Society would not by any means 'rest and be thankful'.

Gladstone, now member for South Lancashire, but still Chancellor of the Exchequer, remonstrated that the implication of these words was, 'The Church is safe within these walls so long as you keep the nation out of them' – a *mot* which was enthusiastically received by the Nonconformists. With even greater emphasis, however, he declared that he could never support the 'simple', that is to say, unconditional abolition of Church Rates. This would throw the needs of the rural Churches completely upon their Clergy and subject them to financial hardship. He was willing to support the Bill if there were added in Committee three clauses – these, he felt, involved but a small sacrifice on the part of the Church:

1. That the legal right of determining the appropriation of subscriptions or voluntary payments for ecclesiastical purposes be confined exclusively to those who have contributed to the fund.
2. That the parochial machinery be left as it is that it may be worked by voluntary energy and liberality.

[1] He showed that in 1772 there were 1,160 chapels in England; in 1850, nearly 20,000. In 1865 the total sum collected by annual voluntary subscriptions among Dissenting bodies for Ministers' salaries, support of schools, repairs, etc., was £3,000,000. As a Churchman, he thought his Church could easily likewise raise the £250,000 which was supplied by the Church Rate. Cf. *Nonconformist*, 14.iii.66, p. 207.

13

3. That those declining contribution to the fund substituted for the rate, be charged a higher fee for burial in the Church yard.[1]

The main Opposition speech came from Spencer H. Walpole (M.P., Cambridge University), an effective spokesman in view of his position as an Ecclesiastical Commissioner and former Home Secretary under Lord Derby. He contended that Church Rates was no longer a religious objection, but a political one. He made good use of the local taxation returns for 1865, which, according to his analysis, revealed that Church Rates were refused in only 10 per cent of the 12,074 parishes. Although Dissenters firmly challenged the truth of these facts, he confidently stated that there was no overwhelming evidence to show parishioners unwilling to keep their own churches in serviceable condition. With the exception of £1,000,000 at the end of the French Revolutionary War, Parliament had never granted anything to the Church. The fact that her grants had resulted from private voluntary donations indicated that the voluntary principle needed endowments behind it to work permanently.

John Bright (M.P., Birmingham) thundered that compromise was absolutely impossible. He had the satisfaction of seeing in the measure before the House the substance of what he had proposed four years previously – abolition of the intervention of the magistrates, the summons, and the bailiffs. The measure was for the benefit, not the harm of the Church of England. He then paid tribute to the Established Church, which he hoped might live as long as it could convey the truth of religion and teach the morality of the New Testament to a humble member of the community. The response of the House to this was a moment of great personal triumph for Mr Bright.

In a fiery maiden speech Samuel Morley (M.P., Nottingham) vindicated the evidence which he and Dr Foster, as members of the Liberation Society, had given before the Lords' Select Committee. Disraeli followed with a terse summary, admonishing the House to see behind Gladstone's diverting ideas to the real issue. The House then divided. The result was announced, 285 for the second reading and 252 against it. It was the Abolitionists' and Liberationists' turn to cheer in the Commons. Conservatives and Churchmen, however, went away consoled by the fact that they still had a House of Lords.

Although Gladstone's clauses appeared to put Church Rates directly on a voluntary basis, the Parliamentary Committee of the Society was cautious – at first withholding opinion until actually seeing the final proposal in print. John Bennett, the Society's legal adviser, laid a copy of the drafted Government Bill before Counsel, to obtain an opinion on its effect on the rights of parishioners. In the opinion by Sir James Parker Deane and Dr J. Freeman Norris, both of the Temple,

the effect of the clauses would not be to deprive the parishioners of certain rights, and of no other common law rights; while the rights of disqualification

[1] Hansard (3rd series), clxxxi, 1667.

could at any time be recovered by the payment of three years arrears of voluntary rates.[1]

With the apparent abandonment of 'compulsory exactions' the way was clear for the Liberation Society to urge support of the Government Bill. At the annual Council meeting, on 5 May 1866, Mr Miall declared that Gladstone's proposals did not involve a compromise of their grievance. The Council thus passed a motion 'sincerely desiring a joint settlement of this long debated question' which, while acceptable to Episcopalians, 'shall not violate the rights of Christian willinghood'.

Meanwhile, the Society conducted inquiries on the extent to which 'voluntary' Church Rates were being levied. Replies were received from 1,500 parishes, 284 of which were given in the Local Taxation Returns as levying Church Rates, although not enforced. Of the remainder, the report showed 900 parishes in which Rates were abolished, 200 parishes in which expenses were met by endowments, and 150 parishes in which the Rate was compulsory. The Annual Report for 1867 showed that out of 9,186 parishes making a return in 1864, there were 4,912 which did not make a Church Rate that year. The facts were placed in the hands of Mr Hardcastle to use at his discretion.

The Liberal Government was defeated on 4 July 1866, in a Committee division on the Reform Bill, and the Russell Ministry resigned. When the Conservatives came into office with Disraeli as the new Chancellor of the Exchequer, the Liberation Society promptly asked that Gladstone proceed with his Bill. Whereupon Hardcastle withdrew his Bill, reserving the right to re-introduce it.

When Gladstone introduced the second reading of his Compulsory Church Rates Abolition Bill on 18 July, a curious thing happened, more amusing than distressing to the Abolitionists. Shortly before the debate the former Chancellor of the Exchequer had word from the Government that it received his proposal in a 'conciliatory spirit' and would not therefore oppose the second reading, but it probably would propose amendments in Committee. This was on the understanding that no further proceedings should be taken after the second reading during that session, in order to consider fully the details of a satisfactory solution in the following session. Some skilled Parliamentarians saw this as a delaying manœuvre to enable Disraeli to avoid the certain defeat of the new Government. Newspapers such as the *Daily Telegraph* stated that Disraeli had played 'a very cunning card' but that he would have to 'finesse even when his cards are laid upon the table'. In the long game, Gladstone's hand seemed to be gaining more strength.

> We fear that the only real objection to Mr. Gladstone's Bill is that it was Mr. Gladstone's, together with the natural perverseness of the human heart when after long strife it is offered terms of peace.[2]

Gladstone's motion was therefore talked out by the Conservatives and fell

[1] Their statements are recorded in full in Executive Committee Minutes, iv, 372: 24.v.67.
[2] *Spectator*, 21.vii.66, p. 791.

into the position of a dropped order. Because of the lateness of the session, there was no chance of renewed debate.

At the Church Congress in Wolverhampton in 1867, Lord Lyttelton led a discussion on the best means of bringing Nonconformity into union with the Church. In the same year, however, Mr P. A. Taylor (M.P., Leicester) forwarded a petition from James Brighton Grant, a prisoner in the pauper ward of the debtor's prison, Whitecross Street, London, which concluded:

> Your petitioner therefore prays your Honourable House to pass such laws as will make it impossible for one religious order to claim supremacy over the others by making them pay towards the expenses of its worship, so that your petitioner may be the last person imprisoned for resisting a Church Rate.[1]

C. *Abolition Victories*
'Due to an unfavourable reception of Mr Gladstone's Bill by those whom it was intended to conciliate', Mr Hardcastle re-introduced his measure at the opening session in 1867. Because of this, Gladstone withheld putting forward a separate measure, and voted for Hardcastle's Bill – with the insertion of additional clauses which

> authorize the assessment of voluntary rates, and the payment of voluntary contributions, for the purposes to which Church-rates are now applicable, and also give those who furnish such funds exclusive control over the expenditure.[2]

Thus, on 20 March, Hardcastle's Bill was read a second time by 263 to 187 votes. This being the largest majority recorded in its favour, the end of the issue was now clearly ahead.

In contrast to others, this debate had been uninteresting, and little that had been said was really new. Hardcastle contended that if a Clergyman lived in the affection of his people as he ought to do, he would find no difficulty in raising the sum necessary for repair of his church. Mr Beresford-Hope (M.P., Stoke-on-Trent) said that Nonconformity was fast becoming a second Establishment of England – a far thing from its original position in society – and that it should now be satisfied. Gladstone challenged Walpole's charge of 'sentimental objections' to a 'rightful tax' which was on property and not on persons. This was a most crucial point for persons not members of the Church of England, said Gladstone, and the moment Mr Walpole consented to exempt the Dissenter from an inherited charge on his estate, it became useless for him to defend Church Rates as a charge on property.

Because of the lateness of the hour and the smallness of the House, the Bill was rushed through Committee on 25 June without serious alteration, and on

---

[1] At Croydon, in 1867, when the old parish church was burned down, 'the vicar and the chairman of the Anti-Church Rate Party agreed in proposing that there should be no rate but a voluntary subscription, and the Congregational minister promised Nonconformist support. "Is not this", asked Mr. Miall, "a great deal better than sending round a bellman to advertise the seized goods of Quakers?" ' Addison, op. cit., p. 116.

[2] Report of Executive Committee, 1867; quoted in *Liberator*, May 1867, p. 75.

24 July the third reading passed by 129 to 99 votes. Although the country was preoccupied with heated Reform (Parliamentary representation) legislation, the hopes of the Abolitionists that this Bill would pass by the Lords unnoticed proved vain.

The House of Lords showed no more elasticity than it had with previous Church Rate Bills. The defence of the measure by Earl Morley, who introduced it on 8 August, Earl Russell, and Lord Taunton, was not as impressive as that afforded in the Commons. The presence of the measure without the caution clauses which Gladstone had made the condition of his support, made it even less attractive to the Peers. Here again the cry of Liberationists for religious equality was overruled by the call of the Church of England for supremacy. The Archbishop of Canterbury (Dr Charles Longley) declared that the Establishment rather than the Church was in danger. He warned that the opponents would follow up this question immediately to deprive the possessors of tithes, and to separate the Church from the State.

The Lords therefore rejected the second reading by 24 to 82 votes, without, however, ruling out the possibility of 'a fair compromise' in another session. The Church party in both Houses was pressing hard to save as much as possible in the existing law. Gladstone accordingly gave notice that in the next session he would bring forth without fail a satisfactory Abolition Bill. The Society's Executive Committee was not particular which of the two Bills eventually passed – Gladstone's or Hardcastle's – for the voluntary principle was definitely vindicated in both.

The measure introduced by Gladstone in the 1868 session was not without objectionable features. Thus, in a special report of the Parliamentary Committee, the Society gave its judgement:

> Inasmuch as the preamble of the Bill affirms that it is expedient that 'the power to compel payment of Church Rates by any legal process should be abolished', it seems to the Committee to be inconsistent with the spirit of the Bill that it should create a Contract for the payment of a voluntary rate and permit the enforcement of such Contract in a court of Law.

Consequently, a deputation consisting of Messrs Miall, Edwards, Williams, and Hardcastle, together with representatives of the Dissenting Deputies, consulted with the Liberal leader on 15 February 1868. He replied, first, that his Bill would not be pressed against any considerable Tory opposition, in which case efforts might still be turned towards a Bill for total abolition, but held in abeyance in the meanwhile. Second, he declared that the objectionable clauses of his Bill were not open to the construction which the Parliamentary Committee had placed upon them. Unlike other such representations to previous Ministers of the Government, the deputation of leaders went away gratified at the spirit of fairness with which their case had been received.

Two days after the visit, Gladstone gave a speech in harmony with the views expressed by the deputation. He made clear that in his measure the principle

[1] Minute 30: 7.ii.68.

of Church Rates was not now at issue – it was rather the principle of removing irritations in the existing law on Church Rates. He also explained at length the meaning of the crucial fifth and sixth clauses, which had been altered after his consultations with Sir Roundell Palmer and the Society's Counsel, Mr Bevan Braithwaite.[1]

The speech of Viscount Cranborne (M.P., Stamford) on behalf of the agreeable Conservatives meant the end of many years of steady obstruction. Though naturally reluctant 'to give up anything the Church possesses', he believed the terms should be accepted lest they become more harsh in a later settlement. The Bill, backed by Sir George Grey and Sir Roundell Palmer, was read a second time without a division, and promptly went into Committee on 11 March. After sitting for the greater part of the day, arguing on precise wording, the Committee passed the measure intact.

There were, however, last-ditch attempts on 25 March to stymie the Bill's third reading. Mr C. N. Newdegate (M.P., Warwickshire, N.) moved the adjournment of the members, saying the effect of the Bill had been materially altered since it had passed through Committee. The motion was lost without a division, and on another motion of Mr C. Schreiber (M.P., Cheltenham) for adjournment of the debate, the Commons divided for the last time on the issue – 131 noes, and 28 ayes. Liberal members remained until the late hours to prevent devious tactics 'to devise a new kind of voluntary compulsion'. At one o'clock in the morning the Speaker put the question and declared that 'the Ayes have it'.

Although indignant over the clauses originating with the Liberation Society, the Lords gave the Bill an unopposed second reading, on the condition that it be worked over by a Select Committee. Lord Russell rejected the suspicions of Lord Cairns, the Lord Chancellor, and emphasized that no lawyer could frame a clause in which holes could not be picked by his brethren at the bar.

The Report from the Select Committee was brought in on 9 July, when the Bishop of Oxford (Dr Samuel Wilberforce) moved to insert three amendments: (1) Nothing in the Act should prevent any agreement to pay Church Rates from being enforced in the same manner as any other similar contract might be enforced in any court of law. (2) No vote for, nor right to act as, Churchwarden should be given to any person who had not paid up his voluntary rate. (3) Should a Churchwarden make a default in paying a Church Rate for which he might be rated, then a Treasurer not guilty of such default could be elected in his place to employ his powers concerning Rates. The first two amendments were negatived, and the last withdrawn for the third reading.

---

[1] The object of clause 5 was to give the management of the fund for Church expenses to the subscribers; if they chose to appoint a person who had not subscribed, it was not for the law to interfere. The object of clause 6 was to bring these subscriptions within the scope of the general law of Contract and not to hold as binding promises on behalf of any voluntary institution (as in the case of a treasurer of a Dissenting Chapel). Liberationists feared that if any person promised to subscribe and later refused or was unable to do so, he would 'have the pleasure of going into the Court of Chancery' (*Nonconformist*, 22.ii.68, p. 179).

The core of the High Church opposition held on almost like martyrs, to the bitter end. On 24 July Mr Gladstone agreed, and the House with him, to the Lords' amendments. These, said the Society, involved no departure from its fundamental principles. The Bill was read a third time in the Lords on 13 July, and received the Royal Assent on 31 July 1868. Several of the Peers and Clergy expressed their preference for total abolition rather than for this Bill which still made it possible for Dissenters 'to meddle' in the vestry proceedings.[1] But Parliament was tired of the issue and so the Bill became law.

Thus ended the chapter on 'the miserable question' that had baffled the country for forty years. A special minute was passed by the general Committee of Liberationists, expressing satisfaction at the rights vindicated by the new Act, and thanking those who had assumed leadership of the question through Parliament: W. E. Gladstone, J. A. Hardcastle, Sir William Clay, Sir Charles Douglas, and Sir John W. Salusbury-Trelawny. Each of these gentlemen wrote replies commending the Society on the role it had played in the final settlement.

No one, whether Churchman or Dissenter, shall be compelled to contribute, by means of parochial taxation, to the maintenance of ecclesiastical edifices, or of divine worship; and henceforth the Church of England, while permitted to retain the use of parochial machinery, must raise funds for such objects by voluntary instead of coercive methods.[2]

---

[1] The Act, 31 & 32 Vict., cap. 109, permitted everybody to attend the vestry and vote on the question of 'Rate' or 'No Rate', on the amount, and on the purpose to which the Rate would be applied. The parish would continue to be polled in the same way. The Rate having been made, no one who could not pay it could take part in any vestry proceeding on its expenditure or account. However, any person could attend any vestry afterward called to make another Rate, and to 'exercise all the rights which he originally possessed'. Cf. R. W. Dale, *History of English Congregationalism*, p. 623.

[2] Twenty-five years later Sir Robert Phillimore, in his *Ecclesiastical Law of the Church of England*, p. 1446, expressed the following opinion: 'This statute has been found generally inapplicable, and churches are now for the most part supported by voluntary contributions.'

CHAPTER 14

Theological Tests

Tolerance is far more than the abandonment of civil usurpations over conscience. It is a lesson often needed quite as much in the hearts of a minority as of a majority. Tolerance means reverence for all the possibilities of Truth; it means acknowledgment that she dwells in diverse mansions, and wears vesture of many colours, and speaks in strange tongues; it means frank respect for freedom of indwelling conscience against mechanic forms, official conventions, social force; it means the charity that is greater than even faith and hope.

JOHN MORLEY[1]

[Dissent's] demand is not now for toleration, but for ascendance. It has its political league, and its parliamentary tactics, and its confederation of sects, and its agency, active, unscrupulous, and ubiquitous. Its language may be somewhat ambiguous, but its objects are no longer disguised. In its present vocabulary, right of private judgment means resistance to authority; freedom of conscience, dictation to the consciences of others; liberation of religion, the subversion of the National Church and the confiscation of ecclesiastical property.

THE VEN. ARCHDEACON JOHN SANDFORD[2]

THE 'ABSTENTION POLICY'[3] adopted by friends of religious equality for the duration of the Palmerstonian Ministry had been hailed by Conservatives as a sign of weakness and defeat. In the matter of University reform, this illusion was quickly dispelled.

When there were signs of a change of Government in 1864, the names of the heroes of the Radical-Liberal phalanx against Church Rates were replaced by other *dramatis personae*. In this new episode the bulwarks of the State

---

[1] *Life of Gladstone*, i, 577.

[2] Bampton Lectures 1861, *The Mission and Extension of the Church at Home* (London 1862), pp. 70f.; quoted in *Liberator*, Sept. 1862, p. 156.

[3] This policy was adopted after the defeat of the Church Rates Abolition Bill in 1861; see Manifesto, 'Parliamentary Action in 1862', p. 165, above.

Church were assailed by its own members and friends such as Dodson, Goschen, Bouverie, Coleridge and Fawcett. Young Oxford, and not militant Nonconformity, led the attack, but they all gained considerable strength by informal alliance with one another.[1]

Opinions on theological tests were expressed by people of three ecclesiastical classes – Puritan, Sacerdotal, and Rationalist. Edward Miall, in his *Nonconformist*, asked what was Christian education at the Universities, and how was it different from a mere 'aroma of Christianity' which came from compulsory attendance at chapel services? Further, was a declaration of faith a necessary guarantee that he who made it was a Christian? The Rev. W. C. Lake, later Dean of Durham, claimed with the *Guardian* that admission of Dissenters was not to be dreaded so much as the presence of an unsettled and anti-Christian teaching which threatened the ancient religious traditions of the Church. Professor Goldwin Smith in his 'Plea for Abolition of Tests', like the *Spectator*, pointed out that believing and unbelieving parties would always be in the Colleges. The best hope for the religious party in the University lay in a closer union within itself, not to be gained by excluding Nonconformists.

A. *Preliminary Moves and Measures*

Before the introduction in 1868 of the comprehensive Tests Bill applying to both national Universities, the groundwork had been laid in the discussion of two preliminary measures – the University Test (Oxford) Abolition Bill, and the Fellows of Colleges Declaration (or Act of Uniformity Amendment) Bill. The Liberation Society believed that the views expressed on these motions by intellectual leaders would help (1) 'to obliterate sectarian distinctions in social life', (2) 'to generate an atmosphere of catholicity' and tolerance, and (3) to give education free scope to strengthen the nation.[2]

The theological tests required for the M.A. and other higher degrees at Oxford were: subscription to the Thirty-Nine Articles and the three Articles of the 36th Canon, and a declaration of accepting the full extent of the tests:

> I assent to the Thirty-nine Articles of Religion, and the Book of Common Prayer, and the ordering of bishops, priests, and deacons. I believe the doctrine of the United Church of England and Ireland as therein set forth to be agreeable to the Word of God, and in public prayer and administration of the Sacraments, I will use the form in the said book prescribed, and none other, except so far as shall be ordered by lawful authority.[3]

Nonconformists were anxious to get rid of this because, contrary to the

---

[1] An Association of University reformers was formed about this time, to consider ways of nationalizing higher education. Charles Roundell was made Secretary, and J. G. Dodson eventually President. Miall was invited to become a member in order to enlist the support of the Liberationists and Nonconformists. Parl. Com. Minutes, 15.vi.64.

[2] *Liberator*, May 1866, supplement, p. 91.

[3] Hansard (3rd series), clxxx, 636; cf. also Schedule appended to the Clerical Subscription Act, 1865.

function of a national institution, it ruled out Dissent and thus relegated Dissenters to a lower social position at the University. This position fostered contempt on both sides, and gave rise to fanatics and bigots.

The object of the Bill introduced by Mr J. G. Dodson (M.P., Sussex, E.) was simply to abolish these religious tests without making any separate ruling for Nonconformists. 'Tests', he believed, 'were cobwebs which let through the large flies and caught the little ones.' For Churchmen who could not accept these tests for lay Professorships and offices in the University, the Bill provided a simple declaration of *bona fide* membership in the Church of England and Ireland as it was by law established.

The Liberation Society issued a preliminary whip calling for support of Dodson's proposals and, on 16 March 1864, the second reading was carried by 211 to 189 votes. In Committee attempts were made to disqualify Nonconformists from voting in Convocation. The Parliamentary Committee of the Society would not tolerate any such compromise.[1] They promptly drew up a petition signed by 117 leading Nonconformist religious leaders and educators, sent it to all Liberal M.P.s, and urged them to resist all amendments which would alter the fundamental principle of the Bill. After extended correspondence, Dodson assured Carvell Williams that 'Jonah would not be thrown overboard while the vessel laboured in the storm'.

In June of the same year, 106 heads of Colleges, Professors, and Fellows at Oxford presented to the Lords a petition praying that subscription to formularies of faith be abolished:

> . . . subscription . . . has failed to secure unanimity of religious sentiment, or even to promote religious peace in the University . . . has a tendency to perplex the conscience, and leads to ambiguous interpretations of solemn obligations . . . is in danger of losing the services of men of higher character and ability . . .

The Conservatives allowed the Bill to pass through Committee unchanged, hoping that those who had supported it with reservations would oppose it on finding no amendments in the third reading. The first vote resulted in a tie and the Bill lost upon a re-vote that the measure 'do pass'.

On the eve of the General Election in 1865, the Bill was taken over by Mr G. J. Goschen, the Chancellor of the Duchy of Lancaster and M.P. for the City of London.[2] At the beginning of this particular year, similar tests had been abolished at Durham University, and this was interpreted as a hopeful sign for Oxford. In the month of May, a committee of Nonconformists, composed chiefly of members of the Dissenting Deputies and the Liberation Society, supported the Bill and elected Mr James L. Heywood as chairman. It was decided to put the question to all candidates who sought

---

[1] Nonconformists would have the right in this scheme to append 'M.A.' to their names, to wear a separate hood, and to be admitted to the Bodleian Library. Minute 390: 20.v.64.

[2] cf. chart in Hansard (3rd series), clxxx, 203–4, giving a list of the Oxford Colleges, the number of Fellows in each, and the restrictions on Fellowships in favour of the Church of England. Presented by Mr Goschen on 14 June 1865.

the votes of Liberal electors in the General Election, and as a result the second reading passed on 14 June, by 206 to 190 votes.

In 1866, as Cabinet Minister on the Treasury Bench and once again member for Exeter, John Coleridge assumed leadership of the Bill. Fresh with the Liberal victory at the polls, the 'dissatisfied conformists' such as he were ready to ask for more than before. The measure therefore sought to abolish all religious tests as a legal qualification for the M.A. degree and its rights in the University – a seat in Convocation, election of Parliamentary representatives, and eligibility to all professorships and emoluments not expressly restricted to persons in Holy Orders. Charles Neate (M.P., Oxford City) declared that it would 'shake every stone in the edifice' of the Establishment. Coleridge, later Lord Chief Justice of England, maintained that the Church need not fear free and fair inquiry, for when had religious truth been found unequal to its foes?

Sir William Heathcote, senior member for Oxford University, offered a compromise from the other University. This enabled Nonconformists to enter their names on 'the left side of the book' for an honorary M.A. with the privilege of teaching students in a private home only, but without the privilege of sharing in the government of the University. These amendments quickly failed and the Bill passed its second and third readings, but was prevented from going to the Lords by the sudden change of Ministry.

Coleridge's Oxford Bill reached the Lords in 1867 with a motion of Henry Fawcett (M.P., Brighton) to extend the provisions to Cambridge also. It was easily defeated despite the support of the Chancellor of Cambridge University, the Duke of Devonshire.

The Society's Parliamentary Committee had replied to a letter from Heywood early in 1862 and agreed to support plans for opening College Fellowships at Oxford and Cambridge. The measure was brought forward by E. P. Bouverie (M.P., Kilmarnock) and had the backing also of resident Fellows and Tutors at Cambridge. It proposed to repeal that portion of the Act of Uniformity which required certain dignitaries of the Church and Fellows of Colleges in the Universities to declare conformity to the liturgy of the Church of England. Except in cases where persons wished to proceed to a theological degree, the Bill sought to allow existing Fellows in both Universities to elect as Fellows any who distinguished themselves in University examinations, without requiring their declaration to the Anglican doctrine.

The Bill failed in 1863 and 1864, but in his next attempt in 1866, Bouverie cited the case of Henry M. Bompas, a Baptist student of St John's College, Cambridge, who had been fifth wrangler of the University in 1858.[1] While there he had declared his belief in Baptist principles, but attended the College Chapel, and received Communion according to the rites of the Church of

---

[1] He was the son of the Right Rev. William Carpenter Bompas, first bishop of the diocese of Selkirk, subsequently renamed Yukon. He later became a member of the Executive Committee of the Liberation Society and in 1881 was admitted to the Court of Queen's Bench.

England. Before sitting for a Fellowship, it was first necessary to make a declaration under the Act of Uniformity approving all the rubrics of the Book of Common Prayer. Because Bompas could not conscientiously sign the declaration, he could not take a College Fellowship, although some below him academically had obtained one.

But another Nonconformist student, James A. Aldis M.A., of Trinity College, Cambridge, and sixth wrangler in the Mathematical Tripos in 1863,[1] opposed this Bill because it would turn over national property to private college corporations. In a letter to the *Nonconformist* of 19 September 1866, he claimed that the Colleges' tenure of their endowments was overridden by the Act of Uniformity, placing them under the Crown. He therefore urged a 'root-and-branch' University Reform Bill based on thoroughly just philosophical ideas.

An Act of Uniformity Amendment Bill of Bouverie and Fawcett was read a second time by 200 to 156 votes in 1866, but adjournment of the debate on the third reading stalled proceedings for the rest of the session. The Corporation of London petitioned strongly in favour because many scholars of the City of London School 'had been debarred' from honours at Oxford and Cambridge by the declaration. Fawcett gave notice to extend the Bill to Trinity College, Dublin, in the interest of Irish Catholics.

B. *Disputing Parties and Principles*

A group of influential educators assembled in the Free Trade Hall, Manchester, on 6 April 1866, to endorse legislation for a more complete opening of Oxford and Cambridge. In attendance were Dr Frederick Temple, the Headmaster of Rugby School, Dr W. C. Sedgwick, the Warden of Merton College, Oxford, and Oxford Fellows: W. A. Rutson (Magdalen), A. Dicey (Trinity), James Bryce (Oriel), the Hon. George C. Brodrick (Merton), and the Hon. E. L. Stanley (Balliol). One of their resolutions stated:

> That, acknowledging the advantage which has attended a partial emancipation of the Universities from exclusive tests, and a partial restoration of their national character and of their active interest in the education of the whole nation, this meeting regards the further emancipation of the great national schools of learning as an object of national concern, and wishes to unite all denominations and classes of the people, and especially those who are most interested in learning, science, and education, to unite in cordial support of the measures now in Parliament for effecting this object.[2]

Whether they were known as Intellectual Liberationists, Liberal Educators, or Oxford Radicals, most of their number in and out of Parliament acquired the reputation for a high standard of debating. The new liberal logic was

---

[1] His brother, William Steadman Aldis, likewise of Trinity College, had been Senior Wrangler in the Mathematical Triposes in 1861. In 1860 the Senior Wrangler, W. Stirling, also of Trinity College, was a Presbyterian.

[2] *Nonconformist*, 11.iv.66, p. 284.

delightful to the ears of all earnest Dissenters as they carefully studied the working of this reform on the members of the House. These men sought to lift the controversy to a level free from the whine of Nonconformist suppliants, and the superciliousness of Conservative patrons.

The University reformers opposed religious tests on well-defined principles: (1) They had a questionable legal basis, for the University was a lay, not a religious, corporation[1] belonging to the nation, and should come under the repeal of the Test and Corporation Acts. (2) They were an obstruction to many men of great promise, and a hindrance to the progress of free scientific inquiry. (3) They aided enemies of the Church by distressing conscience, prompting dishonesty, and discouraging true theological study at the Universities. (4) They destroyed the social value of the exchange of opposite points of view, so important in the making of a gentleman. (5) They reflected more of a negative fear of 'de-Anglicanizing the spires and towers' than a positive belief in the development of culture and truth.

For those opposing the University reform Bills, all arguments turned on one great fact – the Universities should be guided by distinctive religious teaching. On this point Conservatives hoped to divide the ranks of the Liberals and Nonconformists, for many orthodox Dissenters deplored religious liberalism more than they did the Established Church.

The 'non-political' Nonconformists generally accepted the view that religion could not be taught without basic doctrinal convictions. They therefore preferred a system of education which was closely bound to the teaching of the Holy Scriptures, rather than one which bowed before human reason. For example, the Earl of Denbigh, although a Roman Catholic Dissenter, opposed the Oxford Bill in the Lords on the ground that it was necessary to have public recognition of religion in education. Conservative educators emphasized that even Dissenting educational institutions would not admit members to their governing bodies with no religious test or qualification whatever.

Despite this affinity between Dissent and Conformity, the Conservatives were not by any means disposed to court the favour of Dissenters. Many Anglicans did not mind lay members of the University being freed from a superfluous test, provided that the government of the University was free from the taint of Nonconformists. The social prestige of Oxford and Cambridge was due to their close ties with the ancient religious traditions of the nation.

The views of Church Defenders had certain presuppositions: (1) These reform Bills were but the cloaks of sinister motives – the severance of the connexion between the University and the Church, and the secularizing of educational institutions. (2) Universities were national because they conferred benefits on the entire nation, but they had begun as private associations, using private endowments in conformity with the wills of the benefactors.

---

[1] Confirmed by the opinion laid down by Lord Coke and Mr Justice Blackstone; *Nonconformist*, 28.iii.66, p. 246.

(3) The Universities were not places for free inquiry and 'religious indifferentism', but places where truth was taught with a definite basis of belief. (4) It was a dangerous precedent to change the constitution of the University for the sake of a few Nonconformists, who could effect further radical changes as they had done in the House of Commons. (5) The injustice of which Dissenters complained had been removed by the establishment of London University, free of all religious qualifications.

C. *Disunity in the Anglican Church*
The weight of argument concerning religious tests seemed to favour the Liberationists during this period. This was due partly to the dissension at the heart of the Established Church on doctrinal and theological questions. The consequences of this 'internecine war' made it clear that the existing system for maintaining orthodoxy among well-educated men was not generally accepted. Laws of uniformity would always produce nonconformity inside as well as outside the Church of England.

1. *The Colenso Case*
During the years of this period, 1861–9, the famous Colenso controversy raged throughout the high councils of the Church of England. In certain respects it was but another phase of the struggle between the Tractarian and Liberal parties within Anglicanism.

In 1862, Dr John William Colenso, Bishop of Natal, startled the ecclesiastical world by the publication of a work on the age and authorship of the Pentateuch, which was entirely at variance with the received belief. It contained such statements as: 'The Bible itself is not God's word; but assuredly God's word will be heard in the Bible', and 'The ordinary knowledge of Christ was nothing more than that of any educated Jew of his age.'[1]

Both Houses of Convocation appointed Committees to inquire into the 'heterodox publication'. Archbishop Longley condemned it, and enjoined his Clergy to keep the erring Bishop from their pulpits and from administering the sacraments. Dr Colenso was tried by the South African Synod and on 16 December 1863 was deposed by his Metropolitan, Bishop Gray of Cape Town. He was convicted of teaching contrary to the Articles, Creeds, and Formularies of the Church, and declared 'unfit, so long as he shall persist in these errors, to bear rule in the Church of God'.[2]

On appeal, the Judicial Committee of the Privy Council decided on 20 March 1865 that the proceedings by the Bishop of Cape Town were null and

---

[1] This work, it was alleged, denied the divine inspiration of the Holy Scriptures. In 1861 Colenso had produced a commentary on the Epistle to the Romans, in which were questioned also the received doctrines of the Atonement, Justification – it was stated that all heathen are righteous and accepted before their birth – Original Sin, the Sacraments, Eternal Punishment and Universal Salvation. See Moorman, *History of the Church of England*, pp. 379–80.

[2] Charles Gray, *Life of Robert Gray*, ii, 104.

void. Their judgement was made on the ground that the Crown had no power to constitute a Bishopric in any colony possessing an independent Legislature.[1]

The excommunicated Bishop thus continued to exercise his Episcopal functions in Natal for some years, in spite of the opposition of the Rev. W. K. Macrorie, whom Dr Gray had nominated in 1869 as his successor. The outcome of these events was the existence for a time of two rival communions. One was the Church of England in South Africa which amounted almost to an independent religious association (Clergy and laity together in Council) under the headship of the Crown; the other was the Church of South Africa which asserted the freedom of the Church from State control, the exalting of Episcopal jurisdiction, and the authority of Convocation.

2. The 'Essays and Reviews' Controversy

A further uproar was caused at this time by the appearance in 1860 of another controversial volume, *Essays and Reviews*, written by leading Anglican liberals, among them Dr Frederick Temple, the Rev. H. B. Wilson, and Dr Rowland Williams. The report of the Joint Committee appointed by Convocation condemned the book for containing latitudinarian views which were contrary to the doctrines of the Church of England and 'the whole Catholic Church of Christ'. In a review of the *Essays*, Frederic Harrison said that there remained little but 'a revised Atonement, a transcendant Fall, a practical Salvation, and an idealised Damnation'.

When the Primate (Dr Longley) hesitated to take the action urged against the authors, the Bishop of Salisbury (Dr Walter Hamilton) commenced proceedings against Dr Rowland Williams and the Rev. H. B. Wilson in the Court of Arches.[2] In the judgement of Dr Stephen Lushington the defendants were found guilty on four of the twenty-seven charges, condemned in costs, admonished not to offend in like manner in the future, and suspended *ab officio et beneficio* for one year.

Appeal was made to the Judicial Committee of the Privy Council, which considered the case on 8 February 1864, with Mr Gladstone and the Duke of Argyll present. Dr Williams was charged on statements in his review of 'Bunsen's Biblical Researches', contravening the Articles and Formularies of the Church in regard to Inspiration, and Justification by Faith. The Rev.

---

[1] The entire judgement is given in *Nonconformist*, 22.iii.65, pp. 223–4. It was similar to that in *Long v. The Bishop of Capetown*. In 1853 the Diocese of Cape Town was divided, but in the same year the colony became self-governing. The bishopric therefore came under the Crown instead of the Archbishop of Canterbury, and the Metropolitan was divested of coercive legal jurisdiction. Cornish, *The English Church in the Nineteenth Century*, ii, 252–3. When the trustees of the Colonial Bishoprics Fund discontinued his salary, the Bishop obtained a judgement in his favour (*Colenso v. Gladstone*), maintaining his hold upon the temporalities of the see of Natal.

[2] In the case of *Gorham v. The Bishop of Exeter* it had been decided by the Judicial Committee of the Privy Council that the Arches Court had no jurisdiction to settle matters of faith and doctrine, but only to determine the legal sense of the Articles and Formularies as by law established.

H. B. Wilson was charged on selections in his essay, 'Séances Historiques de Genève – The National Church', impugning the authenticity of certain parts of the canonical books of the Bible, and expressing disbelief in the eternity of future punishment. The Judicial Committee, with the exception of the two Archbishops, held that the passages, extracted from their context and condemned by the Court of Arches, did not sustain the indictment made against them. This judgement, Canon E. B. Pusey angrily asserted, was 'a victory for Satan'.[1]

The Privy Council decision on *Essays and Reviews* was regarded by many as a great step in the progress of religious thought, and by others as a mere step towards easier accommodation within the Church. The *Nonconformist* made the most of the tangled situation, stating that Established orthodoxy could not be entrusted to the guardianship of law.

To the Tractarians especially it was degrading to have their creed interpreted by mere lawyers in the Privy Council and not true clerics. To decide therefore upon a counter-move to the action of 'the lay tribunal', a committee including Dr Pusey and Archdeacon Denison issued a circular requesting the attendance of members of the Oxford University Convocation in the Sheldonian Theatre. A gathering of 524 dissatisfied Anglicans assembled on 25 February 1864, when a formal declaration was accepted that the punishment of 'cursed' souls was 'everlasting', and that 'the whole Catholic Church maintains without reserve or qualifications the plenary inspiration and authority of the whole Canonical Scriptures as the Word of God'.

Backed by this Oxford Declaration, the Bishop of Oxford (Dr Samuel Wilberforce) introduced a motion in the Upper House of Convocation on 19 April 1864, calling for synodical judgement upon the mischievous writings. One month later, largely as a result of the activity of the intrepid Archdeacon Denison, the Lower House accepted the recommendations of the examining committee of the Bishops, and the *Essays* stood officially condemned. The stormy debate was thereupon conducted to the House of Lords on 15 July, when Lords Houghton and Westbury challenged the authority of Convocation to make such a judgement.

The general verdict was now against the offensive book, but Dissenters pointed out how the controversy had weakened the case for theological tests at the Universities. Two irreconcilable judgements on Anglican teaching, one civil and one ecclesiastical, had been brought before the country. Who were the nonconformists here, and which authority determined what was and what was not the doctrine of the Church? All of these problems seemed to confirm the arguments of the Liberationists.

3. *Teaching and Ritual Offences*
The Convocation at Oxford became once more involved in a dispute which

---

[1] quoted in *Liberator*, Oct. 1864, p. 151. Shortly after the judgement, Bishop Gray of Cape Town, in a letter of 19.xii.63, called the Judicial Committee 'that masterpiece of Satan for the overthrow of the Faith' (Charles Gray, *Life of Robert Gray*, ii, 113).

reflected upon its sense of judgement, and further proved the necessity of University reform. On 8 March 1864, this governing body voted on a statute for an endowment of the Chair of the Regius Professor of Greek, Professor Benjamin Jowett. The statute, recommended by Congregation, was that Professor Jowett's salary should be raised from £40 to £400 per year, with a proviso, suggested by John Keble, that the University pronounced no judgement on the Professor's theological writings. Jowett had written in 1858 to his friend Dean Stanley:

> We do not wish to do anything rash or irritating to the public or the University, but we are determined not to submit to this abominable system of terrorism, which prevents the statement of the plainest facts, and makes true theology or theological education impossible.[1]

In a crowded and restless Convocation, Archdeacon Denison on behalf of the Anglo-Catholic section, delivered a speech in Latin, strongly opposing the statute. The voting took place immediately afterward, and the Senior Proctor announced the loss of the statute by 467 to 295 votes.

Nonconformists disdained this action as smacking of the spirit of the Vatican. Sir Stafford Northcote wrote afterwards that he could not conceive of 'a more unfortunate mode of testing the opinion of the University upon the fearfully important questions which now agitate the minds of Churchmen'.[2]

In 1867, the Royal Commission on Ritualism issued four reports in all, presenting the Queen with information relative to liturgical practices in the Church of England. In 1868, partly in consequence of the findings of these reports, several famous court cases came to light. In that referred to as the St Alban's Case, *Flamank v. Simpson* and *Martin v. Mackonochie*, the principal charges were: (1) excessive kneeling during the celebration of the sacraments, (2) the use of incense, (3) mixing the wine with water, (4) adoration of the elements, and (5) the use of lighted candles on the altar.

The delivery of the judgement by Sir Robert Phillimore in the Arches Court occupied four and a half hours, but the accused were let off lightly. The Rev. A. H. Mackonochie complained that the action of the court cut them off, as far as a civil tribunal could, from true Catholic tradition. The *Nonconformist* referred to such treatment of 'the spouse of Christ' by the court of law as 'spiritual aduitery'.

In another case, *Sheppard v. Bennett*, the Vicar of Frome, the Rev. W. J. E. Bennett, was charged similarly with violating the Act of Uniformity. In his letter to Dr Pusey in 1867 entitled, 'A Plea for Toleration in the Church of England', he stated his 'blasphemous' views on (1) the real objective presence of Christ in the Eucharist, (2) the sacrifice offered by the Priest, and (3) the adoration of the elements due to the visible and actual presence of Christ therein. Dr Lushington in the Privy Council in 1872 decided that it was not

---

[1] Cornish, *The English Church in the Nineteenth Century*, ii, 218.

[2] *Nonconformist*, 16.iii.64, p. 205. Following the line suggested by Prof. E. A. Freeman, the Dean and Chapter of Christ Church, Oxford, in September 1865, raised the income of the Greek Professorship to £500 out of their own revenues.

illegal to hold the first two beliefs, but that it was unlawful to require the third.

In themselves these practices and beliefs seemed harmless, but to liberal-minded educators, they tended to produce 'superstition and idolatry'. Because of their origin in the Church of Rome, it was feared they might lead the Church of England back to the religious temper of pre-Reformation times. But to suppress them, the leaders of the Oxford Movement maintained, was a denial of freedom of worship.

On this point of religious liberty the Ritualists were in accord with the policy of the Liberation Society. But Disestablishment, they believed, should come not by their secession, but by agitation from within.

4. *Unity with Nonconformists*
By 1865 the swift advances of public opinion on religious tests baffled political prediction and upset the foundations of party discipline. People were experiencing, actively or passively, a process of education so rapid that their convictions, which formerly could not have matured in years, were now reformed in months.

As this problem of higher education approached settlement, individual leaders from the three principal theological streams discovered common interests and objectives. Overtures were made by the High and Low as well as the Broad Church party within the Church to gain unity with parties of Dissenters. The Church of England seemed anxious to make good her boast to 'open wide her portals', but so wide, some feared, as to make her teaching self-contradictory.[1]

The Anglo-Catholics began by seeking out the old body of Wesleyan Methodists, which many thought was closer and therefore easier to win back to the Anglican Establishment. Dr Pusey therefore wrote to the President of the Wesleyan Conference, offering two alternatives for co-operation with the High Churchmen:[2] (1) to substitute for subscription to the Thirty-Nine Articles an acknowledgement of the Faith according to the Nicene Creed, and (2) to the founding of new Colleges out of the revenues of the old ones 'for the different bodies who hold the faith in our Lord Jesus Christ'. The Conference answered satirically by adapting a popular song of the day:

[1] Lord Salisbury was one of those not liking the idea of enlarging the boundaries of the Anglican Church. He disapproved of Lord Ebury's Bill in 1862 for alterations in the Prayer Book to enable the more orthodox Dissenting bodies to unite with the Church of England. In the *Quarterly Review*, July 1862, he compared the injury of this proposal with the aim of the Liberation Society. Mr Miall, he said, would destroy our religious community as an Establishment whilst Lord Ebury would change the distinctive character of the Church. One would take her money, and the other her Faith. Lady Gwendolen Cecil, *Life of Robert, Marquis of Salisbury* (London 1921–32), i, 331–2.

[2] See the copy of the letter in *Nonconformist*, 19.viii.68, p. 814. The Rev. S. H. Hall, President of the Wesleyan Conference, had remarked in his address of 1868 that the *Via Media* (between Anglicanism and Dissent) was their proper designation: '. . . whilst we hold this midway position, we are still prepared to regard . . . with respect and affection the State Church, so long as she remains faithful to her calling.'

You offer one hand to the Papal band,
  And the other to us extend,
Can you really hope that we and the Pope
  Can acknowledge a mutual friend?
You tell us our bark is not an ark,
  We don't believe that's true,
We'd trust a raft before your craft,
  Just paddle your own canoe.[1]

Shortly after this, on 8 June 1868, Evangelical Churchmen under the presidency of Lord Alfred Churchill sought an alliance with Dissenters against Ritualism, in the formation of the Evangelical Church Union. The Union sought (1) to preserve the Evangelical principles of the Reformation, and (2) to purge all phrases of doubtful Protestantism from the Book of Common Prayer.

As for Broad Churchmen, they were willing to ally themselves with Nonconformist educators where the alliance did not violate the just position of the State Church. In an address at Sion College on 13 February 1868, before an audience including Edward Miall, the Rev. James Martineau, and the Bishop of London (Dr Tait), the Dean of Westminster (the Rev. Arthur P. Stanley) outlined his ideas for a State Church comprehending men of diverse opinions: (1) admitting Nonconformists and Anglicans to preach in one another's pulpits with the permission of the local Bishop (but not to administer sacraments); (2) including Nonconformists with Anglicans in a committee to revise the authorized version of the Bible; and (3) recognizing the unity between Nonconformists and Anglicans by free admission of the former to the Universities.

At this stage it was apparent that the dogmatic differences between the Church and Dissent were not greater than the discordance between various types of Anglicans. The fierce competition among the Church parties was, however, by no means an omen of the internal collapse of the Establishment. Most of these Churchmen firmly believed that protection of the law alone was a safeguard for freedom of interpretation of the accepted creeds and formularies within the Church. Instead of individual liberty, the Establishment favoured the virtues of corporate liberty. This prevented rivalling parties from seceding one from another, as they had in the Nonconformist Churches.

Nonconformists would never believe that any other freedom was as worthy as theirs. It was better to inquire than to acquiesce. Religious liberty was meaningless where patronage and grants were enshrouded in religious regulations. Matters of truth and dogma should be left to the sympathies of those who cared for them, while the law of the nation should be used to protect every subject from injury and injustice. Reliance on secular authority and social privilege made for a Church lacking in moral and spiritual vitality. Without sacrifice and struggle in the world, the message of the Church turned

[1] A. L. Drummond, *The Churches Pictured by 'Punch'* (London 1947), p. 13.

into polite ethics. The only true pattern for the Church, simple and separated from temporal power, was to be found in the New Testament.

D. *Gladstone and Comprehensive Bill*

In University Tests, no less than in all the other prominent ecclesiastical questions of the day, Mr Gladstone's ideas received close attention. Behind the strife of the orthodox and liberal parties in the Church and Universities was his quiet confidence that all would be well in the end, and that 'time and the social forces are with us'.

Gladstone was a firm believer in the denominational system of education as most sound and sensible. To reconcile his position, however, as loyal Churchman and representative of Oxford University with the claims of the Liberal party at his back, he had to occupy the role of mediator.

He believed that the course of 'relaxation' in the matter of religious tests was the best. Although he was prepared to open the portals of Oxford as far as those at Cambridge, he was not prepared to allow 'extraneous influence' in the governing bodies of these Anglican strongholds. But he could not see why the same tests of adherence to the Thirty-Nine Articles and Prayer Book for the teachers and clerics of the Church of England should be applied also to the 3,000 laymen constituting the majority of the Oxford Convocation. In order that Dissenters might feel less excluded from regular privileges within the University, he favoured removing all obstacles for establishing their own private Halls.

The stern policy of 'indiscriminate resistance' within Conservative ranks was openly condemned by Gladstone. He believed this was as fatal to the principles of social justice as it was to the best interests of the Church of England herself. These views were not at all pleasing to the high Tories, and it soon became clear that their widening difference with Gladstone would lead to a breach. A private meeting of Conservatives led by Lord Robert Cecil was called in May 1864, with the intention of replacing Mr Gladstone as member for Oxford University.[1] From the floor of the Commons on 1 June, Mr C. Neate (M.P., Oxford City) rebuked the dissatisfied Peer and described Gladstone as a great intellect who had humbly submitted to the doctrines of the Church. His comparison with Virgil, although somewhat rhetorical, was well received:

Si Pergama dextra
defendi possent, etiam hac defensa fuissent.

---

[1] In 1890 Gladstone visited the Oxford Union and delivered an eloquent address on Homer. In his reply to the vote of thanks proposed by Mr C. F. Garbett, the President, he said: 'To call a man a characteristically Oxford man is, in my opinion, to give him the highest compliment that can be paid to any human being. I fear I do not and cannot accept such a compliment, but . . . there is not a man who has passed through this great and famous University that can say with more truth than I can say, I love her from the bottom of my heart.' *Proceedings of the Oxford Union Society*, Thursday, 19 May 1898 (being the day of Mr Gladstone's death), Oxford, p. 9.

Gladstone's speech in 1866 on Coleridge's Bill made moderate concessions to the Nonconformists, but they were not impressed. The Universities, he contended, could not break faith with the parents of England by affording secular instruction only. Allowances, however, could be made to Dissenters without sacrificing the religious education of the University. Obtaining a Fellowship was the crowning of a University career which should not be enjoyed solely by Anglicans. Honour, emolument, and government at the University should be given to Dissenters, so long as it was consistent with the accepted religious teaching in the University. But instead of 'piecemeal legislation' and 'nibbling by Parliament', it was essential to have a comprehensive scheme which applied to both Oxford and Cambridge.

The petitioning for and against the question was unusually prevalent in 1868. A notable deputation presented to Dr Tait, the new Archbishop of Canterbury, a petition, addressing him as 'the chief guardian in Parliament of the religious interests of the realm', and bearing 1,600 signatures – 700 of them graduates, Fellows, and Divinity Professors of Oxford. The University Tests Bill as contemplated, it declared, would destroy unity of faith and worship for the youth of the nation. The battle was not between Church and Dissent, it 'is for Christian faith and Christian morals: it is for our very life'. Should 'a definite creed and . . . a common form of prayer' be overthrown, 'the very basis of a Christian education will disappear among us'.[1]

The Primate responded that he entered fully into their feelings on the matter. Shortly afterwards, he received an appeal from four Baptist Ministers of Cambridge asking him to do all that he could to encourage Nonconformists to enter the Universities and to promote their religious interests. Another circular signed by seven Dissenting graduates and undergraduates of Cambridge was addressed to Nonconformist Ministers, urging them to stress before their congregations the importance of the issue.

The House of Commons received petitions emphatically against the Bill from the governing bodies of Oxford and Cambridge, with their respective University seals affixed. In the Lords, on the other hand, the Earl of Kimberley presented petitions for the removal of religious tests from a large number of the Fellows, Tutors, and Lecturers of Oxford.

At the joint Parliamentary Breakfast of the Liberation Society and the Dissenting Deputies on 10 March, Edward Miall announced that he did not oppose the new Bill. It would grant full privileges of the University to all students entering, but would leave Colleges free to decide privately on their Fellowships.

Introducing his measure, John Coleridge started a series of debates abounding with classical quotations of learned men. His proposals were a combination of the Bill of the previous session and Mr Bouverie's Fellows of Colleges Bill. The result, he hoped, would allow Dissenters to take all degrees free of tests, except in divinity, and repeal the part of the Act of Uniformity

---

[1] *Nonconformist*, 7.iii.68, p. 220.

restricting non-clerical Fellowships. He ended with a passage from Tennyson's *The Passing of Arthur*:

> The old order changeth, yielding place to new,
> And God fulfils himself in many ways,
> Lest one good custom should corrupt the world.

Spencer Walpole, speaking for Cambridge, declared that the Bill would make it necessary to send the theological students to special Colleges for definite religious training, thus depriving the Universities of the common education of Clergy and laity together. Gathorne Hardy insisted amid loud cheers that the Bill was a repudiation of the grand old Oxford motto: *Dominus Illuminatio Mea*. The majority felt otherwise, and so on 1 July the Bill passed by 198 to 140 votes. It was withdrawn on 22 July, because of the lateness of the session and the prorogation of Parliament.

After the Liberal party victory in the 1868 General Election, Sir John Coleridge (as he was now) entered Gladstone's Cabinet as Solicitor-General, and the measure was now supported by all the members of the Government. Thus, on 15 March 1869, the second reading passed without a division, but in Committee two qualifying clauses were added: (1) The Bill should not interfere with the lawfully established system of religious instruction, worship, discipline, otherwise than as expressly enacted. (2) In deciding the conditions governing Fellowships within Colleges, the matter should rest in the hands of the Bishop or the College Visitor, who might give assent to a statute, as the occasion arose, to throw open the Fellowships to Dissenters.[1]

When the Bill came to the House of Lords, the Earl of Carnarvon put forward a new idea, without warning. Since only half the number of Fellowships were required for the working of a College, he thought it best to retain that portion with ecclesiastical tests. The remainder he proposed converting into University Fellowships, and throwing them open without regard to religious opinions. In cases of a Dissenter seeking to become a Fellow, this plan would save the Colleges from embarrassment, and ought not to disturb the security of their religious foundations.

On the proposition that 'the question be put', the result was: content, 54 votes; non-content, 91 votes. The Bill was accordingly thrown out. Some observers thought that their Lordships had done this to soothe their consciences over their passage of the Irish Church Bill. Others felt that it was simply intended 'to keep the Gentiles waiting for a while yet in the outer court'.

---

[1] Hansard (3rd series), cxcii, 209–20; cxcvii, 1090–104.

CHAPTER 15

Religious Revolt in the Colonies

Dissent, as a rule, never compromises. In that she is like Romanism. She will have all, and push her demands to the utmost; and will be satisfied, she says, with nothing less than the overthrow of the Established Church. . . . Equality, that ominous word of revolution, is the grand thing to be gained. Let Churchmen thoroughly know the danger, and there is no fear of the result.

THE VEN. ARCHDEACON GEORGE A. DENISON[1]

The present Prayer-Book represents the exact state of religious knowledge in an age so barbarous and ignorant, that poor helpless girls were roasted to death by arch-bishops, old women were hung as witches by judges on the bench, . . . The confused and contradictory mass of theology contained in our Book of Common Prayer has been permitted to supersede the Word of God in our National Church, and it becomes the duty of every man to consider whether or not he is justified in remaining in it.

THE REV. CHRISTOPHER NEVILE[2]

THE IRISH CHURCH ACT established a precedent for calling Church Establishments into question throughout all parts of the Empire. Thus, in Victoria, British Guiana, Ceylon, Honduras, Sierra Leone, Jamaica, and the Bahamas, discussions arose in the legislatures reflecting the impatience of many colonists with the 'interference' of the Home Government in their religious and educational life.

The unrest between the natives and immigrants vitally affected the State Church question in the Colonies. The Nonconformists, representing several denominational Missionary Societies, were usually more numerous than the adherents to the Church of England. Because of their more democratic form of Church government, the Nonconformists in many cases were in closer sympathy with the aspirations of the native population. The Anglican Church naturally represented the authority of the Crown.

[1] *Church and State Review*, Aug. 1864, pp. 37–8.

[2] From a letter to the *Stamford Mercury*, communicating his decision to resign his two livings; reproduced in the *Liberator*, Sept. 1862, p. 151.

The religious life in the Colonies often revealed the same social and political divisions that existed at home. The Church of England, therefore, was frequently looked upon as 'the Planter's Church', and the other Churches as mainly for the underprivileged and working classes. The Missionary enterprise was hindered and relations between the Churches were strained where it was believed that taxes were wrung from the blacks for the support of the religion of the whites.

A. *The Jamaican Rebellion*

In the case of Jamaica the Disestablishment question came to the fore following the rebellion of subjects against rulers at Morant Bay on 11 October 1865, in the parish of St Thomas-in-the-East. An unruly mob assembled in front of the Court-house, demonstrating against the decision of one of the local courts concerning 'the rights of negro settlers', and defying the order to disperse. After the Riot Act was read, the protesters were fired upon by a handful of volunteers who killed and wounded many. The infuriated Negroes rushed upon the soldiers and overpowered them by force of numbers. Others seized arms from the police barracks, burned the Court-house, and killed or wounded its occupants. They then dispersed over the countryside, joined by Negroes of those plantations pillaged, putting to death and in some cases mutilating the owners.

This savagery was met by terror in retaliation. Reprisals and punishments ordered by Governor Edward J. Eyre, were swift and severe. Within a few weeks 438 rebels were executed, 600 were flogged, and at least 1,000 homes were burnt.[1] The incident which had the most serious consequences was the hanging of Mr George W. Gordon, a member of the local Assembly and defender of Negroes' rights, who was charged with instigating the uprising.[2]

Like the atrocities in the Indian Mutiny in 1857, religious causes were partly involved. After a visit to the island some time before the rebellion, Dr Edward Underhill, Secretary of the Baptist Missionary Society and Executive member of the Liberation Society, had written a letter to Mr Edward Cardwell (M.P., Oxford), Secretary of State for the Colonies, complaining of unjust taxation in Jamaica. The letter attracted wide attention, and the Governor placed considerable blame for what happened upon the Baptist Missionaries who endorsed the views of Dr Underhill. Sir Morton Peto (M.P., Bristol), Treasurer of the Baptist Missionary Society, indignantly denied a similar allegation in a leading article in *The Times*:

> In the old days of slavery the Jamaica negro was noted among his race for his dangerous character, and he rose against his masters under the guidance of the Baptists, on the very eve of Emancipation.[3]

[1] Edward B. Underhill, *The Tragedy of Morant Bay* (London 1895), pp. 64–5.

[2] Correspondence printed in the *Liberator* (March 1866, p. 38) between the Rev. W. Dendy, of Montego Bay, and Mr Gordon, revealed that the latter was the first member of the Jamaican Assembly to bring in a Bill for the purpose of putting an end to the ecclesiastical Establishment in the Island.

[3] *The Times*, 13.xi.65; cf. Peto's evidence in the *Nonconformist*, 22.xi.65, p. 996.

Further ferment was caused when the authorities in Jamaica devised a Bill 'to preserve the worship of God from scandalous abuse, superstitions, practices and seditious purposes'. Mr J. Carvell Williams, Secretary for the Liberation Society, promptly prepared an abstract of this measure and argued that such legislation worked against the religious liberty of the natives and their Churches.[1] In response to appeals by native Jamaicans, the Society submitted evidence for them in home inquiries, and tried to prevent the offensive Religious Worship Bills from receiving the sanction of the Crown. This 'moral pressure' in Parliament increased the influence of the Nonconformists upon the government of the Colony.

The public feeling aroused over the whole Jamaican affair eventually demanded Government action, and Lord John Russell first recalled Governor Eyre, and then authorized a Royal Commission of Inquiry. Mr Charles S. Roundell, a frequent supporter of the Liberation Society, was appointed Secretary to the Commission. The summary findings of the Report, released on 18 June 1866, were: (1) that martial law, suspending the normal constitutional privileges, had been in full force too long, (2) that the punishments inflicted were excessive, (3) that the punishment of death was unnecessarily frequent, (4) that the floggings were reckless and at times barbarous, and (5) that the burning of 1,000 houses was wanton and cruel.[2] The *Nonconformist* insisted that compensation should be made in cases of needless destruction of property and illegal execution of families. The local legislature was replaced by a more compact body, over which Sir John P. Grant was appointed the new Governor.

Ex-Governor Eyre and his subordinates were charged in 1867 with being responsible for the illegal murder, under martial law, of George Gordon. The plaintiffs were John Stuart Mill (M.P., Westminster) and Peter Alfred Taylor (M.P., Leicester), who both acted on behalf of a committee seeking justice for Jamaica.[3] The results of two court trials served less to incriminate these men than to stand as a warning to other harsh-minded colonial administrators.

The Liberation Society had issued a circular in the *Liberator* in January 1866, with a resolution affirming

That as, in consequence of recent lamentable events, the state of Jamaica is likely to become the subject of thorough investigation, the Committee is of opinion that such inquiry should embrace the application of the revenues of the

[1] *Liberator*, Feb. 1866, p. 127: 'If [the religious leaders] require the aid of law to put down religious practices which they deem to be wrong, they, in our judgment, either lack faith in the power of truth, or faith in themselves as its expositors.'

[2] *Report of the Jamaica Royal Commissioners* (Session 1866), xxx, 530–1. The Commission concluded their Report by expressing their regret at the tone of levity found in the letters and language of some of the officers while engaged in serious and responsible duties.

[3] Thomas Carlyle, the literary philosopher, in his *Occasional Discourse on the Nigger Question* (London 1853), written mainly against idleness, defended Eyre as something of a national hero. See reprint of articles on Jamaica from the *Eclectic Review*, Sept.–Oct. 1866, pp. 25–7.

island to ecclesiastical purposes, and that advantage should be taken of the present opportunity for putting an end to a system fraught with injustice.

The special committee appointed to implement this resolution was headed by the Rev. Frederick Trestrail, Executive member of the Baptist Union and the Liberation Society, and assisted by Dr Underhill. The committee reported early in 1867, asking: (1) that the Colonial Office make public any communication with the new Governor on the question of reducing local taxation for the Anglican Establishment,[1] and (2) that a motion be made in the Commons to strike out of the Parliamentary Estimates in England the amount voted for the Jamaican Bishops.

In the Annual Report of 1867, the Society warned that at the expiry of the Jamaican Clergy Act on 31 December 1869, there would be a crisis in these matters. It must be decided by then whether the objectionable taxation would continue or whether Jamaica would be among those Colonies where Churches existed by voluntary means. Mr J. Remington Mills (M.P., Wycombe, Chepping) provided startling statistics: (1) £20,300 per annum went out of the Consolidated Fund for religious purposes in the West Indies; (2) £45,000 per annum was spent by the Jamaican Government for ecclesiastical purposes, and of this £28,000 or one-tenth of the whole revenue of the island was raised in taxes from the people; (3) £37,378 per annum were the average expenses of the Church of England there; (4) £4,600 per annum was paid jointly from the Consolidated Fund for the Bishops of Kingston and Jamaica, neither of whom was a permanent resident of the island; (5) there were 87 Anglican Churches with 39,710 attendants, or one-eighth the population, but 261 Nonconformist Chapels with 127,660 attendants.[2]

The West Indies Bishops and Clergy Bill of Mr Mills, although unopposed by both Derby's and Disraeli's Government, was withdrawn because of the crowded Order-book in the Commons. It would relieve the mother country of ecclesiastical charges for the West Indies Establishment and transfer the responsibility partly to Episcopalians of the island. Meanwhile the Liberation Society pressed the government of the Colony toward a policy of 'complete cessation' of State aid to religion. The Society also put forward a scheme for total Disestablishment and Disendowment in Jamaica.[3]

Rumours were heard that the Governor favoured the policy of concurrent endowment and a 'pay all principle' for all Missionary bodies doing relief work in Jamaica. The Society therefore sent, on 30 June 1869, a strong deputation to Earl Granville, warning that such a policy would fail utterly to

---

[1] When the new Governor first announced a new policy for making the Episcopalian congregations responsible for the expenses hitherto defrayed out of the annual vote of the local Assembly, Bishop Courtenay issued a circular to his Clergy urging them to accept this 'with all readiness of mind' (*Liberator*, Jan. 1867, pp. 11–12). The Liberation Society alleged that the bishop had been absent from his diocese for twenty-three years. *Liberator*, Jan. 1866, p. 3.

[2] Hansard (3rd series), clxxxi, 1268–9; *Nonconformist*, 8.v.67, p. 365.

[3] *Nonconformist*, 9.i.67.

promote peace and prosperity in the island.[1] The Colonial Secretary said that the Home Government wished any legislation on the subject to be based on the principle of 'giving moral culture' to the subject race, and not of giving exclusive advantage to any religious body.

Finally, the Governor proclaimed that he had abandoned his policy of local State support for all general missionary purposes. Furthermore, he declared:

> Whereas the 'Clergy Act of 1868' has expired by efflux of time . . . it is expedient to facilitate by Law the organisation . . . of a Church to be supported on the voluntary principle. . . .[2]

The new Governor had capitulated less because he believed that it was a good thing, than because he feared that the Dissenters and Voluntaryists would perpetuate the dissatisfaction of the natives if their demands were not met. A statement of the course taken by the Nonconformists of the island, and the action of the Liberation Society through its supporters, and a summary of the dispatches of Sir John Grant and Earl Granville, were subsequently published by the Colonial Office.

B. *The South African Discord*

In the case of the Bishop of Cape Town against Long, in 1865, the Judicial Committee of the Privy Council decided on appeal that the Bishop (and Metropolitan), Dr Robert Gray, had no legal jurisdiction over the accused. Whereupon the local 'synod' met and passed a series of resolutions that the Privy Council had no proper authority over them. This appeared to make the local inhabitants independent of the ecclesiastical law of England. According to the Liberation Society, only one thing remained to make the break complete, and that was to tear up the letters patent which gave Bishop Gray his authority.

> The colonists of all denominations are sensible of the advantages which they enjoy in being able to obtain the services in positions of influence of men who have received a first-rate English education, and it cannot be pretended that their ability to do so depends on the readiness of the Crown to grant letters patent. . . .
> That practice is a relic of a former colonial system, under which the ideas of old communities were unhesitatingly transferred and applied to new countries, without regard to the immense difference existing between the state of society in the colonies and at home.[3]

Bishop Gray and the Episcopalians of South Africa were rendered almost the status of Free Churchmen by another judgement of the Privy Council in the case of Bishop Colenso of Natal. In effect, the judgement was: (1) the United Church of England and Ireland was not a part of the Constitution in any colonial settlement, (2) its Clergy could not be recognized by the law of

---

[1] Minute 375: 22.x.69; 400: 3.xii.69.
[2] *Constitution and Canons of the Church of England in Jamaica* (Jamaica 1883), p. 100.
[3] *Daily News*, quoted in *Liberator*, Oct. 1865, p. 170.

the Colony other than as members of a voluntary association, and (3) their authority was merely spiritual, without real legal power. Thus neither the Bishop of Cape Town nor his 'synods' could depose the Bishop of Natal for his teaching, nor did the latter owe them canonical obedience.

For once, the Liberation Society hailed the words of Dr Pusey when he wrote to the *Churchman* newspaper on 28 March 1865: 'The Church of South Africa, then, is free, and this freedom is far better than a temporal juris-diction created by the State.'[1] Even the indefatigable Tractarian, Archdeacon Denison, in his *Church and State Review* for April 1865, applauded this fair working of the Voluntary principle and its future implications. That same year, in charging the Clergy of his diocese in the Cathedral of Cape Town, Dr Gray made a statement which caused some stir:

> What the Church of England would be, were the views of the Liberation Society carried out, that we are . . . It is the State, not the Church, which has declined to extend the support of the Church at home to the colonies.[2]

The Bishop went on to express his belief that the Church in the Colonies generally was apart from the British nation, however closely it might be in communion with the English Church. He declared further that the Church of England was hindered by various legal complications from throwing off the yoke of national tribunals and governing itself by its own 'synods' or convocations.

In answer to these 'unorthodox' views, the Rev. Frederick Denison Maurice wrote a letter which appeared in the *Spectator* magazine on 18 March 1865. Only the acknowledgement of the Church by a nation could be a worthy witness of Christ to other nations of the world.

> Let the Liberation Society say as loudly as it will that no one sect, be it Episco-palian or what it may, has any right to call itself the Church of Christ. But if all it can do is to uphold a multitude of sects, it may succeed in spreading the doctrine abroad that the nation is a secular and godless society; . . .

Edward Miall replied on behalf of the Liberation Society. The Society had never contended that the State should not act, in all things in which it was qualified to act, upon the highest and holiest motives. Nevertheless, it was to the Church and not the nation that Christ had committed the sacred trust of representing his spiritual claims upon men. Liberationists did not identify the Church of Christ with the nation; neither did they identify it with religious denominations or sects. The Society, he continued, did not regard its organi-zation or separate denominations 'as having a more sacred or more godly character than the whole body over which Queen Victoria reigns'. But there were certain realms which no Sovereign could control – freedom of worship and liberty of conscience. The Society did not cherish the ideals of the Puritans and Covenanters, who knew no toleration for diversities of religious

---

[1] Charles Gray, *Life of Robert Gray*, ii, 197.
[2] Robert Gray, *A Charge to the Clergy* (Cape Town 1865), pp. 10–11.

thought and practice, and would have had the Sovereign coerce all subjects into a profession of their creed. Rather, the Society honoured the hope of Christian men that union with their Lord might consist of a great variety of forms in which the same great central truth of revelation might be held.

To Christian Socialists like Maurice, there were two essential elements in every nation – spiritual and temporal – neither of which could work happily or safely if it existed apart from the other, or usurped the functions of the other. At the root of controversies as to whether the Ministers of the Christian Gospel should be supported by their congregations or salaried by the civil Government, lay crucial inquiries as to what the true functions of the State and Church actually were. To this Maurice answered in a concluding letter to the Liberation Editor:

> If the Liberation Society will help us to extricate *these* inquiries which concern our very life from those which concern either our private interests or the merely economic interests of Society, we may indeed hail it as our benefactor. I hope it is one of God's instruments for that purpose; for I feel in myself how much we need to be reminded every day and hour that the riches of a church may become its curses; . . .
>
> I believe that every Dissenter in the land will be in a worse, not in a better position, . . . if we were to announce ourselves members of a sect; if we were to give up the witness which we bear, however feebly, that the State and the Church are united, not by a money tie, but by Divine and eternal bonds which we may set at nought, but which we cannot break.[1]

Two basically different viewpoints therefore emerged from the South African unrest. Maurice believed that Church and State must work together. The Society believed that by such an alliance each would weaken the true nature of the other, and represent even less than before.

C. *The Bahaman Difficulty*

The Liberation Society was pleased to hail the abolition of a third Church Establishment in the year 1869. On 1 June of that year there was passed by the Legislature of the Bahamas an ecclesiastical laws amendment Act, which (1) relieved the revenues from all charges for the erection and repair of churches, (2) terminated the salaries paid to the Episcopal and Presbyterian Ministers of the Colony, (3) revoked all the financial arrangements that regulated the affairs of the Church of England in the Bahamas, (4) relinquished to the local Church full liberty in the conduct of its own affairs, and provided for appointment of Commissioners in whom the legal estate of the Churches would be vested.[2]

The Bill embodying these features did not become law, however, without considerable resistance by the State-Church party. When the Legislative Council first rejected the measure in March 1869, the House of Assembly

---

[1] *Nonconformist*, 5.iv.65, p. 266.

[2] See Preamble setting forth reasons for disestablishment and a summary statement of the provisions of the Act: *Liberator*, March 1870, pp. 36–7.

requested the Governor to dissolve Parliament and order a fresh election. His Excellency declined the request as an infringement of the prerogative of the Crown. Whereupon the Assembly forced the issue by adjourning for three months, and on 8 April the Governor capitulated.

In the ensuing election a close alliance emerged between government officials and the Anglican Church leaders. The supporters of Disendowment were referred to as 'enemies of the Queen', and money was freely spent to oppose them in the constituencies. The final result of the ballot throughout the Colony was that sixteen Dissenters (Liberals) were returned to the House, having polled 5,568 votes, and twelve Churchmen (Conservatives), having polled 3,315 votes.

When the Disendowment Bill was introduced again, it suffered the same obstruction as before by the Legislative Council. Shortly afterwards the Governor, Mr R. Rawson, was replaced by Mr James Walker, who was more sympathetic to the will of the majority on this issue. Upon the third attempt the Legislative Council gave way and accepted the measure as part of the new Governor's 'retrenchment' policy.

The Bahamas Church Act resembled the Irish Church Act by giving to the Episcopalians the edifices in which they had worshipped. It differed in the provisions made for compensation of the Clergy, who would receive their salaries for only seven years after the passing of the Act. The principal promoter of the Bill, Mr R. H. Sawyer, wrote to the *Nonconformist* at the conclusion of the controversy,

> It is clear to every impartial observer, that the exclusive system of ecclesiastical State patronage which has hitherto obtained in the Bahamas has been fraught only with evil to the best and purest interests of the colony. Its natural tendency has been to make the Anglican haughty, and the Dissenter jealous. It has served to inspire both with sentiments and tempers contrary to the Divine precepts of our holy religion. . . . when the heat and passion of the late controversy shall have subsided, and the era of religious liberty and equality shall have been inaugurated, a more substantial union and harmony will subsist between all classes of Christians than has heretofore been known.[1]

---

[1] *Nonconformist*, 2.vi.69, p. 521. The practical effects of this legislation are also described in this letter.

CHAPTER 16

Permissions for Public Service

Anti-State-Church encroachments increase and multiply. This we also read in the manifold attacks on our grammar-schools, universities, burial laws, and qualifications for offices . . . no concessions satisfy . . . the Liberation Society goes from little to more . . . no sooner is one point carried, than it becomes the base of operations and the rallying-cry for other demands, larger and more importunate.

RICHARD MASHEDER[1]

The nature of our institutions and the genius of our people while they sanction and promote the utmost freedom of discussion, are adverse to needless change; and it therefore behoves every friend of progress to wait with patience and to argue with calmness, till public opinion is fully convinced, and the national mind puts its seal on the measures introduced into the Legislature.

LORD JOHN RUSSELL[2]

A. *Nonconformist Burials*

THE COURSE of this legislation during these years brought disclaimers that the Liberation Society had any part in it. Sir Morton Peto and his backers insisted that the proposals were based, not on any blue-print of the Society, but on Burials procedure which had been successful in other parts of the Kingdom. His Bill proceeded on the simple assumption that there should be no monopoly in the burial of the dead.

But the Society did not sit back meekly. Early in 1862, Dr C. J. Foster, of the Parliamentary Committee, wrote to Sir Morton offering to put the best facilities of the Society at his disposal. But the Baptist Baronet, fearing radical associations,[3] decided to keep matters under his and the Dissenting Deputies' supervision.

---

[1] *Dissent and Democracy*, pp. 283–4. This work is almost wholly devoted to amassing facts against the Liberation Society.

[2] Speaking at a banquet given in his honour at Newcastle in 1862. Spencer Walpole, *Life of Lord John Russell*, ii, 399.

[3] The Society in turn dissociated itself from him for his being a holder of patronage in the Church of England. The benefice of the Rectory of Oulton, near Lowestoft, was worth £500 a year; in 1862, when Sir Morton appointed the incumbent, the Society smiled at

Soon afterwards, Peto proposed that the right of Nonconformist Ministers to conduct burials in the Churchyard should be contingent on the permission of the parish Clergyman, provided that the refusal of permission was given within twenty-four hours. The Bill also provided that the cause of refusal should in each case be stated in writing to the applicant, to the Bishop, and to the Secretaries of State. The measure was read a second time and went into Select Committee. The Liberation Society announced that it had as much to do with the design of this Bill as it had to do with the Budget of the Chancellor of the Exchequer.

When the Bill came back from Committee, it gave absolute power of refusal to the incumbent, without regard to time limits. The Nonconformist Minister could not in any way perform a burial service for a member of the Established Church. In burial of his own members, the name of the Dissenting Minister and denomination and description of the intended service, should all be included in application to the Parish Priest. Such a service, if not in accord with the accepted ritual, should consist only of prayers, hymns, and Scripture readings.

In the correspondence between the Society and the Deputies in 1863, Dr Foster objected to the amendments and urged a different measure with a broader basis.[1] In reply, Sir Morton stated that he felt bound to go ahead with his Bill as amended because of a pledge he had given to the Dissenting Deputies. In a future session he would feel at liberty to introduce a different measure.

When voted upon, the Bill lost decisively. The provision calling for the incumbent to put in writing his reason for refusing burial was the most unfavourably received. Lord Robert Cecil declared that this would lead to permanent records in which the Clergyman would reveal to his Bishop nothing but his experience of the Liberation Society in his parish. He feared that these collected opinions would then be permanently placed in Paliamentary Blue-books by the Secretary of State.

> When they considered that these blue-books would be published to all the world, that their racy passages would be transferred to the columns of the *Liberator* and the *Nonconformist*, and that their contents in a still more garbled form would gradually find their way into the local newspapers, he asked them, whether the Bill, which was to introduce so much peace, harmony, and unity, would really have that effect in most of the parishes in England?[2]

The Society lapsed into silence on the subject until an entry in the Parliamentary Committee Minutes on 27 February 1867. It was then reported that Lord Redesdale had brought into the Lords a Bill providing that where land was added to a consecrated Churchyard, it also should be considered conse-

---

what they called the 'anomaly' of the choosing of a Church of England rector by a 'dissenting patron'. *Liberator*, Feb. 1862, p. 23.

[1] Parl. Com. Min., 8.i.63; Executive Com. Minute 176: 30.i.63.

[2] Hansard (3rd series), clxx, 147.

crated. The purpose of the measure was to facilitate the extension of existing Churchyards by dispensing with the cost and trouble of a consecration deed, which conveyed the ground for burial according to the rites of the Church of England exclusively.

The Parliamentary Committee resolved that when the Bill reached the Commons, a qualifying clause should be inserted. This was that whenever any ground was added to a Churchyard, a portion thereof should remain unconsecrated – the extent of it to be determined by the parish vestry meeting, subject to confirmation by the Home Secretary. The opinion of Mr Braithwaite, Counsel for the Society, approved of this clause, and John Remington Mills (M.P., Wycombe) was asked if he would bring in a Bill for opening such Churchyards to Nonconformist Ministers.

Lord Redesdale's Consecration of Churchyards Bill was withdrawn on 30 July, when the Bishop of Oxford, Dr Wilberforce, introduced a similar Bill which rendered the presence of the Bishop within the Churchyard necessary for the rite of consecration. The Society therefore instructed Mr C. Gilpin (M.P., Northampton) to move the above qualifying clause on the grounds that the new portion of Churchyards should make the same allowances for Dissenters as were in the provisions of the Cemetery Act. The clause was defeated when Mr Gathorne Hardy, the Home Secretary, argued that this would in effect attach two kinds of burial grounds to the Church.

During the height of the struggle on the Irish Church Disestablishment in 1868 and 1869, Nonconformists were looking for 'lessons' in any Irish legislation which could be claimed as precedents for their agitation in England. The Act of the 5th of George IV, cap. 25, declared that the Parish Minister of the Church of Ireland might (upon application in writing by any duly authorized Dissenting Minister) permit a burial service at the grave of a Dissenter in the Parish Churchyard. In cases of permission being withheld, the incumbent of the Parish was required to send a statement of reason to the applicant and the Bishop of the diocese – the latter transmitting it to the Lord Lieutenant of Ireland.

So long as the permission was generally granted, the working of the Act was satisfactory. But there were numerous cases of arbitrary refusals, which naturally provoked irritation on the part of the Roman Catholic population whose Priests were excluded from ancient burial places that had originally belonged to them before the Establishment of the English Church.

Accordingly, in 1868, Mr W. Monsell (M.P., Co. Limerick) brought into the Commons and carried without difficulty a Bill establishing as a right what had previously been enjoyed as a favour in Ireland. It was passed by the Lords, with slight limitation in regard to the Churchyards of modern date.

Mr George Hadfield (M.P., Sheffield) introduced a measure in 1869 which aimed at a similar settlement in England. The Executive Committee of the Liberation Society appealed for petitions in support of the Bill especially from Wales where, owing to the preponderance of Nonconformists, the hardship of the law was most severely felt. Surprisingly, the *Guardian*, the High Church

15

journal, conceded the justice of the main propositions of the measure; but the pressure of other public business before both Houses prevented an adequate discussion of the matter.

Soon after, Mr Hadfield decided to retire from charge of this Bill because of failing health.[1] A special sub-committee was appointed by both the Dissenting Deputies and the Liberation Society to revise the Bill thoroughly and to secure his successor. They agreed upon Mr Osborne Morgan (M.P., Denbighshire), whose name was to be linked prominently with all burial legislation during the rest of the century.

B. *Endowed Schools*

In this legislative undertaking the Society's leaders made it quite clear that it was one for which they actually *were* responsible. There was no attempt to hide their role in its progress. In the paper, 'Parliamentary Action in 1862', the Bill of Mr L. L. Dillwyn (M.P., Swansea) which opened Endowed Schools and ancient charities to Dissenters, was described as a preparatory measure for future struggles.

Dillwyn, however, who was personally in charge of the measure, refused appointment to the Executive Committee to which he had been elected at the Fifth Conference of the Society. A year later, in response to Dr Foster's pledge for more thorough co-operation on the subject by the Society, he expressed his desire to work with the Parliamentary Committee. They eventually agreed upon the proposals that (1) no Endowed School of Royal foundation should be deemed to be a Church of England School, (2) the admission of scholars, and appointment of Masters, should be without distinction of sect, (3) no school should be considered a Church of England School unless it had been founded for the exclusive use of members of that Church.

The Society's Executive said that the Bill would open to Nonconformist scholars and Masters those institutions of great educational value, while it would take from Episcopalians nothing to which they could equitably lay claim. But because of the celebration of the Oxford Commemoration on 17 July 1863, and his Bill being on the order for that day, Dillwyn did not proceed further with it.

The Schools Inquiry Commission was formed in 1867, and legislation on the Endowed Schools was therefore delayed until the release of its report. The findings of this Commission caused the Gladstone Government to take up the question in 1869. A Bill was brought in by Mr W. E. Forster (M.P., Bradford) and Mr H. A. Bruce, the Home Secretary, which was broader than that of Dillwyn but achieved much the same object. Forster's Bill of fifty-eight clauses authorized Commissioners to deal with all the educational endowments so as to meet all needs in reconstructing Endowed Schools.

---

[1] Irritated at the intransigence of the Lords on his Burials measure, Hadfield gave notice of a motion in 1869 to exclude bishops from the House of Lords. He later withdrew it in favour of a similar motion by Mr Somerset Beaumont (M.P., Wakefield).

Eventually the Government Bill passed through all its stages in both Houses without undue disapproval, and with surprising ease. Had Parliament not been preoccupied with the Irish Church Act, and had the Schools Bill been in the hands of any other person than the Vice-President of the Committee of the Council of Education, this reform measure might have encountered serious difficulty. It was significant that Mr Forster and Mr Miall sat together as Liberal colleagues for the Bradford constituency. Through Miall it was possible for Forster to determine the mind of the Liberationists, and this was a wise preliminary to offering educational proposals in the name of the Liberal Government.

The proposals provided an increased opportunity for children from the lower classes and for reform in the management of the endowments. Where schools were intended by their founders to be denominational,[1] they should continue to be so, but in other cases: (1) trustees should not be disqualified on sectarian grounds, (2) laymen as well as clergymen should be eligible for masterships, (3) jurisdiction of the Anglican Bishops should cease, and (4) scholars should not be required to receive religious instruction or to attend places of worship to which their parents might object.

Although these provisions were modified slightly in the Committees of both Houses, the substance of the measure remained intact and was approved by the Parliamentary Committee of the Society. Lord de Grey led the Bill through a smooth passage in the Upper House, and it received the Royal Assent on 2 August 1869. Summarizing the significance of the Act, the *Nonconformist* commented:

> The Endowed Schools Bill is second only in importance, and in breadth of purpose, to the Irish Church Bill, to which, indeed, although in relation to a different object, it bears some analogy. It has its Commissioners as that has, and, under the responsibility and control of the Council of Education, it vests in them extraordinary powers.[2]

C. *Qualification for Offices Oaths*

Debating in the House of Lords on 13 May 1862, the Duke of Marlborough alleged that agitation on this question originated with the Liberation Society. Speaking in its defence, Lord Wodehouse denied that this was so:

> . . . if the members of [the Liberation] Society are the crafty and dangerous assailants which they are said to be, I cannot conceive that they could desire anything better than that the friends of the Church should maintain a small irritating grievance which would enable them to draw over many persons to side with them, who otherwise would stand aloof.[3]

---

[1] A school was 'denominational' where it was clearly provided for in the deed of foundation, or under the authority of the founder, or by statutes or regulations made within fifty years of the founder's death and continued in force to the present. Thus the large number of what were called Edward the Sixth's Grammar Schools ceased to be exclusively Church of England institutions.

[2] *Nonconformist*, 16.vi.69, p. 572.

[3] Hansard (3rd series), clxx, 660: 4.iv.63.

To those who were not members of the Established Church, it often seemed that religious oaths for public offices meant that 'Dissenters need not apply'. A Bill was eventually brought in by George Hadfield to abolish the declaration required for Cabinet Ministers and high positions in Parliament as well as for Mayors, Aldermen, Common Councilmen, and Borough Magistrates. It had been adopted in 1828 in place of the sacramental test in the Test and Corporation Acts then repealed:

> I do so solemnly and sincerely, in the presence of God, profess, testify and declare, upon the true faith of a Christian, that I will never exercise any power, authority or influence which I may possess, by virtue of the office of . . . to injure or weaken the Protestant Church as it is by law established in England, or to disturb the said Church, in the possession of any rights or privileges to which such Church, or the said bishops or clergy, are or may be by law entitled.

In order to give validity to official acts by those who had not qualified themselves by taking this oath and declaration, an Indemnity Bill had been passed annually. The office-holders in question were thereby indemnified against any penalties they might thus have incurred. To Hadfield and his supporters this kind of manœuvre was the best proof that Nonconformists had a genuine grievance. The Opposition felt that the difficulty was 'purely theoretical', and that if the existing law was actually a hardship, then the Bill cloaked sinister motives against the Established Church.

With the support of Gladstone as Chancellor of the Exchequer, the measure passed the Commons on 4 March 1863, but the Lords tossed it aside. Undaunted, the Congregationalist member for Sheffield concentrated upon showing that as a security to the Church of England the declaration was valueless. In one instance his investigation of five corporations had shown that the declaration had been made by only eleven of the officers, but that it had been avoided by as many as 5,300 such persons.[1]

Hadfield's Bill weathered the Select Committee in 1865, and for the sixth time it passed comfortably through all stages in the House of Commons. Endorsed in previous years by Lords Taunton, Russell, and Lyttelton, the measure on this occasion was placed in the charge of Lord Houghton for passage in the Upper House. There the leader of the Conservative party, Lord Derby, acknowledged the uselessness of the declaration as protection to Anglicanism, but insisted that its removal would be a dangerous encouragement to Dissent. On the strength of his argument, the Bill was rejected in the Lords for the fifth time.

For this the *Liberator* denounced Derby as the 'Canute' of the Established Church – 'the half heathen, half Christian King'. The Bill, however, on the next attempt in 1866, as a corollary to a uniform Parliamentary Oath Bill, passed unopposed, and the Royal Assent was at last given on 18 May to the abolition of the declaration.[2]

[1] Hansard (3rd series), clxxxi, 1239–40.
[2] 29 Vict., cap. 21. For the text of the Bill, see *Liberator*, Oct. 1866, p. 170.

For all that, the Act nevertheless did not clear away completely the inconveniences for which the Indemnity Bill had been annually necessary. The continuance of this Bill in a modified form was to Nonconformists a clear sign that the political instincts of the age were still dominated by ecclesiastical fears.

PART FOUR

Trial and Error
1870 – 1886

CHAPTER 17

Introductory

Religious people have already taken sides, and those whom
we have yet to convince, whose opinions are undetermined,
are those whom neither church nor chapel can confidently
reckon as its own—who refuse absolutely to be guided by
sectarian or theological considerations, and who can only
be reached through political argument.

JOSEPH CHAMBERLAIN: from Chairman's ad-
dress at the Annual
Meeting of the
Society, 3 May 1876.[1]

PHYSICALLY the Liberation Society grew into a Leviathan during this
period. Its power expanded considerably beyond that of the previous
period, but its legislative victories were not as striking. Unfortunately
for its supporters, its peak in organization and its peak in Parliamentary
success did not coincide.

In the 1870s, however, the Liberationists were high upon a great wave of
public opinion, moving quickly toward the fulfilment, they hoped, of their
ultimate aims. According to *The Times*, the Established Church was but 'little
more than a moiety of the English people; little more than a third of the
British people'.[2] In 1876 Nonconformists had 20,536 places of worship compared with 15,468 consecrated buildings of the Church of England. Earl
Granville wrote to Mr Gladstone in 1877 that a great mass of the people 'did
not care twopence about the Eastern Question, County Franchise, or anything
else, but only Miall and Disestablishment'.

The broad task of the Society to establish equal justice for all religious
classes was now part of the accepted political theory of the day. Across the
European Continent the same movement was spreading. Debates had been
raging in Russia, Italy, Spain, Portugal, Switzerland, and Austria on the
separation of Church and State. Even Sweden and Prussia, 'now the head-

[1] *Nonconformist*, 4.v.76, p. 448. Before the Meeting he wrote to Jesse Collings: 'I have
agreed to take the Chair in Spurgeon's Tabernacle – Ye gods, think of a Unitarian in the seat
of the prophet! – for the Liberation Society.' J. L. Garvin, *The Life of Joseph Chamberlain*
(London 1932), i, 226.
[2] *The Times*, 18.ix.74.

quarters of Establishmentarianism, feel the earthquake coming'.[1] In the call to re-examine the temporal foundations of the Church of England, there were two kinds of voices – political Dissenters and dissatisfied Episcopalians:

> Day by day, I see the Church gathering more mediocrity within its pale—day by day growing more hostile to learning and intellect—crushing where it cannot answer—preaching where it cannot teach—repeating its watchwords, not fighting its true fight.[2]

> . . . with the present just political toleration of all religious beliefs or unbeliefs in subjects of the realm, all equally entitled to political representation and influence in the secular Parliament and the secular government, the Church must at once face the alternative of either retaining her Establishment and repudiating the Faith, or retaining the Faith and repudiating her Establishment.[3]

A. *Reasons for Failure and Disunity*

The labours of the Liberation Society during this period involved considerable trial and error. Although the wave upon which the Society moved was to sweep aside much that was objectionable, it failed to shift the rock[4] on which the foundations of a Christian nation were built. And so the main bridge between Church and State remained.

The basic reason for this failure was the fact that the strength of Dissenters in Parliament was not proportionate to their strength outside. Four-fifths of the members of Parliament in Gladstone's first Ministry were also members of the Church of England. It is true that at the time of the fourth Gladstone Ministry the Dissenting strength reached beyond this (109 Nonconformist M.P.s), but it was never strong enough to induce Churchmen to desert their Church. Liberal candidates pledging to voters outside Parliament to support a general policy of Disestablishment, and political Dissenters aggressively seeking inside Parliament the actual break between Church and State, were not the same thing.

The second reason for failure in final Disestablishment was the fact that divided counsels arose among the Society's supporters as to how best to fulfil their principles and as to which Parliamentary issue was the best medium. The uncertainty was demoralizing, and it aroused questions to which no final answers could be given: Was the time ripe for concentrating all energies

---

[1] *Church Times*, 20.i.71.

[2] Frederic Harrison D.C.L., LITT.D., LL.D., *Autobiographic Memoirs*, i, 146. Spoken as an Oxford Radical in 1853.

[3] The Rev. John B. McClellan M.A., Vicar of Bottesham, *The Fourth Nicene Canon and the Election and Consecration of Bishops* (London 1870), p. 88.

[4] According to Alfred Illingworth, when Gladstone was once asked how he managed to sit out long, dreary hours of debate in the Commons, he replied, 'I have not so much time for religious exercises during the Session, as I used to have, and I will show you what I do.' Out of his pocket he drew a paper bearing a full Latin translation of 'Rock of Ages'. See pamphlet in the Bodleian Library, Oxford: '*Rock of Ages*': *Interesting Particulars, not hitherto published, of this Favourite Hymn of the Rt. Hon. W. E. Gladstone*, by the Rev. J. Brown, of Wincanton (Bristol 1898).

against the English Establishment? Would it not be better to disestablish in Wales and Scotland first, and continue gradually in England? Would not a strong policy of State education in the schools be a better way of working toward this idea of Disestablishment?

The third reason was the diversion of the people's attention to the nation's foreign and military affairs. On 'the Eastern Question'[1] the Nonconformists protested against Britain's 'pagan' foreign policy that supported the anti-Christian Turks. Many Anglican Clergy, however, were inclined to favour Lord Beaconsfield's alliance against Russia. Mr Gladstone was reported, on 15 September 1877, in the *Daily News*:

> The conduct in this matter [the Eastern Question] of many persons of superior Christianity, and in particular of the majority of the clergy, as contrasted with that of the Nonconformists, will to my dying day be to me a subject of great grief and astonishment.

The Peace Society loudly contended that war had been waged without the sanction of Parliament. The Boer and Afghanistan Wars in 1880, followed by Khartoum and the unrest in Egypt five years later, called for emergency economic measures. The net result of these events was a national depression in trade and a loss in agriculture. Shortage of money made it difficult for voluntary societies to gain new subscriptions in support of their work.

Fourthly, during the Ritualist controversy within the Anglican Church, the Liberation Society made the great mistake of *waiting* for the Establishment to crumble. This period roughly coincided with the return of the Liberals from 1880 to 1886. In the editorials of the *Nonconformist*, the Society made a great issue of Ritualist and Sacerdotalist offences. They insisted that 'mutinous public servants' should be given punishment for breaking the law and not the crown of martyrdom. But the consequences of the imprisonment of a few Priests were not as devastating to the unity of the Church as many had expected. The Society had reckoned that Disestablishment would follow upon dissension among the three Church parties. Instead of secession there was an alliance of two to keep the third party from gaining ascendance.

Churchmen realized that internal dissension without the protection or control of the law of the State would mean the disintegration of the Church of England, and loss of national prestige for each of its parties. Englishmen feared that Disestablishment of the Church of England would eventually mean the re-establishment of the Church of Rome. And so the most that the Evangelical and Liberal Churchmen would concede to the Anglo-Catholics was 'remodelling' and 'reconstruction', but not Disestablishment. This made it impossible for the Society to achieve ultimate success through an alliance with any of these three parties.

The fifth and most apparent reason for the failure of English Disestablishment was that the two greatest Parliamentarians of the age were opposed to it.

---

[1] The Rev. R. W. Dale and the Rev. J. Guinness Rogers curtailed their large lecture tour on Disestablishment as a result of the national crisis.

Gladstone and Disraeli acting together made the task of their political adversaries practically hopeless. Churchmen and Clergy everywhere had been long preparing for the final attack, and in these two devotees they had their most reliable defence.

Gladstone's defence, however, was the more unshakeable, because he was more ready than Disraeli to admit the weaknesses of the Church. In a letter appearing in the *Liberator*, the man who once considered becoming an Anglican clergyman wrote:

> I admit that the Church is losing ground in this respect relatively to the lay mind of the country; but when I look to moral tone, if nobleness is repelled from Holy Orders, I know not where it takes refuge. . . . If the Establishment is hard to maintain, it is harder to destroy. But I do not anticipate that reforms of it such as you desire will ever appear anywhere except on paper. I have one advantage over you. The Church of England was, in my view, founded not 300 years ago, but 1800, and I am persuaded there is that in her which, with Establishment or without it, will keep or find for her, great as are her sores and her sins, a place and a name in the final record of God's dealings with mankind for their salvation.[1]

In Disraeli's opinion the Romanizers and Radicals both threatened the national Constitution and belonged to revolutionary movements that drew instinctively together. He therefore despised the Liberationists, and did what he could to thwart the Tractarians.

Because the Liberal Premier went along with both streams, he had the best of both possible worlds – vast numbers of the Clergy and the rank and file following him. What might have happened, had the Nonconformist forces succeeded in converting him to the 'Unauthorized Programme',[2] as they had expected? The Liberal party might have avoided later internal strife between Rationalists and Ritualists, and English history might have taken a dramatically different turn. But as it was, the extreme deployments of the Disestablishers were politely ignored by Mr Gladstone, and a tired Mr Miall declined to return to Parliament in 1874.

A Church calling itself National must reform itself to recognize differences of opinion and become 'as creedless as possible', said Sir John Coleridge.[3] Churchmen from both sides of the House were anxious that this work be wrought by their own hands and not by outside interference. And so the Conservative Government from 1874 to 1880 also produced ecclesiastical reforms – the Increase of Episcopate Bill, the Public Worship Regulation

---

[1] *Liberator*, Sept. 1875, pp. 145–6.

[2] This was the name given by G. J. Goschen to 'the little red volume' edited by John Morley and Joseph Chamberlain in 1874 (from articles in the *Fortnightly Review*), later known as 'the Radical Programme'. Its main features were: Free Land, Free Trade, Free Schools, Free Law, and Free Church.

[3] Speaking on 'Free Inquiry in the Established Church' at Sion College, on 13 January 1870: *Macmillan's Magazine*, March 1870.

Bill, and the Bill to amend laws relating to Simony, Patronage, and Exchange of Benefices.[1]

The Society might easily have expended its energy by pressing its principles in minor Bills, and many Church Defenders hoped that this would happen. During the 1882 session alone, twenty-nine ecclesiastical measures were brought in – fourteen of them specifically for the reform of the Anglican Church. Liberationists accused Gladstone of crowding the debates with small measures to forestall major motions on Disestablishment. But Nonconformity as a whole advanced on a broad front in three basic Bills – Burials, University Tests, and State Elementary Education. These were in the hands of promoters who consulted with the Society's leaders, but the specific Bill for extended Disestablishment lay solely with the initiative of the Liberation Society.

The failure of the Disestablishment motions of 1871–3, together with the success of the Government Education Bill of 1870, brought a breach between the Nonconformist-Radicals and the rest of the Liberals. When the former made their spectacular withdrawal through a policy of 'Give no aid', the ardent Dissenters' dream of political supremacy was spoiled. The Radical Nonconformists therefore formed a somewhat independent wing closely under the guidance of the Liberation Society. As such, it held a certain balance of power in the Liberal party, and on several occasions by its obstruction it threatened the downfall of the Gladstone Ministry.

All through the second Disraeli Ministry, efforts were made within the Opposition party to patch up their internal quarrel. The Editor of the *Fortnightly Review*, John Morley, contended in 1876 that the Liberal party could be reconstructed along the lines of the Liberation Society. Disestablishment was the one subject on which there was the certainty of a crowded meeting in any large town throughout the country. Once this ground had been broken, Morley and his friends confidently expected the arrival of new allies for the Disestablishment campaign – dissatisfied elements in the three Anglican parties, the Wesleyans, the Labour leaders. The Marquess of Hartington and his Whigs would follow 'as soon as a compact and vigorous body of men had put the Liberal rank and file into line'.

As matters turned out this was expecting too much. Many of the Whigs and Moderates, at one time sympathetic with the stand of the Society, turned away when it openly decided 'to go for the Church' and disendow her. When the question became narrowed to a direct struggle for mastery between Nonconformity and Anglicanism, the effective sympathy of the country inclined to the traditional Church. Thus in the ebb and flow of politico-ecclesiastical issues during this period, the breach widened, taking the Liberal party further and further from a united attitude on the English Establishment question. By 1886 the question was virtually out of sight, and there was never again to be

[1] At this time the following Societies were intent upon reform within the Church: the Church Association, the Church Reform Union, the National Society for the Abolition of Purchase in the Church, the Prayer Book Revision Society, the Curates' Alliance, and the Church Defence Association.

an effective representation in the House of Commons for the total separation of Church and State.

In that year the Nonconformists and Radicals were themselves split on whether or not Ireland should be given Home Rule, and the Government therefore was defeated. On this issue the great Liberation doctrine of religious equality for all fell short in its application to the Roman Catholics in Ireland. Some observers wondered if this disunity had been used by Gladstone as 'a great diversion' to break the power of the Disestablishers and save the Church.

> The Nonconformists had won all the battles except the last, and now the two wings of the alliance were separated by an impassable gulf. 'The Irish Question' had settled 'the Church Question' and saved the Establishment. Between them, 'Captain Boycott' and 'Captain Moonlight', Parnell and the Irish Party, John Bright, Joseph Chamberlain and their forty-four followers, had so wrought that, sixty years after, the Church of England still survives as an Establishment and the Book of Common Prayer still remains, . . .[1]

As the Society fell more in line with the Radicals and the secular principles of the day, it moved further away from the traditional Nonconformist pattern of behaviour. The policy of the Society now seemed more clearly political than religious. The 'Nonconformist Conscience' and the 'Radical Programme' had come to a parting of the ways.

The first signs of more than ordinary dissatisfaction within the Liberation Society was revealed as early as 1868 in the correspondence between Canon Girdlestone of Bristol and Mr Samuel Morley, a hosiery millionaire and newly elected Liberal M.P. for that city. At the time of the 1868 General Election, the Canon expressed his approval of Gladstone's policy on the Irish Church, but was dubious of voting for Morley because of his connexion with the Liberation Society. Mr Morley answered:

> I have thought many times that my want of concurrence in some of 'the objects' of the Society, as defined in the prospectus, and my dislike of extreme statements made by some of its supporters, render it doubtful if I ought to belong to the Society at all, but I am not accustomed to be overscrupulous in helping societies which in the main are doing good.[2]

He expressed full sympathy with most of the aims of the Society, namely: (1) the separate functions of Church and State, (2) the spiritual nature of the Church, and (3) the education of public opinion on the harm of State-controlled religion. Although supporting Disendowment of the Church of Ireland, he flatly rejected the secularization of all national property held in trust by the Church of England – 'the two are entirely different.'[3]

[1] Addison, op. cit., p. 163.

[2] Minute 204: 4.xii.68.

[3] The Rev. Charles Williams and the Rev. Marmaduke Miller, two ardent supporters, put a resolution before the Tenth Triennial Conference that the Society did not intend to deprive the Church of England of its private endowments. The resolution was first shelved, and later passed with many abstentions. Minute 990: 14.iv.71.

In the view of the Liberation Society this was a false stand. Consequently, Morley, who had long been one of the Society's most generous donors, requested the withdrawal of his name from the Executive Committee in order 'to place myself in an attitude, not of antagonism, but of friendship, with all truly devout men by whose co-operation the religious future of England may be determined'.[1] The Society replied that it had no rigidly defined scheme of Disendowment, and that it had a responsibility for 'assisting to extricate' the Church from its difficulties.

The Education Bills before Parliament had divided Nonconformists into two parties – those who believed that the State should share in the religious instruction given in the national Schools, and those who believed that the religious education should be voluntarily entrusted to the various denominations. Most of the members of the Liberation Society took the latter position, but a minority dissented. Mr William Edwards, the Treasurer and Chairman of the Executive Committee, resigned in 1872 because of a 'violation of the Society's policy of neutrality' in the controversy.

The trouble began with a report in the official organ of the Society, the *Liberator*, concerning the Nonconformist Conference in Manchester on 24–25 January which enthusiastically favoured compulsory secular education by the State and voluntary religious education by the various Church bodies. The article deprecated the policy of neutrality on the issue and described the Conference as 'the greatest and most important Nonconformist gathering which has been witnessed since Nonconformity came into being'.[2]

The report also included parts of the address of the planning Secretary, the Rev. R. W. Dale, also a member of the Executive Committee of the Society, who was described as 'the moving spirit of the Conference'. Under his guidance the proceedings were the beginnings of what was later described as the 'Nonconformist Revolt'.[3] Nonconformists who shrank from the principle of 'combined secular and separate religious instruction' in the State, said Dale, made it impossible for them consistently to object to the control of religion by the State. He believed that local Nonconformist Associations organized around this principle might (1) promote a movement for Disestablishment of the School instead of the Church, and (2) succeed better than the Liberation Society at securing the election of 'dependable' M.P.s.

Edwards took this as a rebuke to his leadership of the Society. His letter contained the following paragraph:

I am one of those who still believe that a good moral training can only be secured in our primary schools by Biblical instruction being combined with secular education, and I should be sorry to take any step that would tend to disunite them. The last resolution of the Conference, inasmuch as it asks the force of law to prohibit the teacher from giving religious instruction, is as much a

[1] Edwin Hodder, *The Life of Samuel Morley*, 2nd ed. (London 1887), p. 280.
[2] *Liberator*, Feb. 1872, p. 25.
[3] A. W. W. Dale, *Life of R. W. Dale*, pp. 286–99.

violation of our Liberation principle, I think, as is support of religious teaching of the State . . .[1]

When asked by a deputation of the Society to reconsider his resignation, he declined, but agreed to give help in an unofficial capacity. The Executive Committee presented to him a testimonial of appreciation for his services of eighteen years as Chairman and twenty-two years as Treasurer.

Thus two 'pious benefactors', Mr Morley and Mr Edwards, withdrew their membership when the Society moved toward entire secularization of national religion and education. Such individuals, who liberally invested their private money in voluntary agencies and institutions, could appreciate the anger of Anglicans at plans to re-appropriate the private endowments in their Schools and Churches.

B. *Extension, 'Agency System', and Allies*

Although the 'unattached Christian' often considered himself a member of the Church of England, the censuses of places of worship in 1881–2 which were conducted by sixty newspapers decidedly favoured the Free Churches. The increased numbers in Nonconformity made possible a wider extension of Liberation principles.

Furthermore, the expansion of the Society was indirectly assisted by several kindred organizations which agitated for greater freedom within the Church of England: the English Church Union, attempting to win back 'former liberties' of the Church; the Church of England Working Men's Society, calling for 'liberty with Establishment'; the Laymen's Association for the Restoration of Church Rights, urging self-government within the Church; and the League for the Separation of Church and State, seeking Disestablishment without Disendowment. The last-named body, composed of Ritualists and High Churchmen, most nearly approximated to the work of the Society.

In spite of all these favourable circumstances, however, the Society began to encounter a stiff resistance. A great deal of this was due to the counter-action of the Church Defence Association, also called the 'Association for the Defence and Promotion of National Religion'. This Defence Association, with its monthly organ *National Church*, operated in much the same fashion as the Liberation Society, but exclusively for the benefit of the Church of England. For example, the Secretary of the Yorkshire branch of the Association, Mr Sales, once corresponded with Mr Miall:[2]

Sir,
    In consequence of the erroneous statements concerning the Church of England made by persons who profess to be representatives of the Liberation Society, I am requested to invite you, as the leader of the disestablishment movement, to

---

[1] Minute 1166: 12.ii.72. Philip J. Crellin Jr and Henry M. Bompas also resigned at this time from the Executive Committee because of this issue.
[2] *Nonconformist*, 27.xii.71, p. 1262.

a public discussion in Leeds, of the union of Church and State, with the Rev. Dr. Massingham. . . .

As the Church of England has nothing whatever to fear from the fullest discussion, and as it is most desirable that the working classes should have an opportunity of hearing a debate, free from the clap-trap of the platform, I earnestly trust that you will accept this invitation.

> I am, your obedient servant,
> Henry H. Sales, Secretary.

Sir,

I beg to decline your invitation to "a public discussion in Leeds of the union of Church and State, with the Rev. Dr. Massingham." I never knew platform discussions on controverted questions before an excited audience contribute anything worth speaking of towards the elucidation of truth, nor kept free from what you describe as "the clap-trap of the platform." So long as the House of Commons remains open to me, I shall not want a more suitable sphere for honest debate than that which you have invited me, nor do I imagine that my views will be subject to a less formidable scrutiny in that House than they might have to encounter under the critical skill of even the Rev. Dr. Massingham.

> I am, Sir,
> Yours faithfully,
> Edward Miall.

The circulation of the *Liberator* during this period was between ten and twelve thousand subscribers. By 1881 it was placed in a hundred coffee houses throughout London. For fuller coverage of its activities, the Society in 1878 purchased additional space in the *Nonconformist* newspaper, and three years later spent £150 yearly for advertising in the *Edinburgh Daily Review*. The Publication Committee boasted that it was able to insert its communications and letters in 200 journals of the nation. Opportunity was now taken to use 'mural advertising' on placards, particularly in railway stations.

Throughout the latter half of 1871, efforts were made to arrange a series of 'respectable' lectures in London by Dr Hugh Cairns of Berwick, Prof. J. E. Thorold Rogers of Oxford, Prof. James Bryce of Oxford, Profs. Sheppard and Seeley of America, Henry Fawcett M.P., George Trevelyan M.P., and Neville Goodman M.A. The lectures were to be supplemented by special publications to answer arguments of the 'better informed people'.[1]

The philosopher and literary critic, Frederic Harrison, lectured on Disestablishment under the auspices of the Society from 1875 to 1877 in London, Manchester, Bradford, and Liverpool. His essay in the *Fortnightly Review* in May 1877, 'Church and State', was reprinted by the Society. Before 14,000 people at Bingley Ball, Birmingham, on 25 January 1875, John Bright gave a

---

[1] Mr J. H. Gordon, of Darlington, became the Society's 'special lecturer' in 1874 at a salary of £250 and later of £350 per annum. The lectures in 1875 numbered 698. By 1876 the number was 957, and the total publications numbered 2,567,000 copies. In 1877–8, 104 lecturers led 930 lectures and meetings, and 3,150,000 publications were issued. The total of meetings and lectures for 1875–9 was 4,281. The Archbishop of Canterbury (Dr Tait) issued a Pastoral Letter in 1881 urging the Church Defence Association to match such efforts of the Liberation Society.

lecture urging Disestablishment on the consciences of all politicians. This also was published as a pamphlet of the Society.

The lecturing for the Society reached its greatest popularity in the Disestablishment tour of the Rev. J. Guinness Rogers and the Rev. R. W. Dale in 1875–6 to Bradford, Leeds, Manchester, Liverpool, Bristol, Norwich, Plymouth, and London. The campaign coincided roughly with that of the Evangelists Moody and Sankey, and adopted a similar mass appeal. At the end of the long railway journey, a dinner was given in honour of Dale and Rogers by the Executive Committee. After many requests, the mission was repeated in the 1876–7 season, extending this time also to Wales.

The imprisonment of the Rev. A. Tooth, Vicar of St Stephen's Church, Hatcham, for contempt of the Arches Court in a suit under the Public Worship Regulation Act,[1] brought two lectures by Rogers at Memorial Hall in February 1877. Soon after this exposition of 'the Hatcham Case and its Lessons', the accused was released. As Liberationists made political capital out of such cases, State authorities seemed hesitant to enforce the full letter of the law.

During this period, the Society drew upon the help of leading Nonconformist Preachers, and made its way into Nonconformist Colleges. Charles Haddon Spurgeon, Joseph Parker, Alexander McLaren, John Clifford, Hugh Price Hughes, and John Howard Hinton were effective speakers at large public gatherings of the Society. Of these men, perhaps Spurgeon was the most open in his sympathy with the aims of the Liberationists. He wrote to the Annual Meeting of the Society in his Tabernacle in 1882: '. . . more strength to the true friends of the Church of England, who would establish her by disestablishment, and enrich her by disendowment.' J. Carvell Williams campaigned in the Colleges, indoctrinating ministerial students at Rawdon, Hackney, New (London), Regent's Park, Lancashire Independent, Spring Hill, Nottingham, Bristol Baptist, Pontypool, and Bala Independent.[2]

The financial prosperity of the Society during this period made it one of the strongest 'political pressure groups' in the nation. The new Treasurer, Mr Alfred Illingworth of Bradford, reported in 1873 the first deficit (£50) in the Society's annual account. He promptly advanced £500 on personal loan to the Society, and within a single year he had completely reversed the financial picture.

The Triennial Conference in 1874 adopted a plan by Illingworth for raising a special Campaign Fund of £100,000. Before the conclusion of the meetings, personal pledges amounted to £22,500. Individual donations were: £5,000

---

[1] *Punch* caricatured this case as that of 'the unsound tooth that can't be stopped'. A. L. Drummond, *The Churches Pictured by 'Punch'*, p. 17.

[2] After twenty-five years as Secretary of the Society, Williams visited the United States in 1872, hoping to acquire practical ideas and financial support. After his return, the Rev. H. L. Wayland D.D., of Philadelphia, and the Rev. Henry Ward Beecher D.D., of New York, were each invited to speak at the Annual Meetings of the Society. Williams lectured on Voluntaryism within the United States and their Constitutional principle of separation of Church and State.

from himself and Henry Illingworth, £5,000 from Sir Titus Salt and sons, and £5,000 from Isaac Holden and sons – all residents of Bradford, Mr Miall's constituency. By the time of the Annual Meetings the next year, £47,500 had been pledged. At the end of the five-year campaign, the final result, including regular subscriptions, legacies interest and dividends, amounted to £84,063.[1]

When Trade Unions were legally recognized in 1871 their style of operation was evident in the organization of the Society. Deputations sent out from the central office at 2 Serjeants' Inn, Fleet Street, influenced Local Committees, newly formed Borough Councils, and larger District Councils of the Society such as those in Manchester, Bradford, and Edinburgh. An Organizing and Travelling Secretary, the Rev. John Fisher of Sheffield, was appointed in 1874 to collate the work of District Agents who in turn supervised the work of Local Agents.

This enlargement of the Agency system gave the Society a vast network of information centres throughout the country. By mid-1875 the Local and Central Committees had commissioned five District Agents, eighteen Local Agents in England and Scotland, four London Agents, and three Welsh Agents. The Agents were responsible for collecting subscriptions, registering electoral statistics, and providing information to voters.

In their attempt to remodel the Liberal party into the proposed Federation of National Liberal Associations in 1877, its architects Joseph Chamberlain (Chairman of the National Education League) and Francis Schnadhorst (Secretary of the Central Nonconformist Agency) were accused of 'Americanizing' English politics by means of the 'caucus idea'. The Liberation Society afforded these men of the Birmingham School an effective example of this idea. It was an association covering the whole country, existing independently of official party control, and holding power over Parliamentary leaders.

The Agency system and its deputations thus afforded a means of direct intervention in the constituencies. Close attention was given to those where a change in representation was possible, or where opponents of the Society might be persuaded not to vote against Disestablishment. Full information was sought from all political clubs with which the Society could act in the constituencies. A record of votes of M.P.s on ecclesiastical questions was kept and issued by the Society's central office.

The *Quarterly Review* for January 1879 in an article, 'Aggressive Nonconformity', dwelt upon the vices and virtues of this Liberation Agency system. The mainspring of the machine, the writer maintained, was 'a handful of Bradford manufacturers and wool-combers'. Backed by a vicious Radical Press and 'the living voice of a vast army of Dissenting ministers throughout the country', it formed 'a powerful propaganda'.

---

[1] The Society's annual income in 1877–8 was £16,353, an increase of £7,789 over that reported ten years before. In 1877 the Society received a legacy of £10,000 left by W. J. Etches of Derby. A portion of the first payment, £4,500, was invested in Railway Preference Stock. Other legacies were £5,000 bequeathed in 1878 by Jacob Ballowby Powell, and £2,500 in 1881 by Samuel Courtauld of Braintree.

Concentrated effort was made to gain new allies throughout the nation, particularly in the industrial areas of the North. The Society therefore set up links with the Nonconformist Associations of Birmingham, Manchester, Liverpool, and London. Under the Rev. R. W. Dale, the Central Nonconformist Committee directed the work of these Associations, which had been formed to repulse the 'evils' of the Education Act of 1870. The leaders in this movement were George Dixon, Joseph Chamberlain, Jesse Collings, Henry Crosskey, Charles Dilke, and Vernon Harcourt.[1] Direct ties were also made with the Scottish Disestablishment and Disendowment Associations of Glasgow and Edinburgh. The Society's own Scottish Council was established in 1877 with an executive of sixty members. The thousands of members of these bodies attended numerous mass meetings and joint conferences in the principal cities of England and Scotland.

Although there was considerable overlapping, the Society often acted as the policy-making body which co-ordinated the electoral activities of the other bodies. At the 1874 Triennial Conference, the Executive Committee was enlarged from 50 to 75 members, including six M.P.s. The Chairman, Henry Ellington, and the Secretary, Carvell Williams, were invited to Birmingham in 1877 for the proposed Federation of Liberal Associations throughout the country. At the Eleventh Triennial Conference that year, 1,200 delegates were sent from 100 groups all over the United Kingdom.

The Society also began earnest work in the rural districts and villages, inasmuch as it was there that the tradition of the Established Church was most firmly fixed. After the 1885 Election, the Society boasted that it had won the newly enfranchised rural counties for the Liberal party.

In order to help the Society extend into these districts, Carvell Williams attended the Congress of the National Agricultural Labourers' Union in 1873 at Leamington. The chief object of the Union was to gain the franchise for their labourers and relief from harsh land laws. The printed organ, the *Labourers' Union Chronicle*, held principles consistent with those of the *Liberator*.[2] Both of these journals spoke out against servility to 'the parson and landlord alliance', and called particular attention to the justice of the labourer's wage claims. Gladstone said in the *Nineteenth Century* magazine in November 1877, that the pro-capital country-Clergy had forced agricultural labourers to turn to sharp Nonconformist agitators and their aims:

Nonconformity, which still supplies, to so great an extent, the backbone of British Liberalism, is now largely intent on effecting disestablishment.[3]

---

[1] See Muirhead, *Nine Famous Birmingham Men.* In addition to Dale – Chamberlain, Crosskey and Collings were members of the Liberation Society. In 1884 Collings declined appointment as the Society's Agent and Lecturer for the Liverpool District Council. Minute 227: 18.ii.84.

[2] The Union comprised 71,835 members belonging to 982 branches in 24 counties. The *Chronicle* claimed 35,000 subscribers and 250,000 readers. In 1880 the circulation of the *Liberator* reached its peak – 13,000 copies at a cost of £960.

[3] *Nineteenth Century*, Nov. 1877, 'The County Franchise', p. 552.

The Society was anxious to take advantage of the discontent among the agricultural classes, particularly on the Tithe question. Distribution of the Tithe in rural areas was crucial in any Disestablishment scheme. Both the Society and the Union called for the secularization of Tithes 'to benefit the entire community'. The leaders of the Union, Joseph Arch and Henry Taylor, believed that such a stand with the Society would lead to a satisfactory Disestablishment. The organizations agreed to arrange lectures and circulate publications by joint house-to-house visiting.

One of the most significant activities of the Society was the promotion of its own labour movement. This was an attempt to organize an effective following not only among the radical philosophers and independent industrialists, but among the poor workers themselves. Labour groups with an Anglican bias arose to compete against Liberation Committees in the factories.

The tactics of this movement were viewed by its foes as seditious and revolutionary. The *Saturday Review* accused the Society's Executive Committee of enlisting the services of Socialist Republicans and Communists. Dissent was 'mercantile' in spirit and able to preach its Gospel only to those who could afford to pay for it. The Society was said to be in a 'violent alliance' with independent manufacturers who were accused of applying a policy of 'Leave the Church or leave the Mill'. The Society replied in the scheme of organization of 'The Working Men's Committee for Promoting the Separation of Church and State':

> Operations of the Committee are to be limited to the object for which it was formed, and in accordance with the Society's constitution, they are to be 'moral and constitutional only.' The Committee is free to adopt its own methods of action, and at liberty to promote the movement by means of local Committees or correspondents.

The members of this Committee were of several trades, including at least a bricklayer, an ironfounder, a joiner, a stonemason, a carpenter, a glassmaker, an engineer, a printer, and a Labour League representative. After an inaugural Conference in London in 1871, demonstrations and meetings were arranged in the large industrial areas. By the time of the 1880 General Election, however, little was heard of this organization.

The Working Men's Committee faced the hard task of reaching and convincing men of plain speech and short tempers. The debates with speakers of the Church Defence Association in Mechanics' Institutes and Temperance Halls occasionally gave rise to wild scenes, either side accusing the other of planting opposition to break up the proceedings. The *Liberator* reported an uproarious incident which took place on 22 November 1872 at Macclesfield, Cheshire. While the Society's lecturer, the Rev. Charles Williams was speaking, cayenne pepper was thrown about to get the audience sneezing, the stove was upset, and the pipes scattered.

> To give a description of the scene is almost impossible. When the chairman rose to order, 'Rule Britannia' would be struck up, and a shower of peas would be

hurled onto the platform. In the scuffles that took place several forms were smashed, and the railing around the school harmonium destroyed.[1]

In the Annual Report for 1876, the Society complained of forged tickets of admission at these meetings, the employment of noisy hooligans to stop speakers being heard, and occasional recourse to personal violence. Several cases of assault were taken to court. The Society regarded the matter as serious enough to issue a leaflet, 'Practical Hints to Promoters of Public Meetings', calling for a strong body of Stewards to deal with disturbers wisely but firmly.[2] Most of the lectures and meetings, however, afforded a fair opportunity to weigh the arguments intelligently.

C. *Leadership of Chamberlain and Morley*

Upon the retirement of Edward Miall from the active political scene, Liberationists were anxious to find some leader who might adequately fill his place. Many looked upon Joseph Chamberlain as 'their man', and so he was for a short time. But when the Irish Home Rule Bill came before Parliament in 1886, he disappointed many who had given him his political start.

Nevertheless, at the beginning of this period, as a craftsman in politics for Nonconformist Radicals, he quickly gained an influential position in the larger Parliamentary circles. His name was first carried to the public in the early 1870s on the education controversy, while he was an officer of the National Education League. Next as Mayor of Birmingham he exerted considerable influence in what was then the Opposition party in the Commons. From there he moved into the confidence of leading Liberals, and represented Liberation policy in the decisions of the party Executive. In his article, 'The Next Page of the Liberal Programme', his formula for reuniting Liberalism was the subordination of the Burials Bill, the crucial 25th clause of the Education Bill, and the Clerical Tests Bill, to general Disestablishment and Disendowment.

Chamberlain wrote to Carvell Williams in January 1875, indicating Gladstone's intention of resigning from the leadership of the Liberal party.[3] Nonconformists, Whigs, and Moderates were anxious over the choice of a successor. Even the 'Radical Triumvirate' could not agree – Dilke was for Hartington, Bright leaned toward his fellow Quaker, Forster, and Chamberlain at first wished Gladstone to remain at the helm.

By 1885, however, the eager Chamberlain had himself become Gladstone's most dangerous rival. Nothing but the providential life of the elder statesman stood between the Unitarian prophet of social reform and the Liberal Prime

---

[1] *Liberator*, Dec. 1872, p. 197.

[2] In *The Liberation Society – a Jubilee Retrospect*, p. 10 (ed. 1894) 'Addison's sketch of the old Tory fox-hunter, in the *Guardian*,' is quoted for the picture it gives 'of the bigotry and intolerance of those times'. He 'describes one of his acquaintances, a publican, as "the best Church of England man on the road". "He had not time to go to church himself, but had headed a mob at the pulling down of two or three meeting-houses." '

[3] Minute 425: 21.i.75.

Ministership.[1] Liberationists expected that when Gladstone retired, the Whigs would drop out, and the great body of the party would rally around Chamberlain. To every member of the House of Commons he was a man to bear watching. A journalist who was present on the occasion of his maiden speech there, on the Elementary Education Bill, on 4 August 1876, wrote:

> From the Gallery I saw the two great imperial statesmen meet. Chamberlain had said that Disraeli never opened his mouth without telling a falsehood. He stood, carefully groomed, eye-glass in eye, . . . Disraeli was fetched, sat down, and put up *his* glass, which he seemed to hold encircled with his forefinger, so that he might be quizzing; and so the two surveyed each other, doubtless exchanging telepathic defiance.[2]

With his gift of quick, incisive speech, Chamberlain was supremely effective before Liberation and working-class audiences. On these platforms he showed all the persuasive guile of Miall. From the Free Trade Hall in Manchester in 1872 he pressed forward the electoral policy of the Liberation Society, commanding 1,900 Nonconformist delegates to withdraw their votes until 'its tamer followers had learned the Liberal alphabet, and could spell out the first words of the Liberal creed'. Presiding at the Annual Meeting of the Society in 1876, he whipped the large gathering at the Metropolitan Tabernacle into a wave of enthusiasm:

> We have successfully assaulted the outworks of the citadel. The time has come to march to the assault of the inner fortress; and we have to rally our forces for this final consummation.[3]

Mr Chamberlain returned in 1877 to act as Chairman of the public session at the Society's Eleventh Triennial Conference. Turning to the Church of England, he repeatedly ridiculed the idea that it 'sweetens the life of the nation'.

> I thought at one time I would write an essay on this subject which should be wholly composed of extracts which I have been collecting from speeches and writings of Churchmen respecting the members of the body to which they belong, and I should call it 'The Church of England as Painted by Her Sons', and I will undertake to say that it would contain an indictment fiercer and more bitter than anything which Nonconformists have ever attempted to frame.

Disendowment, he said, had only been 'whispered in the ear', while Dis-

---

[1] Despite the 'stab in the back' that Gladstone had received from him over Irish Home Rule, the Grand Old Man always behaved toward him and all his other opponents with magnanimity. When Chamberlain's son Austen made his first speech opposing Gladstone, the father leaned forward in his seat with irritated expectancy as the Premier rose to reply. Gladstone gave sincere praise and spoke touching words of the delight which the speech must have given his father. At this the elder Chamberlain lost his composure for a moment. Justin McCarthy, *The Story of Gladstone's Life* (London 1898), pp. 339–40.

[2] Monypenny & Buckle, *Life of Disraeli*, ii, 819–20.

[3] In this speech, published by the Society, he assailed Matthew Arnold's speech that year to the clergy at Sion College against Dissenters. Chamberlain accused him of wanting to maintain the Church 'as a kind of moral police force for the vulgar'.

establishment, which was the fulfilment of the former, had been proclaimed from the housetops. He therefore was glad of the 'Practical Suggestions'[1] of the Society, to which he added his own: (1) under no circumstances should the precedent of the Irish Church Act be followed in the creation by the State of any new corporation; (2) compensation should be awarded to individuals and not to any Church body. Nonconformists based their right to this property on the right of the State to revise periodically the endowments – whether ancient or modern, whether the gift of pious ancestors or the subscriptions of the present generation – which had been acquired 'in favour of an ecclesiastical department of the State'. These views coincided with his later famous 'Ransom Theory':

> I hold that the sanctity of public property is greater than even that of private property, and that, if it has been lost or wasted or stolen, some equivalent must be found for it, and some compensation may fairly be exacted from the wrong-doer.[2]

About the time that Chamberlain declined renomination to his seat on the Executive of the Liberation Society, John Morley first accepted an appointment. For some years before this, however, he had been sympathetic with the Society's programme. He was much more of an uncompromising intellectual than his ambitious friend, and he could wield his pen with as much force as Chamberlain could his tongue.

Morley preached from the pages of his journals and from the tracts of the Society 'as a "refined type" of heretical priest'.[3] Because of his background as an Oxford Radical, he had more in common with Frederic Harrison, Goldwin Smith, James Bryce, Lyulph Stanley, and men of the academic Liberal set, than with the comparatively unaesthetic Radicals of the Manchester school. He enjoyed the select circle of friends in the Metaphysical Society and frequently attended the discussions as one of its members. There he became acquainted with the vigorous minds of Gladstone, Osborne Morgan, Cardinal Manning, Henry Fawcett, and again Frederic Harrison.

'The Church question is the only one I care about in politics', he wrote to Harrison in 1875. Shortly afterwards, the two of them were working together with a special Committee of the Liberation Society to draft a Disestablishment Act.[4] He and other Liberationists, notably Dale, had some misgivings about it. The chief objection was that the proposed scheme tried to fit the principle of congregational freedom into that of Episcopacy by means of some sort of synodical body.

[1] See p. 227, below.

[2] Stephen Gwynn & G. M. Tuckwell, *The Life of the Rt Hon. Sir Charles W. Dilke, M.P.* (London 1917), ii, 182; see also Garvin, *Life of Joseph Chamberlain*, i, 131–2.

[3] Warren Staebler, *The Liberal Mind of John Morley* (Princeton, N.J. 1943), p. 83.

[4] Morley had little confidence in the men on this sub-committee, except the Rev. Henry W. Crosskey. Dr Crosskey achieved great distinction for his scientific researches, mainly in geology. On Disestablishment, Crosskey strongly opposed any compromise dealing with Church endowments.

Undoubtedly through Morley's influence, Gladstone came to view the Liberationists' ideals more seriously. It was once said of Morley that he was the only Nonconformist really close to the heart of Gladstone. If that was true, Morley returned the trust by unflinching loyalty to his chief. At the time of the Irish Home Rule issue, when old friends were deserting the party union, Morley wrote to Dr Spence Watson, the chairman of his constituency committee in Newcastle:

> ... we northern radicals mean to support him tooth and nail—saving supremacy and unity. Much dirty intriguing is going on. I won't be a party to snubbing the Old Man.[1]

D. *Death of Edward Miall*

Mr Miall was the great Nonconformist pioneer of Christian liberalism in nineteenth-century politics. Throughout his life he was exceedingly popular with the host of Dissenting and Radical electors, and on several notable occasions they demonstrated their loyalty and affection for him.

The Liberals of the North of England gave a banquet in his honour at Newcastle in November 1871, and presented him with a testimonial and personal gifts. Responding to the toast to his health, Miall replied:

> I would very gladly at this moment, nay, thankfully, give up the enterprise, if my conscience recommended me to do so. . . . I have seen many things relating to myself, and to my work, that I would rather not have seen, although I must confess candidly that I could use the language of Brutus in reference to these things, and say, 'They passed by me as the idle wind, which I respect not.'[2]

Punch (16 Dec., 1871) presented its own tasteless 'testimonial':

> Miàll, Miàll,
> There once was call
> Foul of the Church for you to fall.
> But now what sect
> Can you select
> To which wise people less object?
> In her fold pent
> You might dissent
> At this day to your heart's content.
> She'd hold you all—
> 'Gainst her 'tis small
> To caterwaul, Miàll, Miàll!

Several personal friends and political associates of Mr Miall met, on 18 July 1873, for luncheon at the Crystal Palace. Henry Lee of Manchester presented to him 10,000 guineas 'in recognition of his public service in the *Nonconformist* newspaper, and as the representative in Parliament of the principle of religious equality'.[3]

[1] F. W. Hirst, *Early Life & Letters of John Morley* (London 1927), ii, 272.
[2] A. Miall, *Life of Edward Miall*, pp. 337–8.
[3] ibid., p. 348.

Miall wrote on 30 October 1873 to Sir Titus Salt, chairman of his election committee in Bradford, that failing health would prevent him from standing as a candidate in the next Election. The news was disturbing to his followers and they unsuccessfully tried to get him to change his mind. His opponents wondered if it were a sign that he was giving up the long fight. To this the *Pall Mall Gazette* replied that 'he was about as little likely to tell his constituents a series of falsehoods about his health to cover a retreat as any public man in the country'.[1]

On Miall's seventieth birthday, 8 May 1879, a party of old colleagues including John Bright, Henry Richard, and J. Carvell Williams, visited him at his residence at Honor Oak to present him with an address of congratulation, and to assure him of their great affection. His reply, his last addressed to the public, was characteristic:

> My great and enduring solace is this—that the movement for the liberation of religion from State patronage and control, is now far beyond the reach of personal changes. It is a moral force which has its life and vigour in itself; it is sure of triumph, though many of us perhaps will not live to see it.[2]

The final thrust of the Disestablishment campaign thus suffered a great loss in Miall's death on 29 April 1881.[3] There was no man of comparable zeal and perseverance in Liberation principles to take his place. While he was living, he was the 'brain-power' of the movement, dominating most spheres of its activity. The worth of his work found its place in the Statute Book of the Realm, and in what many statesmen believed to be healthier relations between Church and State.

To some observers he seemed to be the incarnation of the obnoxious Nonconformist. Many of the severe remarks about the Church of England, which opponents dwelt upon, were taken from his *Nonconformist's Sketch Book*, first published in 1841. Twenty years later, Miall published a new edition to disown the damaging passages:

> Were [the writer] called upon in his maturer age by sense of duty to go over afresh the same lines of thought, his disposition would incline him to bear himself more gently, and in a somewhat more modest, kindly, charitable spirit than he did when he was a controversial novice. In regard to both taste and temper, there are many phrases and several passages in the book which he could wish had never been written, and more particularly than those which apply to large bodies of men rather than to the systems with which they are associated.[4]

---

[1] ibid., p. 349.

[2] ibid., p. 354.

[3] See his obituary in the *Liberator*, June 1881, pp. 94–8. Other deaths during this period were setbacks to the cause: the Rev. John Howard Hinton, author (1873); Samuel Morley, philanthropist, who had declined a peerage (1886); Herbert Skeats, editor of the *Liberator*, historian (1881); Henry Richard, 'apostle of Wales', pioneer of International Law (1888); John Bright, champion of the Peace Society (1889).

[4] *The Nonconformist's Sketch Book* (ed. 1867), p. vi.

E. *'Practical Suggestions' of the Society*

A secret Committee was appointed, on 18 November 1874, to obtain the legal and other information required for the preparation of a plan of Disestablishment, and to offer suggestions to aid in framing such a Bill for Parliament. The Committee members were: Henry Ellington, Alfred Illingworth, Henry Lee, Guinness Rogers, Henry Leonard, Henry Crosskey, Carvell Williams, and Edward Miall. When they finally drew up recommendations two years later, John Morley agreed to try 'to smooth out' several of the unresolved differences of opinion. Crosskey wrote: 'It will be time to consider what is generous when we understand what is just.'[1]

The Committee privately employed Frederick Martin, editor of the *Statesman's Year Book*, who gave a full statistical report on the nature, origin, and amount of the property in possession of the Church of England. The work, *The Property and Revenues of the English Church Establishment*, formed a volume of 200 pages and was published by the Society in 1877. It formed useful facts for drafting the 'Practical Suggestions'. Professional legal opinion was given on the 'Suggestions' by Frederic Harrison, who had been commissioned to have 'all possible holes driven into them and repaired'. Harrison himself prepared for the Society in 1878 a Disestablishment and Disendowment Bill which was adopted as an authorized plan of the Nonconformist-Radical party, but was never actually put before Parliament.

The 'Suggestions' were kept confidential during the various stages of revision and were officially released at the Eleventh Triennial Conference in 1877.[2] The contents of the document were discussed privately in 1878 with the Dissenting Deputies, who concurred with them and urged a plan for general acceptance. With the return of the Liberals in 1880, the 'Practical Suggestions' provided the substance of a measure also for Disestablishment of the Church of Scotland.

1. *General Principles*

It was desirable that Disestablishment and Disendowment should take place, not by a gradual process, but at a fixed period in accordance with the precedent set by the Irish Church Act. By that Act the Church ceased to be established on 1 January 1871, every ecclesiastical corporation was dissolved, the Bishops ceased to sit in Parliament, the ecclesiastical courts and law were abolished, and all the property of the Church was transferred to Commissioners immediately.

The scheme for Disendowment should give due regard to the just claims of all concerned. But in the payment of compensation for loss of income,

---

[1] Pamphlet published by the Society, 1875; see also Richard Acland Armstrong, *Henry William Crosskey, Ll.D., F.G.S., His Life and Work* (Birmingham 1895), p. 269.

[2] The Rev. J. Guinness Rogers later wrote in the *British Quarterly Review*, Jan. 1886, p. 114: 'The people have been told that it is the intention of the Liberation Society [in its "Practical Suggestions"] to turn Westminster Abbey into an aquarium, and St Paul's Cathedral into a Stock Exchange.'

office or vested rights, the State should deal only with the individuals concerned therein.

On the occurrence of Disestablishment, Episcopalians should be placed in the same legal position as the members of other religious communities not possessing legal claims on the State. They should consequently be able to organize their Church as a voluntary institution or congregation, no longer constituted as an ecclesiastical body by the State. The buildings and endowments appropriated to the Church of England by the State should be absolutely at the State's disposal.

2. *Compensation for Losses*

The Bishops, Deans and Chapters, and other members of the capitular bodies, the beneficed Clergy and permanent Curates should be compensated according to age. If such person were aged 70 or over, he should continue to receive the yearly net income which he received before Disestablishment. If he were aged 35 or less, he should receive half such amount. If he were between the ages of 35 and 70, the annual payment should be reckoned on a scale proportioned to his age. Provision should be made for gratuities to non-permanent Curates, in cases deemed to be entitled to compensation.

No commutation of claims should be made by the State. But where claims were admitted, Bonds for the annual amount should be issued to the individuals entitled, and the sale or transfer of such Bonds should be legalized. The owners of next presentation and advowsons should be compensated according to the market value of their several rights. Collegiate and other corporate bodies not dissolved by Disestablishment should be compensated for the loss of their patronage. No public officer, or person in whom patronage was vested on behalf of the public, should be compensated.

3. *Disposal of Property*

The Liberation Society did not recommend any particular mode of appropriating the surplus wealth which might ultimately be at the disposal of the State after compensation. But as to how the Church property should be dealt with specifically, the Society recommended:

Cathedrals and Ancient Churches

a. Cathedrals, Abbeys, and other monumental buildings should be retained for national uses, under national control, and maintained at public cost.

b. With the exception of these national monuments, the Churches should be transferred to the parishes in which they were situated, and vested in a Board elected by the parishioners. (Buildings which were in the nature of proprietary Churches should be exempted from this provision.)

c. Such Boards should have power to dispose of the buildings, either by sale or letting, as they may think fit.

d. The price of the Churches, if sold, should be determined with regard to the interests of the parishioners generally, but there should be a power to remit rental for any public purpose which was regarded with general approval.

e. Provision should be made for an appeal to the Commissioners in regard to the price or rental of the buildings, as well as to afford security against the unfair sectarian use, or other abuse of the buildings.

f. The term for which any Church should be leased should not exceed seven years.

g. The proceeds arising from the sale or rental of the buildings, could be appropriated to parochial purposes.

h. Subject to the foregoing conditions, the congregations using the Churches should have a prior claim either to purchase or rent of the same. A set period of months should be allowed them for that purpose.

Modern Churches

a. If a Church had been built at the expense of any person who was living at the date of Disestablishment, the Commissioners could, on his application, vest the same in him or in such person, or persons, as he should direct.

b. Where district or other Churches, not being parish Churches, had been rebuilt and erected by voluntary subscriptions exclusively, within fifteen years of the date of Disestablishment, they could be used by the existing congregations free of rent, and subject to the maintenance of the same, for a period of not exceeding fifteen years after the date of Disestablishment. At the expiration of this period they should revert to the parish and be subject to the conditions already named.

Parsonages

a. As the annual value of the parsonages and glebes would be taken into account in estimating the annual income of the Clergy, they could be dealt with in the same way as the other property of the Church which would come into the hands of the Commissioners.

b. The Clergy, however, should not be dispossessed until the expiration of two years from the passing of the Establishment Act.

c. Where a congregation agreed to purchase or to rent a Church, they should also have a prior claim to purchase or rent the parsonage.

Recent Endowments

a. If an endowment had been created solely by a private individual and he were living at the date of Disestablishment, the Commissioners could, on his application, vest the same in him, or in such other person or persons, as he should direct.

b. When endowments had been created, by voluntary subscriptions exclusively, within fifteen years before the date of Disestablishment, they could continue to be employed for the purposes to which they were then applied, for a period of fifteen years. At the expiration of this period, they could be subject to the same conditions as the other property of the Church.

c. Where such modern endowments had been created, partly by subscriptions, and partly by grants from national funds, the amount of the latter should be deducted from the endowment to be dealt with by the Commissioners.

Churchyards

In all cases, parochial burial grounds attached to the Churchyards should be transferred to the Church Board of the parish, or some other parochial body, for the continued use of the inhabitants who should have equal rights therein.

Tithes

The Commissioners should have power to set the tithe and rent charge, and powers of redemption should also be given them.

The *Church Times* made a Shakespearian comment concerning all these suggestions: 'Gross as a mountain, open, palpable.' The great mistake of the Society lay in prematurely identifying itself with a scheme that was too comprehensive and severe. Directing people's attention to many particulars meant increasing the chances of open disagreement, especially in the question of dividing the spoils. It might have been a vastly different story if the specific proposals for Disestablishment had come first through Parliament rather than from Serjeants' Inn. The Society might have then departed safely from its general view and given a united lead to Liberationists in the details for achieving their final aim.

F. *General Elections and the Society*

Leading the Parliamentary Dissenting opposition to the Education Act of 1870, Miall drew from Gladstone the outburst, 'If he cannot give us his support, in God's name let him take it elsewhere.'[1] The words were not forgotten. When the Government dissolved Parliament without making peace with its Nonconformist allies, their support was withdrawn, resulting in the Liberal defeat of 1874. The feeling of Nonconformists, however, about the futility of ecclesiastical debates in that particular House of Commons was shared by Gladstone. In a letter to a friend, written at the close of the final Session he expressed the fear that the House of Commons might 'become a debased copy of an ecclesiastical council',[2] and to Lord Harrowby, on 1 October 1874, he wrote:

> I am convinced that the effect . . . of one or two more Ecclesiastical Sessions of Parliament, such as the last, . . . will be to disestablish the Church. I do not feel the dread of disestablishment which you may probably entertain: but I desire and seek, so long as standing-ground remains, to avert, not to precipitate it.[3]

These words pointed to the great indignation of the national education leaders. Because of the 'miserable dodge' of the Liberal Government Education Amendment Act of 1873, Dr Dale urged his followers 'to run another man whenever a mere Ministerialist invited their suffrages'. Liberal candidates were not to be accredited unless they endorsed (1) the abolition of the 'clerical monopoly' in the Churchyards of England, (2) religious equality in

---

[1] G. M. Young, *Early Victorian England 1830–1865* (Oxford 1951), ii, 84. In a conversation with Charles S. Miall, Edward Miall's son, seventeen years later, Gladstone expressed regret at the *rencontre*.

[2] Morley, *Life of Gladstone*, ii. 81.

[3] D. C. Lathbury (ed.), op. cit., i. 396.

the Universities and Endowed Schools, (3) the amendment (25th clause) of the Elementary Education Act, and (4) the Disestablishment of the Church of England.

A circular was issued a short time later by the Executive Committee, condemning the election address of Gladstone as wholly inadequate. The Society refrained from finding candidates to replace retiring members whose votes had given dissatisfaction. The Parliamentary Committee backed only 149 candidates, 64 of whom were elected. A bloc of 52 M.P.s who had voted with Miall did not return to their seats, and the final result was: 351 Conservatives and 302 Liberals in the new House of Commons.

While it was out of office, the Liberal party welcomed Nonconformists and worked in closer harmony with them. Unusual cordiality, for example, was displayed at the lavish banquet, on 18 June 1878, for the 50th Anniversary of the Repeal of the Test and Corporation Acts, when leading Liberals and Nonconformists ate and drank together.

The great success of Nonconformist-Radicals at the hustings in 1880 caused them to regard the new Parliament as almost theirs. Many journals admitted that the return of the Liberal party to power was due to its reconciliation with the Nonconformists.

Many of the political Dissenters were still under the spell of the former Premier, whose integrity they believed was unmatched by rival party leaders. Gladstone was invited to Memorial Hall in 1878 to receive an address of sympathy and congratulation from leading Nonconformist Ministers. In the home of Dr Newman Hall he also met a select party of Nonconformists and talked with them on questions of common interest.[1] His election address acknowledging the immense services of the Nonconformists as 'the largest section of the Liberal party',[2] made them forget the shabby way he had treated Miall in the Disestablishment debates.

Having no wish to boycott their friends again, the Society had started planning for the 1880 Election two years before. Acting in conjunction with the Leeds Nonconformist Union, it was decided, on the advice of Carvell Williams, to conduct a Nonconformist party caucus. Invitations went out to selected Liberation leaders with notice of a two-point agenda: (1) What attitude should be taken by the Nonconformists toward the Liberal party at the next General Election? (2) What change should be made in the mode of conducting the programme for Disestablishment?

This Conference of the Society's friends was set for the day after the annual meeting of the National Federation of Liberal Associations on 22 January 1879. At that time the Liberal party under the Marquess of Hartington, Earl Granville, and Mr Gladstone, would not accept Disestablishment of the English Church as part of the platform. To pacify the Liberationists, however, they agreed tacitly to Disestablishment of the Scottish Church. The Leeds

---

[1] J. Guinness Rogers, *An Autobiography*, p. 216; cf. also Chapter XI, 'Some Personal Relations with Mr Gladstone'.

[2] Speech to electors on 27 February 1880: *Liberator*, April 1880, p. 49.

Conference of Nonconformists accepted the compromise and the breach was healed.

In the meantime, the Scottish Council of the Society drew up its 'Practical Suggestions'. The policy was that of pulling away another buttress before finally removing the main Establishment. Liberationists had taken careful heed of the assurance given by the Marquess of Hartington to the Society's Scottish representatives:

> As soon as Scottish Liberal opinion respecting the question is sufficiently formed, the Liberal party will be prepared to deal with it irrespective of possible consequences to the English Establishment.[1]

As in 1868, when the whole Liberal party decided in favour of Irish Disestablishment, it was hoped that unanimity on Scottish Disestablishment would reap real results.

The Dissolution of Parliament took place on 24 March. The Triennial Conference of the Society was postponed until June, and £1,000 was authorized toward the election campaign expenses. The result gave the Liberals a majority of 114 over the Conservatives (351–237), independent of sixty-five Irish Home Rulers. The Liberation Society emerged as a small political party of its own, eighteen members of its Executive Committee having been returned. These included advanced Liberals such as Joseph Chamberlain (Birmingham), Alfred Illingworth (Bradford), E. A. Leatham (Huddersfield), Hugh Mason (Ashton), Henry Richard (Merthyr Tydfil), and E. Lyulph Stanley (Oldham).[2] In all, forty-seven platform speakers and subscribers to the Society had been elected, and four of their M.P.s were from Scottish constituencies. Approximately 139 M.P.s were favourable to Disestablishment in both England and Scotland. With Irish support the Disestablishers numbered 150, or forty more than in the first Gladstone Government.

Disestablishment measures, however, did not get very far in the new Parliament. Scottish Disestablishment was considered but half-heartedly, for barely half of the Scottish Liberals favoured it. Carvell Williams advised shifting the weight for Disestablishment in Scotland back to England, when it seemed that the Burials legislation was the most Nonconformists could hope to glean from the Administration.

The only non-Anglicans awarded posts in the Government were: Chamberlain (Unitarian), President of the Board of Trade; Bright (Quaker), Chancellor of the Duchy of Lancaster; and the Duke of Argyll (Presbyterian),

---

[1] Minute 43: 12.xi.77. This statement was in advance of Gladstone's declaration in a letter to the Rev. Robert Rainy D.D., Principal of New College, Edinburgh: 'I certainly desire that this question, which has been recognised as pre-eminently one for the Scottish people to consider, should not be raised by the party until the Scottish people shall have pronounced upon it in a manner which is intelligible and distinct.' *Nonconformist*, 25.vi.79, p. 637.

[2] In 1883 John Morley, a member of the Executive since 1877, was returned as M.P. in the by-election at Newcastle.

Lord Privy Seal. The new Parliamentary leader of the Nonconformists, Henry Richard, as reported in the *Liberator*, said:

> We shall not sulk if we think [our] claims have not as much attention as they deserve; but on the other hand, we cannot surrender our principles.[1]

In the early 1880s the Society realized that it was approaching the climax of its long endeavours, and that it was a case of 'now or never'. And there were encouraging signs. Among the policy makers of the Liberal party the climate of opinion began slowly to shift toward Liberation ideals.

In preparation for the 1885 Election, Liberationists were extremely confident. Important London Electoral Conferences were convened on 13 January and 24 March 1885, in Memorial Hall, with special invitations to representatives of Liberal Associations throughout the country. Rather than defining either a uniform or independent course for Parliamentary action, the Parliamentary Committee of the Society decided to co-operate with the Liberal Associations. By working with them and dealing with each constituency according to local circumstances, the Society hoped to bring Disestablishment openly into the programme of the National Liberal Federation.

The co-operative spirit was rewarded at the National Liberal Federation Conference at Bradford on 1 October 1885. Owing largely to the plea of Joseph Chamberlain, a resolution was passed in favour of a policy of Disestablishment and Disendowment. It was the first occasion on which it had been officially included in the Federation platform. Because of this, the Liberation Society identified itself with the 'Radical Programme'. Edited by Morley, Chamberlain, and Dilke and circulated by the Federation at the time of the appearance of the 'Gladstone Manifesto', it was more far-reaching than the declaration of the Prime Minister. Among the Radical plans that it offered were: (1) manhood suffrage, (2) equal electoral districts and payment of M.P.s, (3) National Councils for Scotland, Ireland, and Wales, (4) progressive taxation of incomes and realized property, (5) reform of land tenure, and (6) Disestablishment and Disendowment of the Church of England. As a sign of the inevitability of the last plan, Liberationists pointed to a concession in Gladstone's declaration:

> I cannot forecast the dim and distant courses of the future. But, like all others, I have observed the vast and ever increasing development, for the last fifty years, both at home and abroad, in the Church to which I belong, of the powers of voluntary support.

As the Election day approached, the fever rose and the bidding for new votes ran high. Much of the Society's energy was directed toward the two million electors in the rural areas of the country which had been newly enfranchised by the 1885 County Franchise Bill. Motions adopting Disestablishment without compromise came from Liberal quarters in all parts of the United Kingdom. The Church Defence Association indulged in their

---

[1] *Liberator*, June 1880, p. 86.

17

share of harsh invective, and hundreds of pulpits voiced the cry of 'The Church in danger!' Both sides drew up their 'black lists', but those connected with the Society seemed to be depicted more darkly than usual.

The Society announced that out of 599 Liberal candidates there were 492 more or less favourable to Disestablishment, classified under three heads: (1) those who were in favour of Disestablishment without any reserve; (2) those who were willing to support it when proposed by a Liberal government, or adopted by the Liberal party; and (3) those who at present were prepared to support Disestablishment in Wales and Scotland only. Candidates directly connected with the Liberation Society itself numbered 82.

On 11 September, the *Record*, an Evangelical journal, prophesied:

> The returns which we publish to-day are probably destined to mark an era in the history of the English Church. The facts . . . constitute at once the most startling and the most important news which it has been our lot to chronicle for many a day. They prove beyond doubt that the overwhelming majority of the Liberal members in the reformed House of Commons will be men who desire Disestablishment. . . . It may mean, though not necessarily, the immediate separation of Church and State; but, in any event, if the present Opposition succeed at the General Election, it means the beginning of the end . . .

This view was confirmed by the actual outcome: 333 Liberals, 251 Tory Conservatives, and 86 Irish Nationalists. Of the Liberals, 171 favoured English Disestablishment, 228 favoured Disestablishment in Scotland or Wales or both, 63 were doubtful or 'opportunist', 13 were non-committal, and 29 were against Disestablishment. Of the 30 Liberals returned from Wales, 29 were 'avowedly in favour'. In Scotland, however, where the Election was dominated by the personal influence of Gladstone, only 30 of the 72 Scottish Liberals pledged tangible support.

The future prospects seemed ideal for the Society, for from its Executive the Chairman of the Parliamentary Committee, Carvell Williams, was returned as M.P. for Nottingham, John Morley was appointed Chief Secretary for Ireland, and Joseph Chamberlain was re-appointed President of the Board of Trade. Nonconformist-Radicals now appeared to control nearly half of the Commons, thus permitting the Society to boast a little:

> . . . whatever else it may be, the English Establishment is one of the most powerful forces at the command of the Conservative party, and that so long as it exists Liberalism will be liable to be checked, and for a time defeated. That leaven has already begun to work, and we shall see the result on a large scale before any of us are much older.[1]

But what the Liberationists proudly regarded as the first truly national Parliament lasted less than six months. The Dissolution announced by Gladstone came to them as an unpleasant shock. In the confusion of the political scene which ensued, it was not clear whether Disestablishment would be more or less favoured by a defeat of Gladstone's Irish policy.

[1] *Liberator*, Jan. 1886, p. 10.

In his search for the right answers the Prime Minister banked on the solid support of the Nonconformists, but they divided miserably. The Rev. J. Guinness Rogers made a vain appeal for loyalty to the chief at the National Liberal Federation meeting which would have forced Chamberlain and his cohorts out of the party. Dr R. W. Dale flatly declared later on, 'I hope the country will never give a blank cheque to any statesman.'[1]

Before matters could be smoothed out, another Election had gone by swiftly. The Liberals had lost 68 seats and returned 30 fewer members in favour of Disestablishment.[2] The Society derived some consolation from the fact that it had not suffered in the defeat to the same extent as the Liberal party.

---

[1] N. Murrell Marris, *The Right Honourable Joseph Chamberlain: the Man and the Statesman* (London 1900), p. 262. Gladstone once asked Rogers if this split over Home Rule for Ireland had spoiled Rogers's friendship with Dale. When told that it had not spoilt it in the slightest, Gladstone exclaimed, 'I am delighted.'

[2] Out of 266 Liberals, 150 favoured Disestablishment, 22 were against, 29 were doubtful, 48 wished it for Scotland or Wales only, or for both, and 17 gave no information. Parl. Com. Min., 18.x.86.

CHAPTER 18

English Church Disestablishment

Hail to the State of England! and conjoin
With this a salutation as devout,
Made to the spiritual fabric of her Church!
Founded in truth, by blood of martyrdom
Cemented; by the hands of wisdom reared,
In beauty of holiness, with ordered pomp,
Decent and unreproved. The voice which greets
The majesty of both shall pray for both,
That, mutually protected and sustained,
They may endure, long as the sea surrounds
This favoured land or sunshine warms her soil.

WILLIAM WORDSWORTH[1]

The first forked flashes of revolutionary fire are sure to be
attracted, and always have been attracted, by political
Churches.

EDWARD MIALL[2]

UNDOUBTEDLY the Disestablishment campaign of the Society was more stubbornly resisted as it became clear that this Disestablishment meant general Disendowment as well. Had simple Disestablishment been the sole object in its agitation, the Society might have won numerous supporters among those who felt cramped by the Prayer Book and the anti-Ritualist decisions of the law courts. However, Disendowment was the price to pay for Disestablishment. Liberationists generally said that after the satisfaction of all life interests, after compensation for personal losses, and after the reservation to the Church of England of that portion of her property which was derived from private resources, there must be an appropriation of her endowments to secular purposes in which the whole nation could share. These were hard words to those who loved their Church.

Most Anglicans believed that the separation of Church and State would imply a rejection of Christianity by the people, and an act of national

---

[1] 'Excursion', as quoted by Sir Roundell Palmer, speaking in the Commons on 9 May 1871. Hansard (3rd series), ccvi, 520.

[2] Speaking on the same occasion for his Disestablishment motion; ibid., ccvi, 497.

apostasy.[1] But not all. Henry Alford, Dean of Canterbury, had written in his *Essays and Addresses* in 1869 that 'the State is what she *is*, not what she calls herself'.[2] Furthermore, he said, there was not necessarily any departure from the faith in denying Anglicanism to be the religion of the State.

> Rather does it appear to us the bounden duty of every responsible body of men, as it is of every individual man, to remove from itself all inconsistency of profession with practice: not to suffer obsolete theories to keep their hold on outward forms . . .

The arch-contestants dealing with these problems behind the scenes in the Disestablishment controversy were the lawyers and theologians of the nation. For many it had now become a matter of deciding which should be the guiding force in society – the law offices of the Crown or the divines of the Church. Primacy had to be given either to the will of the people or the minds of the priests. The rivalry arising between Clerical authority and Royal supremacy brought disagreements between the House of Convocation and the chambers of the Judicial Committee of the Privy Council. Thus, in the 'Clewer Judgement' in the case of *The Queen v. The Bishop of Oxford*, delivered on 8 March 1879, Lord Chief Justice Cockburn declared that

> as an institution maintained and endowed by the State . . . the Church exists for the benefit of the Laity.[3]

The objection of the Liberation Society was that this laity, in the eyes of the law, included only members of the Anglican Church. Disestablishment would therefore have to be an authoritative declaration on the part of the State that it ceased to take responsibility upon itself in regard to the affairs of the Church. Disendowment would be a simple resumption by the State of the national property which had hitherto been especially appropriated to fulfil that responsibility. Merely to relinquish to one denomination (the Episcopal) the ecclesiastical wealth belonging to the whole nation, would constitute a greater re-establishment and not Disestablishment.[4]

[1] The Bishop of Bath and Wells, Dr Arthur C. Hervey, at a Diocesan Conference in 1875 declared of Disestablishment: '. . . then I believe the Church's days are numbered, and . . . at any moment a sudden crash may announce to a startled world that . . . the empire of England is without a God, and without a Church'. *Liberator*, Nov. 1875, p. 178.

[2] *Essays and Addresses: Chiefly on Church Subjects* (London 1869), p. 169.

[3] *Law Reports*, part v, p. 277. Canon Trevor stated in a letter to the *Guardian* (31.x.77): 'The laity of the Church of England are the English nation. The Church is established and endowed for the whole population . . . its clergy are the national pastorate. . . . To set up an *esoteric* laity within the Christian nation is to denationalise the Church and reduce it to a denomination.'

[4] cf. articles by Prof. E. A. Freeman in the *Pall Mall Gazette* from July 1874, stating that Church property – that for ecclesiastical purposes – was not 'national property' in the same sense as that held by city guilds or corporations. It was mainly 'the property of the clergy as the office-bearers of the Church' (*Nonconformist*, 5.viii.74, p. 738), like the trustees of Dissenting bodies. Frederic Harrison replied in the *Pall Mall Gazette* (2.iv.75): 'If you give property nominally to the Church of England, but prescribing a specific ritual, or the like, you are only founding a new Nonconformist sect; the reason being that the political

A. *Effects and Causes Involved*

Liberationists did not always admit the full implications of Disestablishment and Disendowment: (1) The ecclesiastical coronation of the Sovereign would come to an end, and the wearer of the Crown might be of any religion or no religion. (2) The Bishops would depart from the House of Lords. (3) The coercive jurisdiction of the ecclesiastical courts would cease, and the Church would exercise its discipline like any other religious body. (4) The Act of Uniformity would be repealed. (5) The revived Convocation would be left to do what was right in its own eyes, so long as its decrees did not touch the civil rights of any man. (6) The Crown would no longer have the right of appointment of Bishops. (7) Persons having the powers of patronage would be deprived of them and compensated. (8) The disestablished Church would no longer be open to Dissenters, and the ideal by which every man of the country was held to be a member of the Church of the country would come to an end. (9) Soldiers and sailors would no longer be assumed *prima facie* to belong to the Church of England. (10) Schoolmasters of all ancient schools in the country would no longer be required to be members of the Church of England. (11) The Incumbent would no longer be *ex officio* chairman of the Parish vestry meeting. (12) All payments out of public funds, out of taxes or rates, for religious purposes, would cease.

The Society had never officially asked for as much as this, although its opponents implied that it did. Not all Radical-Nonconformists were by any means agreed as to the wisdom of all these points, even though they could not deny that the consequences of what they sought would be drastic. In most of the schemes for Disestablishment[1] during this period the crucial question was, Should the Church be entitled to hold its endowments or property as an independent institution, or as the organ of the State for general religious purposes?

The principal concern of the Society in 1870 was 'to keep the ball rolling' following the Irish Disestablishment. The initial shock of the idea to Churchmen was now past, Liberationists believed, and the time was ripe for planning another resistance movement. It was difficult to decide where the Society would gain most in exciting the national feeling to resist the State Church.

Scotland, first thought to be the next target, was ruled out temporarily in 1870, because the Voluntaryists there were divided in their theory of religious

---

authority alone is competent to direct to what religious uses the property of the Church shall be devoted, and it does so direct from time to time. Non-Church endowments on the other hand are dedicated to such uses as the creator of the trust has specifically directed.'

[1] Some of the current schemes in periodicals were: (1) *Macmillan's Magazine*, April 1873: 'Proposals for a National Church of England', by Alfred R. Wallace f.r.s.: (2) *The Nineteenth Century*, Oct. 1878: 'A Suggested Act for the Separation of Church and State', by A. H. Mackonochie, Rector of St Alban's Holborn – analysed in five issues of the *Nonconformist*, Oct. 1878; (3) *The Fortnightly Review*, June 1883: 'The Legal Aspects of Disestablishment', by Prof. A. V. Dicey; (4) *The Contemporary Review*, March 1887: 'The National Church as a Federal Union', by Dr James Martineau.

establishments, and because no major dissatisfaction with the Established Church was felt by the general populace.[1] In Wales, until the working classes really held the franchise, intervention was considered premature, and therefore likely to bring serious losses to the Liberal party in future elections. Thus, the Liberationists hoped to save time by concentrating on the Establishment in England, ending as quickly as possible the one cause of all the grievances bothering them.

During the 1870s the Society saw that much of the final battle would be against those who were keen upon the reform of the Church of England. The advanced philosophical Radicals and advanced liberal Churchmen were competing during this period for the intellectual leadership of the country. The Evangelicals were not seriously contending. The Ritualists eliminated themselves from the field by obstructing practical experiments in tolerance.[2] The great principle of the Radical-Nonconformists was that good government was handicapped when it became bound to a powerful religious institution. The State would not become unrighteous or unholy in standing by itself. The great principle of the Broad Churchmen was that religion was too powerful a force for good or evil to be ignored by wise Government. The Church of England was too much a part of the nation's life to be denationalized.

Many of the advanced Liberals became sympathetic with a formidable body known as the Church Reform Union. The organization and its organ, the *Church Reformer*, advocated a threefold programme: (1) the admission of the laity to the administration of the parishes and a defined share of power in Church affairs, (2) the removal of impolitic and narrow restraints, and (3) the promotion of practical improvements. To remove the Church from the State would take with it the vital element in the Monarchy and the House of Lords, and thereby mutilate the British Constitution. Church Reform was best achieved in lieu of Disestablishment, and not by means of Disestablishment.

The great absurdity in such a position, said the Ritualists and others, was that the slightest reform of the least important rubric or liturgical practice had to run the gauntlet of an involved legislative Act by Parliament.[3] Fanatical

---

[1] Minute 360: 1.x.69.

[2] The Bishop of London in 1875 (Dr John Jackson) threatened Canon W. H. Fremantle with legal proceedings if he accepted an invitation to preach from the pulpit of the City Temple. In 1870 a Memorial to the Archbishop of Canterbury was signed by 1,500 Ritualist Clergymen protesting against Dean Stanley's invitation to members of the Bible Revision Committee, which included several Nonconformists, to a special Communion Service in Westminster Abbey. An article in the *Church Review*, 13.vii.70, referred to this as the 'Westminster Scandal'. On the occasion of Dr Robert Moffatt's sermon in the Abbey on St Andrew's Day, 1875, the Dean was accused in the *Church Times*, 3.xii.75, of converting the nave of the Abbey into a lecture room 'in which Nonconformist Ministers may disport themselves'.

[3] In 1878, revised statutes were put forward for the Prayer-Book of the disestablished Irish Church which Church reformers desired also for the English Church: removal of the Ornaments Rubric; determination of vestments by special Canon; settlement of the position

Church defenders cried that Disestablishment of the Church meant 'over-throw' as certainly as it would if applied to the Throne, the Army or the Navy. For Evangelicals, it was perfectly right and proper for the State to recognize the strongest single Church of the nation; moreover, it was the only way to prevent an open merger between the Ritualists and the Roman Catholics. To disestablish, the moderates feared, would bring the High, Low, and Broad parties into open rivalry and create fresh sectarianism.

The Liberationists answered that the greatest mischief would be, not doctrinal and ecclesiastical anarchy if the tie between Church and State were severed, but political anarchy if it were retained. They suspected liberal reformers of opposing Disestablishment in order to have legal protection for unorthodox theology. The only real remedy to religious disunity was a return to simple New Testament Christianity with its dynamic of love and not of law. The only alternative to the compulsory system was the voluntary one.[1]

In the international crisis 1878–80, because of Liberal opposition to Lord Beaconsfield's policy of alliance with the 'Godless' Turks against the Russians, there were frequent references to Britain as 'a Christian nation'. Such references often supported the picture in people's minds of a national Church. During their period of Parliamentary Opposition, most of the Liberal chiefs appeared to be following Gladstone's lead in the party line on Disestablishment. He had challenged the Liberationists first to win support from the majority of the citizens before he would throw in his lot with them.[2]

In 1876 Gladstone received a plainly spoken letter signed by a citizen 'from the plough'. He prayed, with thousands of farm workers, that Gladstone might be 'an instrument in the hands of God' to bring benefit to the Anglican Clergy by Disestablishment:

> We know, sir, and these poor men know, who are their enemies; and though there are individual clergymen who are humane and kind-hearted Christians, yet I can assure you, from an intimate acquaintance with a large number of rural parishes, that many of the clergy of the Established Church are tyrants of the worst class . . . This could not continue if the Church were disestablished—if

---

of the celebrant at Holy Communion; omission of reading of the Athanasian Creed; omission of Absolution in the Visitation of the Sick; replacing of words of certainty in the Burial Service by words of hope; simplification of the Marriage Service; alteration of the Catechism so as to lend no countenance to Transubstantiation; affirmation against auricular Sacramental Confession.

[1] In Nov. and Dec. 1877, Canon G. H. Curteis and the Rev. J. Guinness Rogers had a 'friendly tournament' in the *Nonconformist* on basic differences in Anglican and Free Church history. Curteis condemned the American policy of 'State indifference' in religion. If institutions rooted in history could be levelled by such as the Liberation Society, 'the victory of Communism is as good as won'. Rogers said that Dissenters, like Churchmen, feared sacerdotal control of the Church more than Erastian control; but the latter evil was present as long as there was a State Church.

[2] cf. 'Mr. Gladstone and Disestablishment': notes on Gladstone's attitude to this question. *Liberator*, July 1884, p. 103.

there were no "royal road" to the pulpit; for then men would have to preach to live, and would have to conciliate their parishioners, and not be their autocrats. . . .

Gladstone replied in a manner which was not unworthy of a broad-minded leader:

> With regard to the petitions which you wish me to present, I have no objection to do this . . . but I cannot promise concurrence in their prayer. In my opinion, the Establishment of England (not of Scotland) represents the religion of a considerable majority of the people, and they do not seem to desire the change you recommend. . . . Among the classes of our mixed society, I hold that the clergy are, with reference to their training, manners, and social station, as a class, rather under than over paid; and that they are also, as a class, the most self-denying and the most devoted to the education, consolation, and elevation of their poorer brethren.[1]

Lord Hartington's 'benevolent neutrality' was doubtless less vexing to Liberationists than Mr Gladstone's 'polite scepticism'. In a declaration to Scottish Liberals, his Lordship had less to say in defence of Establishments. Goldwin Smith, invited from America to address the Leeds Nonconformist Union in 1877, described Hartington's statement as merely saying, 'that if they had really made up their minds for Disestablishment, he would walk behind them'.

Earl Granville, speaking at Bradford the same year, was as cautious on the subject as his colleagues in the party executive. Although he believed the Established Church was a curse to Ireland and of no great advantage to Scotland,

> I do not agree with a famous landscape gardener, that every tree, whether well grown or not, should be cut down if it be not in a place where if the thing was to be done again you would not plant it.

On the same occasion, by way of contrast, W. E. Forster, the former Vice-President of the Privy Council, said that Disestablishment was highly dangerous because the consequences could not be accurately judged. Moreover, it would destroy a parochial system which placed in every quarter of the land State servants 'whose business it is to care for the highest good of every man'.[2]

Principal Tulloch, apostle of that 'higher rational religion' across the border, condemned the 'dogmatism of Dissent' in the publications of the Liberation Society: 'one rises from the perusal of them, so to speak, with a bad taste in one's mental palate.'[3] As Moderator of the Church of Scotland, he stoutly defended Church Establishments as the preservers of culture, refinement, tolerance, and liberality.

[1] *Nonconformist*, 22.iii.76, p. 277. Gladstone had been invited by the writer to address 20,000 fellow workers at a Whit-Monday demonstration in Yeovil, Somerset, in the old Roman amphitheatre.

[2] T. Wemyss Reid, *Life of the Right Honourable William Edward Forster* (London 1888), ii, 182–4.

[3] *Blackwood's Magazine;* answered by Frederic Harrison in *The Contemporary Review* Oct. 1878, 'The Dogmatism of Dissent', p. 572; cf. *Nonconformist*, 6.xi.78, p. 1097.

In his letter to the Annual Meeting of the Liberation Society in 1879, Professor Thorold Rogers of Oxford provided Disestablishment with a sound rationale from the Puritan interpretation of history. The Non-established Churches also had preserved a noteworthy heritage from their predecessors.

> It has become impossible for Parliament to assume any longer that control over the doctrine as well as the conduct of the clergy which it was the aim of the Reformation to establish. To this object, Gardiner and Bonner were equally committed with Cranmer and Hooper. Such a control was the object of the Puritan party from the time of Elizabeth to the Restoration.[1]

Disestablishment, Rogers continued, was the only remedy to the anarchy caused by the Church in its disobedience to the laws of a lay Parliament. Disestablishment was also the answer to the growing apathy toward the Christian beliefs which the founders of the English Reformation put in the place of religious superstition.

It was now no longer a question to Liberationists of showing *why* the Established Church should be disestablished, but of showing *how* this was to be accomplished. Some leaders inside the Establishment were impressed by the show of strength outside, and therefore talked of a reunion between Anglicanism and Dissent by a process of 'absorption'. But Nonconformist-Radicals who were jealous of their role as agitators or 'purifiers' remained aloof from all overtures that fell short of complete Disestablishment.[2] A politically oppressive Church must be overthrown by political weapons and 'the hotter the war, the sooner the peace'.

B. *Miall's Motions Debated*

At the beginning of this period, tremendous optimism prevailed in all Non-conformist quarters. The Society's founder, Edward Miall, hoped at first to wear down the opposition by the introduction of an annual motion. He intended in this way to reduce gradually the votes of his political foes, and to force settlement in a later Parliament. Such strategy might have proved successful, had he been from the outset in command of a larger Parliamentary bloc.

After lengthy deliberations as to the most suitable time to introduce the first major motion for Disestablishment, the date was eventually fixed for 9 May 1871. The Tenth Triennial Conference of the Society convened a few days before in high spirits. A joint Conference of the Society, the Congregational Union, and the Dissenting Deputies sent to Mr Gladstone their resolutions in favour of Miall's motion:

> That it is expedient to apply the policy of Disestablishment and Disendowment

---

[1] quoted in the *Liberator*, June 1879, p. 91.

[2] In exasperation over Liberation tactics, Disraeli wrote to Queen Victoria on 2 July 1876: 'It is no use attempting to conciliate the Dissenters. They will take all you offer, and, the very next minute, will fly at your throat.' Monypenny & Buckle, *Life of Disraeli*, ii, 824.

carried out by the Irish Church Act of 1869 to the other Churches established by law in the United Kingdom.[1]

At last came the day for which Liberationists had long dreamed. Months before, Miall had prodigiously combed through his arguments, and in true Victorian fashion had exercised severe self-discipline – 'even the customary pipe was laid aside.' But the Churchmen were well primed and ready. Ironically, before the debate opened, Gathorne Hardy (M.P., Oxford University) lodged a petition against the motion, signed by 24,000 ratepayers in Bradford, Miall's own constituency.

As Miall rose to speak, his friend, George Hadfield (M.P., Sheffield), admonished him, 'Miall, fear God, and you need not fear any man.'[2] His speech contained the condensed thought of a lifetime. Its force of logic and intellectual depth surprised those who had expected a radical harangue. Unfortunately, in Disraeli's words, 'Parliament is governed by rhetoric and not by logic.' Miall examined the claim of the Church to be national. It was meant to be the Church of the nation, but it was in fact the Church of about half of it. Frequently it had relied on other Churches to do its work. In most cases the State had not built the national churches, nor had it endowed them, but had simply absorbed them into the system 'as by law established'. The truly great work of the Church of England had been achieved by its individual leaders and supporters and not necessarily by Parliament.

The competence of Parliament to act as a tribunal for testing the worth of religious opinions was next disputed. Suppose that the formulations of science, like those of theology, had been established by law, highly endowed, and protected by statute against the smallest alteration. Religious universality and unity could never be achieved by political instruments. A man's religion was an affair between himself and his God. The law of the land must deal impartially and justly with all subjects and refrain from creating ecclesiastical caste with degrees of respectability.

Miall pointed to the endowments of the Church as a matter of concern not only to Anglicans and Dissenters, but to 'Absenters' who gave no allegiance to either party. Revenue for ecclesiastical purposes was drawn from the upper, middle and lower classes, but chiefly for the benefit of the top two. The Church was failing to reach the working classes with a satisfying ministry. America and the poorer population in Wales gave convincing evidence that the small rural parishes in England would not disappear with the abolition of endowments. A religion that was worth anything would always find the means of its own sustentation and extension. The disappearance of State endowments would be followed by a rush of voluntary efforts to fill up the vacuum.

In the ablest reply from the Opposition, Sir Roundell Palmer (M.P., Richmond) insisted that the good influence of the Established Church extended as well to Dissenters. It was not true that the Church of England was

---

[1] Gladstone acknowledged this communication. Minute 1000: 21.iv.71.
[2] A. Miall, *Life of Edward Miall*, p. 320.

remote from the working classes. Concerning Miall's analogy between science and religion, it was better to remove from religion the incrustations of the science of theology than to repudiate it altogether. To argue that any State institution intended for the public good was not just unless everybody equally participated in it, was to advocate Communism.

Disestablishment created many problems, said Sir Roundell. It would not make any easier the solution of the Education question, for denominations would be set at rivalry with one another. There would be an even sharper cleavage between religious educationists and secularists. The conciliatory spirit of the Church, which the State safeguarded, would be imperilled. The national Courts would have to decide more than ever upon denominational disputes, the national Church would become disunited, and the State would be weakened in its power to thwart national dangers.

Able supporting speeches, free from defiance and complaint, came from J. D. Lewis (M.P., Devonport, and an Anglican), Watkin Williams (M.P., Denbigh), and Henry Richard (M.P., Merthyr Tydfil). E. A. Leatham (M.P., Huddersfield) produced an effective quotation from Dean Alford's essay on 'The Church of the Future':

> Whether years, or decades of years, be taken for the accomplishment of this [the severance of Church from the State], however it may be deprecated and however opposed, accomplished it will certainly be. History has for ages been preparing its way; in past changes, it has been conceded over and over again; God's arm is thrusting it on, and man's power cannot keep it back.[1]

Speaking for many Tories, Disraeli referred to the Puritans who, although they abolished Bishoprics and destroyed liturgies, upheld the connexion between Church and State and resorted to the civil arm to maintain their spiritual predominance. The present-day Puritans, he maintained, were the descendants of this revolutionary party, now supported by philosophical revolutionists. The influence of the Church of England though not so great in the large cities, was predominant in the vast country districts. Let the Church remain tolerant, temperate, comprehensive, and it would then be truly national. The more the Church appealed to various types of people – some looking for ceremony, some for enthusiasm, some for learning – the less chance there would be of Miall's annual motion succeeding.[2]

After complimenting Miall for raising the question to a fair trial in a 'clear, thorough, and manly manner', Gladstone (M.P., Greenwich) pledged his unrelenting opposition. The Church had not stood as a deterrent to liberty of thought, but had been careful to distinguish it from unbounded licence. It was true that the Nonconformist element was strong enough to shatter the Liberal party, but this fact was not a worthy consideration for those who were dealing

---

[1] Alford, *Essays and Address*, p. 166.

[2] Years before, in *Coningsby* (London 1849) Disraeli had stated the opposite – that the union of Church and State would bring 'perpetual interference' by the State, and a 'sedulous avoidance' by the Church of its principles (pp. 351–2).

crucially with national institutions. Although returns of public worship showed an equality of members belonging to the Church and other bodies, the statistics took no account of a great body of people on the fringe of religious persuasion who occasionally observed Anglican ordinances. Before Miall could convert the House of Commons to his opinion, he must convert first the opinions of the majority of the people of England.

In closing, Miall ventured to predict that the minorities of today would become the majorities of tomorrow, and in this question, if not under Gladstone, then under his successor. After seven hours' debating, the result was 89 to 374 votes against the motion. Most of these M.P.s were without strong opinions of their own, and wished to retain their seats, which they risked losing if they committed themselves to this vote.

The Society was far from disheartened. It was determined not to submit to the first rejection in the House of Commons. In preparation for a second attempt, Liberationists everywhere set about the task of organizing their activities with greater gusto. Meetings passing resolutions in support of Miall were held by the hundred.

The form of Miall's next motion was changed twice, and after numerous ballots he secured 2 July 1872 as the date for its debate. It was criticized by Churchmen as a move deliberately designed to gain information for subversive ends, and to embarrass the Liberal party at the next General Election. The motion was in fact much less severe in what it sought to accomplish than the previous Disestablishment motions:

> That a humble address be presented to Her Majesty, praying Her Majesty that by means of a Royal Commission, full and accurate particulars may be procured of the origin, nature, amount and application of any property and revenues appropriated to the use of the Church of England, with a view to furnish requisite information bearing upon the question of Disestablishment and Disendowment.

All the words after 'the Church of England' were dropped when Thomas Hughes (M.P., Frome) said that he would replace them with an amendment asking the Commission (a) to rearrange the system of parochial benefices and (b) to improve the laws of patronage on such benefices.

Miall began by insisting that surely there should be no fear of a factual inquiry into Church property and revenues, for such an inquiry had already been conducted along similar lines in 1832. Nothing could be gained by refusing inspection or concealing the exact extent of the enormous wealth of the Established Church. Because the Church of England belonged to the whole nation, the people had a right to know: (1) the number, origin, and estimated value of Church edifices and parsonages in town and country; (2) the funds by means of which Church buildings were kept in repair; (3) the working of the voluntary rate system; (4) the average annual amount of clerical fees and Easter dues, and where the former were obtained; (5) the amount paid under various Church Building Acts in the form of pew rents; (6) the amount obtained in the metropolis by rates on householders in lieu of tithes; (7) the value and extent of property in the hands of Queen Anne's Bounty, the Bishops, and the Ecclesiastical Commissioners.

The Nonconformist leader hoped that this information would help to answer important questions: (1) Did the State confer her ancient parochial endowments – and the system of tithe rent charge – upon the Church? Did the system originate out of private liberality or public law? (2) In the parishes where glebe lands constituted part of the ecclesiastical endowments, what proportion was given by private liberality, and what from public sources?

On this occasion Gladstone was not inclined to regard the proceedings with great seriousness: 'We are called on tonight to discharge the functions of a debating Society rather than the ordinary duties of the British Parliament.' To him, Hughes's amendment virtually asked for a redistribution of the property of the Church. Miall's motion asked for too much at one time. The discussion had aroused too many theoretical ideas on the question of ecclesiastical property.

The motion was lost by 94 to 295 votes, and the amendment by 41 to 270 votes. For the second year the 'ayes' had included such names as Lord E. Fitzmaurice, Sir C. W. Dilke, Sir H. O. Hoare, and Mr G. O. Trevelyan. Liberals who were not present to cast their votes numbered 160. On 13 July 1872, a few days after the debate, a cartoon appeared in *Punch* under the heading, 'Extinguished', together with a verse entitled 'Miall's Misadventure':

> Miall, the battle, fought of yore,
>   For reason and for right,
> Against the Church that overbore,
>   Is now another fight.

> By rigid tests, without the fold
>   Of England's Church when pent,
> For liberty belief to hold,
>   With good cause strove Dissent.

> But now by tests there's nothing meant,
>   If what they mean we search,
> A narrow faction, wars Dissent
>   Against a liberal Church.

> Dissenters of all shades, O Laud,
>   Thy shade may whoop, or wail!—
> The Church, High Churchmen, Low, and Broad,
>   Includes within its pale.

To which the *Nonconformist*, 17 July 1872, answered:

> O Punch, the battle that we fight,
>   Is the old fight of yore,
> Wherein good men, to set things right,
>   Much persecution bore.

> By rigid test still crampt and pent
>   Within the Church's fold,
> Think you her priests will leave the tent
>   Where hides the wedge of gold?
>
> Unearth the wedge, or else the search,
>   Grown hotter in intent,
> Will number searchers from the "Church"
>   As well as from "Dissent."
>
> At present, "94" may fail
>   To find out Achan's hoard,
> The time will come when, at their tail,
>   You'll find "High," "Low," and "Broad."

The Liberation Society was gratified with the results of the 1872 debate. It had afforded a serious consideration of the radical principle of the right of the State to deal with the property held by the Established Churches. Nonconformists hopefully looked ahead to a third division in 1873 with its prospects of a few additional votes. Two weeks after the division in 1872, Mr Miall had announced his motion for the following Session:

> That in the opinion of this House, the establishment by law of the Churches of England and Scotland involves a violation of religious equality, deprives those Churches of the right of self-government, imposes duties on Parliament which it is incompetent to discharge, and is hurtful to the political and religious interests of the community, and therefore, ought no longer to be maintained.

The effects of this motion were more sweeping than Miall's previous two, and again provoked excitement in all religious circles. Its tone was repellent to Anglican sobriety, but Nonconformist zeal was undiminished. Mass assemblies, *pro* and *con*, were held in every quarter of the country. The Society sought for any new position of prominence and every means of political influence at its disposal.

The speech of Miall on 16 May lacked the eloquence required before a House that was somewhat bored with the subject. Miall did not lack the courage needed to face the restless murmurs of members sitting in the House, but his words betrayed an unfortunate 'minority complex'. To begin with, he spent time tediously proving that religious equality was not an abstract principle. What was religious equality? '*Vide* the Irish Church Act *passim*', came his answer. The recurring call for reform in the Church indicated a dissatisfaction with the law on the Church.

> We have tried to substitute manufacture for growth. We have laid our main stress upon the perfection of our machinery, and have depended too little upon the spirit, the life, and the energy with which it should have been worked.[1]

Let the House tell the nation that it ought to recognize Christianity, he concluded, but first let it place all Christians on the same footing.

[1] Hansard (3rd series), ccxvi, 31.

Carefully chosen statistics were presented by Duncan McLaren (M.P., Edinburgh) in a seconding speech that measured the growth of Voluntaryism in Scotland. There were 1,290 Established Church Ministers, 957 Free Church Ministers, 510 United Presbyterian Ministers, and 301 Ministers of smaller Presbyterian bodies – all of whom adopted substantially the same creed and form of worship. One of the main objections that had been made against the Disestablishment in Ireland, that Protestantism would be destroyed, could not be applied in Scotland.

Gladstone's response was courteous and without condescension.

> With respect to my hon. Friend the member for Bradford himself, I have often had the pleasure of hearing him; and must admit that whether on occasions on which I could cordially agree with him, or on occasions when I could not, I found, and am always certain to find in his speeches great ability, careful examination and research, and evident and palpable goodwill towards all men.[1]

But Miall's propositions were of enormous sweep and volume. He had been misled by what had happened in the case of the Irish Church, and its lessons were many-sided. Gladstone then quoted the German scholar Dr Ignaz von Döllinger, who had stated that the Church of England was ahead of other European Churches in vitality.

Gladstone now routed the Radicals with a ring of oratory that was delightful to the ears of Churchmen on both sides of the House. To take the Church of England out of the history of England would leave behind a bleeding and lacerated mass. Disestablishment and Disendowment in all its phases would cost the country £90,000,000 in compensation to the Church of England. The public would be reluctant to see this wealth in the hands of a voluntary organization. Liberal men should feel no duty to join this crusade led by one who was playing the part of Peter the Hermit.

The reporter of the *Nonconformist* admitted blushing with shame as he heard 'cheer after cheer proceeding from the Tory benches, and felt the cold silence of the men who have made the Liberal party what it is. . . . Caesar addressed his own troops, and all Pompey's legions shouted response'.[2]

To heap more ignominy on Miall's men, the Opposition abruptly closed the debate. The backers of the motion were either caught napping or none of them had the heart to face the large number of confident Churchmen. A sizeable number of Nonconformists had at the moment left the floor and the lobby. John Bright, making one of his infrequent visits to the House, did not rise because it had been prearranged for others to respond. In the moment of hesitation no one came forward, the division bell rang, and the doors closed.

The result was a crushing defeat for Liberationists by 61 to 356 votes. Had the debate proceeded according to plan, they had hoped to register as many as 100 votes. The Opposition trick, the Society complained, had been deliberately planned to create the impression that such motions had lost their

[1] ibid., 38.
[2] *Nonconformist*, 21.v.73, p. 535.

momentum. This concluded the first great Parliamentary offensive for total Disestablishment of the Church of England – an outcome the more frustrating because of the abounding confidence with which it had begun.

C. *Enthusiasm Weakened*

Several desperate Disestablishment attempts were made toward the end of this period. By then, however, the programme of the Society had become so sprawling that it was difficult to manage its attack with uniform thoroughness. In some respects its operations became over-extended, and its enthusiasm began to lag. Supporters in Scotland, England, and Wales were pleading for a priority upon the Society's resources. The necessity of pacifying conflicting demands prevented the Society from making up its mind where to throw the whole of its weight.

Sensing the end of their 'golden opportunity' in 1883, the Society pressed three Disestablishment motions at once, expecting that at least one would pass. By 1885 Mr Henry Richard (M.P., Merthyr Tydfil) had declined to proceed in the coming Session with his motion that the English Church 'should no longer be maintained'. Mr J. Dick-Peddie (M.P., Edinburgh) was prevented by pressure of Government business from moving his motion that the Scottish Church was 'indefensible on public grounds'. The Government was defeated on the Budget before Mr L. L. Dillwyn (M.P., Swansea) found an opportunity with his motion that the Welsh Church was 'an anomaly and injustice which ought no longer to exist'.

The latter two motions were debated in the reformed Parliament in 1886, but failed because of the heavy abstention from voting and the neutrality of many English Liberals. The Society valiantly backed a motion in 1884 on the expediency of excluding Bishops from the House of Lords, but it was narrowly defeated by 139 to 150 votes. The majority included sixteen Liberals, of whom eight were members of the Government.

Gladstone believed that Disestablishment was now being put forward indirectly by the Tories, in order to force the Liberals to vote on ecclesiastical questions on which his party was badly divided. Nevertheless, he did not appear worried, writing to a friend: 'The controversy is real beyond the Tweed, and is rising in Wales; in England it is, and may long continue, little more than what is termed academic.'[1] In a later letter he wrote: 'I have never been in the habit of blowing the trumpet for battles in which I could take no part.'[2] But by the end of his third government not even Gladstone fully realized how close the country had come to another Disestablishment. The branches of the national Church had been shaken to the point that it nearly resigned itself to the cutting of the trunk.

---

[1] Lathbury (ed.), *Correspondence on Church and Religion of William Ewart Gladstone*, i. 183.

[2] ibid., i, 184f.

18

CHAPTER 19

Elementary Education

> Dissent is not picturesque, but it possesses a heroic political
> record. It has little in the way of splendour and state, but
> it has a consistent legend of civil enlightenment. It may
> lack mild majesty, but it has always shown honest instincts.
>
> JOHN MORLEY[1]

> Dissent, as a religious movement of our day, would be
> almost droll, if it were not, from the tempers and actions
> it excites, so extremely irreligious.
>
> MATTHEW ARNOLD[2]

THERE WAS no department of the Government in which the difference between a Liberal and Conservative Ministry was felt more keenly than that which had to do with elementary education. The question between the two parties, broadly stated, was, Shall popular education of the nation be managed principally by the Clergy or by the laity, and with a view to sacred or to secular ends? The opinion in the nation itself was roughly divided between the National Education Union, pressing for religious, compulsory, and denominational schools, and the National Education League, eager for national, voluntary, and non-sectarian schools.[3] The attempts to resolve these positions convulsed English society at its centre.

National Education in the nineteenth century therefore became another phase of the controversy on the proper relations between Church and State. In a speech in June 1875, before the National Society (for the Promotion of Elementary Instruction according to Doctrines and Principles of the Church of England), Lord Shaftesbury warned that

> if religion be severed from national education, national education must be
> severed from the Church and from the clergy; and one-half of their duties will be

---

[1] *The Struggle for National Education* (London 1873), p. 7; this work was compiled from articles in the *Fortnightly Review* during August, September and October 1873, with an additional chapter on 'Free Schools'.

[2] *Literature and Dogma* (London 1883), p. xviii.

[3] The League was backed by John Stuart Mill and the chiefs of the 'Birmingham School' – Joseph Chamberlain, Jesse Collings and George Dixon; cf. Francis Adams, *History of the Elementary School Contest in England*, pp. 197–207.

taken from them. . . . If the time ever arrive when the clergy are driven from the schoolroom and confined to the functions of the pulpit, one-half of the argument for maintaining the Established Church will have been destroyed, and that half will be transferred to the balance of our opponents, who will turn it against us with vigorous effect.[1]

In 1870 the English public was being told that education apart from religion was deprived of the better half of its civilizing power, and that to be morally and intellectually fruitful, education must be religious. Not many Englishmen quarrelled with this general principle. To Nonconformists, however, it was not its truth, but the wise application of it which required careful consideration. They saw religious education in the public elementary schools as creeds, collects, and catechism that were 'crammed' into the memory, without meaning to the understanding or effect upon the conscience. Nonconformist leaders spoke no less bluntly on this matter than on other questions relating to the Established Church. Ever since the origin of the Dissenting Academies out of the conformity legislation of 1662, they had stood stubbornly against the dominance of State religion in education.[2]

The Anglican aim was mainly to preserve the schools of the country as nurseries of Church principles. The whole schooltime of a child should lead to one object – the training of the young Christian for full Communion, and, as a preliminary to that, the training for Confirmation. The parochial system was too deep in the soil of English life to be removed without severe damage. Any educational system freed from the influence of the National Church was suspected of being potentially non-Christian.

The Nonconformist or Liberationist theory (as represented by the National Education League, the Liberation Society, the Dissenting Deputies, and the Central Nonconformist Committee) was one of combined secular and separate religious education of the pupils in schools of the State. There ought to be a distinction between theology as dogmatic teaching and other branches of knowledge. What was required by religious communities for the proper education of children in public elementary schools should be kept distinct from what was required by the State. In this way both the voluntary and the compulsory religious systems would have their allotted time. But it was unfair for public money to be privately devoted to sectarian interests.

> Father Brown of his great bounty
> Built this school at the expense of the county.

A. Forster's Education Bill

This Bill applied to England and Wales only, and enacted that the power to run the new educational machinery would be given to the Education

[1] *Nonconformist*, 16.vi.75, p. 614.

[2] According to Irene Parker, *Dissenting Academies in England*, pp. 45–7, these Academies were among the finest schools of Tudor England. Many of the Oxford and Cambridge teachers and clergymen ejected from their livings turned to these schools and directed their energies to making them far in advance of Church-controlled schools and colleges.

Department. The main objects were: (1) to provide sufficient elementary schools, (2) to arrange for their maintenance and efficiency, and (3) to compel the attendance of children. School Boards were created to administer the accommodation in existing denominational schools, and to build new National schools where that accommodation was inadequate.

One of the great Nonconformist personalities to emerge as a national leader in the National Education struggle, was the Rev. R. W. Dale of Birmingham. Implementing the objects of the Nonconformist Associations, he ceaselessly sought: (1) to amend the provisions in Forster's Education Bill, (2) to secure refusal of national aid to all schools under denominational management, (3) to prevent development of denominational systems of education in Ireland and Scotland, (4) to resist legislative encroachments on the rights of Non-conformists, and (5) to prevent rate schools from becoming institutions for propagating denominational creeds. Some advanced Liberals felt that if Liberalism in education had been entrusted to Dale and not Forster, it would have spared the country years of 'inimical controversy'.[1]

At first the Liberation Society found itself out of step with such proposals because of its policy of neutrality on State education.[2] When the Society came under pressure to take a stand, a special sub-committee was appointed, in March 1870, to look into the matter. It was divided on the question of whether the State might rightly interfere with education, but unanimous in declaring the Education Bill contrary to the principles of the Society. The majority of this committee concluded that the principle of Government inspection of 'dogmatic religious instruction' was harmful. The Executive Committee kept a united front by stating that this was a question not within the scope of the Society's objects. Plans for action in Parliamentary lobbies on the Education Bill were therefore dropped.

Gladstone announced alterations in the Bill in June 1870, and sent the following letter to Lord Shaftesbury:

> I have given it a deliberate assent, as a measure due to the desires and convictions of the country, and as one rendering much honour and scope to religion, without giving fair ground of objection to those who are so fearful that the State should become entangled in theological controversy. Energetic objection will, I have some fear, be taken in some quarters to our proposals; but I believe they will be generally satisfactory to men of moderation.[3]

The Society now relaxed its neutrality and declared: (1) The Parliamentary grants to denominational schools would perpetuate that system of education and would needlessly tax the Imperial Exchequer. (2) In schools created by School Boards, the Bill would permit that kind of religious teaching determined by the ratepayers. (3) With both classes of schools, communities

---

[1] For Morley's opinion of Dale, see his *Recollections* (London 1917), i, 150.

[2] Not until the lively Nonconformist Conference in Manchester on 23 January 1872 did the Society adopt a policy clearly in support of the League.

[3] G. W. E. Russell, *William Ewart Gladstone*, p. 214.

would be compelled to support religious education authorized by the State, to which they might object.

At the Parliamentary Breakfast of the Society and the Dissenting Deputies that year, R. W. Dale and Henry Richard both warned that the Bill meant the endowment of the Established Church in the agricultural districts. Religious instruction in day schools often created religious prejudice instead of religious life. They predicted that, unless concession were made to the Nonconformists, the Liberal party would split. On 18 March, however, George Dixon's amendment summing up their views was rejected in the Commons without a vote.

1. *Miall v. Gladstone*

The breach between Nonconformist-Radicals and Liberals was most dramatically apparent in the third reading of the Bill on 22 July. The leaders of both parties clashed openly and used the language of reproach. Mr Miall sternly defied the Government. Mr Gladstone rarely lost his patience as he did on this occasion.

The M.P. for Bradford first lashed out at the contemptuous indifference of the Government to Nonconformist feelings. 'They laugh who win', especially those who had 'friends at Court'. He did not wonder that the opponents of the Nonconformists took a rather jubilant tone on this occasion. The victors turned round and gave the most discreet advice to those who passed through the 'Valley of Humiliation'. However, he continued, the Administration occupied the position it did mainly in consequence of the 'warm, enthusiastic' support given by the Nonconformist body to the policy announced by the Prime Minister in the 1868 General Election. They were not the sole agents for putting the Liberals where they were, but they were at least 'the hands and heart' of the Liberal cause. Yet in this question which so vitally affected them, consideration was not paid to their objections – they were not even consulted. He admitted that they had been beaten and divided. This was the lesson they had to learn from that Session. But there was far more division of opinion among Dissenters in the House than outside it. There was scarcely a Dissenting organization which had not condemned the Bill. The Liberal party had pointed to the principle of social equality in the measure, but the party had not honoured its pledge to the doctrine of religious equality.

Gladstone's reply was mainly directed at Miall, although Henry Richard had also accused the Premier of 'throwing the Nonconformists overboard'. Gladstone fearlessly denied Miall's attack that the Government had not fulfilled the great expectations for which they had been brought into office.

> We have been thankful to have the independent and honourable support of my hon. Friend, but that support ceases to be of value when accompanied by reproaches such as these. I hope my hon. Friend will not continue that support to the Government one moment longer than he deems it consistent with his sense of duty and right. For God's sake, Sir, let him withdraw it the moment he thinks it better for the cause which he has at heart that he should do so. (Cheers)[1]

[1] Hansard (3rd series), cciii, 745.

So long as Mr Miall was willing to yield support, the Liberal chief went on, the Liberal party would co-operate with him in every purpose held in common. But when it felt that he looked too much at the community which he adorned, and not to the nation at large, he would be reminded that theirs was the Government of the Queen. High administrators must forget the parts in the whole, and the measures they introduced must seek no narrow, no mean, no other object than the welfare of the Empire at large.

The Bill was not partial to the Church of England, said Gladstone. Mr Miall could not deny that in excluding catechisms and dogmas, and in making the Bible a textbook, the Government had excluded something from the schools which was peculiarly characteristic of the Church of England. On this, Anglicans had as much right as the leader of the Nonconformists to say that they had been marched through the 'Valley of Humiliation'. The enormous system of parochial education already in existence ought to be reformed and turned to good account. The measure was far from perfect, but the Government had striven to bring unity in the community of which they were all a part. Special parties should be willing to make sacrifices for an urgently needed measure of National Education.

Parliament heeded Gladstone and so the Bill became law. Two years later, Earl Russell wrote to the Secretary of the British and Foreign Bible Society, expressing the hope that the Birmingham League would be successful in repealing the 25th clause of the Act. The former Premier reflected on the above debating duel:

> The Bishops and Clergy, and the congregations committed to their charge, must be worth their weight in gold in the eyes of our present rulers to make them count as nothing the hostility of Mr. Miall.

In his letter to Mr Forster, admitting the justice of the objections of Nonconformists, the Earl advised, 'such men as Mr Miall and Mr Winterbotham ought surely to be conciliated by justice, and not overpowered'.[1]

2. *Bible Reading and Taxation*

The first round of the education controversy in Parliament caused Nonconformists to come out strongly in favour of 'the ultimate absorption of the denominational system into a really national system'. Generally speaking, Nonconformists had lost respect for the 'conscience clause', which enabled Dissenting parents to remove their children from religious instruction in the Church of England. It was alleged that the children of these parents frequently became child-martyrs in the village community. Many working men preferred leaving their children in the classes on catechism, rather than having trouble with the Church incumbent for writing the 'protest'.

---

[1] Winterbotham (M.P., Stroud) turned a political somersault in 1871 by joining the Ministry. He then urged that Dissenters accept the Act and make the best of it, lest a Tory Government come in with more drastic ideas. For this he was visited personally and challenged on his stand. Garvin, *Life of Joseph Chamberlain*, i, 132.

A truly national system of education, whatever it was, could not avoid oppressing the conscience of someone. But Nonconformists were not willing to stand by and see their social and political gains lost in a 'blanket scheme' for educating the future citizens of the nation in the principles of the Church of England. Nonconformists did not require Liberal leaders to adopt all their principles; they simply asked them to be loyal to their own. They were suspicious of that loyalty because the Education Bill had been carried with strong Conservative support.

As time went on, the wrong in the Act to which Nonconformists pointed became more intolerable to them. They saw an increase in State subsidies and extension of denominational schools, curtailing the building of mixed schools (Anglican and Nonconformist) under School Boards. They saw the School Board system failing to be one of the main features of the National Education programme. The advertisements for teachers in the educational journals were especially galling:

> Wanted, a master for a mixed school (certificate provisional or otherwise), salary £30, school pence, and Government grant. Good Churchman, able to play harmonium in Church occasionally.[1]

To the distressed Dissenters the abuse arose from the working of two faulty clauses in the Act. Clause 14 prohibited in School Board schools the teaching of catechism or religious formularies distinctive of any particular denomination, but it left open the matter of reading and teaching the Bible. Clause 25 permitted the school authorities to pay for the fees of poor children out of local rates.

It was incredible to Churchmen that the greatest objection to reading the Bible in schools should come from those who valued it most highly. Most Nonconformists, however, objected to it being read by a 'legally authorized person' who could proselytize the children of the poor to his own faith. The question was not whether the facts of the Bible should be taught, but whether the State schoolmaster was the best agent for teaching them. Puritan and Calvinistic educators generally believed, as did their Catholic rivals, that religious truth was of a special order 'not of this world', and that therefore the separation between the spiritual and temporal power was as inevitable as between the human and the divine. Spiritual understanding came not from the enterprise of the State, but from the personal instruction of the individual, the family, and the Church.

Other Nonconformists scorned the idea of the Bible as a separate textbook, and regarded reading of the Bible and its explanation by the Schoolmaster as a necessary safeguard against non-Christian influences. This need not involve teaching particular dogmas of Christianity. An Evangelical 'Declaration' was drawn up in 1872 by 500 Dissenting Ministers that deplored the exclusion of

---

[1] Hansard (3rd series), ccxxx, 1203; cf. 1198 ff. Speech by Henry Richard in the Commons on 10 July 1876.

'the Word of God' by law from public elementary schools.[1] For them the ecclesiastical domination of the past was not to be feared as much as secular intolerance in the future.

Liberals in the Anglican Church believed that religious education fitted better into the pattern of general education when both were in the hands of the same person. This prevented a duality in the child's mind – sacred truth as distinct from secular truth – and overcame any tendency to look upon the Christian faith as something separate from ordinary life. The formal separation of the Church from the State would make this task of relating religious faith with natural environment more difficult.

A further Nonconformist educational party was represented by John Morley, one of the philosophical Radicals in the school of John Stuart Mill. In *The Struggle for National Education*, Morley charged the Government with protecting sectarianism at the risk of protecting national ignorance. Worthy secular learning had been regarded too lightly and its standards remained comparatively low.

> The old-fashioned moderation of doctrine is changed into enthusiasm and excess, and our age of science is also the age of deepening superstition and reviving sacerdotalism.[2]

The 'obnoxious 25th clause', which permitted aid from local rates to denominational schools in the case of children of poor parents, aroused the greatest excitement among Nonconformist-Radicals. Disraeli referred to this clause as a symbol of the National Education controversy:

> The school board may, if they think fit, from time to time, for a renewable period not exceeding six months, pay the whole or any part of the school fees payable at any public elementary school by any child resident in their district whose parent is, in their opinion, unable from poverty to pay the same; but no such payment shall be made or refused on condition of the child attending any public elementary school other than such as may be selected by the parent.[3]

The operation of the clause was optional and was left to the local School Board to decide. The debates in the major School Boards of the country attracted wide attention. In numerous cases the Board voted in favour of such payments – the Anglican, Roman Catholic, and Wesleyan Board members usually standing together.

The 'non-sectarians' were alarmed when it was found that most of the applications for assistance were coming from Anglican and Roman Catholic parents. With Dissenters it was never proper for one man to pay for another man's sectarianism. It meant reviving Church Rates in a new guise, and at the same time transferring the struggles from the Vestry to the School Board –

---

[1] The chief sponsors were the Reverends C. H. Spurgeon, Newman Hall, Thomas Binney, and J. Guinness Rogers. Rogers published a pamphlet entitled, *Why Ought Not the State to Give Religious Education?* (London 1872).

[2] *The Struggle for National Education*, p. 63.

[3] 33 & 34 Vict., cap. 75, clause 25.

beyond the reach of Dissenters. They complained of now having two State Churches to fight instead of one.

In militant Anglo-Catholic quarters there was more than a little dissatisfaction with this provision. Thus, Archdeacon George Denison of Taunton wrote in a letter to the Liberation Society:

> The entire 'success' of the [1870 Education] Act turns upon the power of imposing 'School-rate'. 'School-rate' is a 'grievance of conscience'. 'Church-rate' was abolished because it was alleged to be a 'grievance of conscience' to Nonconformists. 'School-rate' is a 'grievance of conscience' to all religious bodies alike. If a 'School-rate' is imposed upon me, I shall not pay it, nor allow it to be paid on my account, except by way of 'distress'. You can make any use you please, private or public, of this letter.[1]

George Dixon (M.P., Birmingham), the Chairman of the National Education League, voiced these objections to the Education Act in his resolutions in the Commons on 5 March 1872: (1) it did not provide proper election of School Boards in rural areas where the prestige of the Anglican Church and its school was strongest; (2) it allowed School Boards to pay rate-money to schools over which the ratepayers had no control. The resolutions were lost by 95 to 355 votes, and Forster's amendment that insufficient time had elapsed since the passing of the 1870 Act to review its provisions profitably, was carried by 328 to 98 votes.

3. *Amendments and Compulsion*

The Government put through an Elementary Education Act Amendment in 1873, described by the *Nonconformist* as 'the expiring effort of an effete and palsied administration'. The Amendment Act provided for several administrative changes in the education law. It left the relations between the indigent classes and the School Boards untouched, but provided for the compulsory education of the children of all 'outdoor paupers' through the machinery of the Board of Guardians.

The opponents of this measure feared that such machinery would lead pupils more easily to parochial schools, and that there should be a corresponding increase of School Board schools. In a speech at Carr's Lane Congregational Church, Birmingham, on 26 June 1873, under the auspices of the Central Nonconformist Committee, the Minister, Dr R. W. Dale, termed it 'a piece of legislative bungle'. It meant the existence of two separate bodies – School Boards and Boards of Guardians – to deal with assistance to poor parents in cases of two separate classes of schools. In 1876 the Education Committee of the Privy Council estimated that there were still 1,387,400 poor children practically outside the compulsory system.

---

[1] *Liberator*, Nov. 1871, p. 194. In his *Notes of my Life 1805–1878* (Oxford 1878), p. 183 Denison stated that because the principle of the Establishment had done so much injury to true religion, he had joined the Church League for the separation of Church from State; cf. also the Society's pamphlet, *Voices from Within, or Disestablishment Viewed by Churchmen*.

An important attempt to repeal the 25th clause was conducted by Henry Richard (M.P., Merthyr Tydfil), early in Disraeli's last Ministry. In the ensuing debate in June 1874, Forster explained that the celebrated clause had been incorporated in his Bill for two reasons: (1) to get children to school when otherwise they could not have gone there, and (2) to take away from the parents any reasonable excuse for keeping their children out of school. Compulsion, even in such a modified form, was impossible without giving the parent full choice.

Instead of the 25th clause, Nonconformists preferred the full operation of the 17th clause, under which certain deprived children might be admitted free. In the extension of this allowance, Richard believed that all children could be given an excellent secular education and separate religious instruction – the reading of the Bible with such explanations as would be suited to their capacities. If the parent wished the child to receive the instruction of a particular Church, he either should pay for it, or send the child to the Church which provided the instruction. It would be no more awkward for Anglicans than it had been for Nonconformists to stand the expense of their religious instruction and to conduct it in their own buildings. Even with the support of the then Liberal leader, the Marquess of Hartington, the second reading of Richard's Bill was lost by 128 to 245 votes.

The only satisfaction Nonconformists seemed to find was that the 25th clause was becoming inoperative in practice. Boards were becoming more reluctant to draw on Rates in order to fill the existing Church schools instead of building new ones.

B. *Lord Sandon's Education Bill*

In an address to his constituents before the 1874 General Election, Gladstone had asserted that no main provisions of the Education Act of 1870 'could advantageously be reconsidered without the aid of an experience such as we have not acquired'. Nonconformist-Radicals said that such utterances had been responsible for the heavy losses of his party at the polls. The Conservatives, moreover, were eager to modify the Education Act to strengthen their position. Without Gladstone's opposition to an alliance between the State and Church schools, the task of the new Tory Government was comparatively easy and the position of the Nonconformists was one of growing frustration.[1]

Feelings on both sides ran high in the heated session in 1876 on Lord Sandon's proposals. For some time Nonconformists had accused the Government of hampering efficient compulsion by intricate schemes for shielding Church of England Schools. Sandon (M.P., Liverpool) therefore extended

[1] About this time the Nonconformists were smarting from the dispute at Perse Grammar School. One of its masters, Mr F. C. Maxwell M.A. (St John's College, Oxford) was a Methodist. He had been appointed by the predecessor of Mr J. B. Allen, who was made Headmaster in 1876. Despite the master's excellent references he was asked by the new Headmaster to leave, because he wished all his colleagues to share the same religious creed. A policy of uniformity, he believed, was socially as well as religiously expedient for the life of the school.

the compulsion, which had just started in the 1873 Education Amendment Act, in four directions: (1) all children whose parents received parochial relief, were compelled to attend schools; (2) free instruction was granted in cases of extreme poverty; (3) the ballot was further extended in the election of all School Boards; (4) the Rate from the Boards of Guardians replaced the School Board Rate in payment of fees to denominational schools.

Carvell Williams, Secretary of the Liberation Society, wrote to Gladstone asking, Did not this last provision mean that such a Rate could in fact become an illegal compulsory Church Rate? Gladstone replied:

> Where a case seems at first view utterly bad, one generally surmises that there must be something in the rear. I am, however, at a loss to conceive what it can be, and I learn with surprise that any one can suppose a payment out of poor's rate for the maintenance of the Church to be voluntary subscription within the meaning of the Compulsory Church-Rates Abolition Act.[1]

Numerous meetings were called to protest at Sandon's measure: the National Education League in Birmingham on 24 May, with Joseph Chamberlain in the Chair; the United Nonconformist Committees in Crewe on 26 May, with R. W. Dale in the chair, and the joint Committees of the Liberation Society and Dissenting Deputies in London on 12 June, with Alderman MacArthur M.P., in the chair. A deluge of petitions from Dissenting denominational bodies were lodged, describing the measure as the most reactionary ever presented to Parliament and beyond hope of satisfactory amendment.

In the debate which began on 15 June, however, an array of amendments were presented.[2] The most outspoken antagonists were Sir Charles Dilke, Joseph Chamberlain, and Henry Richard. Richard's amendment stated that any compulsion to attend schools was grossly unjust without placing public elementary education under public management. He attacked the Bill for its Conservative and Anglican leanings, and cited illustrations of the kind of catechetical teaching it would sponsor:

> Q. Why cannot we look for salvation out of the Church? A. Because God's promises are only made to His Church. Q. Is it not then very dangerous to leave the Church? A. Yes, and it is also a very grievous sin. Q. What is this sin called? A. A schism or division. Q. Are we warned against this sin in the Bible? A. Yes, St. Paul tells us to mark them which cause divisions, and to avoid them (Conservative cheers). Q. What are those who separate from the Church of England commonly called? A. Dissenters. Q. Are there different sorts of Dissenters? A. Yes, Baptists, Independents, Quakers, and many others. Q. Is it wrong to join in the worship of Dissenters? A. Yes; we should only attend places of worship which belong to the Church of England. Q. Why? A. Because

---

[1] *Liberator*, July 1876, p. 122.

[2] *Nonconformist*, 12.vii.76, pp. 688–94. The account of this one-day debate received more coverage in its columns (21 in number) than that on Miall's Disestablishment motions. In Hansard (3rd series), ccxxx, it filled 82 columns, 1186–1268.

it is the branch of the true Church which God has placed in the land. (Hear, hear.)[1]

Lord Hartington and other like-minded Liberals deemed it improper to cite instances of petty persecution. He maintained that it was not a measure to arouse the passion of religious animosity and bigotry. Strict enforcement of the 'conscience clause' would meet the difficulties of the case. Mr Richard's amendment lost by 99 to 317 votes.

Two days later, on the motion for the third reading of the Bill,[2] Richard summed up the righteous indignation of his followers:

> I wish . . . to record my last protest against it, and declare my convictions that it is the worst bill, the most unjust, the most reactionary, the most tyrannical in spirit that has been brought before Parliament since Lord Bolingbroke proposed his Schism Bill in the reign of Queen Anne.

After its passage on 7 August, the Parliamentary Committee of the Liberation Society condemned it in the *Liberator* in equally strong terms:

> The Committee now counsel their supporters to watch with the utmost vigilance the operation of the Act, in their several localities, with a view to counteract, as far as possible, its mischievous tendency; to prepare for such efforts as will be needed to reverse the policy which it embodies; and to labour with increased energy to put an end to an ecclesiastical establishment, which, in regard to education, as well as other important objects, hinders wise legislation and occasions social irritation and discontent.[3]

C. *Consequences and Conclusions*

The Society saw in these Elementary Education laws two concessions to Nonconformists: (1) the insertion of a clause requiring that infractions of the 'conscience clause' should be reported immediately to the Education Department; (2) the withdrawal of the authority of local Education Committees

---

[1] Hansard (3rd series), ccxxx, 1199. By 1888 the catechism of the Rev. F. A. Gace M.A., Vicar of Great Barling, Essex, entitled *Some Questions of the Church Catechism and Doctrines Involved Briefly Explained* (London 1870), had run into its 10th edition. Some of the other questions and answers included: '85. We have amongst us various Sects and Denominations who go by the general name of Dissenters. In what light are we to consider them? A. As heretics; and in our Litany we expressly pray to be delivered from the sins of 'false doctrine, heresy, and schism'. 86. Is then their worship a laudable service? A. No; because they worship God according to their own evil and corrupt imaginations, and not according to His revealed will, and therefore their worship is idolatrous.' In 1889, the Archbishop of Canterbury (Dr Benson) condemned Gace's Catechism as not in keeping with the mind of the National Church.

[2] It now had a further change: Sandon moved to repeal the 25th clause, and to omit the words in the 14th clause which had created distinction between School Boards and other forms of district administration. This, he said, would help to eliminate some of the red tape of which Liberationists were always complaining. They reported that the 25th clause at least left the payment of fees optional, but his amendment would make it compulsory. It was nevertheless repealed by 192 to 91 votes.

[3] *Liberator*, Sept. 1876, p. 157.

which did not have some members who belonged either to Town Councils or Boards of Guardians for 'poor' children.

Nonconformist political agitators now turned to the School Boards as the most suitable spheres for furthering their educational interests. In the rural districts the Board system was unpopular with the Squires and Vicars, but most of the agricultural labourers had confidence in it. In the cities the Boards were strong and could influence the educational future of the country. The Society therefore sent out circulars in November 1876, urging its subscribers to vote in the London School Board Elections for candidates supporting national, unsectarian education. The result was the return of thirty non-sectarians and nineteen denominationalists. In the former group were eleven supporters of the Liberation Society.[1] In similar fashion, the Society established a foothold in School Boards in Liverpool, Birmingham, and Manchester.

Liberationists, especially in the Birmingham League, never forgave Forster for his role in the 1870 Act and its subsequent colouring of all legislation on education. Chagrined by his obstinacy and the apple of discord he had thrown into the Liberal party, they made numerous attempts to shut him out of the House of Commons. A bitter critic, Alfred Illingworth, Treasurer of the Liberation Society, wrote in 1878 that he would endorse Forster as one of the candidates at the next General Election, if he would place himself in the hands of the Bradford Liberal Association. Forster scorned the working of the caucus principle,[2] and decided as the standing member of the constituency to deal with the electors directly. This he did and held his seat in Parliament. Illingworth, however, was returned with him to occupy the other seat.

The Society would not admit that Forster's principles were a fixed part of English law, and that Church schools would continue as they were in English life. This meant a renewal of internal party strife after the return of a Gladstone Administration in 1880. Nonconformists, however, no longer felt the necessity to revolt in order to gain their ends. The Society's minutes recorded the resolutions for Free Education passed by the annual meeting of the National Liberal Federation at Bradford in 1885.

That in the opinion of this meeting, the public elementary schools of this country should be placed under the management of duly-elected representatives of the people, and that any deficiency caused by the abolition of fees in the schools under the control of the rate-payers should be supplied from the national Exchequer.[3]

Before the General Election of that year, Carvell Williams issued a final

[1] Minute 839: 4.xii.76. The Society's agents collected names of those supporting their candidates in order to interest them in the Disestablishment campaign.

[2] Illingworth was applying the rule of the Association's constitution, which required the proposer of any candidate to give such candidate's assurance that he would abide by the decisions of the Association. Reid, *Life of the Right Honourable William Edward Forster*, ii, 208–9.

[3] Minute 634: 5.x.85.

statement for the Society which again condemned the consequences of State aid to denominational schools: (1) exclusion of efficient teachers, (2) compulsory powers for clerically controlled schools, (3) additional public cost of £2,000,000, and (4) withholding the right of public management in country parishes.

Many Liberationists and non-sectarians now sealed a compact together. They swore that it was impossible to legislate with common justice concerning popular education, so long as the country was guided chiefly by an Established Church.

CHAPTER 20

University Tests

Who has not observed inferior original power achieving greater results even in the intellectual field itself, where the superior understanding happens to have been unequally yoked with a self-seeking character, ever scenting the expedient?

JOHN MORLEY[1]

I who have been brought up from my childhood in the Church of England and who see no cause to depart from her teaching and practice, cannot shut my eyes to the fact that, in this great strife of public right and wrong, the spirit of Isaiah and all the prophets has rested on the Ministers and Congregations of the Nonconformists in an incalculably higher degree than on the prelates and clergy of the Establishment.

EDWARD AUGUSTUS FREEMAN[2]

THE YEAR of the abolition of Religious Tests at the Universities, 1871, was also the year of the first debate on the Disestablishment of the Church of England. Churchmen were inclined to view the former as conceding to Nonconformists the lesser of two evils, in order to quiet their consciences. The final passage of the Bill, however, was due principally to the persistence of the academic Liberals seeking University reform, and not to the benevolence of the Conservatives.

The state of affairs in the national Universities undoubtedly called for improvements, but conditions were not always so bad as reformers claimed them to be. Their criticisms tended to be extreme: (1) the idle and dilettante undergraduates had multiplied, (2) the College lecturing standards had fallen, and (3) the tutorial system had become too expensive. Sensible Nonconformists looked upon their principles of voluntary effort and free inquiry as a means of correcting such weaknesses. Also the contribution to the Universities, by young men with the steady economical habits and reliable

---

[1] *On Compromise* (London 1886), p. 91.

[2] Special Memorandum Book of the Liberation Society (unpublished document), No. 2, p. 124.

moral influence from the Puritan middle class, would be considerable.[1]

Professor Renn Dickson Hampden, Bampton Lecturer in 1832, had, as we have seen,[2] defined Nonconformity as the 'difference of opinions, arising out of the different conclusions drawn by different minds out of the same given elements of Scripture'. He distinguished between theological truth, as arising from the human mind, and religious truth, as arising from the Divine Revelation in the Scripture. The University Tests – thirty-nine doctrinal statements to which a student must subscribe upon matriculation – fell in the former category and should not be confused with basic religious truths. For this reason, he believed, the practice of subscription could be safely abolished.[3]

Forty years later Professor Benjamin Jowett (Master of Balliol College) led an energetic group of Oxford Radicals who sought to remove the bonds of religious Tests: George Brodrick (Warden of Merton College), Charles S. Roundell, Albert Rutson, (Sir) G. Osborne Morgan, Charles (Lord) Bowen, James (Lord) Bryce, Lyulph Stanley (Lord Sheffield), and Frederic Harrison. These intellectuals united forces with the London reformers and political Dissenters following Edward Miall and John Bright.

> The delicate task of combining the mildest and even 'Churchy' types of academic Liberalism with the Radical Dissidents of the Chapels and the Lobbies, was in the main the work of the organising genius of Jowett.[4]

A. *Oxford, Cambridge, and Durham Bill*

Sir John Coleridge's University Reform Bill for the three principal Universities of the nation had been rejected by the Lords in 1869. The promoters therefore sought in 1870 to get Gladstone to take up the question personally and to introduce a comprehensive measure. They decided that a deputation to the Prime Minister should be supported by Nonconformist bodies representing their own educational interests:[5]

The Liberation Society (2)	United Presbyterians (1)
The Dissenting Deputies (1)	Methodist New Connexion (1)
The Congregational Union (3)	Methodist Free Church (1)
The Baptist Union (1)	New College, London (1)

---

[1] In the election of the President of the Oxford Union on 23 November 1895, J. Allenbrook Simon (Wadham Coll.), a Liberal-Nonconformist, defeated A. Boyd Carpenter (Balliol Coll.), a Conservative-Churchman by 313 to 209 votes.

[2] cf. p. xvii, above.

[3] *Observations on Religious Dissent*, pp. 12–13.

[4] Frederic Harrison, *Autobiographic Memoirs*, i, 159.

[5] Gladstone wrote to Carvell Williams as Secretary of this deputation which included such educators as Dr R. W. Dale, Dr Joseph Angus, Dr James Martineau, and Messrs Miall, Skeats and Samuel Morley. Minute 427: 11.ii.70. The Committee of University Reformers who were consulted on this consisted of James Heywood M.P., J. G. Dodson M.P., G. J. Goschen M.P., Prof. Benjamin Jowett, Charles Roundell, Goldwin Smith, E. P. Bouverie M.P., Henry Fawcett M.P., E. Lyulph Stanley, Sir J. D. Coleridge M.P., G. C. Brodrick, James Bryce, Frederic Harrison.

The London Congregational Board (1)   Regent's Park College (1)
The London Baptist Board (2)   Manchester College (1)
                    Hackney College (1)

The Prime Minister answered them that the time had arrived for the question
to be settled, the measure should be compulsory, and it should be a Government measure. Oxford had been Gladstone's 'native heath' and he had
therefore naturally been a reluctant convert to the idea of emancipating the
Universities from the Church of England.

Accordingly, it was announced in the Queen's Speech in 1870 that the
Government intended to take action on this matter. Sir John Coleridge, the
Solicitor-General, remained in the vanguard, and in May the Government
Bill which he introduced was read a second time. He followed the line of his
previous speeches – that there was no ground for the Church to dread free
inquiry, for when had the Church been found unequal to the conflict when
fairly matched with her foes?

The Opposition now regarded it as useless to continue resistance on the
question in the Commons. In Committee of the House a provision for opening
Headships of Colleges to Dissenters was included, and the third reading
passed by 247 to 113 votes. The Conservative Peers, however, were not yet
ready to admit defeat. In the Upper House the second reading was amended
by the Marquess of Salisbury that there must be 'safeguards' for maintaining
religion in the Universities. This was carried by 97 to 83 votes, referred to a
Select Committee, and shelved until the 1871 Session.

At the beginning of that year the Liberation Society pressed for a provision to allow Dissenters into Clerical Fellowships. When a deputation of the
Society visited Mr Gladstone on 18 January,[1] he stated that such a proposal
could be supported by amendment in Committee, but that the Lords should
have one more opportunity of passing the Bill in its present shape. The
amendment, however, was defeated and when the Bill was re-read in the
Lords a second time, Lord Salisbury again secured appointment of a Select
Committee with the same purpose as in the previous year.

The Radical-Nonconformist party peevishly felt that the proposals of this
Committee were nothing but an attempt to rob the Bill of Dissenting
successes:

1. The imposition of a new Declaration upon every tutor and lecturer at his
   appointment, not to teach anything contrary to the teaching or Divine
   Authority of Holy Scriptures.
2. The exclusion of the College Headships from the operation of the Bill.
3. The prohibition of alterations in College Statutes, particularly those affecting
   Fellowships, without the authority of Parliament.
4. The obligation on the governing bodies of the Colleges to provide religious
   instruction for members of the Established Church.
5. The obligation to maintain Daily Service in College Chapels.

[1] Parl. Com. Minutes, 12.i.71.

19

The Society protested at the discrimination against some of the most brilliant Nonconformist scholars. Was it just and proper to reserve the best Fellowships in the Colleges for those taking Holy Orders? When W. S. Aldis, a former Senior Wrangler at Cambridge, asked this in a letter to Lord John Manners, he answered that if the measure became law, he would 'never send another son'[1] to the University.

The Secretary of the Society wrote to the Prime Minister, informing him of its intention to resist all five of Lord Salisbury's proposals.[2] He replied that the Government would not resist the latter two, but did reject the first three. After the Bill returned to the Upper Chamber, the insistence of some of the Lords upon the first amendment was rejected by 129 to 89 votes. On 16 June the Act 'to alter the Law respecting Religious Tests in the Universities of Oxford, Cambridge and Durham, and in the Halls and Colleges of those Universities' received the Royal Assent:

> . . . no person taking lay academic degrees—*i.e.* other than degrees in divinity— or holding lay academical or collegiate offices, shall in future be required to subscribe any formulary of faith.[3]

Fifteen years later, under the allowances of this Act and the leadership of Dr R. W. Dale, Nonconformists established Mansfield College at Oxford. Speaking at the opening of the College, Professor Jowett, the Vice-Chancellor, described the occasion as 'a great festival of union and reconciliation'.[4]

> 'Our ideal', he said, 'is to show the alumni of the university to make men rather than books the end of their study. . . . The university, in other words, is no longer thought of as ministering to a learned caste, or a cultured oligarchy, but is to be a link between culture and democracy.'[5]

B. *Dublin and St Patrick's Bill*

The Liberal doctrine that all people of a country ought to be equally dealt with by the State, without reference to religious beliefs or ecclesiastical organizations, encountered serious complications in Ireland. What was good for England was not necessarily good for other countries as well. Most Irishmen could not view the State or school as in any way separate from their religion – at least the Irishmen so minded had most of the political influence in their land.

The weakness in the position of many English Dissenters was that they held a traditional distrust for Roman Catholics anywhere. Although the Irish

---

[1] *Nonconformist*, 8.ii.71, p. 123.

[2] Minute 1026: 22.v.71.

[3] R. W. Dale, *History of English Congregationalism*, pp. 629–30. Divinity degrees and professorships were still closed, as were headships of those colleges whose heads were required to be in orders and certain other offices. In 1894 the Liberation Society sought to remove religious tests for professorships at King's (Anglican) College, London University, in consideration of its receiving Government grants.

[4] Skeats & Miall, op. cit., p. 686.

[5] quoted in *Liberator*, Nov. 1886, p. 179.

Catholics were sincere Nonconformists, they were accused of being in greater religious error than upholders of the Established Church. Uncompromising Protestant Nonconformists thus alienated an energetic political body that might have proved a useful ally in Parliament.[1]

The Dublin University Bill of Henry Fawcett (M.P., Brighton) applied the principle of the University Tests Act of 1871 to the University of Dublin. It added not a little fire to the educational controversy raging during this period. Mr Gladstone did not like the measure because it failed to provide a national University and its degrees to Irish students who wanted their religion with their education. This, he believed, was a denial of civil rights on account of religious opinion. The State should provide a University, the character of which should be determined by the religious views rather than the secular wants of the population. Gladstone later denied that this was tantamount to State-endowment of a Roman Catholic institution.

At the same time the Roman Catholic Clergy were pressing for State educational foundations under their own supervision and control. The Liberation Society maintained that the State should be neutral and should confer neither privileges nor power on ecclesiastical grounds upon any section of the community. Accordingly, in February 1873, the Society called a conference of Nonconformists in Southern England, presided over by James Heywood, adopting a policy of 'mixed education' for Ireland:

> . . . the Conference is of the opinion that past experience, in relation to both the higher and the primary forms of education in Ireland, has conclusively shown the superior value of mental training which involves the mixture of various classes holding diverse religious opinions, over separate education, imparted by, or in the interest of, any ecclesiastical organisation.[2]

At the opening of the 1873 Session the Government brought in the Bill which the several parties eagerly awaited. On the face of it the measure made concessions to those who insisted that Universities should be places of secular learning exclusively. It abolished the Queen's University and one of the Queen's Colleges and encouraged Protestants and Catholics to sit side by side wherever possible in the pursuit of an education. To remove Catholic grievances it prohibited the appointment of any University Professorship in Theology, Modern History, or Moral and Mental Philosophy – separately affiliated Colleges could make their own arrangements on these subjects. Endowment for the new University was to be provided by Trinity College, the Consolidated Fund, and the Irish (Disestablished) Church Surplus, amounting to £50,000 a year. Lastly, the governing bodies of the denominational Colleges could elect representatives to a controlling Council of the University which would be undenominational.

Immediately upon introduction of the Bill the Society convened another

---

[1] Out of 36 Catholic M.P.s in 1871, only 4 voted with Nonconformists on the debate for disestablishing the English Church. This was partly due to derogatory references to that Church's tendencies toward Rome.

[2] Minute 23: 17.ii.73.

Irish University Conference of national Nonconformist organizations.[1] Unanimity was reached and it was resolved to support the Bill if amendments were made that the governing bodies of the denominational Colleges should not be given the power of appointing members to the University Council.

In the course of debate the Government was pressed from two sides – English University reformers who demanded amendments for religious equality, and the Irish politicians who said the Bill abandoned concessions to Roman Catholic religious education. Before the division the Government announced that it was dropping the features which had been objectionable to the Society's conference. Miall's Nonconformists and Fawcett's reformers voted for the second reading, but the Irish bloc dissented.

As a result, on 11 March 1873, the Government was unexpectedly defeated by 287 to 284 votes and promptly resigned. Placed in a dilemma, it had failed to achieve a clever victory with both anti-State-Churchmen and advocates of sectarian education. When the Opposition was not prepared to assume office the Liberals immediately came back into power. Mr Fawcett arranged with the Government for a Bill limited to the abolition of ecclesiastical Tests in the Irish University. It was read a second time without a division, carried through the House of Lords on 16 May, and quickly received the Royal Assent. Henry Richard subsequently referred to this defeat and the hasty amends of the Gladstone Ministry as 'the Nemesis of the English Nonconformists'.[2]

> Why was it that our accomplished and adventurous pilot, who had guided the vessel with such consummate courage and skill through so many shoals and straits, on that occasion steered her on the rocks? Because he saw the Vice-President of the Council, like a spectral apparition in the offing, brandishing in his face the English Education Act, for undoubtedly the denominational character of that Act had enormously aggravated the difficulty of the Government in dealing with Irish Education.

Plans for the formation of a thoroughly Irish University, to be called 'St Patrick's', suddenly came to the fore in 1879 in the Bill of the O'Conor Don (M.P., Co. Roscommon). Appropriation for operating costs of one and a half million pounds of money (from the surplus property of the Disestablished Irish Anglican Church)[3] would endow sectarian Colleges within a secular

---

[1] During the Parliamentary recess in 1872 the Society convened a confidential strategy conference on the Irish University question. Representatives met from the Nonconformist Associations in Manchester, Liverpool, Birmingham and London, the Baptist and Congregational Unions, Methodist and Presbyterian bodies, the Dissenting Deputies, and the Society. Little agreement was achieved.

[2] C. S. Miall, *Henry Richard, M.P.: A Biography*, p. 191.

[3] The annual income of the Irish Church Surplus property was estimated by the Society to be £574,219. The total value of the Irish Church Estate was estimated in 1877 to be £12m., a charge on it was estimated to be about £6m., and the Surplus also approximately £6m. sterling, divided thus: Intermediate Education £1m.; National School Teachers £1,300,000; Famine Relief £1,267,000; Landlords and Tenants (under the Arrears Act to assist them to compound their difficulties), £9½m.; Sea Fisheries £250,000; Royal Universities £600,000; Distressed Unions £10,362. Parliamentary Paper C 2288, Session 1879.

University. Outcries against the 'occult intention' of the Bill were heard from the Protestants of Ireland and the usual anti-Catholic sources. Surprisingly, the Government decided on a measure of their own, and the O'Conor Don's Bill was therefore talked out.

The Ministerial measure provided for the charter of a new University in Ireland to be governed by a Senate of thirty-six members, appointed by the Crown and graduates. This University would have power to grant degrees to anyone in or out of College who passed certain examinations in all faculties (except theology). Within two years after granting the charter the existing Queen's University, but not the Queen's Colleges, would be dissolved. Its graduates and students would be merged in the new University, and its property would be transferred there as well. Within a year the Senate was to prepare plans for University buildings and a Library, and proposals for exhibitions, scholarships, fellowships and other prizes to be given to successful students.

The Liberation Society, in company with Mr George O. Trevelyan, Sir C. Campbell, and Lord Edmond Fitzmaurice, condemned this Bill for using the money in a way contrary to the Irish Church Act. Ironically the arch-Conservative and enemy of the Society, Lord Salisbury, found himself in agreement on this occasion with an editorial in the *Liberator*:

> The Irish Lords who have risen this evening practically do not care about degrees at all—they say, 'We want money.' This money question lies at the root of the case. The Irish Roman Catholics insist that they will have no education of which religion is not a part. The people of this country, on the other hand, insist that no money should be given to support the Roman Catholic religion in Ireland.[1]

The Bill passed all its stages on 11 August in substantially the same form in which it was introduced. The question, however, was only partially settled. The Conservative Government had made political capital in outlining a new University system for Ireland, but the difficulties which it entailed were left for the forthcoming Liberal Administration. The Bill therefore became an apple of discord among Liberals when the Beaconsfield Premiership was about to end. If the rising Liberal majority hoped to solve the problem of Irish Home Rule by pushing any more legislation favouring Catholic education, they faced the certainty of alienating the Nonconformists.

C. The Hertford College Case

University reformers and educational leaders of the Society were not entirely content with the Tests Act settlement of 1871. In order to make it satisfactory, the next task facing them was the removal of Clerical restrictions on Fellowships and Headships of Colleges.

In a paper read to the Cambridge Society for Religious Equality, Mr Neville

---

[1] Hansard (3rd series), ccxlvii, 1850.

Goodman M.A. cited a number of interesting statistics.[1] Of the seventeen Heads of Colleges at Cambridge ten were required to be in Holy Orders. At Oxford, it was seventeen out of twenty-four. At Cambridge the Clerical Headships received a gross income of £12,500 per annum, compared with £8,000 granted to the non-Clerical Heads. At Oxford the seventeen Heads of Colleges were annually paid £25,600, and £6,000 was paid to the others. Of the 671 Fellowships in the two Universities, 323 were affected by some kind of Clerical conditions. To become a Priest in order to retain a College Fellowship, according to Goodman, was to make 'sweet religion a rhapsody of words'.

After several unsuccessful attempts in 1876 and 1877 to reduce clerical control and waste of money in the high University positions, attention was shifted in 1878 to the outcome of the Hertford College Case. This case, *The Queen v. Hertford College, Oxford*, became a legal controversy which tested the practical effect of legislation for University reform. The prosecution of the case, which occupied several years, was one for which the Society and its lawyers were chiefly responsible.[2]

The authorities of Hertford College announced, in December 1875, an election for one of its Fellowships, candidates for which would be limited to members of the Church of England. Mr Lyulph Stanley, of the Society's Executive Committee, wrote letters to *The Times* stating that such a limitation was contrary to the University Tests Abolition Act of 1871, and contrary to the Act of 1874 which had converted Magdalen Hall into Hertford College. No published reply was given to his statements. The Committee decided therefore to take legal action against the College and, if necessary, to appeal to Parliament to amend the Hertford College Act.

Mr J. H. Tillyard, of Cambridge, presented himself as a Nonconformist candidate for the Fellowship and was informed that the authorities would abide by their advertisement. Tillyard withdrew, was not examined, and on again tendering himself on the day of election, received a reply repeating the earlier decision.[3] Mr Henry S. Leonard of the Society applied to the Court of the Queen's Bench, and on 26 January Mr Hersonell Q.C. moved for a writ of mandamus to compel the governing body of Hertford College (1) to proceed to a new election for a Fellow, (2) to hold a new examination, (3) to admit the applicant to compete in the examination, and (4) to show whether the Fellowship was founded after the passing of the University Tests Act of 1871.

---

[1] cf. *Report of Lords' Select Committee on University Tests, together with Proceedings of the Committee, Minutes, Evidence, and Appendix* (Session 1870), House of Commons printing, 24.iv.71, pp. 216–25.

[2] In the Minutes of the meetings of the Senior Common Room at University College, Oxford, in the 1800s, is found an account of wagers between faculty members as to whether or not the Church would be disestablished at the hands of the Liberationists within five years' time.

[3] Minute 622: 16.xii.75. The first candidate, Mr T. Scrutton, the son of an Auditor of the Society, was informed that he had failed his examination.

The College authorities were able to show cause on 19 June why a mandamus should not be issued, and the judgement of the Court was accordingly against Tillyard. In December 1876, the College announced another election to Fellowships, which, like the previous one, excluded all but Episcopalians. Mr Leonard was promptly instructed by the Executive Committee to proceed again for a writ of mandamus against the College. Mr Stanley received promises for a Guarantee Fund to pay for the litigation.[1]

The case was argued in the Court of the Queen's Bench on 2 and 6 June 1877, before Justices Lush and Mellor. They later delivered judgement (1) that there had been a real refusal to examine Mr Tillyard, (2) that the restriction of the Fellowship to members of the Church of England was a violation of the University Tests Act of 1871, (3) and that a peremptory mandamus to hold a new examination and new election must be issued. Justice Mellor was of the opinion that the Act applied to all new Colleges and their endowments. Justice Lush confined his opinion to the Hertford College Act. The College gave notice of appeal on the judgement.

The Court of Appeal, on 2 May 1878, reversed the decision of the Judges of the Queen's Bench calling for a new election. The Court further pronounced that (1) the operation of the University Tests Act in regard to Fellowships was wholly retrospective, (2) new Fellowships with ecclesiastical tests attached might be created in Colleges existing at the time the Act was passed, and (3) even in cases of old Fellowships the Courts of Law could not interfere if College authorities chose to ignore the claims of qualified Nonconformists to Fellowships.

The Society claimed that this made it possible for undenominational Colleges to become re-denominationalized merely by the creation of new Fellowships and offices. But instead of an appeal to the House of Lords, the Parliamentary Committee decided to make the judgement the basis of amendments to the original 1871 Tests Act. A full statement of the facts of the case, and a circular summoning a private conference was signed by James Bryce, Charles W. Dilke, D. B. Monro, Mark Pattison, Henry Richard, E. Lyulph Stanley, Carvell Williams, and G. J. Goschen, the chairman.

The outcome of this conference was the preparation of a Bill suitable to meet the deficiencies of the old measure, and to prevent a repetition of the Hertford College incident. New Colleges were to be subject to the Tests Act of 1871, unless Statutes, Regulations, Charters or other instruments of foundation declared them to be exempt. In any contravention of the Act of 1871,

> an action in the nature of an information, shall lie at the suit of the Attorney General, with or without a relator, against the University or College in respect of the contravention, and the High Court of Justice shall have jurisdiction to give such judgment and make such orders as the justice and circumstances of the case require.[2]

[1] Minute 823: 6.xi.76. The Dissenting Deputies voted a sum not to exceed £50, after having previously declined to contribute to the costs.

[2] Minute 220: 8.vii.78.

It was not until 1882, however, that Mr Gladstone heeded and went ahead with a Bill for removing abuses in administration at Oxford and Cambridge. Matters were clinched when Lord Salisbury, speaking for the Conservative party almost with Radical zeal, asked for the end of the 'idle Fellowships' and other academic abuses. The new Statutes, prepared by the Oxford and Cambridge Royal Commissioners, threw open the Headships to laymen and Nonconformists in all but three Colleges. The Clerical restrictions were removed from the Fellowships except in the case of Fellows who were required as Chaplains to conduct College services and to give religious instruction.

Except for one or two skirmishes, the dispute over University Tests dropped out of party politics during the remainder of this period. Nonconformists kept close watch upon the terms of armistice, making sure that they were all lawfully observed.

Considerable indignation developed in the case of the Rev. R. F. Horton M.A., Fellow and Lecturer of New College, who had been chosen as one of the Examiners in the Rudiments of Faith and Religion at Oxford. Although this choice had been confirmed by the Vice-Chancellor and the ancient House of Congregation (the resident Dons), it was strongly vetoed in Convocation (the Masters of Arts) on the ground that he was a Nonconformist. The latter body maintained that the examination in question included the Thirty-nine Articles and was therefore declared distinctly Church of England in character. The Liberation Society strongly protested that (except in certain traditional posts, of which this was not one) according to the 1871 Act no person was required to belong to any specific Church as a condition of holding any official position in the University. Nonconformity, however, was still but a weak force in the University, and so Mr Horton's sympathizers could only meekly accept the humiliating verdict.[1]

The Tests Act settlements were designed to remove prejudice between the two rival religious classes, but it happened slowly. It was left to later historians to judge who would benefit most in the quest for intellectual equality:

It is only since Oxford and Cambridge have been thrown open to all creeds, that men who would formerly have been the leaders of a militant Nonconformity

[1] Sir John Marriott, in Horton's biography (Albert Peel & J. A. R. Marriott, *Robert Forman Horton*, London 1937) writes (pp. 112–13) that the dispute had become national. 'The merits of the cases were hotly canvassed in London clubs, in half the rectories and vicarages, and in all the episcopal palaces in England. . . . On Thursday, December 13th [1883], the streets of Oxford presented the sight of a seething mass of black coats and white ties. On the same afternoon, when the decision was known, Horton left Oxford for good. When his Fellowship at New College ran out four years later, he removed his name from the books. Shortly after, to the satisfaction of his former colleagues, he replaced his name; but he rarely revisited the College.

have been absorbed in the general stream of national life. This change has contributed with other causes to the diminution of the Dissenting bodies both in self-consciousness and power.[1]

---

[1] G. M. Trevelyan, *British History in the Nineteenth Century and after* (*1782–1919*) (London 1937), p. 284. His father, G. O. Trevelyan, had been a conscientious exponent of these University reforms, and in 1883, when he was Chief Secretary for Ireland, the Liberation Society had appealed to him for a Government plan to establish denominational colleges for training teachers in the national schools of that country. The Society also pressed J. Blair Balfour, the Lord Advocate of Scotland, to abolish religious tests and additional grants for theological chairs, in the Universities (Scotland) Bill in the same year. Roman Catholics and Presbyterians were especially sensitive on these issues.

CHAPTER 21

Burial Laws

I recommend this Resolution to you as a Charter of Toleration; as a direct declaration that every man in the community, whatever his religious opinions may be, should
have a right to be interred with the rites of his own
persuasion.

EARL GRANVILLE[1]

To refuse to any and every individual the liberty to dictate
after his death what shall be done and said in a place set
apart for national use, and belonging to the public, is just
the same abridgment of his religious liberty . . . as he has
been subjected to during the whole course of his life. He
has never during his whole life been free to have, in such a
place, whomsoever he likes 'enter the ground and have his
own say.' He is not free to have it after his death.

MATTHEW ARNOLD[2]

A. *Grounds of Difference*

FEW THINGS were more illustrative of the astounding difference between
institutional Christianity and the Faith inspired by its Founder than the
Burials controversy. It became a chapter of scornful sarcasm in the
history of the relations between the Episcopal and Free Churches of England.
The real point of difference concerned the nature of the churchyard as
property. The Anglicans claimed that it was held exclusively by the Incumbent
of the local Parish; the Nonconformists, that it was national property of
which he was but the Trustee.

'To invade the Churchyard with other than Church rites was ecclesiastical
burglary', said the *Church Quarterly Review*.[3] It was but a short step from
secularizing the Churchyard to secularizing the Church. If Dissenters were
admitted in this way they would soon be knocking on the doors of the Church

---

[1] Burial Laws Amendment Resolution, House of Lords, 15 May 1876. Hansard (3rd
series), ccxxix, 604.

[2] *Last Essays on Church and Religion* (London 1877), 'A Last Word on the Burials Bill',
p. 196.

[3] January 1877: 'Modern Dissent: the Liberation Society: the Burials Bill'.

claiming more drastic 'rights'. It was true that everyone had to be buried, but not necessarily in the same place, nor each person in his own way.

Nonconformists challenged anyone who deliberately belittled or flouted their feelings about their funerals. The opponents of reformed burial legislation were not fighting Disestablishment, but resisting the removal of a shocking social scandal. It was rank impertinence for anyone to claim a monopoly of hallowed ground.

> What's hallow'd ground?—Has earth a clod
> Its Maker meant should not be trod
> By man, the image of his God,
>   Erect and free,
> Unscourged by superstition's rod,
>   To bend the knee?[1]

The Liberation Society assented to provisions in various Burial measures in order to conciliate friends rather than opponents. The Dissenting Deputies were also responsible for pressing this question, and were frequently advising the other Nonconformist bodies on policy. The Society co-operated as much as possible, and did so without sacrificing its energy in the contest over questions of wider public interest.

Neither the Liberationists nor the Deputies would agree to the purchase at public expense of additional burial places where silence would not be required of them. They objected in fact to anything which perpetuated among the dead the sectarian divisions of the living. 'God's acre' had become 'Hell's corner' where those unbaptized according to the order of the Church of England were laid away.

> In case of unbaptized persons, the Parochial Clergyman may refuse to read the service of that Church, and the burial must take place without any service. Even when the deceased has been baptized, Clergymen sometimes decline to recognize Dissenting Baptisms and, contrary to law, refuse to officiate. The result is that not only are Dissenters deprived of the solace which they might derive from services performed by their own Ministers, but in many cases the feelings of relatives are deeply wounded by the necessity for burying their dead in silence, and the Churchyard becomes the scene of incidents which are discreditable to a civilized community.[2]

The attitude of Anglicans in this matter was that their Clergy ought to be allowed to refuse to read the Burial Service over the body of one opposed to their teaching without being called into account by those outside the Parish Church. Moreover, because schism was a deadly sin, so was all participation in 'schismatical services'. The consciences of the Clergy would not permit them to condone an act of sin being committed in the consecrated ground of the Churchyard. Moreover, to be compelled by the State to recognize this encroachment amounted to gross religious persecution.

[1] Thomas Campbell, 'Hallowed Ground', as quoted in the *Liberator*, Aug. 1878, p. 139.
[2] Parl. Com. Minutes, 5.ii.72. For examples of the most disagreeable scenes, cf. B. L. Manning, *Protestant Dissenting Deputies*, pp. 322–7.

Not all Anglicans, however, were unyielding to the demands of Nonconformists for open Churchyards and their own religious services at the graveside. The Clerical and Lay Union's proposals, for example, were an attempt to make sensible concessions: (1) none should officiate at the grave save the responsible Minister of a registered denomination; (2) the service should be limited in length and in substance, as follows:

a. either it should consist only of hymns from some recognized collection, and passages selected from the Bible;
b. or of prayers, without any address, compiled by a committee of Nonconformists;
c. or it should consist of the Burial Service of the Church of England, or of a selection from it, as it appeared that the service was used by some Nonconformists (notably the Wesleyan Methodists).

Nonconformist leaders were inclined to minimize honest bids for a compromise. In the meantime the abuses of the law were being resisted in hundreds of parishes throughout the country. In most of these instances public sympathy went to the side of the Nonconformists, who in turn made political capital out of them. Every fresh burial scandal seemed 'to drive another nail into the coffin of the Establishment'.

B. *Three Legislative Phases*

The more interesting and significant phases of this vexing controversy occurred in the years 1870–2, 1876–7 and 1879–80. After the Bill of 1880, it became for Liberationists chiefly a matter of consolidating the hard-won gains. The responsibility of seeking further adjustments in the law, and that of defending Dissenters in the law courts, was entrusted primarily to the Dissenting Deputies. And as their history shows, they did this most conscientiously.

When Mr Hadfield retired from leadership of the Dissenters' Burial Bill in 1869 a special sub-committee was appointed by both the Dissenting Deputies and the Society to revise the Bill thoroughly. They appointed Osborne Morgan to introduce their Burial Law Amendment Act. Parliamentary Returns at this time showed that there were some 13,000 parishes in England and Wales, of which only 531 had cemeteries where Dissenters might officiate. The Bill sought to open parochial Churchyards to such burial rites as the surviving relatives or friends might prefer – 'decency and solemnity being legally enjoined'. The Churchyard would still be vested in the Incumbent, and the changes would not affect his fees. The repairs of the Churchyard would be charged to the poor-rate. Mr Miall and Samuel Morley of the Society served on the Select Committee of the Bill, which easily earned a second reading in 1870 and 1871.

Meanwhile, in the Lords, Earl Beauchamp secured a second reading for a Bill allowing silent services for Dissenters in the Churchyard and additional ground for unconsecrated burial places. Morgan's Bill was also in the

Commons in 1872, but the pressure of other Parliamentary business made it impossible to consider all of its clauses. The result of the petitioning further complicated matters for the Liberationists – 1,657 petitions, signed by 104,214 persons, were presented against their measure, while only 651 petitions, with 6,048 names, were presented in favour.

Morgan on his own responsibility gave notice of an amendment to Beauchamp's Bill, limiting the Burial Service to reading, singing and praying. This was intended to effect the purpose of his own Bill, but it was not satisfactory to the Society and the majority of Nonconformists. The Parliamentary Committee therefore declared that the deadlock could be overcome only by a Government Bill. A memorial so expressed was drawn up by Morgan, signed by 154 Liberal M.P.s, and sent to Gladstone urging his leadership in the matter. The following reply was received:

> 10 Downing St., Whitehall.
> Dec. 12, 1872
>
> My dear Mr. Osborne Morgan,
> The Government has laboured assiduously during the autumn in the preparation of measures for the next session, and I am sorry to say that we do not, in consequence of the great labours of Parliament during the past years, find ourselves confronted by a less formidable array of demands than in former years.
> I have made known to them, as I promised, the request tendered by you to me in the summer, on behalf of a large body of our supporters and friends in Parliament; but we find with much regret that the pressure of engagements which may be considered both prior and, as respects the government, more urgent, renders it impossible for us, in our judgment, to undertake, with any reasonable prospect of redeeming the pledge, the charge of the Burials Bill.
> I remain very faithfully yours,
> W. E. Gladstone.[1]

Mr Disraeli delivered a strong speech against Morgan's Bill in 1873, maintaining that Dissenters, by refusing to pay Church Rates, had publicly acknowledged Churches and Churchyards as belonging to Churchmen. He believed that his 'Nonconformist fellow-countrymen' were entitled to maintain the noble traditions of toleration and religious liberty, but not to make war on the conditions of law and equity governing Church property. When the unrelenting Welsh Liberal brought in another Bill in 1875, the Disraeli assenters again succeeded in defeating it. In the Clerical press the issue aroused more comment than usual, and with more conciliatory views than usual.

In 1876 Nonconformists were somewhat amused to hear Disraeli referring for the first time to the Burials question 'as one of the most important questions of the day'. To a deputation of seventy prominent figures of the Anglican Church he pledged the 'staunch and unqualified opposition' of the Government to Morgan's Burial resolution. That year Carvell Williams wrote a pamphlet, 'Religious Liberty in the Churchyards', attacking the Burial laws

[1] Minute 1522: 23.xii.72.

as a 'two-edged sword' for (1) fortifying the Clergymen who objected to officiating, (2) prohibiting anyone else who might have no objection.

Especially keen in answering the charges of the Liberation Society during this period was a Society for the Rejection of the Burial Bills, with offices in Torquay. Not all Anglicans, however, were eager to support the designs of this group.

> Sir—
>
> In reply to your printed circular inviting my attendance at a public meeting to be held in Exeter on Friday, Jan. 28th, for the purpose of expressing disappropriation of Mr. Morgan's Burial Bill, I beg leave to assure you that I regard the movement in which you display so much activity as mischievous to the best interests of the Established Church, and contrary to the principles of Christian charity. My own impression is that every parishioner has a right of burial in the churchyard of his parish, and I have not the slightest fear that my Nonconformist brethren will ever do anything unbecoming to their Christian character in the solemn act of interment of their departed friends.
>
> I am, Sir, your obedient servant,
>
>   George Porter, Rector of St. Leonard's, Exeter.[1]
>
> W. H. Kitson, Esq.
> Secretary

Lord Selborne admitted the logic of the case of the Nonconformists, but this did not mean that the Disestablishment of the Church would logically follow the granting of this burial concession. Anglicans would fight the battle against Disestablishment on very bad ground, the Archbishop of York (Dr William Thomson) maintained, if they had to fight it beside the grave. The Committees of the Convocation of Canterbury and York were commissioned by Dr Tait early in 1876 to draw up an alternative Burial Service and reform suitably the Burial Rubrics in the Book of Common Prayer. This alternative form was devised for cases of 'extreme difficulty' but was later dropped.[2]

Another sign of an approaching reconciliation of views was the tenor of the debate in the Lords on 15 May 1876. The Primate surprised many of the Episcopal Bench by saying this was not a question of satisfying the Liberation Society, but of ending a real grievance 'though it affects only a few persons'. Taking the view that 'magnanimity in politics is not seldom the truest wisdom',

---

[1] The Secretaries of the Society, W. H. Kitson and J. W. Eastwood, wrote in the *National Church* (18.x.78) that during the last forty-five years 2,760 churchyards were presented as 'free gifts', 1,153 were purchased by 'the parish', 392 were purchased by voluntary subscriptions, and 748 were otherwise acquired. New churchyards numbering 5,053 (not to mention the old churchyards) had been accepted under the law of the land and consecrated to certain fixed purposes. 'It is now planned', they wrote, 'to hand them over to alien purposes.' Sir Stafford Northcote, the Chancellor of the Exchequer, wrote in a letter, which the *Nonconformist* printed on 12 January 1876, that he declined to allow his name on the Committee of this Burial Society.

[2] Concerning this 'Convocation Service', Dr Tait's biographers wrote: 'Nothing could have conceded more precisely what had been so often asked for, and the value of the precedent was made obvious by the Liberation Society's vehement opposition.' Davidson & Benham, op. cit., ii, 405–6.

Earl Granville put forward a solution (1) permitting interment without the Anglican Burial Service in the Churchyard to which the deceased 'had a right', if desired by the relatives, and (2) allowing the relatives to conduct a funeral with such orderly religious observances as might seem fit.[1] Among those supporting were Lords Selborne, Kimberley, Coleridge and the Bishop of Exeter, Dr Frederick Temple, but it lost by 92 to 148 votes. The Government promptly announced that it would prepare a Bill of its own.

When this much-awaited Burial Acts Consolidation Bill was brought in by the Conservatives in 1877 Disraeli (now Lord Beaconsfield) cynically expressed their motive as being one of 'sanitation'. The measure was actually a reworking of Earl Beauchamp's proposal five years earlier. The Liberation Society and the Dissenting Deputies convened an opposition conference at the Westminster Palace Hotel, maintaining that the complex Bill of the Government 'must be got rid of somehow or other'.

An unprecedented action on this Bill occurred in the Upper House on 18 June 1877, when the Lords carried Lord Harrowby's 74th clause by 127 votes to 111 in spite of the Tory Government's strong hostility. The clause allowed other persons than the Established Clergy to officiate in the parish Churchyards and to use 'Christian and orderly religious services' of their choosing, all with due notice being given to the Incumbent. It was openly endorsed by the two Archbishops, the Bishops of Exeter, Oxford and St Asaph, and 21 Conservative Peers. Within ten days a stern protest, procured by the Church Defence Association, was sent to the Government, signed by 13,770 alarmed Clerics – over two-thirds of the nation's Clergy. Somewhat embarrassed, the Conservatives abandoned the mutilated measure.

In the last year of Lord Beaconsfield's Administration a 'batch of burial bills' went before Parliament. These included Morgan's Nonconformist Burials Bill, Balfour's Burial Law Amendment Bill, Ritchie's Interments in Churchyard Bill, Monk's Consecration of Churchyards Act (1867) Amendment Bill, Egerton's Burial Grounds Bill, and Marten's Public Health Act (1875) Amendment (Interments) Bill. The last of these (authorizing the closure of 'full' Churchyards) lay well hidden by the others. When the Nonconformists realized that the Bill had been 'smuggled through', they indignantly accused the promoters of using sanitary precautions as a disguise for burdening ratepayers with the expense of unnecessary new burial-places.

The change of Ministry in 1880 brought the change in political climate necessary for a successful ending of the 'grave conflict'. Members of the Houses were no longer in a mood to express wild fears that 'the Infidel, Free Thinker, the Shaker, and the Mormon Widow' would scandalize the peaceful Churchyard by having access to it. In the *Liberator* of March 1880 (pp. 36–7), however, the Society circulated a story of a centenarian Quaker, Miss

[1] Before this debate, acknowledging the receipt of a pamphlet by Carvell Williams, Earl Granville humorously wrote: 'You have sent me so much ammunition, to use one of those military metaphors so dear to the Church, that if I could manage to hold the gun straight it ought to have an effect.' (Obituary) *Liberator*, May 1891, p. 67.

Mary Travis of Cottingham, who in the previous year had been persuaded 'to submit to be baptized' so that she might be properly buried with Anglican rites.

The Bill of the Liberal Government in 1880 was put in the charge of the Lord Chancellor (Selborne). As an amalgam of Morgan's and Balfour's Bills, and Lord Harrowby's clause, the Ministerial measure was not unsatisfactory to the Liberationists. Their only objections were: (1) the requirement that all Burial Services should be 'Christian', (2) the failure to abolish all legal distinctions between consecrated and unconsecrated ground, (3) the inclusion in the Bill of the Convocation proceedings which relaxed restrictions on the Clergy using the Burial Service.

The Archbishop of Canterbury (Dr Tait), speaking on the Bill on 3 June in the Lords, generously referred to 'our Nonconformist brethren'. Was it, he asked, a dishonour to Almighty God, over the grave of one at present buried in silence, that a Christian prayer be offered up and a portion of God's word read by an unordained person? The Lords reluctantly passed the second reading, but in their Report of the Committee on the Bill they tacked on amendments which turned it into a neutral measure:

1. Proper notice for Dissenting burials to be given to the Incumbent or proper authority.
2. Requirement for all burials to be 'Christian and orderly'.
3. Powers of prevention of disorder to continue as if the burial had been according to the Church of England rites.
4. Altered forms and Rubrics to be permitted for the use of the Anglican Clergy in special cases.
5. Provisions in the Act not to create precedent for exempting the Clergy from censure for violation of other ecclesiastical law.

At this the Nonconformists were ready to get someone to carry on in place of Mr Morgan, who had accepted a seat on the Treasury Bench as a member of Gladstone's Ministry. The Government, however, showed the good faith it had pledged to the Nonconformists at the General Election by discarding almost all of the Lords' amendments.

The debating was outstanding in the exchanges between A. J. B. Beresford-Hope and John Bright. Mr Beresford-Hope (M.P., Cambridge University) referred to Mr Morgan's defence speech as a 'specimen of psychology' by an erudite man who had long devoted complex mental processes to the question. The Anglican Burial Service was not an example of 'clerical monopoly', but a solemn means of bringing Heaven and earth together. The Bill would make it possible for irreligious people to gather to hear a popular preacher using the funeral as an occasion for all kinds of doctrinal excesses. The Common Law right of burial in the parish graveyard for all did not carry with it a religious service for all. It was a fallacy to define silent burial as suitable only 'for dogs'. It was better to be beaten in a dignified cause than to accept any perilous compromise.

In his customary manner, Bright was equal to the occasion. He referred to the main Opposition speech as a 'pleasant comedy on the floor of the House'. The fear that once a Dissenting Minister got into the Churchyard he would burrow into the Church of England was a 'hobgoblin' one. The doctrines of Calvin or the Universalists uttered at the graveside would not inflict a perilous wound upon Christianity. Nonconformists who had been educated in Voluntaryism would contribute more easily than Churchmen to the beautifying of the Churchyards. On the 14th clause, Bright objected to being classed with the unbaptized, suicides and criminals. He and his colleagues appreciated the wisdom of the Archbishop of Canterbury in this matter. It was no longer easy to say anything new on the issue. The time had now come to close the door upon it.

C. *Final Settlement*

Before the Bill was passed in the Lords (126 to 101 votes),[1] shorn of their previous amendments to it, the Archbishop of York made a final attempt to exclude cemeteries from the Act. The Archbishop of Canterbury, however, declared himself against the cemetery system. A cemetery with two chapels in two separate grounds was a proclamation to the world of the insoluble differences between Church and Dissent. The Bill received the Royal Assent on 7 September 1880, with the following provision:

> . . . the Burial Laws Amendment Act made it possible, after notice given to the incumbent, for burials to take place in any parish churchyard or graveyard with any Christian and orderly service, or without any service at all. No anti-Christian or anti-religious addresses were to be permitted. The Anglican clergy might, if they wished, use parts only of the Prayer Book service, and might perform Church of England services in unconsecrated ground, but they were withheld from the unbaptized and the excommunicated.[2]

The Liberation Society sent out to every Nonconformist Minister in England and Wales a paper containing the provisions and history of the Act. They rejoiced that the distinction between consecrated and unconsecrated ground had been 'practically abolished'.[3] However, the Act still left the Parish Incumbent the arbiter of various points of burial procedure – the fees for the services of the sexton and tolling of the bells, the site of the grave, and the propriety of any proposed headstone.

[1] Davidson & Benham, op. cit., ii, 407, record in Chapter XXIX the bitter reaction to this legislation in Anglican circles: 'Many country clergymen wrote or telegraphed to the Archbishop that they intended to resist by force any attempt by Nonconformists to take advantage of the Act (one rector announcing that he had provided pitchforks for the purpose).'

[2] B. L. Manning, *Protestant Dissenting Deputies*, p. 321, concerning 43 & 44 Vict., cap. 41.

[3] 'Consecration', wrote Mr Morgan, 'is simply the creation of modern Acts of Parliament. The ceremony itself is not to be found in the Prayer-book, and, being prescribed by an old ordinance of Convocation which never received the royal assent is, if not absolutely illegal, at least unauthorised. I have, too, the high authority of the late Bishop Thirlwall for saying 'that it amounts only to a civil act of dedication, . . .' (*Nonconformist and Independent*, 18.iii.80, p. 285). In some cases Burial Boards preferred a service of dedication instead of Consecration. *Liberator*, Nov. 1889, pp. 165–6.

The Society now urged Parliamentary supporters to bring the Burial laws into complete harmony with the principle of religious equality. The *Liberator* continued to blazon the stories of unpleasant conduct in connexion with funerals and violations of the new law. In 1884 a Clergyman sent the dead body of a child in the mail to the Home Office because of a dispute over the appropriation of a cemetery.[1] A great deal of legal confusion prevailed. Apart from the private cemeteries, there remained three systems of burial law based on different principles and supervised by different public authorities: (1) Churchyard law, administered partly by the Bishops and partly by the Home Secretary, (2) Burial Board law, administered by the Home Secretary, and (3) Sanitary Authority law, administered by the Local Government Board.

Several abortive attempts were made by Nonconformists during the 1880s to secure more burial privileges. Gladstone's Government eventually agreed in 1886 to sponsor a Burial Ground Bill which was consistent with the wishes of the Liberation Society and the Dissenting Deputies, but was forced to resign before the matter could be taken up seriously. In 1893 Herbert Asquith, the Home Secretary, pacified an imposing Nonconformist deputation, but did nothing to change the law. Finally the Bill of Carvell Williams in 1900 dealt with most of the remaining grievances:

1. Transfer to the local Government Board of all authority exercised by the Home Secretary relating to Burials.
2. Granting compulsory power for the acquisition of land to Burial Boards as well as to sanitary authorities.
3. Amendment of sections of Marten's 1875 Act requiring the construction of a chapel in consecrated ground, the appointment of a Chaplain, and the erection of walls or fences.
4. Dispensing with notices to the Incumbent in certain cases, and the rule on the use of the bell.
5. Amendments of sections of the 1880 Act to remove limitations on (a) the allotment of grave space in Churchyards, (b) hours for Nonconformist burials, and (c) Sunday burials.

The 1880 Bill had, however, removed the chief religious irritations and stood as the major triumph of Nonconformist Radicals in burial legislation. Thus after twenty-eight years of Parliamentary agitation, which had extended over fifteen sessions with no less than twenty Bills introduced on the subject, the Established Church granted the claims of Free Churches in the graveyards of the country:

> Where'er you seek God he is found,
> And every spot is hallowed ground.[2]

---

[1] *Liberator*, Sept. 1884, p. 187.
[2] *Congregational Praise*, Hymn No. 266: 'Jesus, where'er Thy people meet'.

CHAPTER 22

Grants in the Colonies

It seemed at one time a hard lesson for those to learn who had grown up imbued with the notion of a necessary and indissoluble connection between Church and State, that a branch of the Catholic Church, in which all Orders, Bishops, Clergy and Laity, each in his appropriate sphere, might harmoniously work together for the general good, could exist as a voluntary body without legal enactments. But that lesson has now been learnt.

BISHOP W. G. COWIE OF NEW ZEALAND[1]

At any moment a sudden crash may announce to a startled world that for the first time in her existence the empire of England is without a God, and without a Church.

BISHOP A. C. HERVEY OF BATH AND WELLS[2]

UNDOUBTEDLY, questions concerning Disestablishment and Dis-endowment among the Missionaries and Clergy in the Colonies tended to weaken the witness of the Churches there. But why the civil Government should favour a few Churches and Missions above others with special grants of money was a question difficult to explain. Many of the converts were able to judge for themselves what form of Church worship, discipline and government was most compatible to their culture. When greater social and political prestige was attached to one denomination it created confusion in the minds of the natives, and bitterness in the hearts of not a few white Missionaries.

The situation also created considerable ferment among the interested parties in the home country. Those who were detached from the actual circumstances on the foreign field were prone to be harsh in their judgement:

The attempt to convert the heathen to Christianity by means of . . . unctuous phraseology, of hardly-defined parochial divisions, and of claims based on the ecclesiastical laws and the ancient traditions of England—all this seems so grotesque that it might be ridiculed, if no high interests were at stake.[3]

[1] Address to Diocesan Synod, Nov. 1870. *Wellington Independent*, 3.xii.70.
[2] Address at Diocesan Conference, Oct. 1875; *Liberator*, Nov. 1875.
[3] *Nonconformist*, 30.viii.76, p. 858.

The Church of England tried to regard the matter calmly and from a practical point of view. Without some financial assistance from the local revenues of the Government, the Anglicans claimed, the Missionary work probably could not exist. In most cases the natives were so poor that it was impossible to rely upon their voluntary contributions as means of support. By co-operating with the Government it was possible for the Church to do more good than by remaining independent. The grants were also a sign of the mutual concern of the authorities in the task of religious education and not a case of controlling the Church to further their own ends.

As usual, the Nonconformists were looked upon as trouble-makers playing upon the discontent of those outside the Church. However, in answer to the financial concerns of those within the Church, they fell back upon the principles of simple New Testament Christianity. Had not Missionary enterprise always been primarily a venture of faith? And did not the real power of the Christian Gospel depend upon its own inherent vitality?

Because this was the position of the Liberation Society at home it naturally found itself encouraging the anti-State-Church movements in Crown settlements abroad. When the Government of Jamaica suspended ecclesiastical grants in the Island in 1869, the action was imitated later by British Honduras and the Cape of Good Hope. The Governor of Barbados stated to the Legislative Council in 1871 that the Home Government would establish religious equality in the West Indies by extending grants to all denominations. The Society hoped that these steps throughout the Empire would bring Disestablishment closer in England.

A. *Relations with Missionary Societies*

During this period the Liberation Society became involved in several Missionary Society disputes. With the Church Missionary Society and the Bishop of Ceylon the issue was one of conflicting Church government. In disputes with the Wesleyan Methodist Missionary Society and the London Missionary Society the issue concerned their Missionaries receiving Government subsidies. The Church Defence Association pointed to such incidents as proof that the principle of voluntary support was bound to fail with a country's uneducated masses.

The Liberation Society learned of a Bill in British Guiana in 1875 to continue State grants to the Churches for another seven years. The Wesleyans in the Colony had accepted the principle of concurrent endowment and had petitioned the Legislative Council for an additional sum. Carvell Williams wrote on behalf of the Executive Committee to William Boyce, the Secretary of the Wesleyan Missionary Society, expressing displeasure at this action. In his reply in October 1875, Boyce informed Williams that their Methodist Conference had not come to any decision on State grants and that their Missionaries were at liberty to use their freedom of action.

The Methodists were now following what they had done before in the same area. In 1870 the Wesleyans and the Moravians had both asked and received money from the Legislature in Barbados in order to pay off debts on Chapel buildings.[1] In a second letter Williams wrote that he had assumed the possibility of independent action by their Missionaries in Guiana, but had hoped that their Conference would come to a definite stand against State grants to religious bodies.

Six years later the matter arose again when the Wesleyan Missionary Society petitioned the Court of Policy in British Guiana for another increase in a subsidy for seven more years. In June 1881, Williams submitted an article to the *Nonconformist and Independent* which called for an end to this 'mendicant system, which is unworthy of a body so fruitful in good works springing from the spontaneous energy and self-sacrificing liberality of its members'.[2] The objection was rejected by the *Watchman*, the Wesleyan official organ, but the request for the increase was rejected by the Court.

Statements appeared in the *Christian World* and the *English Independent* in 1877 that Missionary work in Madagascar was in part conducted by means of State authority and support, and that agents of the London Missionary Society were involved.

> . . . the churches in Madagascar are under the jurisdiction of an oligarchy, called '*the Church within the Palace*', which is composed of the leading officers of the Government. This '*Church within the palace*' have stationed in the most populous centres around the capital ten of the students educated in the London Missionary Society Theological Institution. Each holds a commission from the Government, and has all the churches in his district placed under his immediate oversight. These trained preachers are supported by '*the Church within the Palace*,' receive State patronage, and send in their reports to the Government.[3]

One of the local Missionaries, the Rev. C. T. Price, defended the system and wrote that in this matter the London Missionary Society was 'not bound to the Liberation Society'. The Missionaries, he claimed, were dealing with people in Madagascar who were little advanced and to whom Voluntaryism was ill suited. The *National Church*, the organ of the Church Defence Association, welcomed these remarks. The Liberation leaders promptly investigated and received a statement from the Directors of the London Missionary Society denying that their Missionaries advocated patronage of native ministers by the State.

In a letter in the *Nonconformist* on 19 December 1877, Joseph Mullens, the Foreign Secretary of the London Missionary Society, sought to explain matters further. The feudal structure of Malagasy society, the patriarchal

---

[1] The Methodist Society was throughout this period suffering from financial hardship, due partly to the change in theology on the doctrine of final destiny 'which weakened the motives arising from the apprehension of the wholesale perdition of the heathen' (G. G. Findlay & W. W. Holdsworth, *History of the Wesleyan Methodist Missionary Society*, London 1921–4, i, 193).

[2] *Nonconformist and Independent*, 2.vi.81, p. 539.

[3] From a letter of Mr Louis Street, a Quaker Missionary of Antananarivo: *English Independent*, 22.xi.77.

character of its institutions, and the powerful tribal feeling could not be completely uprooted by a Missionary Church. Compulsion was a principle to
which the natives were accustomed, and it was part of the religious and social
pattern which they had always accepted. No one married or built a house or
took a journey without seeking the approval of the native Queen. All taxes
were paid 'in service' or 'in kind', and lands were held on condition of
rendering service. The Malagasy Prime Minister, who safeguarded the freedom
of the Missionaries, frequently showed his interest in the Churches by offering
liberal gifts, and he was therefore consulted in the appointment of their native
Ministers. The Missionaries ought to adjust to any system of Church government that promised the greatest good to the greatest number. The third
article of the Society's Constitution declared

> . . . a fundamental principle of the Society that its design is not to send Presby-
> terianism, Independency, Episcopacy or any other form of Church Order and
> Government (about which there may be difference of opinion among serious
> persons) but the glorious Gospel of the blessed God to the heathen; and that it
> shall be left (as it ought to be left) to the minds of the persons whom God may
> call into the fellowship of His Son from among them, to assume for themselves
> such form of Church government as to them shall appear agreeable to the Word
> of God.[1]

A controversy broke out within Anglican Mission circles following the
appointment of the Rev. R. S. Copleston as Bishop of Colombo.[2] The young
Bishop represented the ardour and culture of the High Church party in
England. On arrival he faced two classes of Clergy in Ceylon: (1) Missionaries
to the Singhalese or to the Tamils, belonging either to the Church Missionary
Society or the Society for the Propagation of the Gospel, and (2) Chaplains to
the English residents – some for the military forces and others for the white
planters. In the Bishop's plan of Church order the Chaplains, who were
largely High Churchmen, were placed over the Missionaries, who were
Evangelical.

The Church Missionary Society in Ceylon had been working in co-operation
with the English Nonconformists, particularly in the Tamil Coolie Mission.
This work, which had been ably supervised by an interdenominational committee, was taken over by the Bishop and placed under his authority. When

---

[1] Dr Norman Goodall, in *A History of the London Missionary Society 1895–1945* (Oxford
1954), pp. 335–6, states that the Palace Church honestly acknowledged its own Missionary
calling: 'According to tradition a new monarch was expected to build a new house within
the precincts of the palace, and in token of her Christian dedication, Ranavalona [II]
decided that the first royal building should be a Christian "house of prayer". Some indication of the strength of the native pastorate at this time may be inferred from the fact that it
was at the hands of Malagasy pastors that the Queen received her instruction in the Faith.
(On seeking baptism she and her Prime Minister were required to undergo the normal
period of three months' preparation, followed by a further four months' catechumenate
before being admitted to Communion.)'

[2] Eugene Stock, *The History of the Church Missionary Society* (London 1899–1916), iii,
203–16.

the committee refused to recognize this action, the Bishop revoked the licences of several Nonconformist Missionaries and threatened planters who accepted their ministrations with excommunication.[1] The Liberation Society protested that the state of affairs was one of 'Priestism versus Protestantism'.

Back in England there were cries that a band of Low Church Missionaries had defied the Bishop and were in league with a number of Dissenting planters to resist his authority. Veteran Anglican Missionaries of the Island denounced the 'Boy Bishop' and declared they had left behind them the exclusive 'clerical paraphernalia' of the English Establishment. Native converts said it would take years to heal the injury done to the unity of the Church in the eyes of those who had been taught 'Behold how Christians love one another!'

The matter was eventually settled by 'a document of advice' drawn up by five prelates at home – the two Archbishops, the Bishops of London, Durham and Winchester. Their advice was favourable in the main to the policy of the C.M.S., but was also fair to the position of the Bishop. It disapproved of tests in granting licences to Missionaries, and left some details to be settled by the disputants and urged both parties to

> act in such a manner as will show that they esteem the progress of the Gospel far above the maintenance of their own particular theories as to how the machinery of the Church is to be worked.[2]

B. *Disestablishment in India and Ceylon*

It was small wonder that the wave of Disestablishment in Britain spread to Ceylon and India at the same time, for the ecclesiastical grievances of both Colonies were much the same. The Irish Church had been disestablished because it was the Church of a few, existing at the cost of the many, and standing as an offence to the country in general. The quasi-establishments in India and Ceylon had a greater condemnation inasmuch as they compelled paganism to pay for the maintenance of Christianity.

In Ceylon alone the annual cost of the Establishment amounted to approximately £15,750. This was mainly appropriated for the salaries of the Bishop of Colombo, the retired Bishop, and an Episcopal staff of fifty Clergymen. The money was drawn from the population, two million of whom were Buddhists, Hindus and Mohammedans, while not more than 15,000 were claimed to be members of the Church of England. The Calcutta *Spectator*, in November 1871, referred to this practice as 'a grievance which dims the splendour of Christianity in the eyes of the heathen and prejudices their minds against it'.[3]

It was especially galling to the native leaders that the State-paid Clergy were employed principally to minister to the spiritual wants of the white colonists. This gave a hollow sound to any who professed a deep concern for the 'heathen that were lost in their false cults'. Moreover, they asked, was it not a

[1] *Nonconformist*, 17.xii.79, pp. 1248–9.

[2] Davidson & Benham, op. cit., ii, 354–8. The five bishops were Tait, Thomson, Jackson, Lightfoot and Browne.

[3] quoted in *Nonconformist*, 15.xi.71, p. 1114.

violation of the proclamation made by Her Majesty on assuming the Government of the territories acquired and held by the East India Company?

> We declare it to be our Royal Will and pleasure that none be in anywise favoured, none molested or disquieted, by reason of their religious life or observances; but that all shall alike enjoy the equal and impartial protection of the law.

Believing the ecclesiastical expenditures in India to be excessive and exclusive, a body of Missionaries was formed, in Calcutta on 4 November 1875, holding principles of the Liberation Society. They openly denounced the Government for its patronage and support of particular religious establishments out of public funds. On the question of Chaplains for military and naval forces opinion was divided as to whether or not this special branch of 'State' Clergy should minister to those who were unconnected with Government service. The Secretary of the Indian Disestablishment Society, Mr A. L. Sykes, wrote, in November 1880, to the Liberation Society in London, asking for its assistance in their objects.[1]

With the change of the Home Government in 1880, Mr Gladstone appointed the Marquess of Ripon as Viceroy of India. Being a Roman Catholic, the new Viceroy was suspected of being sympathetic to a policy of State support to religious teaching. The Government, however, gave power to the Indian Council early in 1880 to reduce some of the salaries and allowances of 'the ecclesiastical department of the Government of India'. The measure met with a cool reception from Indian leaders because it had not gone far enough to remove the £300,000 drawn from the local taxpayers for 'the European Church' and the British Chaplains.

Carvell Williams arranged for a deputation of eight M.P.s and three Liberationists to wait on Lord Kimberley, the Secretary for India, on 10 August 1882. Henry Richard (M.P., Merthyr Tydfil) presented the full facts and asked about ecclesiastical grants in India, British Guiana, the Straits Settlements and other Crown-governed Colonies. The Colonial Secretary replied that it was his duty not to adopt a uniform policy on the matter, but to deal with each Colony according to local circumstances.

The responsibility for pressing Singhalese Disestablishment in the Imperial Parliament was borne principally by Alderman W. McArthur (M.P., Lambeth), with the Liberation Society acting in a supporting role. On 1 May 1877, his motion in the Commons condemning ecclesiastical subsidies was defeated by 147 to 121 votes. *The Times* published a leading article the day after the debate, deprecating the grants.

Mr J. Ferguson, the Secretary of the Society to Procure the Discontinuance of Ecclesiastical Subsidies in Ceylon, also the Editor of the *Ceylon Observer*, wrote to the Liberation Society in 1879 calling for strenuous intervention. The Society leaders in London convened a conference on 27 May at the Westminster Palace Hotel with McArthur in the chair. When the former

---

[1] Minute 1257: 15.xi.80. On a motion by Miall, a Parliamentary Return was issued for 1873–4, showing £175,000 for Church purposes in India.

Governor, Sir William Gregory, whom they hoped to enlist, failed to attend, it was decided to send a deputation to the Colonial Office. When the Secretary, Sir Michael E. Hicks-Beach, declined to receive the deputation, it was decided to question him in the Commons concerning the pension to Bishop Chapman of Colombo from the revenues of the Colony.

At length the Government yielded to pressure. In a Parliamentary Return published early in 1881 they disclosed in the official correspondence their decision, which in effect disestablished the Church of England in Ceylon. In a dispatch in 1880, Sir Michael had suggested that the time had arrived for passing a new Civil List ordinance. The Governor, Sir James R. Longden, concurred in this action, suggesting at the same time a reconsideration of the policy on ecclesiastical grants. Lord Kimberley, then Colonial Secretary, wrote expressing the feeling of the Gladstone Government that the 'only fair and practical course' would be to withdraw them gradually. Summary provisions of this arrangement were printed by the *Ceylon Observer*:

1. The Home Government would end State support to Anglican and Presbyterian Churches by an ordinance in the Legislative Council of Ceylon.
2. The incumbents would continue to receive their present benefits and future pension upon retirement.
3. A Chaplain appointed to a vacancy within five years (from 1 January 1881) would be paid by the Government for the unexpired period.
4. All ecclesiastical buildings kept by the Government would be handed over in good repair to the trustees of the Churches.
5. Each Church body would be subject to its own laws and make its own appointments without interference by Government officials.[1]

It must be admitted that the interference of the Liberation Society in Colonial disputes did not always help to pacify relations between the rulers and the ruled. The Liberation press found it easy to work upon the emotions of peoples seeking complete self-government, but difficult at the same time not to jeopardize British interests. Because of the idealistic and reforming spirit of the age there were many Victorian Nonconformists who eagerly styled themselves as ecclesiastical emancipators everywhere.

> Liberation! sound the war-note
> Of our Church's liberty.
> Sound the note that yet shall free her
> From Erastian slavery,
>   Liberation!
> Let our noble watchword be.
>
> Sons of freedom, raise your banner,
> Write the word in lines of gold,
> On her ancient honoured foldings,

---

[1] 12.iii.81. The Society reported in the following January that in another dispatch Lord Kimberley had recommended the adoption of disendowment in the settlements of the Straits of Malacca, on the same terms as enacted in Ceylon. Minute 1557: 9.i.82.

Free and brave, the cause uphold,
Liberation!
Let the cry be onward rolled![1]

The work of Liberation, however, was not always a pompous-sounding sentiment. The burden of unfair taxation was linked with a kind of slavery and subjection from which the 'pagan' was glad to be freed. Power to take money from the purse for religion was as injurious to his faith as any superstition. Thus the action of the Society and its allies proceeded from a genuine humanitarian principle to enhance the success of Christian Missions in underprivileged countries.

[1] *Liberator*, Aug. 1876, p. 138.

PART FIVE

Decline and Recession
1886 – 1895

CHAPTER 23

Introductory

> It is perhaps harder to be a Nonconformist today than it
> has ever been in the history of England. The very decay of
> the disabilities from which our fathers suffered has made
> it harder for us than it was for them to dissent.
>
> THE REV. A. MARTIN FAIRBAIRN, D.D., D.LITT.,
> Address in 1897 as
> Principal of Mansfield
> College, Oxford.[1]

THE JUBILEE celebration of the Liberation Society at the close of the Victorian Age attracted comparatively little attention. Instead of standing as a sign of greater things to come, it marked the end of the Society's unique role in Nonconformist politics. Although the Society continued to turn the wheels of its machine, its great day of production was over. The decline had been apparent since the break-up within the Liberal party in 1886 over the question of Irish Home Rule. The Liberation movement in Britain, however, was definitely doomed by the defeat of the Liberals in the General Election of 1895, when an even deeper schism occurred within their ranks.

There were several good reasons for this recession. First, and most important, was the failure of the voluntary principle in meeting the Society's financial needs. Second, Nonconformity became divided between the religious and political Dissenters – the former centring their attention upon the spiritual nature of Christ's Kingdom, the latter shifting their interest to the National Education question. Third, Liberal dissentients – Socialists, Unionists and philosophical Radicals – looking for wider and more appealing fields of political endeavour, became generally tired of the hue and cry of Disestablishment. Fourth, public opinion was gradually losing its enthusiasm for ecclesiastical issues, and secular concerns were consuming a greater proportion of the time of the House of Commons. Fifth, the Church Defence Institution accelerated its activities under the encouragement of the Archbishops and adopted the techniques of the Liberation Society with equal effectiveness. Sixth, the ideals of the Society became absorbed by new and more advanced political groups. Seventh, few young men came forward to fill

[1] W. B. Selbie, *The Life of Andrew Martin Fairbairn* (London 1914), p. 257.

the places of leadership surrendered by the deaths of wealthy and respected Liberationists.

As far as the Church of England was concerned, much of the fading away of Disestablishment principles was due to the adoption of a more tolerant attitude among an increasing number of the Anglican Clergy. Within the Church there was a relaxation of the strict rulings on the Ritual controversy owing to a general feeling that over-tight clothes were apt to tear. Outside the Church it became less and less 'the thing to do' to speak ill of one's ecclesiastical neighbours. The Archbishop of York (William Connor Magee), speaking at the Church Congress at Leeds in 1891, said a little boastfully:

> As for the Liberation Society, I have no intention to make any unkind remarks about it, but I venture to say that that business, as far as the Liberation Society is concerned, is well played out. I believe that that Society is altogether a waning power in the country.

The Society replied a little sarcastically:

> If Cleric Congresses could only care
>   A little less for the mere Church and Steeple,
> Parochial pomp and power in lion's share,
>   And have one aim—to purify the People,
> They need not shrink from Disestablishment
>   Or any other secular enormity;
> Unselfish love of Man destroys Dissent,
>   True Charity provokes no Nonconformity.[1]

A. *Financial Affairs*

From 1886 onwards the bulk of the Society's activities were related to means of removing financial burdens. What endowments it possessed through Railway Preference Stock and the Legacy Fund had nearly disappeared, and it became obvious that the Society could not carry on its work solely by voluntary subscription. During this time the yearly income dropped from £8,000 to £4,000.

Attacks by Liberationists upon the Church of England for being in possession of large endowments now appeared to arise from feelings of envy. It became abundantly clear to the Society that endowments did at least carry a body through lean times. There was strong evidence for saying that Voluntaryism held good only so long as its cause remained popular with those who were asked to support. Once the cause ceased, Voluntaryism failed woefully. Such a revelation was hard for the Society to face. In 1874 the Society had 130 voluntary collectors and financial agents, but in 1886 it had only 30 such workers.

Church Defenders were now able to argue, if not to gloat over the fact, that Nonconformists often had to leave the poorer sections of the community to

[1] *Liberator*, Nov. 1891, p. 164.

religious bodies which were heavily subsidized. If the Church were disendowed and disestablished, Anglicans asked, what would happen to their work in places where it had been independent of local contributions?

Henry R. Ellington in 1886 resigned one of the two Treasurerships. His successor, Evan Spicer, refused to issue a personal appeal to his friends for a special fund to cover the Society's debts. When Mr Spicer refused reappointment in 1891, six men declined before Benjamin Smythe Olding accepted the office. He remained until May 1896, when Herbert E. Brooks, the last of four men approached, agreed to take the post. It was sadly reported, in April 1898, that Alfred Illingworth was unwilling to accept re-election as Senior Treasurer.

In 1890, both Treasurers issued invitations to 300 persons to a special finance meeting at the National Liberal Club to raise £5,000 over a period of three years. A little more than half this amount was realized. Attempts had been unsuccessfully made to secure the Free Trade Hall in Manchester for a great finance rally to raise £1,000. In 1891 Mr Williams and Mr Spicer pressed upon two of the officers of the National Liberal Federation, Francis Schnadhorst and Dr Spence Watson, the financial claims of the Society upon the Liberal party. The Executive of the Federation decided that the Committee, 'while in cordial sympathy with the work of the Society, is unable to afford it financial help'. Later, for several special meetings, the Society was granted the facilities and rooms of the National Liberal Club.[1]

During this period the Conversazione became a familiar social function among the Society's methods of raising money. Three of these were held in the galleries of the Royal Society of British Artists for especially invited guests in evening dress. After a recital of vocal and instrumental music, the financial needs of the Society were presented by several selected M.P.s and political figures. Some of these were: The Rev. C. Sylvester Horne, Mr Evan Spicer, Sir Walter Foster, Mr (later Sir) Robert W. Perks,[2] the Rt Hon. (later Sir) James Stansfeld, Mr Augustine Birrell, and Mr J. Herbert Lewis. Another social function at this time was the lantern lecture. Under the preparation of the Agency Secretary, John Fisher, collections of slides were frequently shown to select circles of the Society's friends and young people's groups in Nonconformist Churches and Colleges.

Numerous steps were taken to reduce the expenditure of the Society. First the *Liberator*, the monthly organ, was decreased in size and free copies were cancelled. Then came a reduction in the salaries of the official staff, placing financial agents on a commission basis and dropping district agencies which did not bring substantial income to the treasury. The Secretary of the

---

[1] Minute 418: 20.vii.91; Minute 425: 10.viii.91.

[2] It was Sir Robert who uttered the famous declaration: 'Nonconformists can only gain their chief ends by cohesion, by a firm assertion of their demands, and even by the exercise of a little mild terrorism over their leaders.' Denis Crane, *The Life-Story of Sir Robert W. Perks* (London 1909), p. 193. Perks was instrumental in forming the Nonconformist Parliamentary Council, which held its inaugural meeting at St Martin's Town Hall on 3 May 1898. He was elected President; Mr Lloyd George as Vice-President, and the Rev. J. Hirst Holloway as Secretary.

Manchester District Committee, Mr J. F. Alexander, resigned in 1889 after seventeen years' service.

All of this had a damaging effect upon the morale of the Society's staff workers. Moreover, to make up for the loss of their private incomes, it meant taking on outside employment and giving less time to the Society. Twice Carvell Williams relinquished to the Society sums of money from his salary totalling £900. When the printing firm, Barrett and Co., demanded payment of the account on the *Liberator* within twenty-four hours, with the alternative of legal proceedings, Mr Illingworth advanced £1,000. Mr Olding agreed to be one of twenty men donating £50 each to clear the whole of the Society's liabilities. A legacy of £1,000 bequeathed to the Society by James Heywood came at a time when it was direly needed. A special Jubilee fund of £2,300 raised by sixty of the Society's friends in 1894 saved it from complete financial ruin.

The Society never seemed to run short of ideas for acquiring and saving money. The three rooms on the top of the office building at 2 Serjeants' Inn, Fleet Street, were let. Suggestions were made for observing a 'Free Church Sunday' in Chapels, when sermons could be preached on the principles of the Society and collections taken for its work. Executive members were limited to third-class railway fare for travelling. Council members were urged to solicit for funds. To relieve the Secretaries of routine office duty, a clerk was hired at £60 per annum and an office boy at 7s. per week. It was felt that the mailing of the *Liberator* to some subscribers could be stopped without losing their subscription. In 1891 admission was charged to the Annual Meeting in St James's Hall.

B. *Relations with Other Bodies*

One big reason for the decline in the Liberal party in England, which was shared by the Liberation Society, was that Nonconformists of the country began to lose their political conscience. The Society turned to the religious aspects of the Disestablishment question, partly to hold the support of Nonconformist congregations, and partly because Liberal party Associations had undertaken its secular and political aspects. In the last resort the course of the Disestablishment movement lay in religious conviction and religious leaders.[1]

Accordingly, 'the religious aspects' of the Disestablishment question were slanted to the local Free Churches in a variety of ways: (1) Circulars to Ministers suggesting the importance of sermons and addresses on the question, and offering to supply suitable speakers and necessary information; (2) Special projects, essay competitions, soirées and lantern lectures (such as 'The Story

---

[1] cf. *Guardian*, 11.v.87. This was contrary to the contention of R. E. Prothero, Fellow of All Souls College, Oxford, in a paper, 'Aggressive Irreligion – An Appeal against the Liberation Society'. He believed that 'the Liberation Society, without the knowledge or consent of its original supporters, has wholly changed its character and now represents the spirit, not of Nonconformity, but of Secularism'. This paper was read before the Oxford League for the Defence of the National Church.

of the Pilgrim Father') to interest Young People's Guilds and Mutual Improvement Societies; (3) Deputations to gatherings of denominational Unions and Associations, and urging their Secretaries to include anti-Establishment resolutions in the programmes of their annual and half-yearly meetings.

The Society called attention to the Tercentenary of the 'Congregational Martyrdoms' – the commemoration in 1893 of the deaths of Henry Barrowe, John Greenwood and John Penry who stood against the compulsory State religion in Queen Elizabeth's time. Memorial services were conducted at City Temple on 6 April, at which Dr R. W. Dale, Dr Joseph Parker and the Rev. Hugh Price Hughes took part. Open air commemorations also were held at the sites of the executions. In this vein it was decided, however, not to visit the grave of Edward Miall at Honor Oak Cemetery in Forest Hill.

At the suggestion of Dr Joseph Parker, the Society agreed to have a sermon delivered as a regular feature of the annual meetings. The preachers were: in 1892, the Rev. W. J. Dawson, of Southport; in 1893, Dr John Clifford, of Bloomsbury; in 1894, Dr Charles A. Berry, of Wolverhampton; in 1895, Dr Parker, of the London City Temple. It was decided in 1894 to begin the mass meetings, usually addressed by several politicians, with singing and prayer. It became common to hold these in the churches themselves, particularly at the City Temple and Metropolitan Tabernacle.

The Society's relations with the Dissenting Deputies continued to be cordial. Alfred J. Shepheard, Secretary of the Deputies, however, refused an appointment to the Society's Executive Committee in 1895. The annual Parliamentary Breakfasts for the two bodies continued as an indication of their common purpose. At these gatherings, in such places as the Savoy Hotel, Alfred Illingworth, of the Society, usually acted as chairman and William Woodall, of the Deputies, as vice-chairman. A plan of Mr Williams to constitute a Religious Equality Committee in the House of Commons, comprising some thirty M.P.s, was presumably approved by the Deputies. This Committee, it was felt, would compete more successfully with the newly-formed Church Parliamentary Committee in the Commons. An Executive of twelve was duly appointed with Sir Osborne Morgan as chairman, William Woodall as vice-chairman, Carvell Williams and Robert Perks as secretaries. The expenses were borne by the Society.

By the time the Church Defence Association had grown sufficiently to counteract the agitation of the Society there were several other imposing forces in the field. The Liberation tasks were passed along to the Welsh National Council, the Welsh Disestablishment Campaign Committee, and the Scottish Disestablishment Council.[1]

[1] The formation of the first group is described in Minute 1080: 17.x.87; that of the second in Minute 443: 21.ix.91; the account of the formation of the third (together with the Constitution document) is found between pp. 488–9 of the Minute book for 1889. Founded in 1877, the Liberation Society Scottish Council became a co-operating member of the Scottish Disestablishment Council; cf. Minute 906: 1.xii.86, for a list of officers of the latter.

21

Lord Selborne's scholarly *Defence of the Church of England against Disestablishment* was published in 1886. The former Lord Chancellor devoted all his distinguished legal experience to devastating *The Case for Disestablishment*, which had been published by the Society in 1884. 'The great blemish' of his Lordship's book, said the *Quarterly Review* in October 1887, was that it had 'done enough to convince an honest Dissenter that Disendowment would be wrong', but it had 'done nothing to show him that Establishment is right'.

About the same time that the obituaries appeared in the Press on the death of Edward Miall there were charges against the Liberation Society in a pastoral letter to Church Defenders from the Archbishop of Canterbury, Dr Tait. A copy of the 'Practical Suggestions Relative to Disestablishment of the Church of England' (released four years before) having now caught his eye, he called for competent lecturers and adequate funds to combat the Society's operations and to expose 'the fallacies they would palm off on the ignorant'. He felt that Liberationists were jeopardizing the Protestant succession of the Crown and therefore he believed 'the quiet, conscientious discharge of duty' by Churchmen was no longer sufficient.[1] The *Spectator* commented that it was unwise for such an appeal to be made by the head of the nation's Clergy.

Churchmen, however, now seemed to take more notice of the work of the Association. In some instances the Clergy appeared to take the Primate's pastoral as a warrant to deal with Disestablishers as severely as they wished. Speaking at a Church Defence meeting in 1881, the Bishop of Carlisle (Harvey Goodwin) accused the Society of seeking a Disestablishment that would place the Cathedrals under the control of Parliament.

> St Paul's might be turned into a place of recreation, and spirituous liquors be sold there under one Parliament, and under another, when Sir Wilfrid Lawson became Prime Minister, it might be turned into a coffee tavern.[2]

For the General Election in 1895 the Association set a budget of £20,000. After the Election both Primates issued a 'Church Defence Manifesto', urging the formation of diocesan and parochial Committees for propaganda purposes.

C. *Leadership and Electoral Action*

The Society's loss of prestige was not for want of intelligent leaders. During this period three future Prime Ministers appeared upon its platforms and upheld its principles. Henry Campbell-Bannerman (M.P., Stirling Burghs) presided at the annual meeting on 7 May 1890, at the Metropolitan Tabernacle and read a paper on the subject, 'Disestablishment in Scotland and Generally'.[3]

---

[1] *Liberator*, June 1881, p. 103. Presiding at a Church Defence Association meeting on 6 July 1881, he likened the plans of the Liberators to the echoes of the French Revolution; cf. Davidson & Benham, op. cit., ii, 492–3.

[2] *Liberator*, July 1881, p. 124. Lawson was associated with the Liberation Society.

[3] Minute 80: 14.iv.90; Minute 90: 28.iv.90; Minute 187: 20.x.90. He was to have presided at the Triennial Conference of 1889, but was prevented by ill health. J. A. Spender, in *The Life of the Right Hon. Sir Henry Campbell-Bannerman G.C.B.* (London 1923), i. 112, admits that he was quite openly 'a disestablisher' and a visitor at the meetings of the Liberation Society.

Shortly before this, Herbert H. Asquith Q.C. (M.P., East Fife), who had been brought up in 'the rugged school of Yorkshire Nonconformity',[1] went with Carvell Williams to address a large audience in Leicester, on 7 April 1890, on the subject, 'The Political Aspects of Disestablishment'. Mr Asquith occupied the chair on 4 May 1892, at the annual public meeting in St James's Hall and read a paper on 'The General Election and the Liberal Party in Relation to Disestablishment'. The third and most active in the Liberation programme was David Lloyd George (M.P., Caernarvon), a member of the Society's Executive Committee. He took part in the business meetings at the main offices of the Society and was a dependable speaker at many of its public functions.[2]

If any one figure could be said to dominate the Society's activity during this period it was J. Carvell Williams, once referred to by the *Christian World* as the 'Achilles of Disestablishment'. He became Edward Miall's successor as policy director of the Society and chief strategist of the Nonconformist force in Parliament. He had methodically fulfilled the duties of Secretary of the Executive Committee and Editor of the *Liberator* (which he founded in 1853) until 1877, when he became full-time Chairman of the Parliamentary Electoral Committee and Deputy Chairman of the Executive Committee. His wide range of friendships and professional contacts in Parliamentary circles kept the Society alive in the closing years of the nineteenth century. He was returned as M.P. for South Nottingham in 1885 for one year, presented with a cheque for 1,000 guineas and returned for Mansfield, Notts., in 1892, and thereafter until 1900. On 18 October 1897, the jubilee of his connexion with the Society, a testimonial of £1,000 was presented to him by his friends in the Library of Memorial Hall 'in appreciation to him for the work to which he had devoted his life'. 'On this occasion', the *Dictionary of National Biography* records,

> Gladstone credited him with 'consistency, devotion, unselfishness, ability', qualities not rendered less effective by his suave demeanour, his practical judgment of men, and his imperturbable temper.[3]

Other Parliamentary leaders frequently officiated at the Society's public gatherings during this period and by their reputations helped to promote the aims of the movement. Dr R. Spence Watson, the President of the National Liberal Federation, was a speaker on the Society's platform and was elected

[1] Harold Spender, *Herbert Henry Asquith* (London 1915) pp. 80–1. For the text of this speech, see *Liberator*, May 1890, pp. 67–8. Prior to this Asquith had been one of the principal speakers at the annual meeting in the Metropolitan Tabernacle.

[2] One of the most successful of these was on 7 May 1890, at the Metropolitan Tabernacle. Harold Spender, *The Prime Minister* (London 1920), p. 92, writes: '. . . graded by party officialism, he had been given the lowest place in the list of speakers at the Tabernacle. But this was soon forgotten when he once got into his stride. Although the audience had been dismally thinned by a succession of dreary orations, they sat out his speech to the end . . . the cheering and laughter of his audience carried him on . . . the result was that the public soon demanded more.' cf. Minute 339: 20.iv.91.

[3] *D.N.B.* 2nd supplement (London 1912), iii, 677.

to the Society's Executive Committee in 1886. The Rt Hon. (later Sir) James Stansfeld, former Under-Secretary of State for India, also President of the Poor Law Board, presided at the Society's Triennial Conference in 1889, also at the Society's Conversazione in Manchester in 1890 and at the meeting of the Royal Society of British Artists in 1893. The Rt Hon. Sir G. O. Trevelyan addressed the annual public meeting at the Metropolitan Tabernacle in 1888 and presided at the annual meeting in 1891[1] as did the Rt Hon. Sir G. Osborne Morgan, former Under-Secretary for the Colonies, in 1889 and 1893. The President of the Liberal Churchman's Union and the Under-Secretary of State for Home Affairs, the Rt Hon. George W. E. Russell, presided in 1895 at the annual public meeting in the City Temple. In the previous year at the Society's Jubilee observance he had stated:

> We English Churchmen who are also Free Churchmen object to the Establishment because of its evil effect on the Church herself. It engenders an almost indecent hunger for the loaves and fishes. . . .[2]

The deaths among outstanding religious equalitarians during this period left serious gaps in the ranks. The Liberation Society was unable to fill the vacancies with men of the same calibre. Mr Henry Richard, devoted disciple of religious freedom and international peacemaker, died in 1888. He was followed in 1889 by Mr John Bright, 'ornament of the British Parliament . . . firm believer in the self-sustaining power of Christianity'.[3] Sir Edward Baines, Dr Alexander Hannay and Mr Neville Goodman died in 1890; Lord Granville and the Rev C. H. Spurgeon in 1891 and 1892 respectively. The Ministries of the two zealous Liberationists of Birmingham, Dr H. W. Crosskey, and Dr R. W. Dale, ended in 1893 and 1895. Sir G. O. Morgan, Welshman and Churchman of sterling qualities, and Sir Isaac Holden, liberal contributor, passed away in 1897.

The four-times Premier, W. E. Gladstone, never formally identified himself as a member of the Liberation Society, neither did he ally himself with the Church Defence Institution. In his Midlothian tour in 1890, on 25 October, he said at Dalkeith:

> I am supposed, gentlemen, to be a sort of Churchman in my own country, but they never ask me to join a Church Defence Society. I am afraid they consider me totally disqualified, for I am unable to take the preliminary tests.

[1] Both he and Campbell-Bannerman consented to become Vice-Presidents of the newly formed Scottish Disestablishment Council in 1887; Sir George was Secretary for Scotland in 1886 and 1892.

[2] As Liberal Churchmen, he maintained, they wished to see (i) the Bishops removed from the House of Lords, (ii) the Clergy allowed to enter Parliament, (iii) the system of private patronage brought to an end. He stood with Gladstone in repudiating the 'monstrous doctrine of Erastianism' as 'among the most debased systems known to man'. *The Times*, 2.v.94, p. 11.

[3] The Society's eulogy, Minute 1567: 1.iv.89. cf. Miall's obituary: *Liberator*, June 1881, pp. 94–8.

In 1898 the Grand Old Man himself left the scene, bringing to its conclusion a great tradition in Liberal politics.

> He was a man, take him for all in all,
> We shall not look upon his like again.

In spite of its greatly reduced activity the Society was still able to conduct electoral inquiries of Liberal candidates. It was reported in 1890 that of the 495 Parliamentary seats in England and Wales there were 362 Liberal candidates 'already selected for the next General Election'. Of these, 199 favoured Disestablishment generally, 82 desired it for Scotland and Wales only, 13 opposed, and the views of the remaining candidates were uncertain or unknown. The Society prepared 285,000 publications for circulation among candidates and electors. By popular demand a revised edition of *The Case for Disestablishment* was issued in 1893. *A Short History of Christianity in England* was printed in 1896 in a cheap and popular edition, and within the first three months 15,000 copies were sold.

The Liberal party position on ecclesiastical matters was still linked with the position of the Liberation Society. The actual results of the 1892 General Election showed that, of the 276 Liberals elected, 173 agreed upon a policy of general Disestablishment, 89 wished it for Scotland and Wales, and 13 were unclassified. It was assumed that all but a few Liberals were in favour of Gladstone's 'Newcastle Programme'.[1] In the celebrated speech at St Austell, on 12 June 1889, he had openly declared himself in favour of Welsh and Scottish Disestablishment. Nonconformists in the new Parliament numbered 109. Sir William Harcourt invited Carvell Williams to an interview to learn the views of Nonconformists on 'departmental administration'.[2] There were 18 members of the Society's Executive Committee returned, 12 members of its Council, 14 subscribers and 8 who had been speakers – making a bloc of 52 M.P.s.

A curious example of the Society's electoral power occurred in the by-election at Horncastle, Lincolnshire, in 1894. David Lloyd George informed the Society that the Liberal candidate for this constituency, Mr H. J. Torr, had pledged himself to oppose 'tooth and nail' any measure of Disestablishment and Disendowment which did not continue the appropriation of the Tithe to religious purposes. Aware that the Liberal Churchman's Union was working to minimize Disestablishment in the party, the Society decided to make it a test case, lest other candidates follow suit. In a special resolution this candidate's action was condemned as contrary to the Government's promises for the coming session on the Welsh and Scottish Establishments.

[1] Sir G. O. Trevelyan attended meetings in Newcastle on 1–2 October 1891, as the Society's representative, when the National Liberal Federation fixed upon a policy of Disestablishment (Minute 448: 7.x.91). This famous 'programme' included 'Irish Home Rule, church disestablishment in Wales and Scotland, and a local vote on the sale of alcohol (this to please the puritanism of the chapels).' David Thomson, *England in the Nineteenth Century 1815–1914* (Harmondsworth 1950), p. 231.

[2] Minute 640: 15.viii.92.

The resolution was sent to each elector of the constituency and the 'responsibility of the expense' of it was assumed by Lloyd George.[1] Although Gladstone disapproved of this kind of intervention, Torr was defeated on 11 January by a majority of 838 votes – 100 more than the Conservative majority at the previous General Election.

The preparations of the Society for the 1895 General Election were comparatively meagre. The results practically killed Disestablishment in England, and severely reversed its prospects in Wales and Scotland. The seats in the new House of Commons were occupied by 339 Conservatives, 72 Dissentient (Unionist) Liberals, 176 Gladstonian Liberals, and 82 Irish Home Rulers. Some days after the voting the Executive Committee adopted a special minute which expressed a somewhat melancholy mood:

> The Committee deeply regret that, as the result of, among other causes, the unprecedented exertions of those engaged in the production and sale of intoxicating liquors, aided by the supporters of national Establishments of religion, the recent General Election has destroyed the majority in favour of Religious Equality which existed in the last Parliament, and has given a large majority to its opponents . . .[2]

[1] Minute 746: 4.i.94.
[2] Minute 1046: 29.vii.95.

CHAPTER 24

Church Property and Reform

I think I said [in 1885] I considered that the interests of
Established Churches was one of the paramount features of
the conflict that is impending. I now say so no longer. It
is so in Wales; it is so in Scotland. In these places we must
fight with our utmost vigour to maintain the Established
Churches. But, unless I am deceived, in the whole of
England the Established Church has within the last five
years gained considerably in power, and removed to a long
distance the epoch when her existence will be the object
of sustained attack.

LORD SALISBURY[1]

I sometimes read that the movement for disestablishment is
on the wane, and I have seen the Liberation Society compared to one of those half-extinct volcanoes which have
almost burned themselves out, and whose impotent
rumblings are all that remains to them from the byegone
days when they were powerful engines of destruction.
When people are dreaming away their time in a fool's
paradise, it is a cruel but at the same time a salutary process
to awaken them, . . .

HERBERT II. ASQUITH[2]

THE PARLIAMENTARY history of this period began on a note of dissension among Liberals and ended in the same way. There were too
many independent minds. Lord Rosebery resigned the leadership of
the party in 1896 for lack of explicit support from any quarter, and because of
open differences with many Liberals on the Eastern Question. High Churchmen were not pleased with his Episcopal appointments. He followed in
Gladstone's footsteps as a Disestablisher 'of a sort', but disappointed many
because he held that the Established system was a matter of 'local option'. The
magnificent record of the Grand Old Man made it practically impossible for
anyone to fill his place.

By all odds Asquith should have succeeded Lord Rosebery, but the lot fell

[1] Address at St James's Hall, 15 July 1891: *Liberator*, Aug. 1891, p. 122.

[2] Chairman's Address, Triennial Conference of the Society, St James's Hall, 4 May 1892:
Liberator, May 1892, p. 77.

on Sir William Harcourt, to whom leading Nonconformists at this time were more partial. The former Chancellor of the Exchequer, however, was constantly called into question by his Lordship's followers in the House of Commons. In December 1898, Harcourt could bear it no longer, and John Morley left with him. Lord Kimberley had taken Rosebery's place in the Lords, and in the Commons Sir Henry Campbell-Bannerman assumed titular party leadership.

The party never completely recovered from the shock when 96 dissentient Liberals had voted against Gladstone's Irish Bill in 1886. In the General Election that year the Tories registered well with the slogan: 'Stand by your national Church and your national beverage.' In 1892, however, the Liberal party rebounded from the polls with a majority of 47, and that in spite of Mr Chamberlain's prophecy that Disestablishment was 'no longer in the domain of practical politics'. The Liberals were by no means finished, and did what they could to overcome their divisions by renewing the old combination with the Nonconformists.

By backing Gladstone in his Irish Home Rule policy the Executive of the Liberation Society had improved its esteem among his close followers. The organ of the Evangelicals, the *Record*, on 25 June 1886, spoke of rumours to the effect that a kind of 'informal agreement' existed between Mr Gladstone and the Liberationist clique. By securing the support of political Nonconformity for the Irish Bill, so the story went, he would give the Disestablishment question 'a new consideration – to regard it with an "open mind"'. Whatever the truth, the Society had undoubtedly improved its standing, for a former member of its Executive, John Morley, was called to become Irish Secretary. In 1893 he assured the Society that in the Home Rule Bill the Irish Legislature could not make any law respecting the establishment or endowment of religion 'direct or indirect'.[1]

The Liberation Society now was not suffering from want of friends in the Parliamentary lobbies, but rather from a complete lack of daring. Gone were the days of brilliant oratory by the Society's debaters, yielding major Parliamentary triumphs. The best it could do during this period was to prevent undesirable legislation and to consolidate previous gains.

A. *Church Property*

As chances became more remote for a legal separation between Church and State in England, the Society became more concerned about the nature of ecclesiastical property. This mass of wealth – tithes, glebe lands, clerical mortgages, retiring pensions, etc. – became the heart of the State-Church question. Liberationists now therefore turned their eyes more in the direction of Disendowment.

The shift corresponded to the rising Radical-Socialist theory on sharing national wealth for the welfare of all – but with State control. State supervision, at least, was necessary in any such scheme for full 'economic equality',

[1] Minute 829: 26.vi.93.

and in such circumstances it would not be possible to denationalize the Church completely.

As always, the question of the disposal of money attracted serious attention. Careful scrutiny was given to complicated legislation on the sale of tenures and livings, the rights of patrons and the incidence of tithe. But these matters bristled with theoretical points and thus lacked the popular appeal of Burials, Church Rates and University Tests. At election times 'Prop'uty, prop'uty, prop'uty' became a kind of mock chant which Liberals used whenever Tory Churchmen spoke in defence of their interests. But the cry did not catch on as the other cries of the Society had.

If Liberators could not 'properly disestablish' the Church of England, as had been done in Ireland, they were determined to do all in their power to reduce its hold on national property. This raised complex questions to which there were no simple answers. Who should redistribute some of the huge endowments originally intended for the benefit of the entire religious life of the nation? Were Nonconformists entitled to any of the ownership? Of what funds and endowments was the Church of England the sole beneficiary? Were the Anglican Clergy the paid servants of the State or of the Church?

1. *State-payments to the Clergy*

Were the Clergy of the Church of England in fact State-paid? The chief difficulty in answering this question lay in the variety of definitions of the phrase 'State-paid'. Liberationists believed that the State had always prescribed the conditions under which the Church held its property and had altered those conditions at its own pleasure. The question had been answered decisively, they believed, in the disestablishing and disendowing of the Irish Church in 1869, when Parliament applied the property to secular purposes for the whole Irish people.

The Rev. Charles Williams, a Baptist Minister of Accrington, delved seriously into this matter in 1873 when he submitted an interesting case for Counsel to Woolacott and Leonard, Solicitors in Gracechurch St, London. In one of his lectures that year in Macclesfield, as an Executive member of the Liberation Society, he had contended: (1) that the property 'formerly known as Episcopal Estates', but now managed by the Ecclesiastical Commissioners, 'was national property'; (2) that the Sees were the creation of the State, inasmuch as it had always claimed the right to appoint persons to occupy them, had prescribed their duties, and fixed the amount of their stipends; (3) that the fund out of which these stipends were paid was controlled and managed by a State Commission; (4) that the King, as 'Chief of the State', endowed these particular Episcopal Sees and always had the right to appoint persons to hold them.[1]

---

[1] The documents, 'Case for Counsel to Advise: Ex parte the Rev. Charles Williams' and the 'Opinion of Mr Fitzjames Stephen Q.C. and Henry Mason Bompas', taken from the private files of the Liberation Society. Williams referred Counsel to Sir William Blackstone, *Commentaries on the Laws of England* (1765), 16th ed., edited by John Taylor Coleridge

To substantiate his case that these Sees were State-founded and State-endowed, Williams cited: (1) the preamble to the Statute of Provisors, 25 Edward III, Stat. 6, which proclaimed the right of the King and his heirs to appoint to the two Archbishoprics 'and other elective dignities' of the Holy Church of England; (2) the contention that the Sees of Ripon and Manchester were founded by William IV and the Sees of Gloucester, Bristol, Peterborough and Oxford were founded by Henry VIII – both Sovereigns acting as head of the State; (3) the fact that the Crown still claimed the right to present Prelates to vacant Sees, which were paid salaries managed by a State Commission.

Early in 1885 an Accrington correspondent wrote to Mr Gladstone, the Marquess of Salisbury and Earl Granville, and put directly to them the question, 'Are the Clergy of the Church of England State-paid?' The replies appeared in the March *Liberator*. Mr Gladstone simply said that they were not. Lord Salisbury said, 'The Bishops receive no grants from the State, but they receive a revenue from ancient endowments given to the Church.' Earl Granville said, 'Tithes existed in England before Acts of Parliament, though the present mode of assessment and payment were settled by the Tithe Commutation Act, 6 and 7 William IV, c. 71, and subsequent statutes.'[1]

It was inferred from Earl Granville's reply that because Tithes constituted the bulk of Church property, what was true of them was true of Church property as a whole. On the origin of Tithes, Sir Robert Phillimore had maintained that they were at first purely voluntary offerings, and later were made a compulsory charge by the State.[2] This change took place, in Lord Granville's words, 'before Acts of Parliament', but as it was done by the law-making authority of the time, presumably it was the equivalent of an Act of Parliament. In one sense therefore those receiving Tithes and similar Church property were 'State-paid'.

A year later Carvell Williams exchanged letters with the Prime Minister on the same subject.

2 Serjeants' Inn
Fleet Street, E.C.,
January 24th, 1893

Dear Mr. Gladstone,

At the close of last year there appeared in the newspapers a letter, addressed by your direction, to the Rev. J. T. Hurley, of Ashton-Makerfield, in which you stated that 'the Church of England receives no assistance from public funds'. Unfortunately, Mr. Hurley's letter to which you replied was not also published; but a communication of his to the *Liverpool Courier* seemed to indicate that his inquiry related only to money voted annually by Parliament—in regard to which your statement is, of course, quite accurate.

(London 1825), i, 377–82, and to Edmund Gibson (Bishop of London), *Codex Juris Ecclesiastici Anglicani* (Oxford 1761), i, 79, 121. This work 'is still the highest authority on church law' (*D.N.B.*, xxi, London 1890, 275).

[1] *Liberator*, March 1885, p. 43.

[2] *Ecclesiastical Law of the Church of England* (London 1873), ii, 1483.

In some quarters, however, a much wider and, as I believe, an altogether erroneous construction has been placed upon your letter; the latest illustration of the fact being contained in a speech of the Bishop of St. Asaph (Joshua Hughes), at a meeting in defence of the Establishment in Wales, held at Shrewsbury on the 17th inst. For, in support of an argument to prove that the property in possession of the Church is not national property, his Lordship is reported by *The Times* to have said:

'The present Prime Minister had stated that the clergy of The Church of England were not State-paid, and within the last few weeks had said the Church of England received no assistance whatever from public funds. Therefore, the man who could stand up and say that the property of the Church belonged to the nation was ignorant and unprincipled.'

I am very reluctant to trouble you at the present juncture; but it is important that you should not be misunderstood in regard to such a matter. I therefore venture to ask you to be good enough to inform me whether I am not right in assuming that, in stating that 'the clergy of the Church of England are not State-paid,' and that 'the Church of England received no assistance from public funds,' your statements were limited to the fact that the Church does not now receive State-assistance in the form of Parliamentary grants; and were not intended to support the contention that the endowments in possession of the Church are not national property.

When favoured with your reply I hope to give it the same publicity as has been obtained by your previous letters on the subject.

I am yours, very faithfully,

J. Carvell Williams

The Right Hon. W. E. Gladstone, M.P.

10 Downing Street, Whitehall

January 25th, 1893

Dear Mr. Carvell Williams,

Some of the words quoted in your letter, and said to have been used by me (but I am not aware of having myself used ambiguous words) are perhaps of disputable meaning. But I have declared again and again that the funds of the Church, understanding the words as they were generally understood by the Irish Church Act, are national property. And this remains true, although it be also true that the Established Church in England does not, like that in Scotland, draw anything as an Establishment from what I may call Parliamentary sources.

I trust that this explanation meets your purposes, and

I remain, Faithfully yours,

W. E. Gladstone.[1]

2. *Return, Tithes and Charities*

Surprisingly, the Government, on 20 June 1887, agreed to a motion by Mr A. J. Picton and Mr J. G. Hubbard (later Lord Addington) calling for a Parliamentary Return on the following property and revenues of the Church of England: (1) the Archepiscopal and Episcopal Sees of England and Wales; (2) the Cathedral and Collegiate Churches of England and Wales, including

[1] Minute 743: 6.ii.93.

the property of the minor canons, vicars choral, and others; (3) Ecclesiastical Benefices, including donatives, perpetual curacies; (4) the Ecclesiastical Commissioners for England; and (5) the Corporation of Queen Anne's Bounty. The Return was to classify the property and sources of revenue, giving the gross annual value of lands, tithes, house property, mineral property, manorial and other receipts and income derived from stock and other securities. The property, whether from ancient endowments or private benefaction, was to be listed by counties and to identify its sources since 1703. The year 1703 was fixed because the fund known as 'Queen Anne's Bounty' was established then, and in general, modern benefactions commenced from that date.

The Return was issued in separate instalments and completed in August 1891. The Liberation Society described the twenty-odd pages of the report as 'unintelligible to all but financial experts'. It revealed a gross Revenue of £5,753,557, of which £5,469,171 was derived from 'Ancient Endowments', and £284,386 from 'recent Benefactions' since 1703. Allowing for the omission in the Return of all fees, pew-rents and voluntary offerings, these figures were close to those compiled in 1876 by the Society. The information thus became 'official', and justified the impression in some circles that the Church of England was 'the richest Church in Christendom'.[1] The time was past, however, when Liberationists could use the statistics as effective propaganda against the Established Church.

In the opinion of the Society, the depressed state of agriculture at the outset of this period made it necessary to alter the law on the payment of Tithes. No change would satisfy Liberationists which did not reduce the Tithes by an amount corresponding with the fall in the price of agricultural produce. But who was to endure the consequent loss – the Clergy, the landowners, or the State? Were the incumbencies of the Clergy to be deprived, or was compensation to be granted? Was the national estate, of which Tithes were a part, to be reduced? If the obligation to pay Tithes were transferred directly from the tenant to the landlord, would the amount of the Tithes be added to the rent? Would the landlords accept the obligation with all its attendant risks, without an equivalent relief from taxation?

In answering these questions, the Society kept four points constantly before the public mind: (1) Tithes were national property; (2) they were appropriated to the ministers of only a portion of the population; (3) they should be applied to purposes that would benefit all classes (free education, support of the poor, or general reduction in taxation); (4) they created problems which could be solved only in the process of Disendowment – the inevitable corollary to Disestablishment.

The anti-Tithe agitation stemmed mainly from Wales where numerous illegal Tithe distraints were alleged. The Executive Committee of the Society considered a statement from the South Wales Liberal Federation, on 18

---

[1] Minute 430: 10.viii.91. See p. 227 above, for comments on Frederick Martin, *The Property and Revenues of the English Church Establishment* (London 1877); cf. also explanatory article in the *Liberator*, Aug. 1891, p. 121.

November 1889, concerning the 'harsh and exasperating treatment of Welsh farmers'. It was reported that steps were being taken to test the legality of proceedings by appealing to courts of law. To help 'the victims' in the litigation and to protect them against loss, the Federation was raising a Tithe Defence Fund. When the Society voted to assist in these efforts, Mr H. S. Leonard, its counsel-at-law, resigned from the Executive Committee. To him such assistance amounted to encouraging Tithe-payers to resist and break the law.

The great weakness in the system of Tithe support for the Anglican Church was that the clerical Tithe-receiver had to take a loss of income and to suffer dishonour in attempting to enforce his legal rights. The Clergy possessing glebe lands, which they could neither rent nor cultivate during the depression, were in even greater straits than those dependent upon the Tithes alone.

The Salisbury Government brought in its fourth Tithes measure in 1891. As a simple Tithe Rent-charge Recovery Bill (not touching the subject of redemption) it was less objectionable than the previous ones and received the Royal Assent on 26 March. In substance the Bill made the landowner directly responsible for the payment of the Tithe, regardless of any contract with the occupier to the contrary. It provided for the recovery of the Tithe through the County Court by the provisions of the Tithe Commutation Act in 1836. Where the Tithe exceeded two-thirds of the annual value of the land, the excess was to be remitted by the County Court, 'and shall not be recoverable'. Some landlords now began to view the 'established system' with an irritation formerly felt by their tenants.

During the latter part of the nineteenth century the City of London became a congeries of huge business premises animated by day, but after working hours became a 'barren solitude'. In this vast metropolitan area possessing no less than sixty-one churches, its parochial charities

> represented a lavish income, ill administered by a miscellany of trustees, church-wardens and vestries, who expended part of it in demoralising doles and some of it on purposes entirely obsolete, such as sermons of thanksgiving for the defeat of the Spanish Armada or the frustration of the Gunpowder Plot.[1]

Liberation M.P.s and certain civic leaders began in 1872 to investigate the careless application of charities.[2] In April a group met at the Westminster Palace Hotel to deal with inquiries by the Educational Endowments Committee of the London School Board and the Royal City Parochial Charities Commission.

Mr James (later Lord) Bryce succeeded in 1883 in carrying his important City of London Charities Act (46 and 47 Vict., cap. 36). This was to be in

[1] H. A. L. Fisher, *James Bryce* (*Viscount Bryce of Dechmont, O.M.*) (London 1927), i, 187–8.

[2] On 1 December 1878 an investigator visited fourteen of Sir Christopher Wren's City churches, and found that the sum total of the congregations they contained was under 300 – about 20 persons in each church. The population resident in the City declined from 28,000 in 1870 to 21,000 in 1880. Society Memo. Book, No. 6, pp. 85–6.

effect till 1887, with the possibility of two years' extension. The object of Bryce's Bill was to remove the traditional restrictions upon these charities, and to make them available to the poor of the City under plans to be devised by a Board of Commissioners. Traditionally much of the money had gone to the restoration of City Churches and to Clergy in need of special assistance. Mr James Anstie Q.C., a leading Nonconformist, became one of the two new Charity Commissioners created by the Bill. The Liberation Society emphasized that those managing the funds should have (1) the full knowledge of popular wants and feelings, and (2) the confidence of the public in their strict impartiality.

The management of the City of London Parochial Charities under the provisions of Bryce's 1883 Act became law in 1891. Mr James Stuart (M.P., Shoreditch, Hoxton) failed in a motion to expunge the ecclesiastical portion of the scheme. These funds amounted to £90,000 per annum, and of that sum £56,000 was commissioned to general purposes and £35,000 to ecclesiastical purposes.

B. *Church Reform*

The position of the Society seemed paradoxical on the question of the liberation of the Church from the regulation of Parliament. The official title, 'The Society for the Liberation of Religion from State Patronage and Control', made it clear where the Society should stand on these matters. Nevertheless, it would not accept ideas for an assembly of Anglican laity acting together with the clerical assembly in both Convocations of the Church to reform its ecclesiastical laws and practices.

> The question of Church Reform has apparently entered into a new and very important phase. The hope of reforming the Church by a series of legislative measures is apparently abandoned, and instead, the idea now entertained is that the Church should itself frame measures of reform, by means of a representative body, and that Parliament should possess only the power of veto. This would practically be, to a large extent, Disestablishment without Disendowment; and, however impracticable it may appear in the eyes of politicians, it has great attractiveness for earnest Churchmen, and will seem plausible even to some opponents of the Establishment. There may be a danger of the present Government moving in that direction.[1]

The Society tried to obstruct movements in this direction for two reasons: (1) they believed that it was an attempt to silence Nonconformists on religious issues in Parliament; (2) they believed that it was an attempt by the Church of England to gain the right of self-government while maintaining the privilege of the Established national Church. And the Church ought not to have the best of both worlds.

Ever since the reign of Henry VIII, the State had asserted its right of control

---

[1] Minute 1405: 5.vii.97. cf. Montagu Burrows, *Parliament and the Church of England* (London 1875) pp. 132–9.

over ecclesiastical affairs.[1] The State, through Parliament, had constantly given notice to all its subjects by statutes of Mortmain that if men gave property to the Church, and the Church took it, the property was given and taken subject to State control. Moreover, this transaction took place on State terms – upon conditions laid down from time to time by the State, and liable to alteration by the power which had laid them down.[2] And the Church of England, the Liberation Society maintained, must accept these incumbent difficulties as long as it remained the Established Church of the State.

The Society seemed unreasonable in its insistence that all ecclesiastical reform should be accomplished through Parliament rather than through a revived Convocation. The Society was against removing Parliamentary control, even though it was in the interest of thorough reform, unless it could be removed on their own terms. The reformers believed that the Liberationists preferred to see a system working badly, rather than see it righted by a plan which would be more beneficial to the Church of England.

The only permanently satisfactory reform, Liberationists believed, was the total abolition of State patronage and control. The futility and uselessness of State control was manifest in the desire of Anglican parties themselves for greater freedom of action. High Churchmen would centre supreme control in exclusively clerical assemblies, Broad Churchmen would confer it on parishioners, and Evangelical Churchmen would seek it in a revised Protestant Prayer Book.

1. *Ecclesiastical Courts*

Policy had been formulated and discussions provoked on the subject of Church reform since the Report in 1883 of the Royal Commission on the Ecclesiastical Courts. Later study of its proposals made it clear that the reconstruction of these courts involved a fundamental change in the relations between Church and State.

The grounds for the inquiry had been the 'scandals' arising from legal proceedings against Established Clergymen for alleged violations of the law concerning doctrine and ritual. The effect of the Report was to encourage new demands for freedom from the existing judicial and legislative restraints. It was therefore recommended that the Church Discipline Act, 1840, and the Public Worship Regulation Act, 1874, be repealed.

---

[1] 26 Henry VIII, cap. 1: 'Be it enacted by authority of this present Parliament, that the King our Sovereign Lord, his heirs and successors, kings of this realm, shall be taken, accepted and reputed the only supreme head on earth of the Church of England called *Anglicana Ecclesia*. . . . And that our said Sovereign Lord, his heirs and successors, kings of this realm, shall have full power and authority from time to time, to visit, repress, redress, reform, order, correct, restrain and amend all such errors, heresies, abuses, offences, contempts and enormities, whatsoever they be . . .' The preamble to the Act of Firstfruits, 26 Henry VIII, cap. 3, speaks of the King as being 'now recognised, as he always indeed hath heretofore been, the only Supreme Head on earth, next and immediately under God, of the Church of England'.

[2] Lord Chief Justice Coleridge, in *The Nineteenth Century*, March 1870, pp. 110–12.

The reaction against the Report came from both Anglican and Nonconformist sources, especially on the proposal that the Court of final Appeal should continue to be a lay tribunal, its members being appointed by the Crown. In the opinion of Sir Robert Phillimore this state of affairs would enable lay judges 'to dictate to the Archbishop spiritual sentences which he would have, perhaps contrary to his own judgment, to pronounce'. Disestablishment, Liberationists claimed, could eliminate this complexity by enacting that ecclesiastical offences be tried in tribunals presided over by Bishops with judicial authority. The Earl of Chichester, one of the Royal Commissioners, had stated that charges against Clergymen for breaches of the law should be tried by competent tribunals, the Judges of which should be laymen learned in the law of the State.

The Society strongly objected to certain of the recommendations: (1) that every Judge of the Provincial Courts, and every member of the proposed Court of Appeal for ecclesiastical cases, should declare himself to be a member of the Church of England; (2) that the Judges in the Court of Appeal should not be bound to state reasons for their decisions, and that their actual decrees alone should be of binding authority; (3) that the Bishop should have absolute power of refusing to allow legal proceedings against a clergyman of his diocese – an action deplored by Lord Chief Justice Coleridge, another of the Commissioners, as 'indefensible in theory . . . and intolerable in practice'.

The *Church Times*, on 12 October 1883, was amazed at the '*naïveté*' of the protest against the exclusion of all but Anglicans from the judgeships of the proposed Provincial Court and Court of Appeal:

> When Churchmen complain that they are excluded from the Wesleyan Conference, or from the Congregational or Baptist Union, it will be time for the Liberation Society to claim a place in the courts of the Church of England.

2. *Church Patronage*

The practice of patronage in appointments to Anglican Church livings had long aroused the indignation of those Nonconformists who knew only the advantages of congregational control in the appointment of their Ministers. To them there was something strangely irreligious in advertisements in the public press, such as these:

> For Sale, Advowson Rectory. Eastern counties; near sea; large, modern house, extensive gardens and grounds, good stables. Tithe, commuted, £725; net, about £600. 30 acres glebe. Small population. Excellent shooting neighbourhood. Present incumbent over 70. Price moderate. Apply Cobbold, No. 21, Tower-street, Ipswich.[1]

> Next Presentation to a valuable Living for disposal. The present Incumbent is upwards of 70. The rectory large, with excellent garden. Most healthy situation, near railway station in Midlands. Population small. Net income about £700. Good society, &c. No agents need apply, as principals or their solicitors will

[1] *The Times*, 10.vii.96.

only be treated with. Address Messrs. Fishers, Solicitors, 24, Essex-street, Strand, London, W.C.[1]

A Church Patronage Bill passed in 1887 in the House of Lords. The Parliamentary Committee of the Society did not recommend that it should be opposed, but that it should be freely criticized. The features of this Bill became the substance of many variations in subsequent Bills: (1) While a person may not sell the next presentation to a living, he may sell the advowson to a 'qualified parishioner' – meaning a landowner in the parish. It might also be sold to a public patron – that is, to a Cathedral body, a University, a College, or the governors of any school, hospital, charity, 'or any body corporate', and any person whose office entitled him to exercise the rights of Church patronage. Further, it might be sold to a Council of public patronage under the provisions of the Act. (2) Advowsons were not to be mortgaged or sold by auction, but 'it shall be lawful for such persons to sell the same by private contract'. (3) Patrons were required to make religious declarations which were to be registered. (4) Bishops could refuse to institute presentees, who had the right of appeal to the Archbishop. (5) The parishioners might also object on certain grounds.

The annual Council Meeting of the Society in 1893 heard the criticism (1) that the Church Patronage Bill of the Archbishop of Canterbury (Dr Benson) 'would give fresh legislative sanction to "traffic in livings" ' and (2) that the Bill 'would only abate the grosser scandals of an utterly indefensible system'. In 1894 this Bill was put before the House of Commons on the report of the Standing Committee on Law to which Carvell Williams had been appointed. He summoned a private caucus of Liberation M.P.s in the House of Commons to consider his amendments which would abolish the sale of all Advowsons, as well as next presentations. At the time of the second reading of the Bill, Mr Williams spoke with considerable conviction for total prohibition, but did not vote. In his view, patronage could be reckoned as a trust, but not a trust to be exercised as a marketable commodity. Several Clergymen wrote to him afterwards thanking him for his judicious criticisms. The Government resigned before the Bill could get beyond the Report stage.

The Society adopted a similar position on a very different Bill – the Clergy Discipline (Immorality) Bill introduced in 1892, also by the Archbishop of Canterbury. The Bill came down from the Lords and was referred promptly to the Grand Committee of the Law. Mr Lloyd George pressed opposition on the Report stage, but ultimately the closure was applied, and the Bill went into operation on 27 September 1892. With a slight air of superiority the Society's leaders declared that they had

refrained from opposing, or impeding the progress of, the Bill for better enforcing discipline in the case of crimes and other offences against morality committed by clergymen. They, at the same time, believe that the measure will, in its

[1] *The Times*, 9.iv.97.

22

operation, afford fresh proofs of the impossibility of regulating, by legislative and judicial machinery, the relations between ministers of religion and those to whom they minister—machinery necessarily belonging to a church establishment, but for which non-established religious bodies find no need.[1]

[1] Minute 608: 30.v.92.

CHAPTER 25

Nonconformist Marriages

. . . an honourable estate, instituted of God in the time of man's innocency, signifying unto us the mystical union that is betwixt Christ and his Church; . . . It was ordained for the mutual society, help, and comfort, that the one ought to have of the other, both in prosperity and adversity.

Service of Solemnization of Matrimony[1]

. . . And I do declare, that no foreign Prince, Person, Prelate, State, or Potentate, hath or ought to have, any Jurisdiction, Power Superiority, Pre-eminence, or Authority, Ecclesiastical or Spiritual within this Realm.

Bishop's Oath of the Queen's Supremacy[2]

UP TO THE BEGINNING of this period the Liberation Society was not convinced that the law on Marriage was an urgent Nonconformist grievance. It had been left rather to the Wesleyan Committee of Privileges to deal with the major difficulties of Dissenting Marriages. Prior to 1890 the Society had made one or two minor advances in this direction.

In that year the trouble among the Churches in Malta on Marriages caused the Society to reflect more seriously upon the related problems at home. Liberationists now saw a new and excellent opportunity to make the most of their arguments and principles. As in the case of Nonconformist Burials, the agitation on Marriages inevitably touched upon the social privileges of the Established Church.

The chief complaint of Nonconformists was that under the existing Marriage laws the ceremony could be performed with greater facility and at less cost at the Anglican Churches than at either Registrars' Offices or Dissenting places of worship. Added to the difficulties of giving notices of Marriage and obtaining certificates, the presence of the Registrar was required at Nonconformist Marriages, and not at Anglican Church weddings. This was both a violation of the principle of religious equality and an unnecessary inconvenience.

---

[1] Book of Common Prayer of the Church of England.

[2] Book of Common Prayer of the United Church of England and Ireland (also used in the Form for the Ordering of Deacons).

Nonconformists, however, were divided on the answers to the inconvenience and the violation of principles. Some would compel the attendance of Registrars at every solemnization of Matrimony, whether Dissenting or Church of England. Others would prefer a complete separation of Church and State in the performance of Marriage – in other words, the legal ceremony to be conducted by civic officials, and the religious service left to the choice of the contracting parties.

A. *Parliamentary Measures*

In 1886 Carvell Williams steered his Marriage Hours Extension Bill with comparative ease through Parliament and it promptly became law. The measure had been previously submitted by the Government to the Primate (Dr Benson), who merely suggested that the hours should be limited to the period from 12 noon to 3.0 p.m. instead of from 12 noon to 4.0 p.m. An extension would enable working-class families to have their weddings on Saturdays without losing the half-day of work and wages. When the Act went into effect, difficulties cropped up in connexion with the 62nd Canon which required that all Marriages should take place between 8.0 a.m. and 12 noon. Certain Clergy refused to recognize the new law until the Canon Law was altered by Convocation and brought into harmony with Statute Law. The *Topical Times* of 15 May sized up this situation with a quippish rhyme:

> Three loud cheers for C. Williams, who brought in the Bill,
>   And, what's more to the point, got it carried,
> To enable poor yokels like Jacky and Jill
>   After twelve of the clock to be married.

In 1887 the Society simply recorded its objections to the Marriages (Dispensing with the Attendance of Registrars) Bill brought in by the Attorney-General, Sir Richard Webster (M.P., Isle of Wight), on behalf of the Government. The Bill limited the right to officiate to registered Ministers who were recognized by and responsible to a denominational Committee set up for that purpose. It was withdrawn on 25 July.

After the second reading of the Marriage of Nonconformists (Attendance of Registrars) Bill in 1891 without a division, a conference was called by the Dissenting Deputies at Memorial Hall on 13 April. Mr Williams then read a paper objecting to this Bill and to the amendments of Sir Richard, the Attorney-General. The Chairman of the Liberation Society admitted that the ideal solution would be the severance of the civil from the religious ceremony, but did not think that public opinion was yet prepared for it. He also urged the appointment of a Select Committee before further altering the Marriage Acts. When the Chairman of the Deputies, William Woodall (M.P., Hanley), asked in the House if the Government would propose such an appointment, the reply was that there was no necessity for it. The Bill was dropped through failure to report progress before the end of that Session.

The most the Society had to say about Marriage law reform was contained in a special Minute on 12 December 1892. This had arisen from a request of the Nonconformist Consultative Committee that those who had been a party to the Nonconformist Marriages Bill in 1888 (backed by Messrs Henry Richard, Alfred Illingworth, Henry H. Fowler, and S. D. Waddy) should express their separate opinions on its contents.

In the eyes of the Liberation Society the Bill of 1888, which became a guide for Nonconformist legislation during this period, had certain distinct advantages: (1) It dispensed, when the parties concerned desired it, with the attendance of Registrars at Nonconformist places of worship. (2) It was a permissive measure only, and therefore satisfied Ministers and others who were not willing to officiate without the attendance of a Registrar. (3) It did not confer any authority upon Nonconformist Ministers as such, but recognized only 'the person officiating at a marriage', whether he be a Minister or layman. (4) It made the Superintendent Registrar solely responsible for the registration. The responsibility of the officiating person ended when he returned the completed certificate of the 'functionary'.

The Society favoured the reintroduction of such a Bill in the 1893 Session, provided that it was adapted to existing circumstances. It had to be free from any loopholes for escaping legal obligations, and it should not encourage unjust discrimination between the wealthy and poor inhabitants of a community. Hopefully, some of the objections could be met by administrative changes on the authority of the Registrar-General, without the necessity of legislative sanction.

Mr (later Sir) Robert W. Perks, of the Society, obtained in 1893 the appointment of a Select Committee – in place of his Bill with the above considerations. The Committee consisted of four Churchmen and seven Nonconformists – four of whom were members of the Society's Executive Committee. The findings became the substance of the Act of 1898 which allowed an authorized person (not necessarily a Minister) to substitute for the Registrar, providing that he did the registering properly. The solemnization of a Nonconformist marriage was thereby permitted in all registered places of worship and rendered less expensive, less complicated and less discriminatory.[1]

B. *The Malta Affair*

The Society became considerably interested in the negotiations arising between the British Government and the Vatican on the relations between Church and State in Malta. In this Crown possession the Established Church was the Church of Rome. Its alleged violations of principles of religious freedom occasioned strong reaction by Nonconformists of the island and in Britain.[2]

---

[1] Denis Crane, *Life-Story of Sir Robert W. Perks*, pp. 207–8.

[2] cf. correspondence in 'Sir L. Simmons's Special Mission to the Vatican relative to Religious Questions in the Island of Malta' (Miscellaneous Parliamentary Paper No. 1, 1890).

Sir Lintorn Simmons in 1890 was appointed Envoy Extraordinary and 'Minister Plenipotentiary of high rank' to the Pope (Leo XIII). With the approval of Sir James Fergusson, the Under-Secretary of State for Foreign Affairs, Sir Lintorn consulted with Cardinal Rampolla, the Papal Secretary of State, and the following arrangements were made: (1) On the vacancies of Bishoprics, the special envoy proposed that 'an understanding should be come to confidentially as to the nomination by His Holiness of a successor'. After the appointment had been made, Her Majesty's Government should then publish their 'concurrence' in the appointment. In reply the Papal spokesman declared that while His Holiness could not consent to his liberty of action being curtailed, he would treat Her Majesty's Government with all the consideration compatible with that liberty and therefore 'would not be averse to assure himself of its concurrence'. (2) On the celebration of marriages, it was decided that marriages,

> whether both contracting parties be Catholics, or whether one of them be a Catholic and the other a non-Catholic, are not and shall not be valid if they are not celebrated according to the form established by the Council of Trent.[1]

Consistent with these declarations, the Home Government therefore introduced in the Council of the Maltese Government a new 'Project of Law'. Its object was to regulate the civil status of marriages celebrated there in the past, and those taking place in the future. Licences had been issued since 1801 by the British Government to non-Roman Catholic Ministers, enabling them to celebrate marriages between Maltese Roman Catholics and foreigners. These marriages had been duly celebrated under such licence and had been legally recorded in the Registry office. The sacred validity of these marriages was simply not recognized by the Roman hierarchy.

The Executive Committee of the Society protested that the new policy of the British Government was shaped 'in accordance with the views of ecclesiastical functionaries, instead of with those of the people for whose government they are responsible'. Liberationists insisted (1) that the same freedom in the matter should exist in Malta as in other countries having Established Churches, and (2) that Roman Catholic or Protestant residents should be allowed to marry with the religious rites of their own choice, provided that legal formalities were observed. Much of the dissatisfaction arose, Lord Salisbury admitted, from engagements of the Government which had the effect of enforcing Roman Catholic Canon Law. The only conclusive answer to the problem, said the Society, was Disestablishment.

The Salisbury Government soon published the two proclamations by which these ecclesiastical affairs in Malta had been previously ordered. On 25 July 1890, in the House of Lords, the Archbishop of Canterbury (Dr Benson) raised the issue and disputed the notion that the Canon Law of the Catholic Church was the Civil Law of Malta.

---

[1] Draft Minute 129: 30.vi.90.

The issue was again discussed in the House of Commons on 11 August, on the consideration of the Foreign Estimates. At a 'Wesleyan Dinner' at the National Liberal Club on 30 July, Mr Gladstone declared the situation to be one of danger to religious liberty.[1] Mr Williams penned a letter of protest which appeared in *The Times* on 11 August. By the time of the advent of the new Liberal Government in 1892 legislative proceedings had been held in abeyance in order to obtain a decision from the Judicial Committee of the Privy Council as the actual state of the law. In the meantime arguments were aired in the public press concerning the wisdom of establishing regular and permanent diplomatic relations between the Pope and Her Majesty.

The official deliberations on the Malta situation dragged on behind the scenes until the defeat of Rosebery's Ministry on 21 June 1895, by which time it had been almost forgotten by the Liberationists. During the interim period the Archbishop of Malta warned that any deviation from the decrees of the Holy See at the instance of Her Majesty's Plenipotentiary would be a grave insult to the Pope and would excite Roman Catholics against the Government. The case was cautiously resumed by the Conservative Ministry in July 1895, when the Privy Council decided that mixed marriages in Malta were legal. The new Colonial Secretary, Joseph Chamberlain, accordingly instructed the Governor of Malta to renew the issue of licences for such marriages.

Feelings flared up again a few months after this dispatch. The Legislative Council of Malta passed an ordinance which contradicted the Privy Council decision and carried out the provisions of the earlier 'Project of Law'. The Society adamantly declared that the Assent of the Crown ought to be withheld from this proposed law because (1) it was an admission by the British Government of a doctrinal claim of the Roman Catholic Church, (2) it would cause great domestic distress if mixed marriages already celebrated were rendered invalid, (3) it would be impossible for Nonconformist Ministers of Malta to perform marriages as hitherto, (4) it was a denial to Protestants of Malta of the liberty enjoyed by Roman Catholics in Britain.

Carvell Williams handed a statement with these views to Chamberlain and on 7 August put a question to him in the House of Commons. He replied that (1) the ordinance to which the Society objected had not been brought in with the concurrence of the Home Government; (2) it had not been supported by the official members of the Council of the Maltese Government; (3) it was still under consideration whether or not to withhold Royal sanction.[2] Mr Chamberlain informed Mr Williams privately that it would be unwise to raise a discussion on the subject in Parliament for the present, chiefly because of the feelings of Irish (Roman Catholic) Liberals. The Society agreed not to give publicity to the matter for a while.

On 14 October, the Colonial Secretary sent a dispatch to Malta reasserting the correctness of the opinion of the Privy Council Judicial Committee that mixed marriages in Malta celebrated otherwise than in accordance with the

[1] Minute 152: 11.viii.90.
[2] Hansard (4th series), xliv, 107–8.

rites of the Roman Catholic Church were valid. The sanction of the Crown to the ordinance was withheld, and no further legislation on the subject was proposed. The matter of diplomatic representation between the Vatican and the Crown was also considered closed.[1]

---

[1] In 1896 Pope Leo XIII decreed that the validity of Anglican ordinations should form the subject of an historical and theological investigation. Mr Gladstone wrote a letter welcoming this step in the interest of 'the historical transmission of the truth by a visible Church with an ordained constitution' such as practised by the Roman, Orthodox and Anglican bodies. Dr J. Guinness Rogers, of the Society, 'declared himself puzzled to know how a great and subtle intellect like Mr. Gladstone's could occupy itself for a single moment as to whether the Pope did or did not recognise the validity of Anglican orders.' Justin McCarthy, *The Story of Gladstone's Life*, pp. 371, 373.

CHAPTER 26

National Education

[Free] Education is just and right in itself, and I do not
shrink from—nay, I court and gladly meet—the controversies which this question must necessarily raise. But these
controversies are very vital, and we must be prepared to
fight; and, fighting it out, in the first place we must insist
that every farthing that is given shall go into the pockets
of the parents themselves, and that not one farthing shall
go to bolster up those schools which usurp the name of
'national'.

SIR GEORGE TREVELYAN[1]

With regard to religious instruction in schools, it has long
been the steady aim of educational legislation in England
to remove all causes of offence or friction, and to secure,
as far as possible, that differences of religious belief shall
not unduly restrict the diffusion of educational benefits.

Report of the Royal Commission on Secondary Education[2]

WITH THE GROWING unpopularity of Disestablishment as a
politico-religious ideal, the Society during this time became more
closely identified with the national and unsectarian education
movement. State grants and favouritism to denominational schools had now
acquired first place among the grievances of well-informed Nonconformists,
and English Disestablishment became identified with a passing phase of English
Liberalism. The School replaced the Church as the main arena in which the
struggle for religious equality was to continue into the twentieth century. The
Liberation Society thus naturally became parent to the National Education
Association.

In their change of role the leaders of the Society did not express themselves
less frankly than before. They feared that their existence as a Liberal social
force would be negated if the Anglicans won over the schools of the nation.
At the Society's Jubilee celebrations Dr Joseph Parker, of the London City
Temple, stated: 'to teach theological dogmas at the public expense is "an

[1] Chairman's Address, Annual Meeting of the Liberation Society, St James's Hall,
6 May 1891. *Liberator*, June 1891, p. 87.
[2] Minute 1113: 11.xi.95.

infamous unrighteousness". We should suspect the priest wherever we find him.'[1]

But behind these polemics there loomed the great problem of the right of the Government to govern the minds of its citizens. To some the problem could be solved by segregating the teaching of the State Church from the schools provided by the community. To others, the problem could be solved by preparing the State Schoolmaster to teach religion as the other subjects. Which benefited the minds of the young the most, the Church Catechism or the syllabus approved by the School Boards?

> Over all those issues the religious wrangled interminably and very angrily, presenting a spectacle unedifying before God, and infinitely wearisome to men. . . . Yet the central point of the old Dissenting position was freedom of men's minds and consciences from state control; and who shall say with confidence that they were wrong?[2]

A. *The Royal Commission*

The Royal Commission, appointed in January 1886 to inquire into the working of the Elementary Education Acts, came mainly from a request of Cardinal Manning. He acted primarily in the interests of the Roman Catholic Church, but he was also supported by the leaders of the Church of England schools. Their joint purpose was expressly to secure an improved status for denominational schools as distinguished from those under School Boards. The Conservative Government had asserted through its Home Secretary, Sir Richard Cross, that 'the voluntary schools were suffering very greatly from many of the provisions of the Act [of 1870] and ought to be placed in the same position as Board schools'.[3]

The constitution of the Commission corresponded with its origin. Sir Richard (later Viscount) Cross was made the Chairman. The Duke of Norfolk and Cardinal Manning (who represented the Roman Catholics), and those representing the Anglicans (Lords Harrowby, Beauchamp, Norton, and the Bishop of London, Dr Frederick Temple) were all in the majority. The advocates of an unsectarian system of national education formed a decided minority; among them were Sir John Lubbock, Henry Richard, Dr R. W. Dale, and the Hon. E. Lyulph Stanley.

The full report, which appeared in 1888, assumed the form of three separate reports, owing to the obvious disagreements. The Commission sat for 146 days, examined 151 witnesses, and as many as 51 days were devoted to the overall report which filled 500 pages. The first report came from fifteen of the twenty-three Commissioners, and the second from the eight remaining ones. The purely Nonconformist point of view was prepared by five of the eight dissenting Commissioners. This was described by Dr R. W. Dale in a letter to Henry Richard as universal School Boards, free education, and pure secu-

---

[1] *The Christian World*, 2.v.94, p. 326.
[2] G. Kitson Clark, *The English Inheritance* (London 1950), p. 137.
[3] *The Times*, 16.xi.85; quoted in the *Liberator*, Feb. 1888, p. 20.

larism'.[1] Both minorities, however, pronounced a general condemnation against the policy determined by the majority.

The Majority Report contended that the cost of the maintenance of voluntary schools had been largely increased by the competition of rate-supported schools. School Boards had the 'power of the purse' to draw upon, thereby placing the managers of voluntary schools at a financial disadvantage. That power should at least be shared with voluntary schools, to help them meet the costs incurred by this rivalry.

According to traditional usage, the term 'voluntary schools' and 'voluntary system' in the above context were misleading. 'Voluntary', in the sense employed in the Majority Report, referred to denominational schools that were originated or largely supported by 'private' endowments and donations. Liberationists, however, denied that all national religious endowments were necessarily private and they therefore denied that all schools receiving such money were of a truly voluntary character. The word, as conceived by the Liberal-Nonconformists, who were mainly responsible for its introduction into the Disestablishment controversy, meant enterprise that was free from the compulsory controls of the State and wholly dependent upon 'individual liberality'.[2] For them Voluntaryism (like the word 'Independency') had been almost synonymous with *laissez faire* and belonged distinctly to the Liberal political creed.

This 'juxtaposition' or usurping of vocabulary confused the issue not a little, for the Anglican 'voluntary schools' were supported by State grants and children's pence. Frequently these were the only schools existing in rural districts and all children were compelled to attend them. While known as 'Public Elementary Schools', they were in fact under private management. Of some 14,000–15,000 such schools in England and Wales, nearly 12,000 belonged to the Established Church.

The recommendations of the Majority Report, said the National Educationalists, aimed at discouraging the School Board system, and making the extension and improvements of education subordinate to the interests of ecclesiastical organizations. This favouritism was, as alleged, shown in the following ways: (1) the structural improvement of the so-called 'voluntary schools'; (2) the limitation of transfer of 'voluntary schools' to School Boards; (3) the support of 'voluntary schools' out of the rates, as well as by State grants; (4) the allowance of denominational catechisms and formularies in religious instruction; (5) the registering of school attendance before commencement of religious instruction; (6) the fixing of school fees and their exemption from public control; (7) the continued exclusion of Nonconformists from denominational Training Colleges; (8) the definition of subjects of instruction and the exact determination of the limits between primary and secondary instruction.

[1] A. W. W. Dale, *Life of R. W. Dale*, p. 549.
[2] C. S. Miall, *Henry Richard, M.P.: A Biography*, p. 368.

B. *The National Education Association*

The Society called upon all Nonconformists interested in the momentous task of educating their children to improve the existing system and to advance the cause of undenominational schools. Liberationists admitted that it would be unwise to seek the entire abolition of State grants to denominational schools and Training Colleges. But the true basis of sound educational policy, they believed, lay in the recommendation of the Minority Report.

> . . . in districts where there can be only one efficient school, that school should be under public management, and ought not to be used as an agency for maintaining the religious faith of any particular denomination.[1]

National Educationalists looked forward to the time when there would be no enforced attendance at privately managed schools, but only at schools under the control of the elected representatives of the ratepayers. The majority of the Commissioners were willing that 'some parents' should be admitted to school management, as long as they did not become a 'preponderating element'.

The Liberation Society in 1888 helped to convene a conference *en masse* to consider means of defeating the recommendations of the 'Reactionary Report'. Invitation circulars were sent out signed by fifty prominent National Educationalists. On 20–21 November, some 800 delegates from 170 bodies throughout the country met together at Exeter Hall, with the Rt Hon. H. H. Fowler, Mr Alfred Illingworth, and the Rt Hon. A. J. Mundella presiding over the proceedings. Resolutions of opposition which had been drawn up by the Society's Executive were passed with little hesitation.

The conference expenses of £250 were met by subscriptions sufficient to leave a surplus for the formation of a permanent organization. This was eventually known as the National Education Association, consisting of 250–300 permanent members. The Executive body of thirty-three elected members included thirteen members of the Liberation Society. It was decided to open offices at the Outer Temple opposite the Law Courts, to appoint Mr T. E. Minshall and Mr Bernard Wishaw as joint Secretaries, and to draft a constitution.[2] All operations were to be based upon the fundamental principle that grants of public money involved the necessity for public management.

C. *Free Education Bill*

The Society heard rumours early in 1890 that the Government was thinking of appropriating £2,000,000 from national funds for purposes of 'free education'. At this stage the Executive leaders of the Society refrained from expressing an official opinion on the expediency of free education. They did

---

[1] Minority Report, p. 241. In more than 10,000 parishes in England and Wales, children of Nonconformists were compelled to attend Church of England schools, because there was no other public elementary school available. Minute 2: 13.i.90.

[2] Minute 1299: 3.xii.88; Minute 1305: 17.xii.88. The Constitution was printed in the *Liberator*, Feb. 1889, p. 22.

state, however, that it was not their wish to discourage broad attempts to remove obstacles to 'the culture and enlightenment of the whole people'. Moreover, if the principle of free education was to be adopted by Parliament, a practical distinction must be drawn between sectarian and non-sectarian schools. The Society feared that the monopoly of the Anglican Church would be extended if its schools received, in lieu of existing school fees, further grants of public money. There must be guarantees that the 'Nonconformist Conscience' would be respected in the management and teaching of State-financed schools.

The way for the Government free education Bill was prepared in 1891 by the Chancellor of the Exchequer, Mr G. J. Goschen (M.P., St George's, Hanover Square). He announced that he had in mind a measure for abolishing, from 1 September of that year, the payment of fees in public elementary schools in the four parts of the United Kingdom. The cost was estimated at £2,000,000, as rumoured.[1]

'To be forewarned is to be forearmed', said the *Liberator*, and so when the Elementary Education Bill was formally introduced by the Vice-President of the Committee of Council on Education, Sir W. H. Hart Dyke (M.P., Kent, Dartford), the Society released a lengthy criticism. The measure was no better than previous ones of a similar kind because the authors admitted it to be their aim to place 'voluntary schools' in an 'impregnable position'. Although professing to relieve parents from the payment of fees, which it did only partially, the Bill authorized an additional Parliamentary grant of 10s. per head for pupils between the ages of five and fourteen years.

The feelings of National Educationalists on this occasion became more anti-clerical. They ridiculed the denominational schools where 'the management practically falls into the hands of a single manager, most frequently the clergyman of the parish'. They resented the selection of teachers 'with a view to other than educational qualifications', and their retention or dismissal depending upon their degree of co-operation with the clergy. They regarded the power of the Conscience Clause, in the words of Patrick Cumin, the Secretary of the Education Department, as a 'thing on paper'. Besides, he told the Royal Commission, 'everybody who manages a school knows that the real thing is the power of appointing the teacher'.[2]

These sentiments, however, did not prevent the Bill from passing by an overwhelming margin (318–10 votes).[3] In the Commons on 20 June, Henry H. Fowler (later Lord Wolverhampton) moved a final Instruction to the Committee that

[1] S. Maccoby, *English Radicalism 1886–1914* (London 1953), p. 478, comments: 'Disestablishment probably became completely inexecutable after Conservatives decided in 1891 to finance "Free Education" from the taxes rather than have Church revenues held up continuously as a "bait to the poor".'

[2] See *Liberator*, July 1891, p. 99.

[3] The debate lasted for three days. Hansard (3rd series), cccliv, 1099–1157, 1216–1303, 1315–1359.

they have power to make provision, in the case of districts where there exists no school under public control, for the introduction of the principle of local representation in the supervision of schools receiving the fee grants.[1]

Mr Fowler asserted that nine-tenths of the seven and a half million pounds' cost of Elementary Education would be dipped out of the public purse. Very little more than one-tenth of the cost would come out of voluntary contributions. Under these circumstances, he believed, the British people would not entrust such an enormous amount of money to irresponsible private organizations. In placing free education upon the Statute Book, he said the Liberals 'would make the Tory party the hewers of their wood and the drawers of their water'.[2]

Ironically, Joseph Chamberlain argued that to vote for this Instruction would give more power to the most sectarian of the existing denominational schools. To go for general control and universal School Boards would postpone free education indefinitely. To justify the change of policy he had championed in the 1870s and '80s as a leader of the Birmingham Education League, he read a portion of a letter from Dr R. W. Dale:

> For my part, I am well content that for the present no attempt should be made to secure public control. Those of us who believe in it are not strong enough to insist on any effective application of our principle, and I do not care to have a mere illusory arrangement. . . . At present the denominational schools are too strong for it to be possible to transfer the power of their managers to School Boards. We may regret this—I regret it very much—but the fact cannot be denied; and the question is whether, if this fact is recognised, any fairer and less objectionable measure for securing free education can be constructed than that which has been proposed by the Government.[3]

The Instruction was rejected by 267 to 166 votes. The Bill, without serious alteration, received the Royal Assent on 5 August (54 and 55 Vict., cap. 56) and went into effect on the date originally set.

The opposition of the unsectarian National Educationalists fared better in the case of the Government Education Bill in 1896, which, they maintained, virtually extinguished School Boards. A mass protest at Queen's Hall, presided over by the former Home Secretary, Herbert Asquith, insisted on no more public money for denominational schools without some degree of local control. Another huge demonstration was chaired by Alderman Evan Spicer M.P., addressed by leading Free Church Ministers,[4] and attended by the

[1] Hansard (3rd series), cccliv, 1730.

[2] Edith H. Fowler, *The Life of Henry Hartley Fowler, First Viscount Wolverhampton* (London 1912), pp. 243–4.

[3] Hansard (3rd series), cccliv, 1763–4. This letter brought a storm of denunciation and charges of 'apostasy'. Dr Dale, however, answered in the *Independent*, 23.x.91, that he had not forsaken the great Nonconformist principle in the Education struggle: '. . . not the mere "*supervision*" by a local representative authority of schools receiving public grants, but the transfer of the *management* of the schools to a local representative authority . . .'

[4] Six months afterwards, Dr John Clifford addressed his famous letter to the Liberation Society, 'A Call to Free Churchmen', marking a new chapter in the history of British Nonconformity. Minute 1479: 24.i.98.

National Council of Evangelical Free Churches, the National Education League of the Free Churches, the Three Denominations of Dissenting Ministers, the National Education Association, the London Nonconformist Council, the Dissenting Deputies and the Liberation Society.

These organizations were animated by one mind – to prevent the absorption of their children into the orbit of the Church of England. The School Boards would be superseded by a new education authority under County Councils, which, in addition to administering grants, appointing managers, and fixing rates, would merely 'permit' arrangements for separate religious instruction 'if required by a reasonable number of parents'.

Inside Parliament some 1,200 amendments descended upon the measure from both sides of the House. The Speaker ruled out of order eleven Instructions on which notice had been given. The speech of Carvell Williams bristled with the Liberationist objections. After heated discussion in Committee for five days, only two and a half lines of the first clause passed. The Cabinet at an emergency meeting decided to have the Bill withdrawn. Therewith, the legions of defiant Nonconformity were not denied.

Postscript

Survivors there were, and are, from the Gladstonian age; the Liberation Society still exists and there are still Churchmen who dread Disestablishment. But after the deluge the great world passed them by amused or disgusted at finding the old melodrama still on the boards.

WILLIAM GEORGE ADDISON[1]

AND WHAT of Disestablishment in England? The Liberation Society frankly, though not openly, admitted that such a goal could be realized only by a new approach.[2] This was not to say that the old way had failed to upset the Establishment. A revolution in public sentiment had definitely taken place.

The Society had disestablished the Church of England in that it had established national power and prestige for the Free Churches of England. It had established a firm place for a free and fair inquiry into the teachings of the Church. In one sense the Preface to the Thirty-Nine Articles of Religion had been abrogated, especially the injunction on differences of interpretation, 'We will, that all further curious search be laid aside, and these disputes shut up . . .'[3]

The removal of the worst Nonconformist grievances over the years had, of course, amounted to a progressive or gradual Disestablishment. But perhaps the final goal of disentangling Church and State was most naturally achieved in a medium where it was least expected – Sir Henry Fowler's Local Government Act of 1894 with its establishment of Parish Councils in England and Wales. By this Act, Sir Henry said, English men and women

> had slain Bumbledom and Vestrydom, and no one shed a tear over their graves. They believed that class would co-operate with class, that they would meet together on a common platform for a common object.[4]

Through the passage of his measure, with which the Society had very little to

---

[1] *Religious Equality in Modern England 1714–1914*, p. 172.

[2] A sign of the new way open to a later generation occurred during 1887, the year of Queen Victoria's Jubilee, when Episcopalians and Nonconformists more than once joined in the same commemoration service.

[3] The Book of Common Prayer. 'Agreed upon by the Archbishops and Bishops of both Provinces and the whole Clergy in the Convocation holden at London in the year 1562 for the avoiding of Diversities of Opinions.'

[4] Edith H. Fowler, op. cit., p. 282.

do, there came a partial Disestablishment in areas where the Church of England had been strongest. The Rev. Joseph Parker at the Society's Jubilee, maintained that by means of the Parish Councils Bill 'Nonconformist Councils' should be set up in every town. In effect, the new law diminished the legal powers of the Established Clergy and officials, and recognized the principle of separation between civil and ecclesiastical matters in parochial affairs. It was the last issue on which Mr Gladstone addressed the House of Commons. Concerning that speech on 1 March, George W. E. Russell observed:

> . . . he bequeathed to his party the legacy of a nobly-worded protest against the irresponsible power of the 'Nominated Chamber'; and then . . . he simply disappeared, without ceremony or farewell. In my mind's eye I see him now, upright as ever, and walking fast, with his despatch-box dangling from his right hand, as he passed the Speaker's Chair, and quitted the scene of his life's work for ever.[1]

In his letter of farewell to Mr Russell, the nephew of his old Liberal chief, Gladstone wrote:

> Of one thing I am, and always have been, convinced—it is not by the State that man can be regenerated, and the terrible woes of this darkened world effectually dealt with.[2]

Liberal-minded men who remained at the threshold of the twentieth century were likewise dubious of the role of the State Church in national crises. While honest thinking men of all parties and opinions could feel some doubt or searching of heart, apparently the State Church would have to stand by the Government in its moral judgements. No words of censure, according to the new humanitarians, could be too strong when the national Church stooped to the status of a domestic chaplain for the governing class and cried with the poet, 'Theirs not to reason why.'

> A church, a creed which can chant such a requiem as this over the grave of the Nineteenth Century need trouble us no more. It is left henceforth to faith in humanity to do what it can to curb the passions of the strong who are thirsting to crush the weak; . . . These high priests of the New Imperialism have forsworn their own religion and forgotten their own sacred books.[3]

The time of the Society's greatest usefulness, beginning in 1844, ended fifty years later with Gladstone's retirement. The *finale* to the Society's great cry in Victorian politics, however, took place in the House of Commons on 9 February 1897, upon the vote of a motion by Mr Samuel Smith (M.P.,

---

[1] G. W. E. Russell, *Fifteen Chapters of Autobiography* (London 1915), p. 281. Charles S. Roundell, *Recollections of Mr Gladstone* (Skipton 1898), p. 14, wrote that after Gladstone's last speech 'the glory of the House had departed'. 'There was in this old man a never-failing dignity, reaching to majestic proportions, a dignity reaching up to and embodying the very dignity of the House of Commons itself. When he rose to his feet, there was a visible hush throughout the House.'

[2] G. W. E. Russell, op. cit., p. 282.

[3] Frederic Harrison, 'Christianity at the End of the Nineteenth Century', in J. Vyrnwy Morgan (ed.), *Theology at the Dawn of the Twentieth Century* (Boston, Mass. 1901), p. 17.

Flintshire). The Society's whip went out to all Liberal M.P.s, and a letter to 7,000 of its most influential friends, pleading for all possible weight of influence in Parliament on the motion: 'That it is expedient to Disestablish and Disendow the Church of England both in England and Wales.'

The debate was in some ways pathetic. Supporting speeches came from Mr E. J. C. Morton (M.P., Devonport) who was a Churchman, Mr J. Herbert Roberts (M.P., Denbigh, W.) and Carvell Williams (M.P., Mansfield, Notts.). A solitary speech from the Ministerial side, that of Mr A. J. Balfour (M.P., Leeds, Central, and Chief Secretary for Ireland), seemed all that was necessary. Including tellers the resolution was routed by 206 to 88 votes.

The criticism so often made of Disestablishment was that it had failed because it was too negative. It had been too much looked upon not in its own positive right, but as a stepping stone by those ambitious politicians who instinctively appealed to the dissatisfied elements in society.

> Indeed, it may be claimed that the nineteenth-century Dissenters saw too much in a mirror that distorted the features of their fellow countrymen. The distortion came not only from party politics, but from real grievances reasonably resented, from anger at social privilege and the insolence of class, and from the old Puritan vice of imputing base motives to the other side and dividing the world sharply and inaccurately into the godly and ungodly, . . .[1]

This is not to imply, however, that the Disestablishment cause is a closed chapter in history. The possibility of its revival, although in a different form, remains as long as its unrealized objectives are discussed by the public. Disestablishment ideals will come to an end: (1) when the Sovereign is free, like any other national leader, to choose the Church in Britain to which he/she will belong; (2) when the Coronation is conducted by the Church or Churches of his/her choice; (3) when he/she has ceased to summon Convocation or to nominate Bishops; (4) when the Bishops have ceased to sit in the House of Lords; and (5) when Parliament has ceased to regulate in Church matters and has repealed outmoded conformist ecclesiastical legislation. The judgement of Sir Lewis Dibdin in these matters is well applied:

> The Establishment has survived so many modifications that, whatever we may think, it would be rash to assert that the irreducible minimum has now been nearly reached.[2]

And so it seems that the subject is not without significance to present-day Church history. For the more the Ecumenical Movement spreads and the intercommunion of Churches increases, the more the Christian people of Britain will have to decide whether Episcopacy is to be made more flexible – Prelacy *ex hypothesi* having been abandoned. Has the Act of Uniformity really been taken seriously by the Church of England today?

Today we hear of discussions by some leaders concerning 'readjustment' between Church and State, which others are afraid means self-government

---

[1] G. Kitson Clark, *The English Inheritance*, p. 128.
[2] *Establishment in England: being Essays on Church and State*, p. 116.

for the Anglicans while maintaining their position of State supremacy.[1] Disestablishment of the Church of England in the twentieth century may mean a re-establishing of the major Reformed denominations of the nation into a new and stronger National Church. Further, disestablishing rigid Anglican Episcopacy may have such a revolutionary effect as to make possible a modified Episcopacy working together with the Methodism of the Free Church and the Presbyterianism of the Church of Scotland in establishing a United Church of the United Kingdom.

The disturbing tensions today between the State and the 'Christian conscience' on moral and social issues – trying to determine what is right and what is wrong through the laws of the Realm – make it imperative that there be an *entente cordiale* between the Free Churches and the Established Churches.[2] The maintenance of a Christian Establishment and its mission in a highly secular society is uncertain without it. The real influence of the Christian message cannot be maintained today where one Christian body stands aloof from another. A positive answer lies in Reunion, and this should be possible, even though it means the Free Churches retracing some of their steps, and the National Churches doing the same.

> The time has come when you should admit that you made a great mistake, and we should admit our sin in losing the sorrow of our fathers in their ejectment and in being content and proud in our isolation. Is it not possible that if we approached the matter in the right spirit . . . we might celebrate . . . a day of national humiliation and reconciliation? I am not without hope, for it seems to me that what is true and worthy and great in our Congregational and Free Church tradition is not antipathetic to most of you.[3]

[1] Cyril Garbett, *Church and State in England* (London 1950), p. 5; cf. the evidence of Bernard Lord Manning, *Archbishops' Commission on Church and State* (London 1935), ii, 90–1.

[2] cf. the evidence of the Rev. Prof. Norman Sykes before the *Archbishops' Commission on Church and State*, pp. 287–304, esp. p. 300. On Reunion, Prof. Sykes states (p. 304): '. . . the operation of the law of periodicity within the Church of England, which has governed so markedly the series of religious movements within its communion since the Reformation, may evoke a school of thought attaching particular value to the official relationship to- wards the state-dominated Establishment, and anxious to further that end by a reunion with the non-episcopal reformed Churches of the realm.'

[3] Nathaniel Micklem, *The Church Catholic* (London 1935), p. 49: from an address, 'The Proper Treatment of Byegones', delivered at St Edmund's (Anglican) Church, Lombard St, London, on 14 December 1933.

INDEX